McGRAW-HILL SERIES IN

Sociology and Anthropology

RICHARD T. LaPIERE
Consulting Editor

THE AMERICAN CITY

McGRAW-HILL SERIES IN
SOCIOLOGY AND ANTHROPOLOGY

RICHARD T. LaPIERE, *Consulting Editor*

The American City

STUART ALFRED QUEEN
Washington University

DAVID BAILEY CARPENTER
Washington University

1953   NEW YORK   TORONTO   LONDON

McGRAW-HILL BOOK COMPANY, INC.

Preface

In the fourteen years since the McGraw-Hill Book Company published *The City* by Stuart A. Queen and Lewis F. Thomas, the pace of urban change has quickened under the impact of World War II, the Korean incident, and the threat of an atomic World War III. As the barriers of space and distance have been shrunk by ever faster means of transportation and communication, hinterlands have increasingly been drawn into the life of the city. Now more than ever before, the conditions of city living set the pace of our civilization. He who would understand contemporary society must first understand the city.

Although the late Lewis F. Thomas was not able to participate in a revision of the book he originally coauthored, his influence continues to be reflected throughout the present work. The approaches of the urban sociologist and ecologist continue to dominate the treatment, though heavy reliance has been put on materials developed in other fields.

The present book is for the most part new, reflecting the great amount of pertinent research done in the past decade and a half and the far-reaching changes which have occurred and are occurring in city life. The rising degree of integration of metropolis, city, town, and country into a common metropolitan community has made the older dichotomy of rural and urban unrealistic. We have sought to measure degrees of urbanism and urbanization and to analyze their correlates in social life. Diversities within cities and between cities have concerned us as much as features characteristic of city life in general. Our interest in the factors affecting cities and the processes through which they change has carried over to an interest in predicting and controlling the future of cities.

We cannot in brief space mention all those who by their research and writing have made this volume possible. Both to those cited by name and to those unnamed, we are deeply indebted. For all inadequacies, however, we assume full responsibility.

St. Louis, Missouri　　　　　　　　　　　　　　*Stuart A. Queen*
January, 1953　　　　　　　　　　　　　　　　*David B. Carpenter*

Contents

Contents

PART 4. *The Social Life of the City Dweller*

PART 5. *Social Change and the City*

PART 1

Mounting Significance of the City

CHAPTER 1. *Importance of Studying the City*

Ever since their first appearance several thousand years ago, cities have been the objects of pride and of suspicion, of envy and of fear. Books have been written about "The Shame of the Cities" and about "The City the Hope of Democracy." Orators have extolled cities as "the vanguard of civilization" and condemned them as "blots on the landscape." In our own land hostility between city and country is suggested by the pitting of Baltimore against the Eastern Shore, New York against Upstate, Chicago against Downstate, Denver against the Western Slope. All these popular expressions imply that there is something distinctive about cities, but none of them tell us what that something is.

Before undertaking a systematic inquiry into the nature of cities, we shall present three sketches of urban scenes in the United States. The first describes some of the irritations, open conflicts, and insecurity of the masses of people in an industrial center. The second portrays some of the circumstances involved in the isolation of individuals and the separation of categories of persons who dwell in the heart of a great metropolis. The third is the story of how a fashionable neighborhood has survived in spite of the usual pressures of an expanding business district and other economic demands.

In offering these brief sketches to our readers we are not joining those who declare that cities are abnormal. We are not proposing nostrums for the complaints of troubled city dwellers. But we are emphasizing the fact that the study of cities is not an academic game invented by curious professors to provide busy work for campus playboys. It deals with real issues that bother real people. These issues are not likely to be resolved without greater understanding than we now have of their nature, origin, and possible alternatives. Our ambition is to provide some of this understanding, in order that the people may attack their problems realistically. With more knowledge of what cities are actually like, how they came to be what they are, and by what means they may be changed, civic campaigns may "generate more light and less heat." They may be less spectacular but more effective in achieving whatever goals the people may seek. At least, this is our hope.

LIFE IN A FACTORY CITY[1]

Up to World War I, Detroit was a stable, Middle Western city, growing steadily from 200,000 in 1890 to 500,000 in 1914. But in the next fifteen years its population trebled. Newcomers poured in from near and far. This dramatic change seems to have started with the Ford Motor Company's announcement that it would pay $5 a day to all its workers.

Within a week of the announcement in January, 1914, there were 5,000 men lined up at the gate at five o'clock one morning. By the time the plant opened, their numbers had swelled to 12,000. The company was not prepared to handle such a crowd. The men were kept waiting outside in the bitter cold. Presently disappointment and anger resulted in open rioting. Hundreds forced their way inside, hurling bricks and other missiles, being finally dispersed after fire hose had drenched them with ice-cold water.

The word about jobs and wages—not about the riot—was spread over the country, especially through the South, where money was scarce and for many people the prospects of getting ahead were dim. So folks started for Detroit from the hills of Kentucky and Tennessee, the pine woods of Arkansas, the cotton fields of Alabama. By 1948 perhaps half a million of Detroit's residents were Southerners who had come looking for jobs with good wages. At first most of them were white folks with limited schooling, "revivalistic" religion, race prejudices, and customs developed in the open country and small towns.

Unaccustomed to the ways of the big city, with its crowding and hurrying, constant facing of strangers on the street, getting food from the store instead of the garden, wondering where the youngsters might be, they worried. The winter was cold and long; the food was different. It was hard to live in light housekeeping rooms, sharing hall and bath and toilet with the families of strangers. The city church seemed cold and inhospitable. The social settlement was an unfamiliar kind of place. The school was big and the lessons were hard. Life was baffling at every turn.

The corner tavern or bar appealed to many of the men. The storefront church, Holiness or Apostolic Faith, attracted some of the women. The children played in the streets. Some of these confused and irritated

[1] Data from various sources including Irving Howe and B. J. Widick, *The UAW and Walter Reuther,* 1949; Alfred M. Lee and Norman D. Humphrey, *Race Riot,* 1943. By permission of Random House, The Dryden Press, Inc., and the authors.

migrants joined the Ku Klux Klan or followed Gerald L. K. Smith. In time, many became members of the United Automobile Workers, but that was a later phase.

Another large contingent of Southerners were dark-skinned, Negroes hoping to escape from sharecropping and Jim Crow, seeking for better jobs, better houses, education for their children, and a chance to be treated "like folks." From 6,000 in 1910 the Negroes of Detroit increased to 150,000 in 1940. Another 60,000 came at the opening of World War II.

These black folks experienced nearly all the difficulties encountered by the poor whites, plus prejudice against people of color. How much or little the old Detroiters disliked Negroes is hard to say. But white newcomers from the South left little uncertainty as to their feelings and probably stirred up others as well. In any case, many thousands of Negroes were crowded into a deteriorated area known as Paradise Valley, where life was far different from that pictured by the hopeful migrants when they left the sunny South.

Among the people most hostile to the Southerners, both white and Negro, were the Poles. There are about 350,000 persons of Polish birth or parentage living in Detroit and Hamtramck, a municipality entirely surrounded by the larger city. They maintain many of their old traditions and customs, their language, and their religion. The Protestantism of the hillbillies, the dark skin of the Negroes, and, it might be added, the retail stores of the Jews are symbols to which Detroit's Poles often react with antagonism.

Other ethnic elements might be mentioned, but these will serve to indicate something of the diversity of Detroit's population and some of the possibilities of conflict in this great industrial city.

The jobs by which Detroiters earn their living are by no means all in the automobile industry, but here is obviously the economic core of the city's life. This means that a great part of the labor force is employed in large factories on assembly lines. This means further that control is highly centralized in a few corporations, relationships are depersonalized, the pace is set by the "line," and workmen are almost part of the machinery. An assembly line may be 100 to 400 yards long; on it as many as 300 men may work. The conveyer belt moves the auto body or chassis along at a steady pace, while each man performs a relatively simple task over and over, several hundred or several thousand times a day. There is not much chance to relax, although a man may "move up the line" a short distance and get ahead enough to smoke a cigarette.

Before and after work many thousands of Detroiters get in their cars and "fight the traffic." Public transportation is crowded and the streets are jammed with private cars. Thus there is an added strain on those who work for a living.

But there are other things that worry the wage earners more than the monotony and tension of assembly line and the irritations of city traffic. Chief among these are fear of layoff, short work week, prolonged unemployment, or speed-up. Experience has taught them that, when new models come out and some operations have to be changed, the pace may be increased. In fact, they suspect management of constantly watching for chances to demand more work without more pay. But some of their most painful memories have to do with unemployment. They remember that in 1927 the Ford Motor Company laid off 60,000 in the Detroit area for periods of six months to a year, while the shops were changed over from the making of Model T to the making of Model A. They recall even more vividly the great depression that began in 1929 when the employees of Detroit's auto factories dropped from 470,000 to 250,000 with most of the latter working only part of the time. Some of them remember being on relief along with 200,000 other hard-pressed citizens. They can hardly forget the long lines at the welfare offices, the $2 grocery orders, and the long-delayed investigation to determine eligibility. Because they had no money for radios and newspapers, they probably did not know much about the wrangling between City Hall, Community Fund, Henry Ford, and others about who was responsible and what was the best way to meet this situation.

Before the National Recovery Act of 1933, few of the automobile workers belonged to trade-unions. The organizations they had were weak and divided. But from that time on, organizers were busy and strikes multiplied. However, a depression does not offer the most favorable opportunities for building unions and winning strikes. Among the workers there was mounting dissatisfaction with the old leadership, and in 1936 many of the auto unionists went over from the AFL to the CIO. In that same year came the famous sit-down strikes in which groups of employees took possession of plants and refused either to work or to leave. Some of these strikes were carefully planned and conducted by union leaders. Others were of the "wildcat" variety, *i.e.*, groups of employees in various plants "spontaneously" stopped work and expressed their grievances without reference to union policy or strategy. Besides, there was strife among union leaders and factions fighting for programs and for power.

Gradually the United Automobile Workers became more unified and built up an effective organization. In 1937 they organized General Motors and Chrysler, and in 1940 after an especially bitter struggle they forced the Ford Motor Company to agree to a union shop, checkoff of dues, grievance machinery, seniority, and time and a half for overtime. The bad feeling engendered in these struggles did not soon die down. Distrust and suspicion filled the minds of both management and labor. Within the union there was continued rivalry between leaders and bitter strife between the communists and their enemies. During World War II, a no-strike pledge was adopted, but it was almost constantly in question.

During the war there was also an intensification of feelings between the races. The tolerance and teamwork which had been developing between Negroes and whites within the automobile union were seriously disturbed by the masses of southern whites who surged into Detroit. Their coming plus the arrival of thousands of new Negro workers also produced a veritable housing crisis. Single rooms in Paradise Valley were renting for $60 a month. In 1941 a a low-cost housing development for Negroes was located in a previously all-white district. This was by order of the Federal authority which presently wavered back and forth between opening the project for Negroes and turning it over to whites. In any case, Negro occupancy began in February, 1942, after the burning of a fiery cross and rioting by bands of white men. After two months and under police and military protection, Negro families actually moved into the project.

But tensions were not relieved. In the spring of 1943 they flared up again. At the Packard plant 20,000 white workers went on strike because some Negroes had been upgraded. From time to time there were minor street clashes. Finally rioting broke out on a large scale and did not end until 34 were killed and 800 injured.

In describing the irritations, tensions, open conflicts, and insecurity of great masses in a factory city there is no intention to deny or ignore the more cheerful aspects of Detroit's life. We are simply calling attention to situations which trouble the people who participate in them. They have not found solutions to their problems and are not likely to stop struggling until they are satisfied or defeated. We do not expect them to turn to sociologists for advice about what to do tomorrow afternoon, how to administer factory or city hall, how to win strikes or stop race riots. But if sociologists provide new insights into the behavior of city folks and their relationships to each other, these insights can be used in many ways by those who assume responsibility for social action.

GOLD COAST AND SLUM[2]—A MOSAIC OF LITTLE WORLDS

Just across the Chicago River from the Loop lies the Near North Side, an area half a mile wide by a mile and a half long, where twenty years

[2] This account is based on Harvey W. Zorbaugh, *Gold Coast and Slum*, 1929. By permission of the University of Chicago Press and the author.

ago lived 90,000 people. For several decades of the nineteenth century this was a fashionable district, but since then "wave after wave of immigrants has swept over the area—Irish, Swedish, German, Italian, Persian, Greek, and Negro—forming colonies, staying for awhile, then giving way to others."[3] Each left an impress and some stragglers. At the time of the study on which this account is based, people of 30 different nationalities were living on the Near North Side.

This was an area of vivid contrasts between old and new, native and foreign, rich and poor, conventional and bohemian. In one year there were 90 contributors to the United Charities in less than a square mile on the lake front, and 460 relief cases in the square mile behind it. From casual observation it could be seen that the Near North Side was made up of three main parts: (1) the Gold Coast with imposing stone mansions and tall apartment hotels, (2) a rooming-house section, and (3) a tenement-house district occupied mainly by foreigners. In addition there was a colony of artists and would-be artists presenting a sharp contrast to the formal and conventional life of the Gold Coast a few short blocks away.

The isolation of the population crowded together within these few hundred blocks, the superficiality and externality of their contacts, the social distances that separate them, their absorption in the affairs of their own little worlds— these, and not mere size and numbers, constitute the social problem of the inner city.[4]

The Gold Coast was the home of the leaders of Chicago's Four Hundred, those who had "arrived." They led lives quite different from those of the rest of the city. To them good form and the amenities of life were of great importance. Those who really "belonged" had their names in the *Social Register,* while others aspired to this distinction. The "climbers" sought to associate with the "right" people, support their pet charities, and sponsor celebrities of title or fame, thus hoping to gain attention and prestige.

The social ritual which separated the elite from those of lesser status included living in the right blocks or at certain hotels, wearing clothes of the prevailing exclusive mode, entertaining with the proper service, never carrying a package or umbrella, avoiding streetcars and Yellow Cabs, and in general displaying an air of complete self-confidence.

In a more serious vein, many prominent men and women displayed a sense of *noblesse oblige.* They actively supported churches, social settlements, nurseries, dispensaries, reform movements in politics, art, and the opera.

[3] *Ibid.,* p. 4.
[4] *Ibid.,* p. 16.

These upper-class folks seemed to have "a more or less common body of experience and tradition, of attitudes and conventions."[5] They felt themselves above all others. Yet among these there was an absence of general acquaintance. Some spent three to five months of every year away from Chicago. While in the city, they associated as members of smart cliques rather than as neighbors. Thus the Gold Coast was a distinctive area with a distinctive population, but without the solidarity an outsider might expect to find.

A little farther back from Lake Michigan the houses were smaller and dingier. In window after window was seen a card reading "Rooms to Rent." In fact, the investigator found over 1,100 rooming and lodging-houses with 23,000 tenants. Nearly three-fourths of all houses in the district kept roomers. These were predominantly white-collar folks between the ages of twenty and thirty-five. About half were single men, two-fifths were couples presumably married, the rest were single women. Children were very scarce.

They were evidently a restless lot for the average turnover was 300 per cent a year. Doubtless this high mobility was one factor in the small number of acquaintances and friends. "One knows no one, and is known by no one. One comes and goes as one wishes, does very much as one pleases, and as long as one disturbs no one else, no questions are asked."[6] Roomers sometimes moved in without giving their names and departed without leaving a forwarding address. While some professed to like this anonymity, others acknowledged that they were lonely. They would go out of their way to buy some little thing at a drugstore "just for the sake of talking a few minutes with someone." Some found satisfaction in a dog or parrot. As to sex, the alternatives for many were prostitution, casual "affairs," or simply frustration. It was "a world of atomized individuals, of spiritual nomads."[7]

Through the heart of the Near North Side ran North Clark Street, "the little white way," with its cabarets, "chili parlors," taxi-dance halls, pawnshops, "lady barbers," and "rescue missions." To one side was Towertown, "the village," or "Latin Quarter," much visited by "slummers" lured by tales of garret studios, long hair, eccentric dress, and free love. Its actual residents included real artists and sincere radicals mingled with

. . . egocentric poseurs, neurotics, rebels against the conventions of Main Street or the gossip of the foreign community, seekers of atmosphere, dabblers in the occult, dilettantes in the arts, or parties to drab lapses from a moral code which the city has not yet destroyed.[8]

[5] *Ibid.*, p. 63.
[6] *Ibid.*, p. 75.
[7] *Ibid.*, p. 86.
[8] *Ibid.*, p. 92.

Farther west was the slum occupied by poverty-stricken stragglers left behind by successive waves of migrants—Germans, Swedes, Greeks, Persians, Negroes, and others. But the largest ethnic group at the time of this study was 15,000 Italians. Many of them had come directly from Sicily bringing their Old World customs and traditions. Living apart, speaking a foreign tongue, hampered by poverty, they took little part in the general life of the city. But their American-born children attended school, sold newspapers, joined gangs, and went into politics. They found themselves torn between conflicting loyalties—on the one hand family and church, on the other gang and job.

During World War I an effort was made to bring these diverse elements together through the Lower North Community Council. Prior to that, social settlements had been established to interpret the privileged and the disadvantaged to each other. The Board of Education started a number of community centers. But none of these seemed to work.

To win and hold the interest of wealthy contributors a note of uplift was maintained. To promote unity and local feeling there were "sings" and forums, committees galore, much talk about tolerance and neighborliness, and organization of block units. But it appeared impossible to arouse much interest in local affairs or to make a community out of native and foreign, rich and poor, educated and unschooled. The Near North Side continued to be a "mosaic of little worlds that touch but do not interpenetrate."

The purpose of a sociologist in studying such a situation as that just described is first to gain acquaintance, to know what is actually there. Then he asks such questions as: How did it come to be? What does it mean to those who are a part of it? What is its significance for the rest of the city? What changes have been attempted? With what success or failure? Finally he moves on to more general questions: Are these things always present in the inner city? If not, how different are the circumstances under which they do and do not occur? Are there regular sequences or directions of change which can be identified and used as a basis for prediction?

BEACON HILL—A FASHIONABLE NEIGHBORHOOD PERSISTS[9]

Beacon Hill is a neighborhood within five minutes' walking distance from Boston's principal retail center. For a century and a half it has retained its reputation as a preferred upper-class residential section, while six other districts in Boston have developed into fashionable neighborhoods, have enjoyed favor for a while, and then have declined. But

[9] Based on Walter Firey, *Land Use in Central Boston*, 1947. By permission of Harvard University Press and the author.

Beacon Hill has continued as an exclusive residential area despite the presence of a slum to the north and business houses to the east and the west. As a matter of fact, it had more upper-class residents in the 1940's than in the 1890's. Very often land use in a large city is determined by the process of economic competition. But this is a case in which sentimental attachment to an area has offset the pressures of an expanding business district and of possible financial advantages to property owners.

The history of this unusual neighborhood may be followed from 1795 when a new state house was erected on Beacon Street. In the same year a syndicate of socially prominent men was organized to buy up land on the Hill and to lay out streets and lots. Houses were to be large mansions. Streets were designed to minimize north and south traffic, since the northern slope was occupied by families of low economic status and varied national backgrounds. Doubtless the winter sunshine and the open space of Boston Common to the south were added attractions.

After its initial development, Beacon Hill became a favorite residential district for statesmen and scholars, poets and novelists. Thus letters and civic achievement were added to economic status as foundations of prestige. The district was described as a "citadel of aristocracy" and "the height of exclusiveness." As late as 1943, over 300 families listed in the *Social Register* had Beacon Hill addresses. Apparently the neighborhood had acquired a halo which attracted and retained upper-class families who otherwise might have fled from the city's center.

Many articles and pamphlets have been written by residents of the Hill referring to its "sacredness, charm, antiquity, and tradition." Ordinarily such documents may be taken with a grain of salt, but the fact that their authors have clung to this area despite the suburban lure and economic pressure indicates that their values are really reflected in their writings. Here are some phrases that suggest their feelings of pride and attachment—"a sense of everything well placed," "an indescribable air of breeding and quality," "gentle and cultured people," "dignified beauty, mellow refinement, and air of comfort."[10] To a Beacon Hill resident it is a matter of pride if he can boast of having been born on the Hill or at least of having grown up there. Continuity of family residence is also a source of prestige. Even the houses have "pedigrees." It means something to live in a house once occupied by a celebrity of long ago.

To some *nouveaux riches* residence in the district is evidently a bid for status. It is a "proper" section in which to live and should help to "place" their subdebutante daughters. Sometimes young couples of "good" family but limited resources may rent a moderately priced apartment in a converted Beacon Hill house. Thus they manage to live in a

[10] *Ibid.*, p. 95.

socially approved neighborhood and symbolize their class position without too great expense. Then there are elderly spinsters who live on the Hill because the house was part of their inheritance; they could ill afford to dwell anywhere else. Finally, on the fringe are a considerable number of clerical workers who have found inexpensive living accommodations with good reputation and near to their places of employment.

But the people of greatest prestige are those of "old-stock Yankee aristocracy," who occupy positions of leadership and authority in financial, educational, artistic, and welfare organizations. Next to them come the newer families who are respectable and well to do but "lack genealogy." In both segments of the upper class there is an unusually large percentage of middle-aged persons, children are few, and unmarried women are numerous. It has been suggested that an upper-class man may marry "down," but an upper-class woman cannot without forfeiting her social position.

There is a complex network of blood relationships which have a great deal to do with one's choice of a mate, an occupation, the schools to which one sends his children, and the clubs to which he may gain admittance. Of course, these relationships are not confined to the Hill, but they do seem to center there. Besides kinship ties there are those of visiting, based on years of friendship often reaching back to childhood. These same people may meet as members of exclusive clubs. Likewise they share in certain ceremonial activities, such as placing lighted candles in the windows at Christmas and going through the district singing carols. Two small groups of friends known as the Beacon Hill Handbell Ringers also share in the holiday festivities. Finally there is a May Day festival which was organized "as a means of furthering good will and neighborliness in the district."

There are two more formal associations. One is the Louisburg Square Proprietors, founded in 1844 to enlarge and ornament the oval plot before their houses and to share expenses. They also have employed a caretaker and take regular steps to prevent the establishment of public rights to use of the square by prohibiting trespass. All purchasers of property within a certain area must join the organization and agree to share its expenses. The other formal organization is the Beacon Hill Association which was formed in 1922 "to keep undesirable business and living conditions from affecting the hill district." We shall have more to say about this organization a little later.

Between 1875 and 1880 some families moved from the Hill to the then new and impressive Back Bay district. This "emigration" was followed by the "invasion" of rooming houses, clubs, and stores. A few apartment houses were built. Private schools took over some of the old houses. Nevertheless most of the families remained. Even at the lowest point, about 1905, there were over 240 Social Registerites living in the neighborhood.

In that year a noted architect returned from Back Bay to Beacon Hill, took over a deteriorated colonial dwelling, and made extensive renovations. He modernized the interior but left the colonial exterior intact. The head of one family that had remained on the Hill bought and improved two old houses, later selling them at a profit. Presently others followed this example. Thus a revival movement got under way. But it was not like a typical real estate boom, for extensive publicity and speculation were absent. But it did spread beyond the confines of the old fashionable neighborhood, bringing it to pass that "tenements, stables, and workshops were gradually displaced by homes, antique shops, and apartment buildings." A "formerly dirty obscure alley, notorious for its vice, crime, and frequent police raids, was reconstructed and . . . designed for 'tenants who appreciate something out of the ordinary'."[11] Little theater and radical political groups appeared and exotic tearooms were opened. A sort of bohemian atmosphere was developing in the immediate environs of the old exclusive neighborhood, and it was viewed with apprehension by the more aristocratic families. One woman in a letter to the editor of the *Boston Herald* warned that "those seeking to find or create there a second Greenwich Village will meet with obstacles" and organized resistance from the residents "drawn together for self-defense."[12] Someone else wrote an article telling of hazards to the neighborhood involved in the purchase of an old house by someone who might demolish it or convert it into a multiple dwelling.

Out of such experiences as these grew the Beacon Hill Association. It opposed an unsatisfactory zoning ordinance in 1924. It succeeded in having Phillips Street rezoned from local business use to residential use. In 1927 it fought against a group which wanted the building height limits raised from 65 to 155 feet to permit the construction of a large apartment hotel. It was argued by the promoters that this change would enhance property values and be a source of financial gain to Beacon Hill property owners. Nevertheless, 500 people turned out at a public hearing to protest this threat to "the consistent character of the Beacon Hill district." The final decision was in favor of the Association. Once again sentiment had prevailed over possible economic advantage. In 1930 and in 1933, the Association succeeded in having building height limits reduced from 80 to 65 feet in certain parts of the district. In 1931 it aroused the citizens to protest against an effort to locate "high-grade

[11] *Ibid.*, p. 121.
[12] *Ibid.*, p. 122.

stores" on Beacon Street. These efforts and others of the sort indicate a high degree of group solidarity and a strong attachment to the district, as a result of which the old fashionable neighborhood persists.

The story of Beacon Hill makes us wonder whether we have identified the most significant differences between it and other exclusive residential districts which lasted much shorter periods of time. Apparently Beacon Hill is a bit unusual, although there are other cases in which old neighborhoods resist the intrusion of newcomers and of new land uses. But since many residential sections do succumb after a generation or so, it is important to discover, if we can, just what factors make for survival and what factors are associated with decline. With such knowledge we would have learned something important about cities in general and could offer something very practical to homeowners and others interested in urban neighborhoods.

WHY STUDY THE CITY?

Obviously the modern city is something very complex. At least in the United States, its inhabitants include many different kinds of people who have varying relationships to each other. Prosperity and bright lights attract country folks who do not know how to live in cities. The outward push of expanding business sends "substantial" citizens to the suburbs. Succeeding waves of newcomers press on the older residents and on each other. The net result is an atmosphere of impermanence, physical proximity accompanied by social distance, with great masses of people who seem unable to unite in common tasks and sometimes fall to fighting. The city is puzzling even to those who know it best. At times it seems utterly chaotic. At other times one catches a glimpse of order and system. At times it is quite disgusting and repulsive. At other times it is strangely alluring. In any case there is need of careful study, if we are to achieve understanding of this enormous, complicated, and changing thing we call the city.

Finally, the importance of such studies is driven home by the large number of cities, their great size, and the increasing proportion of the world's population that lives in urban centers. The details will be presented in a later chapter, but it is worth mentioning here that there are more than 40 cities in the world with populations of 1 million or over, and probably 700 with populations of 100,000 and over. In several countries over half the population is classed as urban, and in the United States half of the people live in 140 metropolitan areas. This degree of concentration is something new. To be sure, there have been cities for five thousand years, but as recently as 1800 they were few and far between. Great Britain, the most urban of countries, had then only 20 per cent of its people living in cities of 10,000 and over. Such facts as these lead us immediately to ask: How has all this come about? What has it done to people? How much further is it likely to go?

SELECTED READINGS

ANGELL, ROBERT C.: *The Moral Integration of American Cities,* Supplement to the *American Journal of Sociology,* July, 1951. A discussion of ends and values with data on efforts made by cities toward achieving the good life as defined.

DAVIE, MAURICE R.: *Problems of City Life,* John Wiley & Sons, Inc., 1932. Deals chiefly with the difficulties encountered by city people in the effort to obtain housing, health, education, and recreation.

MUMFORD, LEWIS: *The Culture of Cities,* Harcourt, Brace and Company, Inc., 1938. A criticism of our present urban civilization, "the insensate industrial town," and "the acquisitiveness of a sick metropolis," with a philosophy of "renewal."

PETERSON, ELMER T: *Cities Are Abnormal,* University of Oklahoma Press, 1946. An uneven collection of essays by editor, novelist, physician, architect, businessman, churchman, social worker, and three social scientists, most of whom condemn our cities for what they do to human relations and personal development.

SERT, JOSE LUIS: *Can Our Cities Survive?* Harvard University Press, 1942. An architect's challenge to plan a way out of "existing urban chaos."

CHAPTER 2. *Definitions and Hypotheses*

The three sketches presented in Chap. 1 are somewhat impressionistic and obviously incomplete. But each is based on a more intimate acquaintance than first appears. The story of Detroit is based on observations and experiences of journalists, trade-unionists, social workers, and sociologists. The accounts of Chicago's Near North Side and of Boston's Beacon Hill are taken from systematic studies of these areas by sociologists.

Members of other professions too have devoted themselves to the study of cities. Architects and city planners have examined the physical equipment, including land use, buildings, and public utilities. Geographers and historians have sought to trace and explain the location and growth of cities. Economists have studied changing ways of making a living in relation to the increasing size of population aggregates. Political scientists have concerned themselves with municipal government and urban politics. Social workers have made surveys of poverty, unemployment, delinquency, and facilities for their treatment or prevention. Specialists in public health and vital statistics have compiled and analyzed data about birth and death, physical and mental disorders, marriage and divorce. Sociologists have concerned themselves with the relationships between persons and groups on the urban scene, with the customs, traditions, and attitudes that characterize city people.

This division of labor has grown out of specialized training and varied professional interests. But we should not ignore the probability that the many aspects of city life are interrelated. Since, however, no one can be an expert in all, we are confronted with a dilemma: How shall we avoid both the Scylla of particularism and the Charybdis of superficiality? Our proposal is this, that we concentrate on human relations as they appear to be affected by the many factors involved in the city and in urbanism. This then imposes on us the responsibility for defining city and urbanism.

First of all, we must decide whether to limit our criteria to such tangibles as number and density of population (urbanism) or to include whatever may be considered a part of the urban way of life (urbanization). Obviously the former are easier to manipulate, are less controversial, and leave little doubt as to what we mean. However, it would be unwise to deal only with materials easy to define, to assemble, and to manipulate, if these should turn out to be not very important, and especially if the neglected materials should prove more helpful in understanding the experiences and behavior of people. But before discussing the relative usefulness of the concepts "city" and "urbanism," defined in such terms as number and density of population, versus the concept "urbanization," described as a complex of traits that are not always well defined and sometimes not reduced to measurement, we shall first consider the simpler question of what we mean by a city.

WHAT IS A CITY?

In the state of Kansas 100 people living near together and meeting certain other requirements set forth by the legislature may incorporate as a city of the third class. A group of Bostonians talking about rural social work once referred to the charities of Northampton (25,000) and Lowell (100,000). Clearly the Kansas lawmakers and Boston social workers had very different conceptions of city and country. Both were interested in enabling the inhabitants of a locality to organize for the carrying on of joint activities. But one group was thinking of the scattered population of the rolling prairies, while the other spoke from the vantage point of a great metropolitan center.

Evidently the concept of a city is conditioned by the point of view of the person who is observing or studying it. Also, plainly it must be a statement in terms of the setting in which cities appear. Thus Massachusetts is a small, densely populated state. The 1950 census classed 84 per cent of its people as urban (living in places of 2,500 and over) and reported 36 places with a population of 25,000 or more. In fact, half the population lived in metropolitan Boston, 2,350,000 of 4,700,000. The density of the whole state was 550 persons per square mile. Kansas, on the other hand, is ten times as large as Massachusetts but has only two-fifths as many people. Less than 10 per cent of its people were classed as urban in 1950. There were only five places with a population of 25,000 or more, and all of them together accounted for only one-sixth of the population. The density of the whole state was 23 per square mile. To a Bostonian, city means a large number of people, perhaps a million, living close together in multiple dwellings, riding to their work in streetcar, subway, elevated, and bus, working in great office buildings, stores, and factories, enjoying the bright lights of movie and dance palace, or possibly the subdued lights of orchestra hall and art museum. To a Kansan, city means any incorporated place with its water tower rising above the prairie, its cottages, stores, schools, and churches, its main street, and its courthouse square, clustered amid trees that break the horizon. Apparently the marks of identification are varied and numerous.

Simply as a preliminary statement, we may say that a city is a collection of people and buildings, large for its time and place, and characterized by distinctive activities. But for practical purposes we need something more definite. As to numbers we might accept 2,500 as the point at which to distinguish urban from rural. In this we would be following the U.S. Bureau of the Census.[1] But there is no agreement between countries. The Netherlands draws the line at 20,000, while Canada sets no minimum. Moreover, there is a question as to what area should be used for the population count. In most cases we have no choice but to accept the legally incorporated unit or municipality. Very often this serves well to differentiate a compact body of people from those who live in the open country. But sometimes the municipal boundaries are extended to include a lot of farming land. At other times we find a cluster of municipalities which, in every sense except the legal, are a single population aggregate.

To meet this latter case the Bureau of the Census used in 1930 and 1940 the concept "metropolitan district" which it defined as a local area containing at least 100,000 people, of whom at least 50,000 live in a central city or cities (incorporated municipalities) and the remainder are found in "adjacent and contiguous civil divisions having a density of not less than 150 inhabitants per square mile, and also as a rule, those civil divisions of less density that are directly or nearly surrounded by minor civil divisions that have the required density."[2] Somewhat different definitions had been employed in 1910 and 1920. Since 1940 another change has been made. The term "metropolitan area" has been adopted to mean substantially the same thing as a 1940 metropolitan district, except that the boundaries are made to follow county lines. Here is the definition as worked out by the Federal Committee on Standard Metropolitan Areas in 1950.

Each standard metropolitan area contains at least one city of 50,000 or more. In general, each comprises an entire county or group of two or more

[1] "According to the definition established for use in the 1950 Census, urban territory has been defined to comprise (a) places of 2,500 inhabitants or more incorporated as cities, boroughs, towns (except in New England, New York, and Wisconsin where 'towns' are subdivisions of counties and are not necessarily densely settled centers like the towns in other States), and villages; (b) the densely settled urban fringe, including both incorporated and unincorporated areas around cities of 50,000 or more; and (c) unincorporated places of 2,500 inhabitants or more outside any urban fringe. All other territory is classified as rural." Bureau of the Census, Current Population Reports, Series P-20, No. 36, p. 5, Dec. 9, 1951.

[2] Bureau of the Census, *Metropolitan Districts*, pp. 5–6, 1932.

contiguous counties that are economically and socially integrated. The outlying counties must meet several qualifications regarding population density and the volume of nonagricultural employment. In New England, standard metropolitan areas comprise groups of contiguous cities and towns.[3]

Note that this last definition adds employment as a criterion and retains density. Earlier students of the city had insisted on the importance of density on the grounds that, if people are crowded very closely together, they must take some account of each other's presence and must give special thought to the requirements of housing, transportation, sanitation, and the like. In the next chapter we shall set forth a scheme not only for identifying rural-urban differences, but for grading local populations as more or less rural or urban, that is, assigning positions on a continuum running from very rural to very urban. In this scheme we shall make use of the percentages of county populations resident in places of varying size. These simple demographic data will be utilized in constructing an Index of Urbanism.

WHAT IS URBANIZATION?

Some thoughtful observers and scholars have taken the position that mere differences in numbers are not very important. They believe that attention should be concentrated on how people live. It is their opinion that significant differences can be pointed out between the behavior, beliefs, organizations, and relationships of rural and urban people. They would join us in discarding the idea of a simple dichotomy and endeavor to establish degrees of difference along a hypothetical continuum. But instead of a demographic index, such as we are suggesting, theirs would be social psychological. In fact, they would define rural and urban in terms of behavior and relationships, while we would seek to discover how these may be related to rural and urban situations numerically defined. In succeeding chapters we shall present evidence bearing on these propositions and procedures. For the present we shall elaborate them as hypotheses.[4]

At one end of the continuum we may expect to find not only small numbers, but homogeneity and acquaintance of each with all. Members of the community are much alike and are in direct personal touch with

[3] Bureau of the Census, Preliminary Reports, Series PC-7, No. 4, Nov. 20, 1951.

[4] In the discussion which follows much use is made of the work of Redfield, Beals, Wirth, Simmel, Sorokin, and Zimmerman. See especially Robert Redfield, "The Folk Society," *Amer. Jour. Sociol.*, 52 (1947), 293–308; Louis Wirth, "Urbanism as a Way of Life," *Amer. Jour. Sociol.*, 44 (1938), 1–24; Nicholas J. Spykman, *The Social Theory of Georg Simmel*, 1925; Pitirim Sorokin and C. C. Zimmerman, *Principles of Rural-Urban Sociology*, 1929; Ralph Beals, "Urbanism, Urbanization and Acculturation," *Amer. Anth.*, 55 (1951), 1–10.

one another. They remain together for a long time with few changes in the conditions of life. Hence they may be assumed to understand each other and to work together on the basis of a coherent system of customs and traditions.

At the other extreme, which we call urban, we look for large numbers, heterogeneity, and "secondary" contacts. From large numbers alone we would expect a greater range of variation in ability and performance. In addition, cities are filled with people from many different places. Urban dwellers are diverse in language, customs, codes of behavior, occupation, education, religion, wealth, appearance, and status. In the city one may face a great many people every day without knowing any of them well. He may meet a wide variety of persons and be intimate with none. Some observers report that urban contacts tend to be temporary, casual, and superficial.

If facts support these impressions as to the relative number, variety, intimacy, and permanence of contacts in places of large and of small population, we may take either of two positions: (1) we may hold that social contacts are more significant criteria of degrees of urbanism than are mere numbers of people, (2) we may report that the character of social contacts varies with the size of population aggregates or with some other demographic index.

At the rural end of the continuum, it is supposed that everyone belongs to a family group which determines his place in the larger social structure. In addition he may also be a member of some special interest groups, but they are presumably less important than kinship and locality in shaping his life and in getting essential work done. Rural interest groups are relatively few in number, small in size, and in any given community apparently have about the same membership lists.

At the urban pole, so runs the usual hypothesis, special interest groups represent the machinery for getting many things done. So we find trade-unions, neighborhood improvement associations, taxpayers' leagues, chambers of commerce, parent-teacher associations, civil liberties committees, athletic clubs, and countless others, each with a more or less well-defined purpose. Sometimes these groups divide the community into warring factions, sometimes into segments that ignore one another. Membership is far from identical, though there is much overlapping. Some individuals represent unique combinations of group memberships; others may participate in none. On the urban scene it is believed that special interest groups have taken over many functions from kinship and locality groups (family and neighborhood) and that the latter are growing gradually weaker.

A corollary of the proposition concerning the increasing dominance of interest groups as we approach the urban end of our supposed continuum is that membership in many groups produces "segmentalization of human relationships." That is, a city person may be said to give just a small part of himself to each of the groups to which he belongs, with-holding many of his ideas, skill, much of his time and energy for other organizations. Thus he reveals only a segment of his personality to his associates in any given group. According to the same corollary, a rural dweller is supposed to be known more nearly as a whole person, sharing membership in several groups with the same persons and thus touching their lives at several points.

If we actually discover situations that differ in the ways suggested, and if these differences vary with the size of population units or with some similar index, we may argue whether number of people or kind of social groups is the better criterion of urban. But perhaps we would use our time more profitably in seeking to learn what other features of social life occur in conjunction with community size.

One such feature has to do with making a living. As we go from one end of the continuum to the other, we may expect to find marked changes in the number, variety, and dominant types of occupations. At the rural pole we find only a few vocations, most of them involved in some phase of agriculture or other extractive industry. At the opposite pole we count vocations by the hundreds; we note their wide variety—from gambler to social worker, from waitress to broker, from tinsmith to musician. In the former case nearly everyone seems to be a Jack-of-all-trades who can do many things for himself, while in the latter case most people are rather helpless outside of their own specialties. As we approach the rural end of the continuum, we find communities nearly self-sufficient, producing much or all of their own food, clothing, fuel, and other necessities. As we approach the urban end, we find people consuming goods from the ends of the earth and distributing their own products far and wide. This means at one extreme general production for home use and local barter, at the other extreme specialized produc-tion for sale in a market. At the one pole, we have residence and work-place near together if not identical; at the other pole, residence and workplace are separated. Again we have a phase of group life which seems to vary with size of population aggregate. Again we have a proposition to test with factual data.

Another feature which appears to vary along with those previously mentioned may be called social control. At the rural end of our hypo-thetical continuum it appears that people are "kept in line" by the inertia of habit and custom, fear of what "they" will say if one transgresses, and the many subtle pressures that can be exerted in a small body of people that puts a premium on conformity.

As we move away from this pole toward its opposite, we find fewer customs shared by all the people in an area, we find gossip and personal pressures confined to small subgroups. More and more aspects of life are dealt with by formal regulations and specially designated officials. We have written rules for sports, constitutions and bylaws for clubs, union rules and company orders, municipal ordinances. These are enforced more or less effectively by umpires, sergeants at arms, parliamentarians, business agents, foremen, police officers. There are office hours, traffic lights, fair prices, innumerable signs forbidding this and requiring that. All in all it appears that places and populations near the urban end of the continuum in other respects are characterized by formal devices for social control. Again we have something to test by objective data in so far as these are available.

Mobility is frequently proposed as a distinguishing characteristic of the city. However, before testing the implied hypothesis we must discriminate between three or four different kinds of behavior to which this term is applied, and deal with each of them separately. Sometimes mobility refers to the daily coming and going to and from work, shopping, recreation, and the like. On the surface this type of movement appears to characterize populations near the urban end of our continuum. But this cannot be accepted without further inquiry. Hard roads and automobiles are enabling rural folks to get about a great deal.

Mobility in the sense of changing residence or employment seems to vary directly with the size of population and other factors which we have noted on the hypothetical continuum. However, there are many migratory agricultural laborers both in the United States and in other countries, and there are some very stable city dwellers. Hence common observation needs to be checked against more precise data.

Mobility in a third sense, that is, change in socioeconomic status, also seems to increase as we proceed from the rural to the urban part of our continuum. Many observations support this proposition, but again we find need of further testing.

Other aspects of human experience and behavior have been suggested for inclusion in a scheme for identifying degrees of difference in rural and urban populations. Among them are personality traits, social institutions, and rates of change. We do not intend to ignore these, but we defer consideration of them until later.

TYPES OF STUDIES

In this section we examine two types of studies dealing with rural-urban differences. The first is illustrated with a field study by an anthropologist, who presents his findings in narrative and descriptive form. The second is illustrated by a research plan tried out in a limited way by two sociologists. It involves an attempt to score behavior and relationships and thus reduce the comparisons of rural and urban to quantitative form.

About twenty years ago Robert Redfield[5] made an important field study in the state of Yucatan, Mexico, in which he compared four "communities" ranging from a tribal village of 100 to a capital city of 100,000. As he went from the smallest to the largest, he noted certain progressive changes. First of all the population became more heterogeneous. There were more contacts with other communities. Custom and tradition were less dominant; individuals displayed a greater variety of attitudes and behavior. That is, there was less and less consistency in the ways of life. Common understandings and expectations gave way to questioning and planned variations. Family and kinship were less important, while contractual and other formal relationships gained in frequency. Predominantly personal ties gradually diminished in number and intensity.

Tusik, the tribal village, was four days by horse or foot from the railroad. Its people rarely went outside of the immediate vicinity, and outsiders rarely came to visit. In fact, travel was not encouraged. There was no school; no one took a newspaper; only two persons could read and write. Maize was raised for home consumption only, but chicle was gathered in the forest and sent away for sale. Tribal government was strictly local and not an integral part of the Mexican governmental system. Most of the inhabitants appeared to be pure Indian with little admixture of Spanish or other blood. Maya was the language of the community.

Chan Kom, the peasant village, was only one day's walk from the railroad. Most of the men had been to Mérida, the state capital, though such trips were infrequent. Traveling merchants came from time to time, and there were a few other visitors. Mail came regularly, though most of it consisted of official communications. Occasionally newspapers were brought in. There was a school in which most of the instruction was in Maya. A good many people spoke some Spanish, but very few fluently. Everyone was an agriculturist raising maize for home consumption. However, a few products were sold or exchanged for textiles, soap, and salt. Isolation was less than in Tusik, though homogeneity was almost as great.

Dzitas a town of 1,200, would probably be called a county seat town in the United States. It was on the railroad and was a shipping center for maize and cattle. Communication was further facilitated by a post office, telegraph, 20 newspapers received fairly regularly, and a movie once or twice a week. While the chief occupation was agriculture, there were a

---

[5] Robert Redfield, *The Folk Culture of Yucatan,* 1941. Summarized by permission of the University of Chicago Press.

number of tradesmen and professional men, most of whom were not natives of the town. Spanish and Maya were both spoken quite generally. The population was clearly of mixed blood.

Mérida, the capital city, had a population of 100,000. All lines of communication converged upon it. It was a center of trade, industry, and finance, as well as of the highly centralized state government. Moreover, it was the seat of all the state's institutions of higher learning. Having contacts with the outside world, it adopted innovations from Europe and the Americas, passing them on to lesser places in the hinterland. Hence it was a focus of social change. The population was rather heterogeneous, including individuals from every Mexican state and from 56 foreign countries. About 100 different occupations were represented, most of them not agricultural. There were fairly wide differences of wealth, education, and social status.

These four communities seem clearly to indicate four points on a continuum. At one end we find isolation, homogeneity, self-sufficiency, stability, and close personal ties. At the other we find many outside contacts, heterogeneity, participation in a world market, social change, and many impersonal relationships. Starting with ecological and demographic criteria of rural-urban differences, Redfield found associated with them differences of social organization and culture.

More recently two rural sociologists, Loomis and Beegle,[6] have presented a scheme for defining the continuum largely in terms of social interaction and relationships. The concepts and procedures of these men are rather different from the ones we have been describing. Hence, even at the risk of not doing them full justice, we shall take the liberty of restating them in our own language.

The end of the continuum which we have called rural they label "familistic *Gemeinschaft*." By this they evidently mean to identify behavior and relationships of the sort we expect to find in a family or somewhat larger group of people who deal with each other informally, intimately, and consistently on the basis of custom and tradition. The opposite end, which we call urban, they label "contractual *Gesellschaft*." By this they evidently mean to identify a system of behavior and relationships that may be called formal, impersonal, planned, and subject to change by agreement. If the family symbolizes the one, the market place may symbolize the other. This is an oversimplified statement of a conceptual scheme carefully worked out by the Americans just named, who drew heavily on the French sociologist, Durkheim, and the German, Tönnies.

The real innovation of Loomis and Beegle is not the idea of a continuum, but the development of a scale for locating positions on it. For

[6] Charles P. Loomis and J. Allan Beegle, *Rural Social Systems*, Appendix A, 1950.

each of 15 items, they rate behavior and relationships on an 11-point scale. For example, one item has to do with interaction between a person and someone in authority over him. If the superior gets the other to respond to him more than he responds to his subordinate, the action is considered relatively one-sided or one-way and is scored accordingly. If there is little or no difference between the individuals in number of responses of each to the other, the score is on the other side of the middle or neutral point. One-way responding represents what we call the urban end and the two-way responding what we call the rural end of the continuum. Another item has to do with relatively voluntary and compulsory actions. If activity under the direction of a superior would have been engaged in if the subordinate were "free," then the score is on the rural side of the mid-point. If the opposite should be true, the score would be on the urban side.

A third item involves considering whether participants in a system have common or opposing interests, values, and motives. A fourth has to do with means of communication. At one extreme there will be common interests expressed directly by word of mouth, tone of voice, facial expression, and gestures; at the other there will be formal and conventionalized symbols like those used by truck drivers in passing. The fifth item is called "sacred versus secular." Deference to certain persons and certain ways of behaving are regarded on the one hand as divinely ordained, on the other simply as means to ends. The sixth is similar in that it runs from acceptance of certain ways because they are customary to evaluation in terms of calculated results. In the seventh, authority is viewed as ranging from one extreme in which it is dependent on personal qualities of the individual concerned to the other extreme in which it is position that is important, while personality is of less consequence.

The foregoing represent "hierarchical" relations as they vary from the familistic *Gemeinschaft* (rural) to the contractual *Gesellschaft* (urban) end of the continuum. Passing to nonhierarchical relations, we find the gamut running from highly integrated roles to roles that have little or no significance for each other. That is, on the rural end one's roles in family, church, and other groups are similar, compatible, generally understood, and accepted; whereas on the urban end what a person does in one group may be unknown, unimportant, or even opposed to his part in another group. Differently stated, at one end of the continuum, roles must be integrated; at the other, they are mutually irrelevant.

At one extreme there is "complete community of fate." Pleasure and grief, loss and gain are presumably shared by all. At the other extreme there is limited responsibility; suffering or advantage of one may have little or no impact on another. On the one hand a member's social interaction and relations are confined to his own "system," presumably his local community. On the other hand he may divide his activities among many separate systems, diverse as to membership, locality, and interests.

In keeping with the preceding items, value orientation may be expected to vary from one end of the continuum to the other. At the rural pole we look for norms that are "so respected and revered that violation results in a general emotional upheaval."[7] At the urban pole we expect to find norms regarded as ways of "maximizing returns and minimizing effort." In the first case goals are rather general and are determined by tradition. In the latter case they are more specific and are determined rationally or by contract.

This is an interesting program for rating forms of interaction in order that quantitative comparisons may be made either of persons or of situations. It deserves much more consideration than we are able to give it here. But, for reasons which will be developed later, we have decided neither to adopt nor to imitate the scheme of Loomis and Beegle. Our own procedure, outlined in the next chapter, involves first an ecological or demographic scale in which we utilize ten statistical series obtained from the United States census. A sample of counties is drawn from all the states in the union. These are then ranked according to their index numbers ($0 =$ completely rural; $100 =$ completely urban). Then we compute the relationship of many other series to the indices of urbanism. Because there have not been many studies of the sort outlined by Loomis and Beegle, we cannot get directly at such things as interaction, relationships, and norms. Instead we must approach them indirectly through such items as are actually available. Admittedly this procedure leaves much to be desired, but at least it has the virtue of being practicable.

Besides relating county data to our Index of Urbanism, we utilize material assembled in other categories, *e.g.*, by cities (usually municipalities); by metropolitan districts or areas; by rural-farm, rural-nonfarm, and urban; or merely by rural and urban as defined by the census. These series are not always directly comparable, but they provide supplementary evidence bearing on hypotheses which we want to test. Whatever form the data may take, however they may be classified, we examine them to see if we can determine the concomitants of urbanism, measured preferably by our index, but when that is not practicable, by other measures of population aggregates.

Finally, we concern ourselves with variations between and within cities, noting again factors that appear together and that go to make up types of local situations. So far as possible we use statistical data and procedures, but we do not ignore narrative and descriptive materials when these are available and when they shed light on the nature and significance of human relations and the settings in which they occur.

[7] *Ibid.*, p. 819.

SELECTED READINGS

BEALS, RALPH L.: "Urbanism, Urbanization and Acculturation," *Amer. Anth.*, 55 (1951), 1–10. Suggests that urbanization is a special case of acculturation; that urbanism in different countries may take on different forms.

LOOMIS, CHARLES P., and J. ALLAN BEEGLE: *Rural Social Systems*, Prentice-Hall, Inc., 1950. Rural-urban comparisons made in terms of variations along a continuum, with proposals for measurement of human relations and value orientations.

MCKENZIE, R. D.: *The Metropolitan Community*, McGraw-Hill Book Company, Inc., 1933. A classic presentation of the concepts: metropolitan region, metropolitan district, central city, nucleation; with quantitative study of trends from 1900 to 1930.

PARK, ROBT. E., ERNEST W. BURGESS, and R. D. MCKENZIE: *The City*, University of Chicago Press, 1925. A collection of papers formulating problems and hypotheses that have been the basis of much sociological research on cities.

REDFIELD, ROBERT: "The Folk Society," *Amer. Jour. Sociol.*, 52 (1947), 293–308. This article set up an "ideal-type" at the opposite pole from the type of society called urban.

WIRTH, LOUIS: "Urbanism as a Way of Life," *Amer. Jour. Sociol.*, 44 (1938), 1–24. This article sets up an "ideal type" of urban life with social organization quite different from Redfield's folk society.

CHAPTER 3. *Urbanism and Urbanization*

Among the tasks we have set ourselves in this book are: (1) developing a yardstick by which to measure the degree to which any given population is ecologically urban, *i.e.*, the degree to which any given population lives in large population aggregates of great density and occupational diversification, and (2) utilizing our measure of ecological urbanism in the analysis of those variations in behavior which are significantly correlated with variations in position on a rural-urban continuum. We are thus distinguishing urbanism from urbanization: urbanism we use to identify the phenomenon of city residence; urbanization we use to identify the distinctive way of life typically associated with city residence. We hypothesize that urban and rural are ideal types and that actual human communities fall along a continuum extending from occupationally unspecialized, sparsely settled groupings at the rural extreme, to occupationally specialized, densely settled population aggregates at the urban extreme. We hypothesize, further, that as human communities are arrayed along this rural-urban continuum, consistent variation occurs in patterns of behavior and social structure. In testing these hypotheses, we utilize data from the continental United States. It is our hope that cross-cultural testing may later be undertaken.

In undertaking our first task, *i.e.*, developing a measure of urbanism, we are limited to available reporting units and categories of tabulation utilized in the 1940 census. Available reporting units include minor civil divisions, incorporated places, counties, and states. Only a minimum of data is reported for minor civil divisions and incorporated places of all sizes. States display great internal heterogeneity with regard to degree of urbanism. Counties have appeared to offer least disadvantages as reporting units in the construction of a useful index with maximum range in degree of urbanism. A very wide range of data is available from the census on a county basis, a much wider range than is available for any unit other than the state.

There were reported in the 1947 edition of the *County Data Book*[1] 3,050 politically organized counties and 49 areas of other types which were treated as counties, a total of 3,099 counties. A randomly representative sample of 100 counties was selected for use in the construction of the Index of Urbanism. Figure 1 identifies the sample counties.

Among data which might have been used in the construction of the Index were: percentage of the population of each county living in incorporated places of various sizes; percentage of the population living in metropolitan districts of various sizes; size of the largest incorporated place lying wholly or partly in each county; size of the largest metropolitan district lying wholly or partly in each county; population density; percentage of the population with nonfarm residence; percentage of those employed in industries other than agriculture; percentage of those employed in industries other than the extractive ones of agriculture, mining, fisheries, forestry, and logging; accessibility to the nearest metropolitan district. As we shall see shortly, these measures appear to be highly intercorrelated and might be combined in a variety of ways into composite indexes with which our Index of Urbanism would highly correlate.

Since our focus is on size of population aggregate, so that we may study behavior correlates of increasing size of centers, population of largest metropolitan district or incorporated place has obvious pertinence to our Index. But equally important is percentage of county residents living in centers of various sizes. The problem is then: How to construct a composite measure which will reflect both the size of a county's largest center and the percentage of county residents experiencing center living in places of various sizes.

Our Index of Urbanism is the arithmetic mean of 10 separate measures of urbanism:

1. Percentage of population resident in places of 500,000 or more
2. Percentage of population resident in places of 250,000 or more
3. Percentage of population resident in places of 100,000 or more
4. Percentage of population resident in places of 50,000 or more
5. Percentage of population resident in places of 25,000 or more
6. Percentage of population resident in places of 10,000 or more
7. Percentage of population resident in places of 5,000 or more
8. Percentage of population resident in places of 2,500 or more
9. Percentage of population resident in places of 1,000 or more
10. Percentage of population resident in places of 500 or more

Places are defined as metropolitan districts and nonmetropolitan incorporated cities, towns, boroughs, and villages. Metropolitan districts are used instead of incorporated places when possible, since the

[1] Bureau of the Census, *County Data Book, A Supplement to the Statistical Abstract of the United States,* 1947.

boundaries of the former correspond more adequately to the effective limits of the center. For centers of less than 50,000 population, no reporting unit other than the incorporated place is available, and it is therefore used. Incorporated places which are within metropolitan boundaries are considered parts of their metropolitan districts and are not treated as separate places.

Figure 1 graphically presents the 100 sample counties arrayed according to urbanism scores. The distribution of scores strongly supports the hypothesis of the rural-urban continuum, *i.e.*, a continuous gradation from rural to urban, rather than a simple rural-urban dichotomy. One sample county, Essex, N.J., which is totally within the boundaries of the New York–northeastern New Jersey metropolitan district, scores the maximum possible, 100; and six counties, none of which has an incorporated place of 500 or more population lying wholly or partly within its boundaries, score the minimum possible, 0. Only seven counties have indices of 50 or more, while 52 counties have indices of less than 10. The positive skewness of the 100 county Indices of Urbanism is shown by Table 1. A pattern emerges of sharp variation among the counties of the United States with regard to degree of urbanism—a kind of urbanism pyramid peaked by a few metropolitan counties and broadly based in a large number of counties in which the great majority of the population reside outside populous centers.

Table 1. Distribution of Index of Urbanism Scores, 100 Randomly Representative United States Counties, 1940

Index of Urbanism Scores	Number of Counties
Total counties scored............100	
0– 9.9.....................	52
10.0– 19.9.....................	25
20.0– 29.9.....................	10
30.0– 39.9.....................	5
40.0– 49.9.....................	1
50.0– 59.9.....................	0
60.0– 69.9.....................	0
70.0– 79.9.....................	1
80.0– 89.9.....................	3
90.0–100.0.....................	3

SOURCE: Figure 1.

To test the validity of the Index of Urbanism, correlations have been run between it and six other commonly used measures of urbanism. As shown in Table 2 and Fig. 2, all six correlations are high, ranging from .75 to .86. Of no less interest than the amount and direction of association is the nature of the association between the Index of Urbanism and the

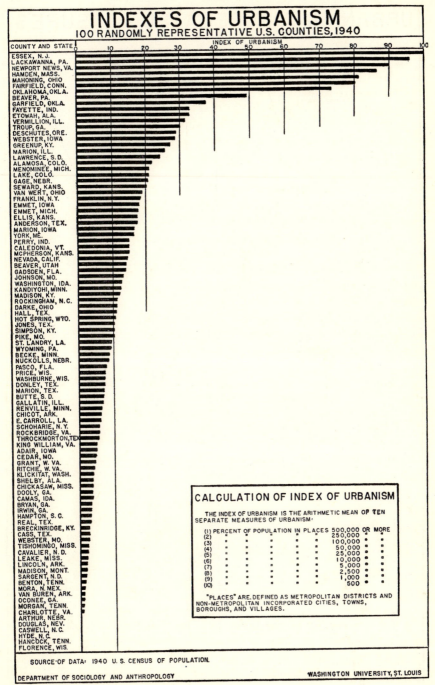

FIG. 1.

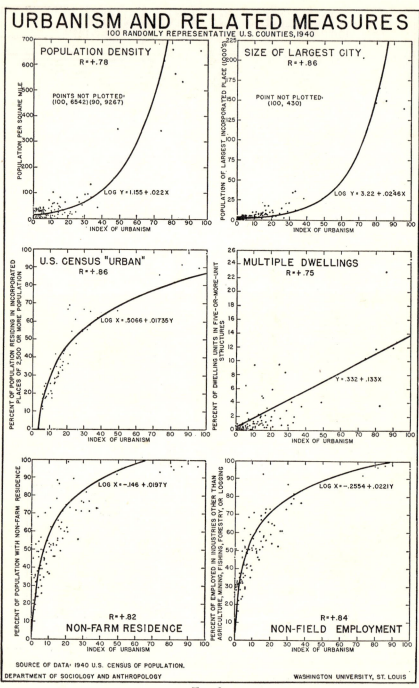

URBANISM AND RELATED MEASURES
100 RANDOMLY REPRESENTATIVE U.S. COUNTIES, 1940

POPULATION DENSITY
R = +.78

POINTS NOT PLOTTED:
(100, 6542) (90, 9267)

LOG Y = 1.155 + .022 X

POPULATION PER SQUARE MILE — INDEX OF URBANISM

SIZE OF LARGEST CITY
R = +.86

POINT NOT PLOTTED:
(100, 430)

LOG Y = 3.22 + .0246 X

POPULATION OF LARGEST INCORPORATED PLACE (100'S) — INDEX OF URBANISM

U.S. CENSUS "URBAN"
R = +.86

LOG X = .5066 + .01735 Y

PERCENT OF POPULATION RESIDING IN INCORPORATED PLACES OF 2,500 OR MORE POPULATION — INDEX OF URBANISM

MULTIPLE DWELLINGS
R = +.75

Y = .332 + .133 X

PERCENT OF DWELLING UNITS IN FIVE-OR-MORE-UNIT STRUCTURES — INDEX OF URBANISM

LOG X = −.146 + .0197 Y

R = +.82
NON-FARM RESIDENCE

PERCENT OF POPULATION WITH NON-FARM RESIDENCE — INDEX OF URBANISM

LOG X = −.2554 + .0221 Y

R = +.84
NON-FIELD EMPLOYMENT

PERCENT OF EMPLOYED IN INDUSTRIES OTHER THAN AGRICULTURE, MINING, FISHING, FORESTRY, OR LOGGING — INDEX OF URBANISM

SOURCE OF DATA: 1940 U.S. CENSUS OF POPULATION.
DEPARTMENT OF SOCIOLOGY AND ANTHROPOLOGY   WASHINGTON UNIVERSITY, ST. LOUIS

Fig. 2.

six related measures. In Fig. 2 are shown the scatter diagrams and one of the two lines of regression for each of the six relationships. In two cases, population density and size of largest city, geometric progression in the related measure is associated with arithmetic progression in the

Table 2. Correlations between the Index of Urbanism and Six Other Commonly Used Measures of Urbanism, 100 Randomly Representative United States Counties, 1940

Measure of Urbanism	Coefficient of Correlation of Measure with Index of Urbanism
Population of largest incorporated place lying wholly or partly in county..	+.86
Percentage of population residing in incorporated places of 2,500 or more population...	+.86
Percentage of employed persons in industries other than agriculture, mining, fishing, forestry, or logging.........................	+.84
Percentage of population with nonfarm residence...............	+.82
Population per square mile.................................	+.78
Percentage of dwelling units in five or more unit structures........	+.75

SOURCE: Figure 2.

Index of Urbanism. In three cases, United States census urban, nonfarm residence, and nonfield employment, arithmetic progression in the related measure is associated with geometric progression in the Index of Urbanism. In one case, multiple dwellings, a linear arithmetic relation obtains between the two measures. It is clear that the Index of Urbanism represents a measure intermediate between the continua related to city size and the continua related to percentage of population living in processing and trade centers.

In subsequent sections of this book, use will be made of the Index of Urbanism in the analysis of direction, amount, and nature of the association between ecological urbanism and patterns of human interaction. Hypotheses proposed in Chap. 2 will, when possible, be systematically tested.

A further test of the hypothesis of the rural-urban continuum is afforded on a more localized scale by field research done by one of the authors in Grays Harbor County in southwestern Washington.[2] This study was made in cooperation with a 1940 community planning project of the Washington State Planning Council, then concerned with the impact of timber depletion on the economy and social structure of communities of western Washington. The locus of the study was the community served by the town of Elma, embracing 250 square miles of mixed farming, logging, and milling territory, peopled by approximately

[2] David B. Carpenter, *Some Factors Associated with Influence Position in the Associational Structure of a Rural Community,* unpublished doctoral dissertation, University of Washington, Seattle, 1951.

8,000 inhabitants.[3] The considerable heterogeneity of this population with regard to residence and occupation—farm and logging camp versus trading town and mill town—affords data pertinent in at least a suggestive way to our problem of urbanism and its behavior correlates. The area is within commuting distance of the Puget Sound cities of Olympia and Tacoma, and the Pacific Ocean ports of Hoquiam and Aberdeen, and presents an intriguing and complex interplay of rural and urban characteristics.

Data were secured from 1,190 households, approximately two-thirds of the area's total. As part of the study, 116 local neighborhoods were identified in the Elma Community, and a series of eight scales were constructed with neighborhoods as reporting units. In addition to a scale to measure degree of rurality, there were prepared composite scale measures of (1) influence position in the associational structure of the Elma Community, (2) participation in the local associational structure, (3) plane of living, (4) occupational status, (5) educational status, (6) continuity of residence and job, and (7) satisfaction with residence and job. Validation of the eight scales was carried on through the Guttman scalogram technique, an empirical procedure for testing for internal consistency of composite with component scale scores.[4] Table 3 summarizes results of tests for validity.

Twenty-four component measures were combined into the composite rurality scale, as follows:

1. Percentage of households resident on farms.
2. Percentage of employed in agriculture.
3. Percentage of employed in agriculture or logging.
4. Percentage of households in which farm magazines are read regularly.
5. Percentage of households in which no magazines or farm magazines are read regularly.
6. Percentage of heads of households employed in agriculture.
7. Percentage of heads of households employed in agriculture or logging.
8. Percentage of heads of households preferring agricultural employment.

---

[3] Findings and recommendations of the planning survey are published in: Washington State Planning Council, *The Elma Survey,* Olympia, 1941. A popular account of the Elma Survey and its planning results as of that date is available in Stuart Chase, "How to Keep Ghosts Out of Town," *Reader's Digest,* 46 (1945), 53–56. For systematic sociological and human ecological studies of this area see Walter Firey, "Factors in Community Receptivity to a State Planning Program," *Jour. Appl. Anth.,* 1 (1942), pp. 7ff.; *Relation of Population Distribution and Redistribution to the Natural Resources of the Elma Service Area,* unpublished master's thesis, University of Washington, 1940.

[4] For a nontechnical presentation of the logic and method of scale analysis, see Louis Guttman, "The Cornell Technique of Scale and Intensity Analysis," *Educational and Psychological Measurement,* 7 (1947), 247–279. For the fullest treatment available, see Samuel A. Stouffer *et al., Measurement and Prediction,* Vol. IV of the *Studies in Social Psychology in World War II,* Princeton, 1950.

9. Percentage of heads of households preferring agricultural or logging employment.

10. Percentage of heads of households self-employed.

11. Percentage of households growing three-fourths or more of own food.

12. Percentage of households growing one-half or more of own food.

13. Percentage of households growing one-fourth or more of own food.

14. Percentage of households growing one-tenth or more of own food.

15. Percentage of households operating one or more acres of land.

16. Percentage of households operating one or more acres of cropland.

17. Percentage of households operating one or more acres of cleared pasture.

18. Percentage of households operating one or more acres of woodlot.

19. Percentage of households having one or more milch cows.

20. Percentage of households having one or more chickens.

21. Percentage of households having 10 or more chickens.

22. Percentage of heads of households preferring farm residence.

23. Percentage of heads of households preferring nontown residence.

24. Percentage of heads of households preferring residence elsewhere than in a town of 2,500 or more population.

Table 3. The Range, Reproducibility, and Predictability of Eight Scales Constructed with 116 Neighborhoods as Reporting Units, Elma Community, Washington, 1940

Scale designation	Range of scores	Reproducibility percentage*	Predictability percentage*
Rurality..............................	0–24	90.8	69.2
Satisfaction with residence and job.........	1–10	86.4	52.5
Continuity of residence and job...........	1–12	92.3	60.5
Influence position in the associational structure...................................	0–30	86.5	69.5
Occupational status......................	1–10	92.1	64.3
Participation in formally organized associations...................................	0–23	88.2	60.1
Plane of living.........................	0–17	86.6	37.8
Educational status......................	1–12	86.0	61.2

* Reproducibility percentage represents the percentage of component scores which are consistent with composite scale scores. Predictability percentage represents the percentage of component scores, excluding the modal scores for each component measure, which are consistent with composite scale scores. A reproducibility percentage of 85 or more and a predictability score of 50 or more are conventionally taken as minimum criteria of acceptable scalability. We have, however, utilized the plane of living scale despite its predictability percentage of 37.8.

Linear correlations were run between scores on the rurality scale and scores on each of the other seven scales, with results as shown in Table 4. Negative correlations were found in all cases except in the associations between rurality on the one hand and satisfaction and continuity of residence and job on the other. Figure 3 presents graphically as correlation profiles the matrix of intercorrelation between all eight scaled variables.

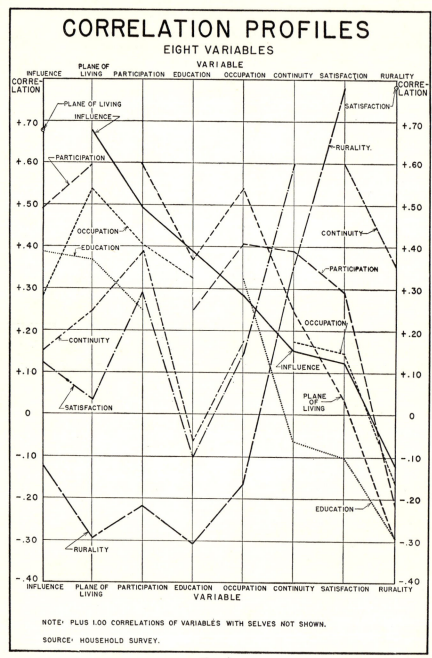

Fig. 3.

It is clear from the profiles that five of the variables cluster around plane of living, suggesting a common attribute of socioeconomic status: (1) educational status, (2) plane of living, (3) participation in formally organized associations, (4) occupational status, and (5) influence position in the associational structure. It is also clear that rurality is inversely related to the five socioeconomic status variables, and that the remaining two variables—satisfaction with residence and job and continuity of residence and job—are directly related both to the socioeconomic status variables and to rurality.

The +.78 correlation between rurality and satisfaction with residence and job is the highest of the correlation matrix and suggests a direct relationship between urbanism and dissatisfaction with residence and job. Possibly the process by which rural Americans are brought into the urban way of life is not unlike the process by which contented primitive peoples are lured into acculturation, and often dissatisfaction and disorganization, by the trinkets and baubles of the trader harbingers of Western civilization.

The intermediate position of satisfaction and continuity, between the socioeconomic status variables on the one hand and rurality on the other, suggests a conflict of values between rural residence and socioeconomic status. It appears in this study that rurality and continuity, valued in themselves, when sacrificed to urbanism and mobility, are given up as a means of achievement of greater income and socioeconomic status.

Table 4. Correlations between Rurality and (1) Satisfaction, (2) Continuity, (3) Influence Position, (4) Occupational Status, (5) Participation, (6) Plane of Living, and (7) Educational Status, 116 Neighborhoods, Elma Community, Washington, 1940

Scaled Continuum	Linear Coefficient of Correlation with Rurality
Satisfaction with residence and job	+.78
Continuity of residence and job	+.35
Influence position in the associational structure	−.12
Occupational status	−.17
Participation in formally organized associations	−.22
Plane of living	−.30
Educational status	−.31

In this chapter, we have attempted to develop a yardstick by which to measure the degree to which a population possesses urbanism. We have, for our purpose, distinguished between urbanism and urbanization: urbanism we use to identify the phenomenon of city residence; urbanization we use to identify the distinctive way of life typically associated with city residence. We have constructed an Index of Urbanism, utilizing a randomly representative sample of 100 United States counties, and 1940 United States census data. We have validated our measure of urbanism by its high direct correlation with six other common measures of urbanism, noting that our Index is an intermediate measure between geometrically associated measures of city size and measures of percentage of population living in processing and trade centers. With our Index and with a related study made in southwestern Washington, we have documented (1) the hypothesis that there is a continuous gradation in the United States from rural to urban rather than a simple rural-urban dichotomy and (2) the hypothesis that as human communities are arrayed along this rural-urban continuum, consistent variations occur in patterns of behavior.

Before proceeding further in the use of our Index of Urbanism in the study of behavior variations consistently associated with position on the rural-urban continuum, we shall turn to consideration of the historical factors which have given rise to cities.

SELECTED READINGS

BRADSHAW, NETTIE, P.: *County Classifications by Size of Largest City, United States, April, 1940,* Bureau of Agricultural Economics, 1944. For summary tables and discussion of characteristics of counties when classified by the size of the largest city, see Margaret Jarman Hagood, "Rural Population Characteristics," Carl C. Taylor, *et al., Rural Life in the United States,* Chap. 12, Alfred A. Knopf, Inc., 1949.

KEYES, FENTON: *The Correlation of Social Phenomena with Community Size,* unpublished doctoral dissertation, Yale University, 1942. Keyes has classified 3,890 United States cities of 2,000 or more population into 10 size intervals, and analyzed the relation to size of the incidence of a large number of social and economic characteristics.

OGBURN, WILLIAM F.: *Social Characteristics of Cities,* The International City Managers' Association, Chicago, 1937. A systematic analysis of the relation to the social and economic characteristics of a sample of United States cities by size, region, city type, and increase or decrease in size.

County Data Book, A Supplement to the Statistical Abstract of the United States, Bureau of the Census, 1947. A convenient source for recent statistical data, including series related to the measurement of urbanism, for all United States counties, metropolitan counties, and metropolitan areas.

"Population by Urban-Rural Classification," *Demographic Yearbook, 1948,* pp. 212–219, U.N. Statistical Office, 1949. The most convenient source of official definitions of urban and rural for 58 countries, together with recent urban-rural population data.

PART 2

The Rise of the City

CHAPTER 4.   *The Rise of Cities*

It is very difficult for a modern person, particularly one who has lived most of his life under urban conditions, to realize that mankind is overwhelmingly rural. In fact, until fairly recently in the evolution of man, our ancestors were exclusively rural. This cannot be stated in terms of dates and percentages, because the chronology of man's evolution is very far from precise. Nevertheless, a few generalizations may be ventured. It is pretty well agreed that there have been human beings of one kind or another for a half million to a million years. For twenty-five to fifty thousand years there have been men very much like ourselves. But until five or six thousand years ago there was nothing which we could recognize as a city. Against the background of man's history, the period of city dwelling is short indeed. But even that five thousand years has found only a small fraction of the human race urbanized. As recently as 1800 only 4 per cent of the population of the United States lived in places of 8,000 or more. In various European countries corresponding percentages ranged from 3 to 21.[1] Today over half the people of the United States and of Europe may be classed as urban. In 1927 there were 182 great cities (100,000 or over) in Europe, as against only 21 in 1801. At the beginning of the nineteenth century, so far as we know, there was no city over 100,000 outside of Europe. By 1927 there were 355 on other continents.[2] But we know that, the great cities of China, Japan, and India notwithstanding, the majority of Asiatics are villagers. The same thing is true of Africa and South America. This means that even today many more people live in villages, towns, and the open country than are found in cities.[3] Perhaps we might sum up the whole matter thus: A short time ago there were no cities at all. Just yesterday they became large and important. Even yet their dominance is not complete.

[1] Adna F. Weber, *The Growth of Cities in the Nineteenth Century*, pp. 144–145, 1899.

[2] Mark Jefferson, "Distribution of the World's City Folks," *Geog. Rev.*, 21 (1931), 446–465.

[3] Weber, *op. cit.*, Chap. 2.

PRECURSORS OF CITIES

Just what points have marked the transition from rural to urban living may never be established. However, we do have some information about various sorts of primitive communities and how they grew up. We need not go back to those distant ancestors who lived in trees and caves, gathering berries, nuts, and roots, killing small animals, and moving about from place to place. Their way of life was about as completely unlike that which we call urban as it is possible for us to conceive. Let us start with men who planted and cultivated grasses, roots, and trees.

Childe has called the cultivation of plants the first great economic revolution. It began to give man more control over his food supply and began to attach human groups to fixed places of residence. Wheat and barley seem to have been especially significant because of their combined food value, ease of storage, relatively high return, and fairly limited labor requirement. With such tillage, and also with the domestication of some animals, came an increase in population. Children could be useful in weeding the crops, chasing away birds, and tending sheep. Now the development of tillage and domestication did not necessarily mean the adoption of a sedentary life. Even today there are in Africa, Asia, and South America peoples who clear a patch in the jungle, reap a few crops, and leave to repeat the process somewhere else when the productiveness of the first tract of land has been used. Nevertheless, cultivation of the soil was a first step toward permanent residence, which in turn had to come long before there could be any such thing as a city.

Once people settled even temporarily, their groups became somewhat larger. Other things appeared which tended to make possible development in the direction of urbanism. One was planned cooperative effort. It was necessary for the whole group to work together in clearing a place in the forest, draining a marsh, making dikes to protect against floods, building irrigation canals, and erecting walls for defense. Through such large-scale activities men must have learned a great deal about the kind of teamwork which must be done if they are to live together in large groups and in permanent settlements.

Thus we have to observe that through most of human history (in the actual, not merely in the written, sense) the way of life followed by human beings might be described as nomadic and collectional. This gave way to a seminomadic and "hoe" economy which was in turn succeeded by primitive agricultural villages. Some of these villages must have grown to towns of a few thousand; some of them developed trade with peoples at a distance, but in general their activities and interests were localized, their numbers were small, and they were very unlike anything we would recognize as a city.[4] Nevertheless they were settled abodes where material goods might accumulate. The relative scarcity of desirable sites, the labor required for their improvement, the time needed for growth of orchards and vineyards, all contributed to stability. So did the storehouses, irrigation ditches, and walls for defense. Living close together within a limited area, forced to act together in military and engineering projects, and dependent on common sources of water and food, these neolithic villagers doubtless developed numerous social institutions. Their standard of living rose; they must have been envied and attacked by nomads from adjacent districts.

THE EARLIEST CITIES

It is probable that the earliest settlements that we would accept as urban appeared in the great stretch of semiarid lands reaching from Egypt to India. They developed along the valleys of the Nile, Tigris, Euphrates, and Indus Rivers. No doubt they started as neolithic villages which developed in one way and another into walled cities, some of which became the capitals of great empires. Their growth was probably associated with the necessity of assembling inside strong walls for defense, the attraction to a common shrine for religious purposes, or the development of a market for the exchange of various goods. These river valleys which were good places for the raising of certain crops were poor in other raw materials particularly stone and timber; hence trade must have developed very early. Now in order that trade might be carried on there had to be a surplus of some local produce for exchange, and it was necessary for a local group to support a body of traders and transport workers. They had to have craftsmen who could work up the imported articles; they needed soldiers to protect goods in transit, clerks to keep records of transactions, and public officials to adjudicate disputes. All these represented developments in the direction of numbers, heterogeneity, and complexity, which we associate with city life. Apparently it was about the middle of the third millennium B.C. that some of these cities became imperial capitals. Doubtless this resulted from clashes between rival cities, union of some sort for protection against hostile forces, the prestige of outstanding warriors, judges, or priests.

In general, the conditions attending the appearance of these first cities have been summarized by Carpenter as: (1) mild climate, (2) growth

[4] The story of cultural development before the appearance of cities and the kinds of communities that preceded the existence of cities have been presented in the following works: V. Gordon Childe, *Man Makes Himself*, 1936; Niles Carpenter, *The Sociology of City Life*, Chap. 1, 1931; Dwight Sanderson, *The Rural Community*, Chaps. 2–3, 1932.

of cereals, (3) relative freedom from attack, (4) soil and climate which favored people's living close together.[5] To Carpenter's list, Gras[6] adds transportation facilities by land and by water, a considerable distance from possible rivals, and a fairly wide free-trade area. In the areas described, these conditions obtained; but whether they were all essential to the rise of cities or whether cities might have arisen under other conditions it is impossible to say. It is at least worth noting that the Incas in Peru, the Aztecs in Mexico, and the Mayans in Yucatan developed many features of an urban civilization in quite different environments. The freedom from attack mentioned by Carpenter was very real in Egypt but far from complete in Mesopotamia. His fourth point seems to us more important. The fertile valleys were narrow and were surrounded by wide deserts. These conditions promoted the cooperation for flood control, irrigation, and other purposes discussed in the preceding section. In any event, further research is necessary before we can assess the importance of the various factors associated with the appearance of cities in the Near East.

Another problem concerning the earliest cities pertains to their dominant functions. It is frequently held that they were primarily places of defense or seats of government. It is observed that they were also centers of worship and to a certain extent headquarters of trade. Which of these functions was primary in time and which was supreme in importance are questions much less easily answered than may appear to the casual student. Again it may be that further historical research will enable us to make more definite statements on these matters. For the present we can merely observe that the earliest cities seem to have performed for their inhabitants these four functions.

CITIES OF THE MEDITERRANEAN WORLD

While some really great cities were appearing in Egypt, Babylonia, and India, Europe was inhabited by rude pastoral peoples whose lives were crude and whose communities were small. However, around the eastern Mediterranean and Aegean Seas cities grew up one after another. Beginning with the seaports of Phoenicia, they spread into the western Mediterranean and then northward into Gaul.

In their development it appears that the usual sequence was something like this: (1) Several clans or tribes settled together for common defense, worship, and trade. (2) A tribal village grew into a big town, retaining, however, the kinship type of social organization with the elders of the

[5] Carpenter, *op. cit.*, p. 21. By permission of Longmans, Green & Co., Inc.
[6] N. S. B. Gras, "The Rise of the Metropolitan Community," *The Urban Community*, edited by E. W. Burgess, pp. 183–191, 1926. By permission of the University of Chicago Press.

clans often forming a council or senate. (3) As trade developed, individuals not important in the clans sometimes came to the fore, sought emancipation from the kinship system, and elevated one or several of their number to positions of authority. Thus appeared the tyrants in Greek city-states. (4) The numbers of ordinary traders, soldiers, and artisans increased; the tyrants were perhaps overthrown, and a semi-democratic government was set up, representing usually, however, only the slaveowners.

Now this cannot be accepted as a universal sequence. In fact, it may not have been followed precisely in a single instance. Nevertheless, something like this order of events does seem to have occurred often enough to warrant our using it as a pattern of the general trend. Whether changes in the physical pattern bore any relation to changes in the social pattern has not been established. But there are some indications that a common sequence was: (1) a defensive hilltop settlement, expanding to include (2) a market place in a valley, and (3) a harbor on a river, estuary, or bay. (4) The original hilltops become aristocratic residential sections or the sites of temples and other public buildings. (5) The lowlands were occupied by residences of poorer people and by expanding business.

There is evidence that some of these cities of antiquity grew to very great size. The Greeks had several cities which undoubtedly reached 100,000 in population. Weber thinks that Carthage may have attained the figure of 700,000. Rome grew to more than half a million and quite likely contained at one time nearly a million people. It is interesting in view of this significant development in the Roman Empire that cities subsequently declined and that by the beginning of the sixteenth century there were only a half dozen in the 100,000 class.

The cities of two thousand years ago were both like and unlike those of today. In Rome some of the streets were paved; water was brought down from the mountains; sewers emptied into the Tiber; there were public baths; and, in the reign of Augustus, systems of fire and police protection were highly developed. First in Rome and later in provincial cities, the concept of a municipal corporation evolved; *i.e.*, Roman cities became legal entities, artificial persons. However, most cities of antiquity lacked some or all of the urban characteristics just mentioned.

The appearance of Periclean Athens (fifth century B.C.) has been described in words which show it to have been a real city, yet something very different from a modern metropolis.[7] On a high hill called the Acropolis were stately temples to the gods, but below it was a "sea of low flat roofs," without a single chimney. There were no attractive houses, but mostly one-story dwellings with blank walls of sun-dried

---

[7] J. H. Breasted, *The Conquest of Civilization*, Chap. 15, 1926. By permission of Harper & Brothers.

brick. They had few windows, dirt floors, no plumbing or drainage, but many beautiful utensils, some lovely furniture, and some books. The streets were narrow, crooked lanes without pavement or sidewalks. All household rubbish and garbage were thrown directly into the streets. There were no sewers and no system of street cleaning. At the foot of the Acropolis was an outdoor theater with wooden seats. Farther down the slope was a market place. The entire city covered the equivalent of about 150 modern blocks, though it was not laid out in any such orderly fashion. Surrounding the whole was a wall, with a double wall reaching down to Piraeus, the seaport. The urban population was perhaps 100,000 including a large number of slaves and some foreigners. Another 100,000 lived in outlying parts of Attica, dependent on Athens as a market, administrative, religious, and military center. But other sections of ancient Greece were much more rural, as were most parts of the Mediterranean world.

Perhaps the change from classical antiquity to the so-called dark ages was not really as great as we sometimes imagine. After all, in spite of the truly great cities that existed, most people were residents of little villages. Hence, when the northern tribesmen and villagers swept down into southern Europe we may say that they were merely making apparent what had been really true all the time, namely, that the bulk of mankind was rural and the city dwellers were rather exceptional. In other words, the mere presence of cities does not mean that a region has been truly urbanized. As Carpenter puts it, "In an urban society the city dominates the scene. It is the center of gravity, politically, socially, and culturally."[8] Moreover, the country is economically dependent upon it. Each city not only dominates its own hinterland but is in close touch with other urban centers. By way of contrast, in nonurban societies cities are small, communication is slow and uncertain, trade is mostly local, the city is economically dependent on the country, but the latter is almost self-sufficing. This hypothesis is worthy of further study. Certainly there is a great difference between an agricultural civilization, with occasional cities as centers of government, religion, and trade, and an urban society like that of present-day England. However, one should not be too hasty in assuming that the cultures of the ancient world were all nonurban.

MEDIEVAL TOWNS

We have suggested that the cities of classical antiquity declined and in some instances disappeared. This was not because the Germans came to destroy the cities but rather because they did not know how to live

[8] Carpenter, *op. cit.*, p. 19. By permission of Longmans, Green & Co., Inc.

in them. This urban decline was likewise bound up with the encroachments of the Mohammedans, so that by the end of the eighth century Charlemagne's empire was inland, isolated, and practically without foreign commerce. Rome itself had declined from a possible 1 million inhabitants to less than 20,000. Now the towns that remained were for the most part fortresses, feudal administrative centers, or ecclesiastical headquarters. Economically they were bound up with the neighboring countryside. They were not part of a far-reaching nexus of commercial activities and relations. Pirenne has said:[9]

It is, therefore, a safe conclusion that the period which opened with the Carolingian Era knew cities neither in the social sense, nor in the economic sense, nor in the legal sense of that word. The towns and burgs were merely fortified places and headquarters of administration. Their inhabitants enjoyed neither special laws nor institutions of their own, and their manner of living did not distinguish them in any way from the rest of society.

Some of these medieval towns apparently grew through their markets, fairs, and otherwise into cities possessing those features with which we are familiar; but the actual urban development of the late Middle Ages and early modern period seems most often to have involved an external stimulus and accretion of strangers. The external stimulus seems to have been bound up with the Crusades and the expanding influence of Venice. Now this city had a unique history. It was founded by people who were fleeing before the advancing Huns. They found a refuge on some barren islands which lacked even drinking water. Hence they were forced to become traders in order to survive. In the beginning they exchanged salt and fish for wheat and other necessities. Thus they escaped conquest by the Germans and remained under the sovereignty and influence of Constantinople; thus they maintained an urban tradition in an era of ruralization. But Venice did not attain importance until the Crusades created a great demand for supplies and ships to carry men and equipment to the Holy Land. She was relatively well prepared to supply these wants, because of her location, because she had many ships, and because she had a business system. While Europe as a whole was engaging in local barter, Venice was carrying cargoes between distant points, operating a credit system, keeping books, making commercial treaties. In due time other Italian cities began to imitate and rival Venice; ere long, merchants from these places were finding their way to the markets of various lands in western Europe.

Thus there came to be a conspicuous number of traveling merchants, peddlers, and foot-loose adventurers who went about in groups for

[9] Henri Pirenne, *Medieval Cities: Their Origins and the Revival of Trade*, p. 76, 1925. By permission of Princeton University Press.

mutual protection, sometimes organized themselves into brotherhoods, and usually invited the suspicion of those who lived settled lives under the feudal order. Now these wandering merchants needed a point to which they could return between trips, during the winter, or otherwise as convenience might dictate, so some of them settled down usually just outside the walls of some burg or episcopal town. Presumably they had not merely a place of temporary residence but one where goods might be stored and transferred. For defense they often erected a wall about their little settlement. Sometimes a "new burg" grew entirely around the old town, and ultimately the public interests and governments of the two tended to merge. To the merchants were added persons who engaged in transportation, the manufacture of boats and vehicles and other accessories of the developing commerce. Industries were drawn in from the country, *e.g.*, working with wool.

These new towns, of course, found it necessary to come to some sort of terms with the feudal proprietors of the soil. The merchants did not fit into the old order. They were a new sort of folks. Pirenne calls them *de facto* free men because their original status was unknown. But many of their servants and artisans came from nearby demesnes whose lords sometimes tried to identify and reclaim them. This made trouble, as did intermarriage of the two groups. Other ways in which feudalism hampered the development of trade included the fees charged for the holding of markets, for the use of bridges, and for crossing the boundaries of petty states. Finding it difficult, if not impossible, to carry on business under feudal limitations, townsmen entered upon a struggle which was basically for four or five concessions. First of all, the city dwellers wanted freedom to transfer and mortgage their property without securing the permissions and paying the fees required of feudal tenants. Second, they wanted a new legal system eliminating the old-fashioned compurgations and ordeals and offering a more dependable, more rational system of justice, to be operated by their own magistrates. In the third place, they wanted to administer some of their own affairs independently and to raise taxes for these municipal purposes, which included water supply and fortification. In general, they wanted the abolition of feudal dues, the regulation of new laws, the appointment of their own officials—in short, a new social status. The acquisition of these prerogatives resulted in the recognition of "free cities" or city-states having more and more of the traits we associate with urbanism. In Germany several score of cities united in the great Hanseatic League to win and defend such concessions as we have just mentioned. In France, England, and other countries they made individual agreements with the nobility or secured royal aid in escaping from ancient requirements. Thus in one way or another there emerged not only a new agglomeration of people and buildings but also a new commerce, a new form of government—in short, a new way of life.

The history of Paris[10] involves many of the features we have mentioned but is unique on account of the important role which government played in its development. Near the convergence of several navigable rivers and actually occupying an island in the Seine, Julius Caesar found Lutetia, the principal town of the Parisii. Two wooden bridges connected the island with the north and south banks, respectively, providing a convenient crossing of the river. During the first century this became a fortified Roman town, which spread out on both banks of the Seine, and included a theater, an arena, baths, an aqueduct, and other tangible evidences of urban development. About A.D. 300 this relatively luxurious town was destroyed, but it was later rebuilt as an island fortress with a fortified bridgehead on each bank.

In the fifth century the Franks gained possession of Paris, and a little later their King, Clovis, made this the seat of his rule. It was a convenient center from which to control the expanding territory which he was bringing under his power. Paris was growing as a political and ecclesiastical center. However, with the Norman invasions of the ninth century and the development of feudalism, Paris apparently suffered a setback which lasted until the accession of the Capetian dynasty toward the end of the tenth century. From that time on the city revived and grew with the power of the monarchy. In the eleventh century there was considerable expansion of trade and by 1200 Paris had become a city of some consequence.

Structurally and functionally it consisted of three parts. The island, now called *La Cité*, was the center of government and the site of the cathedral. It had narrow streets and was connected with the banks of the river by two bridges. On the north bank, where boats anchored, were a market and the houses and shops of merchants, but there were also many empty spaces, orchards, and vineyards interspersed with churches. On the south bank were schools and convents occupied by students, teachers, and writers, together with tradesmen who catered to their needs. In the thirteenth century the group included such illustrious foreigners as Thomas Aquinas and Albertus Magnus. Surrounding the whole city was a wall with towers and fortified gates, started by Philip Augustus in 1180. But the city could not be confined within these limits. The commercial section spread out toward the north so that in a century and a half another wall was needed. Shortly before its erection, a census was taken, in 1329, which enumerated 61,000 "hearths," *i.e.*, households, including possibly 290,000 persons.

[10] A. Demangeon, *Paris: la ville et sa banlieue*, pp. 10–14, 1933; Lucien Gallois, "The Origin and Growth of Paris," *Geog. Rev.*, 13 (1923), 345–367.

Paris had grown from a small town to a great city as a place of defense, the site of religious institutions, a crossing of trade routes, a commercial center, and above all as a seat of government. For over eight centuries Paris has been a capital city.

THE INDUSTRIAL REVOLUTION AND THE DEVELOPMENT OF CITIES

It is impossible in such a work as this to follow the fortunes of other medieval towns as they grew into modern cities. The basic principles of their emergence and growth were established in such ways as have just been indicated. By the end of the eighteenth century there were in Europe possibly 300 towns and cities of 10,000 inhabitants or more; there were 21 cities of over 100,000 inhabitants.[11] The next great culture change associated with the development of cities is that complex series of events which we call the Industrial Revolution. As a matter of fact, this was not only industrial; it was also a revolution in agriculture, in transportation and communication, in social control, and in urbanization.

It is generally agreed that this great social change manifested itself first in England, probably first of all in the textile industry. England had a good climate for textile manufactures, farm lands were being enclosed to provide more wool for the spinners, British imperialism had opened the way for widespread markets for the finished products. Presently under some impetus, improvements were effected here and there in the making of woolen and cotton cloth. One invention followed another until the output was enormously increased and the number of employed workers multiplied manyfold.

Something of the same sort happened in the metal trades. Whether it was the reduced availability of charcoal that necessitated the use of coal and hence forced a change in the process of manufacturing iron and steel, or whether other influences would have brought this about, we need not pause here to inquire. We need only observe that in this industry another series of inventions took place which considerably changed the character of metalworking. The new development of mechanical power may have been stimulated by considerations of economy and the desire for greater output in the industry just mentioned. Perhaps the need for new and greater power to pump water out of the mines, or perhaps still another stimulation should be held accountable. In any case, the latter part of the eighteenth century and early part of the nineteenth saw the rapid displacement of manpower by water and steam. Now this new mechanical power could be utilized most effectively in the operation of large machines or large groups of machines, hence it was natural that

[11] Weber, *op. cit.*, Chap. 2.

factories should appear and mass production should begin. But the development of factories meant the getting to them of great numbers of workers. So factory towns and cities grew up.

The changes that took place during the same period in agriculture facilitated the growth of cities in at least two ways. As new methods of tilling the soil and new farm implements were introduced, as lands were enclosed for the raising of sheep, there was a surplus labor supply crowded off the rural estates and available for employment in the factories. As agricultural production increased, there was a surplus of foods and other raw materials by means of which urban populations could be supported.

Still a third revolution had to accompany the industrial and agricultural revolutions. There was a tremendous change in means of transportation and communication. The earlier roads and vehicles and ships could not possibly have carried from the farms to the cities sufficient food at a price and within a length of time that would have permitted large industrial communities to develop. But with the application of steam to both water and rail, this new urban growth was greatly facilitated. No less important has been the later development of canning, refrigeration, and cold storage. Since the conduct of business was no longer limited to local or even national markets, it required much better communications. The steamboat and the railroad carried people to and fro faster than ever before. The regular mails sped up the transmission of messages, the newspaper printed on a steam press disseminated general information to those concerned with the market. Long after, there came, of course, the telegraph and telephone, the radio, electric railway, automobile, and airway, all of which have made possible the transacting of business over large areas, economically uniting groups of great cities.

One of the first great cities to be developed in the Industrial Revolution was Manchester, England. But its origin was much earlier. Apparently the site was first occupied by a Roman camp. Subsequently a Saxon community grew up. In Norman times it was part of a feudal estate with a market, a fair, and a borough court. There is evidence that the textile industry had taken root here before 1300. This received an impetus from the coming of Dutch and Flemish workers invited by Edward III. Through the sixteenth century the raw materials were wool and flax; by the middle of the seventeenth some cotton was being imported. The stuff was given out to be taken home, carded, spun, woven, bleached, or dyed, and returned to the merchant-clothier—the so-called domestic system. Hence, there was no large population in the town. In 1650 Manchester had less than 5,000 inhabitants.

But the domestic system was not very efficient. A weaver sometimes had to walk 3 or 4 miles in the morning to collect enough yarn to keep him busy through the day. By 1750 there were master weavers who, instead of giving out homework, brought together journeymen and apprentices in shops with 5 to 20 looms apiece. As a result of this centralization, the population of Manchester had grown to 17,000. But industry and urban development were alike hampered by primitive transportation facilities. We read of wagons and caravans of pack horses going weekly to London and Bristol. During the next half century, good roads were built and waterways were opened connecting Manchester with Liverpool and with inland towns.

In 1769 water power was applied to spinning machines, and soon mills were set up wherever there was a good water-power site. Industry was again decentralized, leaving to Manchester certain finishing processes and marketing. But by 1800 available water-power sites had nearly all been utilized. Meanwhile development of the steam engine and of nearby coal fields helped to reverse the trend and to bring about a new concentration of mills in Manchester. By 1800 the city had 70,000 inhabitants, of whom 10,000 were Irish immigrants. Naturally the city spread out, but it also became more congested in the center. New residential districts grew up in outlying sections, but near the heart of the city old houses were turned into converted tenements, where whole families were crowded into single rooms. Newer dwellings were put up in "gloomy little courts and blind alleys," while hundreds of families lived in dark, damp cellars. New streets in outlying districts were wide and straight, but those in the central and older section were narrow, winding, and for the most part unlighted and unpaved. In 1776 there was some widening, but not until 1821 was there a more general clearance. Moreover its purpose was to facilitate traffic rather than to improve the public health. In 1830 the opening of the Manchester and Liverpool Railway brought another aid to urban development. By 1850 the population had risen to nearly 400,000. Thus grew up one of the first great industrial cities.[12]

SELECTED READINGS

CHILDE, V. GORDON: *Man Makes Himself,* Watts and Company, London, 1936. Describes the "neolithic revolution" and "urban revolution" of the Near East as two great turning points in cultural development. A briefer account is found in the next reference.

CHILDE, V. GORDON: *What Happened in History,* Penguin Books, Inc., 1946.

GRAS, N. S. B.: "The Rise of the Metropolitan Community," pp. 183–191 of *The Urban Community,* edited by E. W. Burgess, University of Chicago

---

[12] G. H. Tupling, "Old Manchester: A Sketch of Its Growth to the End of the Eighteenth Century," *Jour. Manchester Geog. Soc.,* 45 (1935), 5–23; R. S. Atwood, "Localization of the Cotton Industry in Lancashire, England," *Econ. Geog.,* 4 (1928), 187–195.

Press, 1926. Depicts the rise of cities in relation to stages of economic development.

MUMFORD, LEWIS: *The Culture of Cities,* Harcourt, Brace and Company, Inc., 1938. Chapters 1 and 2 offer a brilliant, but somewhat biased, account of the development of medieval and early modern cities.

PIRENNE, HENRI: *Medieval Cities: Their Origins and the Revival of Trade,* Princeton University Press, 1925. Describes the breakdown of urbanism during the Germanic invasions of southern Europe and its revival during the commercial revolution.

TURNER, RALPH: *The Great Cultural Traditions,* Vol. 1, "The Ancient Cities," McGraw-Hill Book Company, Inc., 1941. Sketches of man's preurban background and the rise of cities in Mesopotamia, India, Egypt, China, and the Mediterranean world of the classical period.

CHAPTER 5

Recent Urban Development and Associated Factors

In Chap. 4 we pointed out how very recent is the development of cities and urban ways of life. We emphasized this by showing that in 1800, which roughly marks the beginning of the period of the Industrial Revolution, the percentage of our (United States) population that was urban (living in places of 8,000 or more) was less than 4. For all Europe it may have been equally small, though in Great Britain and the Netherlands it was somewhat greater. In the whole world there were reported to be only 21 cities of 100,000 and none of 1,000,000 population.[1] The 21 referred to were all in Europe. There may well have been some equally large cities in Asia, but unfortunately our sources of information are not very dependable. In any case, it is safe to say that the world of 1800 was overwhelmingly rural.

But during the nineteenth and twentieth centuries great changes have taken place. By 1927 Jefferson counted 537 cities in the class of 100,000 or more.[2] In 1944 Masuoka referred to 649 including 37 of 1,000,000 inhabitants or more.[3] In 1948 Gist and Halbert made a tabulation of 721.[4] It should be said in all honesty that these figures are not altogether comparable, and we are not quite sure what they mean. The difficulty arises partly from the varied definitions of what is a city, partly from the lack of recent censuses, and partly from the disturbances of World War II and subsequent years. However, in order to give a general idea of the urbanism that had developed by 1950, we have assembled some rough estimates in Table 5.

These estimates by continents are supplemented by Tables 6 and 7

[1] Mark Jefferson, "Distribution of the World's City Folks," *Geog. Rev.* 21 (1931), 446–465.
[2] *Ibid.*
[3] Jitsuichi Masuoka, "Race and Culture Contacts in the Emporium: A Frame of Reference," *Amer. Jour. Sociol.*, 50 (1944), 201.
[4] Noel P. Gist and L. A. Halbert, *Urban Society*, p. 21, 1948.

indicating the urbanism of selected countries in 1800, 1930, and 1950. However, we have not attempted to bring Table 6 up to date because in many countries no recent data are available. War prevented census taking in 1940, and 1950 data are coming in very slowly.[5]

The three tables presented below indicate the approximate, rather than the exact truth. In some countries no census was taken until long after 1800. The most recent counts have been made at various dates. For the United States we report metropolitan districts rather than municipalities. The boundaries of some countries have been changed, some of them several times. For these and other reasons, the figures must be used with discretion. Nevertheless, they display an unmistakable trend toward urbanization of the world.

Table 5. Estimated Urbanism by Continents, 1950

Continent	Cities of 1,000,000 and over	Cities of 100,000 and over	Per cent of total population in cities of 100,000 and over
Africa..................	1	25	3
Asia.....................	10	170	5
Australia................	2	10	45
Europe..................	15	300	20
North America...........	15	160	30
South America...........	3	35	12
Total................	46	700	

SOURCE: Estimates based on *United Nations Demographic Yearbook, 1948;* advance releases of the United States census, 1950; Noel P. Gist and L. A. Halbert, *Urban Society,* p. 21, 1948; Jitsuichi Masuoka, "Race and Culture Contacts in the Emporium: A Frame of Reference," *Amer. Jour. Sociol.,* 50 (1944), 201.

So far we have been considering urban development without reference to particular cities. In Table 8 we present data which indicate how very large certain cities have become and how they have grown since 1800. However, in detail many qualifications and corrections need to be made. Some of the figures cover the metropolitan district, while others represent only the "inner city," or the political unit. Some data are missing altogether, because no recent census has been taken and no reliable estimate is at our disposal. World War II involved the scattering of populations and the partial destruction of many cities which have not yet been fully restored. Nevertheless, despite serious shortcomings, this table, like the other three, offers convincing evidence of rapid urban expansion since 1800. In that year there were no cities of 1,000,000 and less than 25 of 100,000 inhabitants. Now there are over 40 in the million class.

[5] Some supplementary data are to be found in Kingsley Davis and Ana Casis, "Urbanization in Latin America," *Milbank Memorial Fund Quarterly,* 24 (1946), 186–207.

Table 6. Urbanism in 15 Selected Countries, 1800 to 1930

Country	Per cent of population living in great cities		Number of great cities		Population of great cities	
	1930	1800	1930	1800	1930	1800
Great Britain..............	49	10	58	1	22,900,000	865,000
United States*...........	45	0	96	0	55,000,000	
Australia................	43	0	5	0	3,050,000	
Germany................	30	1	53	1	19,950,000	200,000
Argentina...............	30	0	8	0	3,750,000	
Canada.................	22	0	7	0	2,320,000	
France.................	20	3	17	3	8,625,000	765,000
Italy...................	15	4	22	4	6,175,000	800,000
Japan..................	14	0	21	0	9,200,000	
Brazil..................	10	0	10	0	4,000,000	
Mexico.................	8	0	4	0	1,400,000	
Russia.................	7	1	31	3	11,000,000	500,000
Turkey.................	7	?	3	3	1,000,000	1,000,000
China..................	6	0	112	3	22,000,000	
India..................	3	0	38	0	11,900,000	

SOURCE: Data for this table were derived from Adna F. Weber, *The Growth of Cities in the Nineteenth Century*, 1899; Mark Jefferson, "Distribution of the World's City Folks," *Geog. Rev.*, 21 (1931), 446–465; United States census, 1930; *The World Almanac*, 1937.
* Bureau of the Census, *Metropolitan Districts*, 1930.

Table 7. Percentage of Total Population Living in Places of 10,000 and Over, 1800 to 1950.

Country	1950	1930	1890	1850	1800
England and Wales..........	74*	80	62	39	21
France....................	38	50	26	14	10
United States..............	48	47	27	12	4
Australia.................	74†	45	41		

SOURCE: Data for first three periods are from Adna F. Weber, *The Growth of Cities in the Nineteenth Century*, pp. 144–145, 1899. For 1930 they are based on sources used in constructing Table 2 and are intentionally in round numbers. For 1950 they are based on United States census, 1950; *Whitaker's Almanack*, 1951; *U.N. Demographic Year Book*, 1948.
* Includes Scotland.
† Only cities of 25,000 and over.

Whitaker's Almanack for 1951 lists 40 cities with more than 1 million inhabitants each.[6] In many cases the figures do not cover the metropolitan area. Hence it is reasonable to suppose that the actual number of such population aggregates is somewhat larger. Also the dates reported vary from 1931 to 1949. During the intervening period some cities are

[6] *Whitaker's Almanack*, p. 204, 1951.

known to have increased considerably in size, while others, like Seoul have been almost destroyed. The reader can easily understand, therefore, why it is impossible to present an accurate count of urban populations at any given date.

Data at hand, but not included in Table 8, indicate that some individual cities have grown at an amazing rate. Even old London multiplied ninefold, if we may assume that city and metropolitan district were approximately identical in 1800. Greater New York multiplied a hundredfold and Sydney (not included in the table) nearly five-hundredfold.

Table 8. Largest Cities in the World

City	Estimated population, 1950	Date	Area
New York	12,800,000	1950	Metropolitan
London	8,700,000	1931	Greater London
Shanghai	6,000,000	1949	Greater Shanghai
Chicago	5,500,000	1950	Metropolitan
Tokyo	5,400,000	1947	Prefecture
Paris	5,000,000	1947	Greater Paris
Los Angeles	4,300,000	1950	Metropolitan
Berlin	4,300,000	1946	Greater Berlin
Moscow	4,100,000	1939	
Philadelphia	3,700,000	1950	Metropolitan
Osaka	3,300,000	1947	Prefecture
Leningrad	3,200,000	1931	
Kobe	3,100,000	1947	Prefecture
Buenos Aires	3,000,000	1947	
Detroit	3,000,000	1950	Metropolitan
Calcutta	2,700,000	1947	
Yokohama	2,700,000	1947	
Mexico City	2,500,000	1949	
Rio de Janeiro	2,500,000	1948	
Boston	2,400,000	1950	Metropolitan
Pittsburgh	2,200,000	1950	Metropolitan
San Francisco–Oakland	2,200,000	1950	Metropolitan
Vienna	2,000,000	1948	

SOURCE: Bureau of the Census, Preliminary Reports, 1950; Japanese Census, 1947; *Whitaker's Almanack*, 1951; *The World Almanac*, 1951.

If one examines Table 8 with reference to location of the world's largest cities about 1950, he will find that 8 were in the United States, 6 in Europe, 6 in Asia, and 3 in Latin America. The largest of them all, New York, seems to represent the culmination of a westward movement. In 1800 the largest city was London; in 1600 it was Paris; in 1500 it was Constantinople. Perhaps before the twentieth century is over the lead may pass to some Asiatic city.

One more comment should be made before we turn from world-wide development of urbanism to the growth of cities in our own country:

urban development has been in part an aspect of general increase in population. It has been estimated that the world's population in 1750 was 660 million, that in 1850 it was 1,100 million, and that in 1950 it had risen to 2,300 million. This alone directly implies a great increase in city dwellers. Indirectly it has still further implications, for the improvements in agriculture which added to the world's food supply released surplus rural workers for urban commerce and industry. Hence it is quite natural that cities should grow much faster than their rural hinterlands.

THE GROWTH OF CITIES IN THE UNITED STATES

As might be expected, the growth of cities has been especially marked in our own country. With "a continent to conquer," unbelievable natural resources, a growing flood of immigrants (until 1914), new inventions appearing at an accelerated rate, and a philosophy of "bigger and better," it is not surprising that the United States has had a great urban development. As shown in Table 6, we had in 1800 no city of 100,000 inhabitants. By 1950 we had 150 metropolitan districts ranging from 100,000 to nearly 13,000,000. Another view of the trend toward urbanization is offered by Table 9. Here we see a great and steady increase in the number of places reported as urban and in the percentage of the total population that they contain. These increases are apparent whether one draws the line at 2,500, at 100,000, or at 1,000,000. However, it should be noted that the places reported are incorporated municipalities, whether or not parts of a metropolitan area, and whether inclusive of all the people living close together or having a suburban fringe outside the legal boundaries. These uncertainties are very confusing for some purposes, but at this point they are not very serious, because by every method of counting we find the number of cities increasing, and the urban population increasing both absolutely and relatively. Thus Table 10 shows a steady increase in the number and population of metropolitan districts and in the percentage of the United States population which they contain. Also they have absorbed a disproportionate share of the national increase.

Periods of Urban Development. McKenzie offers an interpretation of urban development in the United States in relation to three periods, each with a dominant type of transportation—water, railroad, motor.[7] The first period, according to his analysis, was that of development along the seacoast, lakes, and navigable rivers. This era lasted to 1850 and was marked by a predominantly rural population living east of the Mississippi River, in fact, mainly east of the Alleghanies. The second period was marked by rapid westward expansion of the railroads, occupation of new

[7] R. D. McKenzie, *The Metropolitan Community*, Chap. 1, 1933.

Table 9. Development of Urbanism in the United States, 1790 to 1950

Year	Incorporated places of 2,500 and over		Incorporated places of 100,000 and over		Incorporated places of 1,000,000 and over	
	Number of places	Per cent of total population	Number of places	Per cent of total population	Number of places	Per cent of total population
1950	3,873	57.0	106	29.9	5	11.5
1940	3,464	56.5	92	28.9	5	12.1
1930	3,165	56.2	93	29.6	5	12.3
1920	2,722	51.2	68	26.0	3	9.6
1910	2,262	45.7	50	22.1	3	9.2
1900	1,737	39.7	38	18.8	3	8.5
1890	1,348	35.1	28	15.4	3	5.8
1880	939	28.2	20	12.4	1	2.4
1870	663	25.7	14	10.8		
1850	236	15.3	6	5.0		
1830	90	8.8	1	1.6		
1810	46	7.3				
1790	24	5.1				

SOURCE: Adapted from Bureau of the Census, *Urban Population in the United States from the First Census (1790) to the Fifteenth Census (1930)*, 1939; and *Historical Statistics of the United States, 1789–1945*, Supplement to the Statistical Abstract, 1949; Preliminary Reports, 1950.

Table 10. Metropolitan Districts of the United States, 1900 to 1950

Year	Number of districts	Total population of districts, in millions	Per cent of United States population in districts	Per cent of United States increase in districts
1950	168	84	55.7	80.6
1940	140	63	47.8	53.0
1930	97	55	44.6	70.8
1920	58	36	34.0	55.5
1910	44	26	28.3	41.9
1900	44	19	25.5	

SOURCE: Adapted from Warren S. Thompson, *The Growth of Metropolitan Districts in the United States: 1900–1940*, 1947; Bureau of the Census, Preliminary Reports, 1950. The 1950 data pertain to standard metropolitan areas.

lands, and the development of cities at junctions and convenient shipping centers. The third period, which McKenzie dates from about 1900, is one of what he calls "city regionalism." Both wholesale and retail trade, the marketing of farm produce, and the distribution of manufactured goods are centered in great cities and handled largely by motor transportation.

A slightly different interpretation, although one not incompatible with

McKenzie's, has been offered by Mark Jefferson.[8] It is graphically presented in Fig. 4. In this chart the name of a given city appears in the period during which it reached a population of 100,000; it appears in the vertical column which represents the major transportation facility at its disposal. Progression from period to period through the development of ocean, river, lake, and railroad transportation is quite obvious from this chart. From checking the chart with the histories of these cities, it is interesting to find that they had been founded in periods following approximately the same order as those in which they reached 100,000. When we view the location of these cities on a map, we wonder why they did not develop first along the Hudson–Mohawk–Great Lakes route.

RISE OF GREAT CITIES IN RELATION TO TRANSPORTATION

	Ocean	River	Lake	Railroad	
1800-1840	New York Baltimore Boston New Orleans				
1840-1870	Philadelphia San Francisco	Cincinnati St. Louis Pittsburgh Louisville	Chicago Buffalo		
1870-1900	Providence Fall River	Memphis	Cleveland Detroit Milwaukee Toledo	Minneapolis Rochester Kansas City Omaha Indianapolis Denver Columbus	Worcester Syracuse New Haven Paterson Los Angeles Scranton

FIG. 4. Rise of great cities in relation to transportation. (*Adapted by permission of The American Geographical Society.*)

Physically this was an easier way to the West than that which crossed the mountains between the Potomac and the Ohio Valleys. Perhaps the conflict between France and England held the English-speaking people back from the Great Lakes region until a strong movement toward the Southwest had already been established. Moreover, the Mohawk Valley has been much more useful as a rail route than as a waterway. The lake cities are all important railroad centers.

Without dividing the last century and a third into periods, McKenzie has suggested another possible basis of classification. On the whole, population has moved from east to west, but more and more it appears to be slowing down; so that instead of the ratio of westward to eastward movement being 9 to 1 as in 1900, it was only 3 to 1 in 1930. A similar

[8] Jefferson, *op. cit.*, p. 462.

change has been taking place in the movement of population between the North and the South. After the War between the States, there was a marked movement into the South. By 1900 more people were moving north than in the opposite direction, and by 1930 the ratio of northward to southward movement was approximately 2 to 1.[9] Still another basis of dividing our urban development into periods is suggested by the census data concerning the percentage of urban dwellers in different regions at various dates. Thus in 1880 New England was the only section that showed more than half the population urban. In 1890 this predominant urbanism was also evident in the North Atlantic states. By 1910 it had extended to the East North Central, and Pacific groups. Undoubtedly this southwestward trend is associated with the development of transportation and other factors previously discussed.

In the early years of our republic, there was a steady stream of settlers pouring into the West, pushing steadily on to new frontiers; but about 1890 there ceased to be any new frontiers to occupy, and in place of dispersion we began to see a very marked concentration of population. To be sure, there had been long before this a definite increase in the percentage of population that was urban, but the end of the nineteenth century seemed to mark a special sort of turning point. So great was this change that by 1930 only 27 counties contained one-fourth of our entire population. Two-thirds of our people lived within 50 miles of the seaboard or the Great Lakes. Nearly one-half lived in our 96 metropolitan districts. Not only that, but of the increase in population, 1920–1930, three-fourths occurred in 63 metropolitan zones.[10] Table 10 displays the continuance of concentration through 1950.

Finally, the development of American cities may be divided into periods according to the dominant ethnic groups which contributed to their growth. In the first half of the nineteenth century, our own rural white folk furnished most of the accretions to our urban population. From the War between the States to World War I, it was immigrants from abroad. Since 1900, rural Negroes from the South have been an increasingly important element in urban growth. These changes will be discussed further in Chap. 10.

Factors Associated with the Growth and Dominance of Cities. McKenzie has effectively summarized the frame of reference into which we may put the many factors believed to bear a significant relationship to the development of urbanism in the United States.

[9] McKenzie, *op. cit.,* p. 12. The manner of computing the data which support these statements is briefly this: Take the census reports for each state, the people born in it and in other states; people born in a state to the east are counted as representing a westward movement. The same principle is, of course, applied to all four directions of the compass.

[10] *Ibid.,* pp. 19–21.

The activities required to sustain any society involve a territorial division of labor of a twofold nature: (1) the field work at the sources from which the basic materials are procured from nature; and (2) the center work where the raw materials are processed for consumption and where group services are performed. As a civilization grows in wealth and complexity, the number and variety of both field and center activities increase correspondingly. Two general tendencies are observable with regard to the spatial aspects of the production of goods and services: (1) the proportion of labor required to obtain the original materials from nature is becoming relatively less than that required to fabricate them and to effect the various services demanded by a population with a rising standard of living; and (2) modern communications have so shrunken space that these center activities may be performed over wider areas than formerly, thereby concentrating territorially these functions and the populations engaged in their performance.[11]

Table 11 summarizes a number of representative changes in agricultural production, manufacturing, transportation, communication, and finance. Just by way of amplifying and emphasizing the data therein contained, we add these further items. In 1820, 71.8 per cent of the persons gainfully employed in the United States were engaged in agriculture. In 1950, the per cent was only 12.8. In 1820, each agricultural worker provided food for 4½ persons; in 1950, for 24. So great were the technological changes in farming that the total number of persons engaged in agriculture declined in number (as well as in proportion) from 10,912,000 in 1900 to 7,138,000 in 1950. As to industry, it is estimated that the productivity per worker doubled between the Spanish-American War and World War II. The production of electric energy increased from 6 billion kilowatthours in 1902 to 270 billion in 1945. In commerce there were in the United States at the outbreak of World War II 200,000 wholesale establishments, 1,770,000 retail stores, and 645,000 service establishments. From 1790 to 1945 our exports rose from $20 million to $10,000 million, and our imports from $23 million to $4,250 million. In the field of communications we did not mention telegraph, television, or the postal system, all of which were greatly expanded.

To sum up this discussion, we do not profess to have located the causes of city growth, but we have pointed out a number of cultural changes that have accompanied the rapid development of cities during the past one hundred fifty years in the United States. Moreover, without having access to exactly equivalent data from other countries, we have evidence that some of these factors are associated with urbanism throughout the world. They include a surplus of agricultural production and farm population; shifting of workers to commerce, industry, the service trades, and professions; expansion of manufacturing, merchandis-

[11] *Ibid.*, pp. 50–51.

Table 11. Changes in Urban Population and Related Phenomena

Phenomena	Approximate dates		Ratio of 1940–1950 to 1840–1850
	1840–1850	1940–1950	
Total U.S. population..............	17 million	151 million	9
Per cent of U.S. population urban....	10.9	63.7	6
Ratio of agricultural workers to U.S. population.....................	$\frac{2}{9}$	$\frac{1}{24}$	$\frac{1}{5}$
Production of corn, bu..............	377 million	3,650 million	9
Production of wheat, bu.............	85 million	1,288 million	15
Production of rice, lb..............	84 million	2,373 million	28
Production of sugar, lb.............	121 million	3,518 million	29
Production of cotton, bales..........	1.3 million	15 million	11
Physical output of manufacturing energy from fuel and water power, Btu.........................	1 trillion	36 trillion	36
Miles of railways..................	100	225,000	2,250
Miles of paved roads...............	100	1,500,000	15,000
Automobiles......................	0	43 million	
Airplane passenger-miles...........	0	6 billion	
Tonnage of merchant marine........	1 billion	33 billion	33
Telephones.......................	0	40 million	
Radio broadcasting stations.........	0	4,000	
Patents issued in decade............	6,000	690,000	115
Number of banks..................	500	15,000	30
Assets of banks....................	$400 million	$175,000 million	437
Stock of money...................	$1 billion	$53 billion	53

SOURCE: Principal sources of data presented in this table are: *Statistical Abstract of the United States, 1950; Historical Statistics of the United States, 1789–1945; The World Almanac,* 1951; *Statesman's Yearbook,* 1950.

ing, and finance; new scientific discoveries and mechanical inventions. We might have added new developments in construction, sanitation, and medicine, which have greatly reduced the crowding, filth, and plagues that characterized cities of an earlier period. Finally, we have noted the increased speed and range of means of communication and transportation, which have made possible not only the supplying of cities from their hinterlands, but also the transaction of business between distant cities and increasingly the dominance over entire peoples by their urban centers. Data in support of this last item will be presented in later chapters.

SELECTED READINGS

McKENZIE, R. D.: *The Metropolitan Community,* McGraw-Hill Book Company, Inc., 1933. This is one of the important monographs prepared under direction of the President's Research Committee on Social Trends. It covers the period from 1900 to 1930, with a sociological analysis supported by statistical data.

SCHLESINGER, ARTHUR M.: *The Rise of the City*, The Macmillan Company, 1933. Chapters 3–5 and 9–11 constitute a narrative of the rise of cities and of urbanism in the United States since the War between the States.

WEBER, ADNA F.: *The Growth of Cities in the Nineteenth Century*, Columbia University Press, 1899. This remains the most important statistical study of the period in question.

Historical Statistics of the United States, 1789–1945, prepared by the Bureau of the Census with the cooperation of the Social Science Research Council, 1949. An indispensable reference.

Our Cities, Their Role in the National Economy, Report of the Urbanism Committee to the National Resources Committee, 1937. An excellent graphic presentation of the development of cities in the United States.

CHAPTER 6. *The Growth of Individual Cities*

In the preceding chapters we hope it has been made clear that in accounting for the rise of cities we must consider geographic and cultural factors and specific historic events. The earliest cities seem to have appeared in the fertile river valleys of the Near East. But the mere existence of these valleys did not create cities. The valleys were there a long time before cities emerged. Medieval towns were usually set on hills or other defensive sites. They were adapted to petty warfare, local economy, and stable population. But the Crusades set in motion great numbers of people who required supplies and transportation, stimulated demand for new wares, and led to a revival of commerce. Along with these specific events, towns grew into cities especially where there were breaks in transportation. The new factories of the eighteenth and nineteenth centuries were first built near waterfalls, but as water power gave way to steam and later to electricity, different sites presented superior advantages. We have seen that great cities in the United States were established successively on ocean, river, lake, and railway.

In the pages which follow we shall attempt to show concretely how geographic features (*e.g.*, waterways, climate, and natural resources) combined with cultural features (*e.g.*, transportation, manufacturing, and propaganda) and with historic events (*e.g.*, the War between the States, depression, digging a canal) to produce great cities. In the case of St. Louis the initial settlement was related to a site providing wood, drinking water, safety from flood, and proximity to navigable water, separate national ownership of east and west banks of the Mississippi River, current interest in the trapping and trading of furs, dependence on transportation by boat, distance from possible rivals, and the activities of certain Frenchmen in Louisiana. In the case of Los Angeles the organized efforts of promoters and engineers served to overcome the natural limitations of water supply, of arable hinterland, of harbor facilities, and of distance from potential markets. In the case of Seattle changing means of transportation shifted the apparent advantages of site from one side of Puget Sound to the other. Changing forms of business organization called for centralization of management and control in one place. The energy, skill, and determination of local businessmen in competition with those of other cities were probably decisive in making Seattle rather than Tacoma or some other city the metropolis of the Puget Sound region. In the case of Fall River geographic factors were first a handicap, then an asset, and later were overshadowed by economic and political factors. In similar fashion we find that the story of city after city must be told in terms of geographic features, cultural traits, and specific events—man and his institutions and his physical environment.

ST. LOUIS

About the middle of the eighteenth century trappers and fur traders were making their way into the Missouri and upper Mississippi Valleys. Near the junction of the two rivers French pioneers established little agricultural villages, quiet and self-sufficient. But there was no hint of a future city until St. Louis was founded in 1764 as a fur-trading post.

Two French officers in Louisiana were rewarded for their services in Indian wars by a grant of trading rights with the Indians in the Missouri Valley. They came up the river to Fort Chartres. Then, learning that the east bank of the Mississippi had been ceded to England, they moved on to a site on the west bank. Near what is now the head of Eads Bridge in St. Louis they found a happy combination of limestone cliffs, which afforded protection against floods, with wood and drinking water. As to location, they were not far from the junction of the Missouri, Illinois, and Mississippi Rivers. They were in a position to tap a great trade area reaching to the Rocky Mountains and into Canada.

About the same time but without knowledge of the settlers, Louisiana Territory was ceded to Spain. However, this seems to have made little difference locally, for the Spanish governors hardly disturbed the life of the French town. Likewise the return to French rule in 1800 passed almost unnoted. But when the United States purchased the Territory from Napoleon in 1803 and Lewis and Clark opened a route to the Northwest, there were signs of a new era. By 1820 it was reported that 30 to 50 wagons crossed the Mississippi every day. Some of their passengers probably remained in St. Louis, but for many it was a start on the overland trails. For these migrants St. Louis was a place to repair and purchase equipment and supplies. Thus it became a gateway to the West. Nevertheless, for another forty years it was the fur trade that gave St. Louis its chief claim to importance.

From 1817 until the War between the States, good-sized steamboats plied the river between New Orleans and St. Louis, while smaller boats carried passengers and freight on the upper Mississippi and on the Missouri. But the blockades of the war helped to change the main trade routes from north and south by water to east and west by rail.

In the 1850's railroads reached the Mississippi from the East. But not until 1874 was there a bridge across the river at St. Louis. Meanwhile Chicago began to overtake St. Louis in population and trade. Six railroads running west from Chicago cut off a large part of the trade area which was earlier linked with St. Louis. The lines through Iowa to Omaha diverted trade from the North and Northwest. The Santa Fe brought the invasion right into the state of Missouri.

St. Louis had the advantage of an early start, but Chicago offset this with the new "water-level" rail lines dominating large areas to the east and to the west. Moreover, the businessmen of Chicago did not leave matters to impersonal forces of competition. They intervened actively to delay the bridging of the Mississippi at St. Louis and to have the first bridge placed as inconveniently as possible. But it was neither villainy nor "the stars" that caused St. Louis to yield its place as third largest city in the United States to Chicago. It was a combination of geographic location, changed means of transportation, disrupting influence of the War between the States, and active rivalry of specific individuals and groups.

However, St. Louis continued to grow. Manufacturing of many kinds was already established and continued to expand. There were foundries, machine shops, brickyards, flour mills, tanneries, chemical works, tobacco factories, plants making shoes, clothing, drugs, and many other goods. With ore from southern Missouri and coal from Illinois there was for a time a prosperous iron and steel industry. A little later came lead and zinc.

These industries distributed themselves over the city and its environs in accordance with various geographic and economic factors. Establishments dealing in furs, hides, and wool retained their location of early days in what is still the main wholesale district. Grain elevators and mills were placed along the narrow flood plains to the north and to the south as well as west in Mill Creek Valley. All three represented routes of easy access and were followed by railroads which brought in most of the wheat and corn. Lumberyards were first established on the northern flood plain, so that rafts of logs from upstream might not disturb shipping activities of the levee. Later, when rafts of northern logs were replaced by southern lumber shipped by rail, there was a corresponding shift of lumberyards and woodworking establishments. Livestock yards and meatpacking plants were built on the east side where plenty of cheap land was available and freight rates were favorable. The early iron and steel industry developed on the south side along the railroads which brought ore from southern Missouri; but when this ore was exhausted, new plants appeared on the east side where there was more room and readier access to other sources of raw material.

With the building of belt lines by the Terminal Railroad and especially with the use of auto trucks, light industry began to scatter over outlying parts of the metropolitan area.

The workers to man these industries and to perform the other tasks of a growing city came from eastern and later from southern states. In the 1840's and the 1850's many immigrants came from Germany and Ireland; in the 1890's from Italy. After 1900 there was an influx of Negroes from the South and Jews from central and eastern Europe. However, St. Louis has never had a large and varied array of ethnic groups such as may be found in New York, Boston, Chicago, and some other cities.

St. Louis's period of most rapid growth was before the War between the States. From 1840 to 1860 its population multiplied tenfold, in spite of fire, flood, and cholera epidemic. In the sixties it nearly doubled. Then, after slowing down in the seventies, it added about 100,000 per decade until 1910. Since then the heart of the city has lost population, St. Louis proper has grown moderately (except during the thirties) and the suburbs have expanded greatly, bringing the metropolitan population to 1,700,000 in 1950.

While the metropolitan district, Greater St. Louis, has been growing in population and wealth, it has been politically subdivided to an extreme degree. The Missouri constitution of 1875 and the city charter of 1876 made the central city independent of St. Louis County and rendered subsequent expansion and annexation almost impossible. Since then about 100 independent municipalities have been incorporated in the county, adding greatly to the complexity and probably to the total cost of government in the area. In addition the Mississippi River is not only a physical barrier, but also a political boundary. Yet many of the principal industries of the metropolitan district are on the east side. Many people go back and forth every day to work, shop, and play. Not until 1950 was a bistate agency finally established to develop plans for the entire area and to acquire and build bridges and other interstate facilities.

For years people have been moving from the heart of St. Louis to its outskirts, commonly becoming voters in the suburbs but keeping their businesses and jobs in the central city. The residential areas they have left behind have gradually deteriorated, yielding fewer and fewer tax dollars but costing the city more and more for police and fire protection and other services. Thus over-all growth is accompanied by internal decline. World War II with its defense industries and doubling up of families brought an increased population to the central city, but the postwar building boom and population growth have been principally in the suburbs.

Earlier we mentioned the reduction of the immense trade area of pioneer times by the Santa Fe and other railroads. This was accompanied and followed by the growth of rival cities at the fringe of the St. Louis hinterland. After Chicago, Omaha, and Kansas City came Springfield, Des Moines, and Little Rock. These have left St. Louis with a trade area 200 to 300 miles in diameter, fairly stable and prosperous, but unlikely to expand.

LOS ANGELES

We turn now to a very different city and a very different setting. The Franciscan Fathers who established a mission and a way station for their trips up and down the Pacific coast probably had no thought of founding a city. But looking backward, we shall seek to identify the factors that may have helped or hindered its development from a sleepy village into a great metropolis.

Los Angeles has been widely advertised as possessing great natural advantages. Many people believe it to be actually natural superiority rather than superior promotion that has produced this metropolitan district of 4 million inhabitants. There is much for us to observe that is contrary to popular impression. Los Angeles started with very serious natural disadvantages. It was in an extreme corner of the country, isolated by mountains, deserts, and great distances. It had a small arable hinterland and a limited water supply. It possessed no natural harbor, and its site was on an earth fault entailing the danger of earthquakes. On the other hand, it had a mild climate and was "at a respectful distance from possible competitors." Throughout the period of the missions, when the Southwest was dominated by Spanish-speaking people, Los Angeles remained a village. By the time of the War between the States it had only 4,500 inhabitants. But in the next twenty years increasing numbers of "Americans" drifted in to engage in small farming. They started the growing of oranges, and after the first railroads came through they began to advertise for tourists. By 1885 they were ready for the first great boom. The Southern Pacific and the Santa Fe railroads were bidding for passengers with amazingly low rates. The next two years were marked by feverish speculation in land and the two following by a building boom. A chamber of commerce was organized and active promotion became a major activity in this nascent metropolis. From 11,000 inhabitants in 1880 it leaped to 50,000 in 1890, doubling again by 1900. During the nineties, however, there was a temporary slowing down. The nationwide depression left its mark on Los Angeles, and many individuals suffered severe losses. But by 1902 a new boom was on, which continued with only a temporary interruption until the opening of World War I. Henry E. Huntington acquired and integrated a system of interurban lines promoting suburbs to furnish passengers for his cars and reaping a large reward from the rapid rise in the prices of real estate. Presently came a new railroad from Salt Lake City and another down the coast from San Francisco.

The population had already reached a point that made the water problem acute. The earthquake of 1906 and the depression of 1907 also contributed to the temporary interruption, but the completion of the aqueduct bringing water from the Owens Valley, the Panama Canal facilitating trade with the Atlantic seaboard and with Europe, the annexation of San Pedro and other water fronts, the building of a breakwater, and the coming of the movies carried Los Angeles forward in an enthusiastic growth which seemed to have no end. This combination of engineering feats—the bringing of water 250 miles and the building of a harbor 25 miles away—with the constant promotional efforts had by 1910 made a city of 320,000 people. Then came World War I. Construction and the real estate business were hard hit, as elsewhere. Middle Western farmers found it profitable to remain at home and raise wheat or corn at high prices; industrialists and laborers found eastern attractions. But once the war was over and the depression of 1921 past, a third boom set in which lasted until the great depression of 1929. The postwar prosperity of the country was revealed in the thousands who flocked into the Southwest to retire or to invest and have an easy living. The automobile made possible the filling in of areas not tapped by the interurban lines. New oil developments, accompanied by excessive drilling and high-pressure salesmanship, drew thousands of new residents and millions of new dollars.

Even through the "depressed thirties" Los Angeles continued to grow. However, some of the newcomers were not wanted and strenuous efforts were adopted to keep them away. Without too careful consideration of legal niceties or of vaunted American freedom, Los Angeles police at the state borders sought to turn back impecunious job seekers.

Then came World War II, the expulsion of Japanese-Americans and the attracting of new labor force for the airplane and other war industries. This was a period of tremendous expansion. From 1940 to 1950 the population of Los Angeles city increased from 1,500,000 to 1,950,000, and of the metropolitan area (Los Angeles and Orange Counties) from 2,900,000 to 4,300,000. Not only was there an over-all growth, in particular there was a marked increase in the number of Negroes, Mexicans, and Jews, accompanied by various manifestations of race prejudice and, in 1943, by open rioting directed chiefly against "zoot-suiters," Spanish-speaking youths who were scapegoats for the insecurity and irritation of the crowded, wartime metropolis.

In the meantime Hoover Dam had been completed, providing a new source of water and power from the Colorado River. But for this it would hardly have been possible to provide for the expansion of industry and population during the war. After V-J Day there was much concern lest there be a serious recession, but instead Los Angeles shared the boom and inflation that swept over the country. Many war workers and ex-service men decided to remain or return to Los Angeles. The backlog of unfilled orders and unsatisfied demand for all sorts of products assured at least temporary work for many and tided the city over until the Korean war provided a new stimulus.

All these trends, which might have gone forward of themselves, were accelerated, if not forced, by the advertising of the Chamber of Commerce and the All Year Club, heralding to the world the "health, beauty, and romance" to be found in sunny Southern California and especially in Los Angeles. Here, then, is the tale of a city built by man's ingenuity in engineering feats and his persistence in propaganda—the two quite overcoming the natural disadvantages which might have prevented the spot from producing any important urban development.

SEATTLE

As to favorable geographic features Seattle resembles St. Louis more than it does Los Angeles. It started off with a good harbor, drainage, wood, and water for domestic use (site). It is nearer than other ports in the United States to Alaska and the Orient, besides being near the center of the Puget Sound region with a wealth of natural resources (location). However, Seattle did not immediately become a dominant center. That did not happen until there were changes in the principal modes of transportation and business organization, development of new industries, and increased traffic to Alaska.

The first white settlers from the eastern part of the United States appeared in this area about the same time they started moving into southern California. But their first settlements were isolated lumber camps. Most of these were scattered around the rim of the Olympic Peninsula. Each town was a center of logging and mill operations. Its products were shipped directly to California or some other distant place. Its material needs were met largely by goods brought directly from places outside the region. Contact between these little towns was irregularly by boat or overland by horseback. There was no hint of a real city or of a dominant center. In 1880 Seattle, the largest of these pioneer settlements, had a population of only 3,500.

But about this time the coming of railroads to the eastern shores of Puget Sound marked the beginning of a great change. The discovery of coal nearby gave Seattle and Tacoma an added advantage. Lumber companies began to separate their functions; logging continued to be widely scattered, but mills were more centralized, and general management often moved into a city. The fisheries likewise were scattered as were the canneries, but the cities were sources of labor and supplies as well as headquarters of management. While regional products continued to be shipped from various points, goods from afar were brought into wholesale houses in the larger centers. This was a period of intense rivalry, especially between Tacoma and Seattle, each of which wanted to be the center of this rapidly developing commercial and industrial life. For a time Tacoma seemed to have an advantage—which so frightened the residents of Seattle that they threatened to build a railroad connecting them with the Canadian Pacific unless their city instead of Tacoma was made the terminus of lines this side of the border. By 1890 Seattle had begun to pull ahead, but the margin of difference was slight indeed. By 1900 it had again doubled its population, while Tacoma had almost stood still.

During this period, agriculture was developing west of the Cascades—hop growing, dairying, growing of vegetables and berries, and large-scale poultry raising. After 1910 the marketing of these farm products was increasingly centralized in Seattle through commission houses and cooperatives. Other business organizations, both regional and national, established headquarters in this rapidly growing city. Paved roads, busses, trucks, and private cars linked to each other and to the metropolitan center towns that had previously been rather isolated and contributed further to the dominance of Seattle.

While the economic development was going on, the population was undergoing changes in character as well as in numbers. The 3,500 inhabitants of 1880 multiplied twelvefold in the next decade, doubled in the nineties, and trebled in the next ten years, reaching 237,000 in 1910. Thereafter, the rate of growth slowed down a bit yielding a population of 470,000 by 1950 plus 165,000 living beyond the city limits. But other changes were making Seattle a different kind of city. It was settled by young men who now were aging and who meanwhile had acquired wives and families. In 1890, 30 per cent of the population was in the twenties; only one-eighth was over forty-five. In 1940, one-third was over forty-five and only 17 per cent was in the twenties. In 1890, the sex ratio (males per 100 females) was 167; in 1940, it was 99. In 1890, 30 per cent of the population was foreign-born, mostly Canadian, British, and Scandinavian, plus a few Chinese. Later came more Chinese, Japanese, and some Italians. But the proportion of foreigners in 1940 was only 16 per cent. In the 1880's hard times and race prejudice led to rioting against the Chinese. In the 1940's, military precautions and popular hysteria led to evacuation of the Japanese.

As in other cities, the land-use pattern was at first undifferentiated. Everything was close together and near the water front. But gradually commerce moved back, while residential areas pushed still farther away, leaving the water front to shipping and factories. Then as business and industry expanded, they invaded residential districts, deterioration ensued, and people who could, moved out to the periphery, even beyond the city limits. At the same time combinations of group cohesion and external pressures produced little islands of segregated minorities, so that Seattle became as other cities, "a mosaic of little worlds that touch, but do not interpenetrate."

During the depression of the 1930's, Seattle practically stood still. There were many stranded laborers, some of whom established a community of nondescript shacks on a tract of vacant land near the business and industrial districts. By common consent, it bore the name Hooverville. World War II brought new life to Seattle through the aircraft industry, shipbuilding, and embarcation for the Far East. These developments did not end with V-J Day, but, as in the case of Los Angeles, continued with the postwar boom and inflation into the new rearmament of 1950.

FALL RIVER

The history of Fall River displays several combinations of geographic and social factors involved in the growth and decline of a once great textile center. Located on an arm of Narragansett Bay at the mouth of the Taunton River, Fall River remained for many years a tiny village, as late as 1800 having less than 100 inhabitants. In the vicinity there were farming, shipbuilding, and ocean shipping, but Fall River played little part in this agricultural-maritime economy. Its harbor was unimpressive and did not provide a basis for competition with Providence and New Bedford. To the east, swamps and ponds formed barriers between Fall River and the farm lands, causing main roads to by-pass the village.

But with the development of the New England textile industry, Fall River came into its own. The Quequechan (Fall) River with a steady flow and a drop of 120 feet near tidewater provided an attractive site for the establishment of mills depending on water power. From 1813 on, companies were organized and factories erected. A little later, ironworks were started for the manufacture of hoops, nails, and other small products. When the limited local supply of ore was exhausted, it was possible to bring ore from New Jersey. When the local supply of charcoal became depleted, coal was brought from Pennsylvania. The textile industry also profited from easy means of transporting cotton from the South and of shipping finished products to Boston, New York, and other markets. As against other possible locations nearer the cotton fields, Fall River was believed to have just the right humidity. By 1845 Fall River had become a thriving factory town with a population of 10,000. It had a well-developed cloth-printing industry, an iron industry, and the beginnings of a textile machine industry. Thirty years later, its population had trebled; its 42 mills with their 1,250,000 spindles made it the leading textile center of the United States. Not even the War between the States had been able to check its growth. Supplies of cotton were partly cut off and markets were disrupted, but the Fall River plants managed to keep going. After the war depleted stocks of clothing, a high tariff and lower prices of raw cotton gave new impetus to Fall River. New corporations were chartered and new mills were built.

In the beginning, it was water power that gave Fall River an advantage over other sites in the region. But after 1870 there was a steady increase in the use of steam engines until in 1900 the mills used twice as much power developed from steam as that developed by water.

About the same time there began to be a little competition from the South. By 1889 the dollar value of cotton manufactures in the South was nearly one-fourth that of New England's. At first the South produced yarn and the coarser kinds of cloth, leaving print goods to New England. But by 1939 the South produced 93 per cent of the print cloth manufactured in the United States. The textile industry continued to grow in Fall River until about 1925, after which it declined precipitately as indicated by Table 12.

Table 12. Cotton Textile Industry in Fall River

Year	Spindles	Looms	Pieces of print cloth
1875	1,265,000	30,000	5,000,000
1899	2,600,000	70,000	10,300,000
1922	4,000,000	90,000	8,200,000
1931	....	50,000	1,800,000
1940	990,000	20,000	

SOURCE: Adapted from several tables in Thomas R. Smith, *The Cotton Textile Industry of Fall River, Massachusetts,* 1944. By permission of Columbia University Press.

This dramatic collapse of a thriving industry is generally attributed to competition with the South. Certain it is that from 1880 to 1930 the South in general, and South Carolina in particular, had lower wage rates, less stringent (or advanced) labor laws, and less pressure from trade-unions. During World War I, the wage differential narrowed, but after

1920, it widened again. As to labor legislation, Massachusetts began to regulate child labor in 1867 and restricted working hours for women and minors from 1874 on. Before 1900 such laws were virtually nonexistent in the South. However, by 1920, South Carolina had enacted compulsory schooling and child labor laws. The disparity was being reduced precisely during the years that the South was winning out over New England. As to the trade-unions, these had shown strength in Massachusetts from the middle of the nineteenth century, having definite influence on wages, hours, and other working conditions. Organization of unions came much later in the South, and by 1920 only about one-tenth of employees of textile mills in South Carolina were members of trade-unions.

During the 1880's and 1890's, there was talk of "bringing the mills to the cotton fields," but it appears that the over-all transportation costs were not very different in the two sections. Perhaps the most significant difference lay in the fact that the northern companies had heavy investments in machinery that was becoming outmoded while the southern mills were being equipped with high-speed spinning machines, automatic looms, and other efficient devices. Some of these could be operated by women and children who were paid low wages, thus offering further financial inducement to investors and managers. The difference in modernization was indicated by the fact that in 1907 only 4 per cent of the Fall River looms were of the new type called Northrop, while in comparable mills of South Carolina, 53 per cent of the looms were Northrops. Some attribute this difference to trade-union opposition; others ascribe it to the attitude of owners—"Why pay out money for new machinery that might be paid in bonuses and dividends?" In any case, the differential was more social than geographic as these terms are usually employed.

Table 13. Population of Fall River

1800	100	1900	104,000
1820	1,600	1910	119,000
1840	6,700	1920	120,000
1860	14,000	1930	115,000
1880	49,000	1940	115,000
1890	74,000	1950	112,000

SOURCE: Bureau of the Census.

At all events the southern textile mills were offering severe competition to those of Fall River and other northern centers. Profits declined and owners became worried. They rebuilt some of the old looms, reduced the piece rate for weavers, and diversified their products. But the situation continued to worsen until World War I gave the entire industry a

new lease on life. Both output and profits were high except during the
short depression of 1920 to 1922. But this prosperity did not last. In 1924
it was announced that two mills were moving to Tennessee. Others were
simply closed. The depression of the 1930's contributed to the decline
although the NRA gave a short breathing spell. During the fifteen years
from 1925 to 1940, 73 mills representing three-fourths of Fall River's
capacity were liquidated.

FACTORS AFFECTING LOCATION AND GROWTH OF CITIES

In the accounts of four cities we have found evidence of what is sometimes called "multiple causation." No single factor is regularly associated
with the location and growth of cities, but it appears that some combination may be. In other words, it seems necessary to consider not only a
number of factors, but also their possible relation to each other as parts
of a complex situation or process. For example, numerous points along
the shores of the Great Lakes might have utilized transportation by water
to assemble raw material (iron ore) and fuel (coal) for industrial uses.
Some of them never did, and none of these points attracted a large population until agriculture was well developed in the surrounding region
and railroads were built to assemble its products. In the face of such an
interplay of factors, it would be rather fruitless to search for a single
cause of a city's location and growth, or even for a principal cause.
Nevertheless, it is worth our while to review some of the elements which
appear frequently in the chain of events associated with the development
of cities.

Starting with geographic factors, it is easy to show that there are no
urban centers of consequence in the arctic regions and not many in the
tropics. Few are found above an elevation of 2,000 feet and few in
desert regions. Down to the present time, most cities have developed in
temperate zones, in areas where rainfall is moderate, where plant and
animal life assure subsistence, where the soil can be tilled, where power
can be developed, and where there are no serious barriers to the movement of people. We observe that the immediate sites of cities provide
foundations, building materials, water supply, accessibility, and sometimes power and raw materials. In earlier times defense was an important
consideration. Today it may be said that all cities are vulnerable to air
attack. Those along the seaboard are also subject to naval bombardment.
Finally, some cities are centrally located with reference to trade, others
with respect to government.

But already we have passed from strictly geographic to cultural
aspects of the environment. As a matter of fact, practically all the physical features of site and location are significant in relation to the technol-

ogy and social organization of the occupants at a given time. We have seen in the case of Los Angeles how the ingenuity of men enabled them to offset the apparent disadvantages of nature. In the case of Seattle the issue of which should be the dominant city of the Puget Sound region was settled through competitive struggle of opposing groups of men. The relative size and influence of St. Louis and Chicago have likewise been affected by the pressures of competing business interests. The rise and decline of Fall River involved competition with the South, the organization of trade-unions, enactment of labor legislation, inventions and investments in power machinery. In other words, we find in all these cases varying combinations of physical features and cultural traits utilized by specific persons and groups.

Various attempts have been made to explain the location and growth of cities in terms of particular characteristics such as "break in transportation" or "service centers in tributary areas," each of which emphasizes part of the process of urban development.[1] But we find it unsatisfactory to symbolize the whole by any single aspect of a situation. As a matter of fact, cities usually are service centers for surrounding regions; also they are dependent on their regions for food and other supplies. Cities usually are foci of transportation facilities; but whether convergence of routes makes a city or a city attracts lines of travel is hard to say.

Sometimes the location of a city can be attributed to the purpose of a specific individual or group as in the cases of Washington, D.C., and Leningrad (St. Petersburg when it was founded). But often a site is chosen for settlement without anyone's anticipating the subsequent development of a city. Perhaps we might say that the resources of a region may be taken as indicating the possibility of a city somewhere within its boundaries, but various circumstances and events seem to share in determining just when and where it will appear. Just as urban development in general has accompanied increase in world population, expanding food supply, improved transportation, and other aspects of modern civilization, so in a given area the growth of a particular city is associated with development of the region's agriculture, manufacturing, communications, etc. We have used the stories of individual cities to give us clues to relationships among these various factors.

SELECTED READINGS

Fall River

Smith, Thomas R.: *The Cotton Textile Industry of Fall River, Massachusetts,* Columbia University Press, 1944.

[1] See, for example, Edward Ullman, "A Theory of Location for Cities," *Amer. Jour. Sociol.,* 46 (1941), 853–864.

Los Angeles

WAGNER, ANTON: *Los Angeles: Werden, Leben und Gestalt der Zweimillionen Stadt in Sudkalifornien,* Bibliographisches Institut (Leipzig), 1935. An excellent account of the rise of Los Angeles by a German geographer. Unfortunately not translated into English.

Seattle

SCHMID, CALVIN F.: *Social Trends in Seattle,* University of Washington Press, 1944. A carefully prepared history and analysis, well illustrated and documented.

St. Louis

THOMAS, LEWIS F.: *The Localization of Business Activities in Metropolitan St. Louis,* Washington University Studies, 1927. Contains much background material prepared by an economic geographer who was coauthor of *The City.*

CHAPTER 7. *Rise of the Metropolitan Region*

Two of the cities discussed in the preceding chapter show vividly the relations between a metropolitan center and the surrounding region. It was St. Louis rather than Carondelet, St. Ferdinand, or Cahokia that became a great city, in part because St. Louis was planned as the trading center for a vast region. Almost from its founding, it was the point where furs were assembled from the whole Missouri Valley and beyond. Later it drew in other raw materials and then distributed manufactured products. When, about 1850, the trade area was divided by railroads leading to Chicago and other cities, the rate of St. Louis's growth declined and its prospects of development were curtailed, but it has not ceased to be the commercial, industrial, and now financial center for a considerable territory.

The early history of settlements on Puget Sound is different from that of St. Louis. At first none of the pioneer lumber towns was planned or operated as a center of regional activity. Each settlement maintained its own trade relations directly with the outside world. Only with the coming of railroads and paved highways did Seattle become the headquarters of lumber companies and fisheries, later of wholesale houses and cooperative societies, operating throughout the region. Now goods from distant points come through Seattle, and the shipment of Puget Sound products is controlled from Seattle. It is definitely the economic center of its region.

Looking back into Chap. 5, we see indications of this sort of relationship developing quite generally. Cities of the modern world have become great, as means of transportation have enabled them to assemble food and raw materials from the surrounding area and to distribute local and imported manufactured goods throughout the same area. This means that a metropolis needs a hinterland rich in natural resources and also serving as a market for urban products. The relationship is not entirely unlike that of a country town to the adjacent farming district, but it does differ in some important respects. Not only is there a greater volume

79

and variety of trade over a wider territory. In addition the assembly of raw materials and the distribution of finished products often pass through intermediate centers en route to and from the open country and the metropolis.

Going back still further, we find cities of medieval and early modern Europe exercising political control over outlying districts, capital cities sometimes dominating wide areas. The world of classical antiquity also displayed the same phenomenon. To be sure, the dominance of most city-states was rather limited, but Rome once ruled a vast empire. Thus wherever we have found a great city, we have found its fortunes bound up with those of an adjacent hinterland or with distant provinces.

On the other hand, rural populations of the medieval and ancient worlds could maintain themselves without help from the cities, even though the latter needed the products and excess population of the country. In the modern world interdependence is more evident, and the ties that bind metropolis, town, and countryside are not only economic, but recreational, educational, and other. Country people go to the city's theaters, museums, and ball parks, while city people go hunting, fishing, and vacationing in the country. Youths from throughout the region attend the same colleges and universities.

THE HYPOTHESIS OF METROPOLITAN DOMINANCE

So far has the United States moved from the relative isolation and independence of folk societies that some students speak freely of urban, or even more of metropolitan, dominance. A generation ago it was still possible to find country districts in the United States from which very few persons had ever visited a city or seen a movie. Today such isolated places and persons are rare indeed. In 1906 Frederic C. Howe sensed the change of which we have been speaking and wrote:

The city has become the central feature in modern civilization and to an ever increasing extent the dominant one. . . . This rural civilization, whose making engaged mankind since the dawn of history, is passing away. The city has erased the landmarks of an earlier society. Man has entered on an urban age.[1]

Twenty years later Charles Beard said:

It is from the urban centers that the national economy of the future will be controlled, whether we like it or not, and it is the culture of urbanism that promises to dominate the future.[2]

[1] Frederic C. Howe, *The City, the Hope of Democracy*, p. 22, 1906. By permission of Charles Scribner's Sons.

[2] Charles A. Beard, "The City's Place in Civilization," *Nat. Mun. Rev.*, 17 (1928), 729–730. By permission of the National Municipal League.

In 1922 N. S. B. Gras[3] presented an economic historical interpretation of cities in terms of stages referred to in Chap. 4 and now reviewed in new perspective. For many thousands of years our ancestors appear to have lived on whatever they could find in the way of fruits, herbs, fish, and game (collectional economy). Then they settled at least temporarily in places where they could care for domesticated animals and perhaps raise a simple crop or two (agricultural nomadic economy). Eventually they established themselves more permanently, with labor invested in vineyards, ditches, storehouses, and dwellings (settled village economy). Some of the villages grew into towns, with a little division of labor and with markets serving the population within a radius of several miles (town economy). Much later came the great cities, each serving and being served by many towns and extensive agricultural areas, "casting a spell" over rural dwellers and developing a way of life for them to imitate (metropolitan economy). Gras has described the economic aspect of this metropolitan dominance in these words.

We may think of metropolitan economy as an organization of people having a large city as nucleus. Or we may put it this way, metropolitan economy is the organization of producers and consumers mutually dependent for goods and services, wherein their wants are supplied by a system of exchange concentrated in a large city which is the focus of local trade and the center through which normal economic relations with the outside are established and maintained.

Just as villages remained when town economy prevailed, so do towns remain when metropolitan economy comes into existence. Towns remain, but in economic subordination to the metropolis. They continue to play a part, but as tributaries to a larger center. A closer examination of these dependent towns would show different types performing different functions, but all subordinate.[4]

In 1933 McKenzie gave us the classic account of the rise of what he called "metropolitan communities," meaning in effect great cities with their nearby satellites and their far-flung trade areas.[5] In 1949 Don J. Bogue restated the hypothesis of metropolitan dominance and undertook to test it with data and procedures which we shall discuss a little later.[6]

The metropolis is usually the largest and most complex (the farthest removed from the "average" city) of all the cities in the territory. Because it is able to assemble cheaply a varied array of raw materials and products from all parts of the world; because a large number of specialized components

[3] N. S. B. Gras, *An Introduction to Economic History*, 1922. See also his article in *The Urban Community*, edited by E. W. Burgess, 1926.

[4] *Ibid.*, p. 184. By permission of Harper & Brothers.

[5] R. D. McKenzie, "The Rise of the Metropolitan Community," in *Recent Social Trends*, Chap. 9, 1933.

[6] Don J. Bogue, *The Structure of the Metropolitan Community*, pp. 5–6, 1949. By permission of the author and the University of Michigan.

and skills are required in the production of the goods required to sustain human beings at their present level of living; because up to a certain point machine production increases in efficiency with an increased scale of operations; and because certain mutual benefits appear to accrue to business enterprises from their location in proximity to each other, the large city is able to produce and distribute more varied goods and services than is a smaller city. The more specialized the goods, and the more the goods are amenable to mass production, the greater these industrial and commercial advantages of large cities seem to become. From these facts it has been concluded that the metropolis, or modern large and complex city, exercises an organizing and integrative influence on the social and economic life of a broad expanse of territory far beyond the civil boundaries, and thereby dominates all other communities within this area. The hypothesis of metropolitan dominance assumes that there is a system of interdependency among cities, and that there are considerable differences between the activities of individual cities. It maintains that the organizing agent, and one of the forces making for intercity differentiation, is the metropolis.

Sufficient evidence has been accumulated to make of this view a very plausible hypothesis. Smaller cities and villages lying in the region about great cities appear to have been drawn into a division of labor with the larger urban center. They exchange for the specialized goods and services of the metropolis such other products as can most effectively be produced from the resources in their immediate locality. Farm operators also appear to have become more dependent upon metropolitan markets, and consequently have regulated their activities to produce, if possible, those products which will yield them the greatest return in the metropolitan market. With these exchanges of material goods has also gone the exchange of ideas and human values. The metropolis appears to have become the focal point not only of our material activities, but of much of our moral and intellectual life as well. Repeatedly it has been pointed out that not only in activities such as non-agricultural production, distribution, and finance, but also in matters of government, progress in the arts and sciences, news dissemination and the formation of public opinion, changed philosophies of religion and the emergence of new human values, the great metropolis is now the dominating center.

EVIDENCE OF METROPOLITAN DOMINANCE

One of the earliest and most impressive measures of metropolitan dominance has been made in terms of newspaper circulation. It is well known that metropolitan dailies (and Sunday papers) are read by people living in lesser cities, towns, and even rural districts far beyond the limits of the great city itself. Such reading means a daily (or weekly) contact with the metropolis, its wares (goods advertised for sale), its political views and activities, its cultural life (music and art), its sports, and whatever else may find its way into print. If the newspapers from one city reach a larger part of the population of a given village, town, or other group than do those from another city, it is probably correct to consider the group as belonging to the hinterland of the first city. Here is the method of determining this. From the Audit Bureau of Circulation we learn the numbers of various metropolitan papers sold daily or on Sunday in a given area. We compare the total circulation of the papers from one city with that of the papers from any other cities involved and with the circulation of local papers, if any. Then, if we wish, we can compute the ratio of newspapers sold to the population of the area in question. Park used this method first in the Chicago region and later applied it to the United States.[7] Now the first advantage of this index

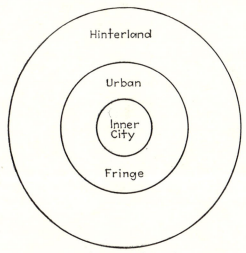

Fig. 5. General pattern of an urban region.

of a city's dominance is that it is rather easy to compute. The second is that the results of its use are very similar to those secured from other studies to which we shall presently refer.

But it is also true that some difficulties have been encountered in using newspaper circulation as one basis of an index of metropolitan dominance. Thus Park found that Chicago papers competed in Wisconsin with those of Milwaukee and in Indiana with those of Indianapolis on such even terms that the results were indecisive. Also smaller cities near Chicago, such as Elgin and Joliet, had their own papers whose circulation in the local district exceeded that of the metropolitan dailies. Another significant factor was the number of commuters going and coming between small cities and Chicago. When this number was great, the circulation of metropolitan papers was high. But in and about industrial

[7] R. E. Park and Charles Newcomb, "Newspaper Circulation and Metropolitan Regions," Chap. 8 in *The Metropolitan Community*, by R. D. McKenzie, 1933.

cities with few commuters, the metropolitan circulation was low. Despite these complications this method does serve in a general way to delineate the sphere of influence of a great city.

Another measure of metropolitan dominance may be made in terms of wholesale trade. While it is true that stores in small cities and towns obtain their goods from many different centers, there is often one metropolis from which they do a large part of their buying. This has been definitely established in the case of groceries.[8] A somewhat different means of identifying the wholesale trade area is by using the home addresses of out-of-town buyers who visit a great city.[9]

Still other indicators of metropolitan spheres of influence are charge accounts at department stores, range of deliveries made by large city retailers, sale of bus and train tickets between the metropolis and outlying points, automobile traffic counts, trucking of livestock, milk, and other farm products, toll telephone calls, counts of radio listeners, and metropolitan bank correspondents. We shall return to some of these a little later when we discuss gradients and patterns in metropolitan regions.

Finally we know that there is considerable migration from the hinterland into every large city. Unfortunately actual counts and analyses of this particular movement are almost nonexistent.

The reality of metropolitan regions has been increasingly apparent to administrators in recent years, even though they have not always been careful to discover their actual extent. In 1917, when the American Red Cross was suddenly confronted with the task of organizing the nation for "home service," it divided the country into 13 parts, each with headquarters in a large city. In other words, it found the whole United States too large to administer without subdivisions, the states too numerous, and large cities the logical centers. However, Red Cross divisions were merely groups of states, without reference to the now well-known fact that a part of a state may be more closely related to a part of another state than to the remainder of its own state. The 12 Federal Reserve districts, like the Red Cross divisions, are much larger than true metropolitan regions, but they do represent social and economic rather than political territories. Odum has assembled maps outlining 20 other administrative divisions of the United States.[10] Perhaps it is neither necessary nor wise that these should all correspond, but their wide variance suggests the importance of determining the natural limits of metropolitan, and possibly other subregions, as thoroughly as Odum has identified 6 major regions of the United States.

[8] *Atlas of Wholesale Grocery Territories*, U.S. Department of Commerce, 1938.
[9] McKenzie, *The Metropolitan Community*, p. 77, 1933.
[10] Howard W. Odum, *Southern Regions of the United States*, pp. 245ff., 1936.

SOCIOECONOMIC PATTERN OF THE METROPOLITAN REGION

We have called attention to several means of identifying metropolitan dominance using newspaper circulation, wholesale trade, telephone calls, traffic counts, etc. We can now add the significant fact that these are not uniform throughout a region nor are they scattered at random. On the contrary, rather definite patterns emerge.

In general, it appears that the influence of the metropolis diminishes steadily as one proceeds from center to periphery of the region. Thus the ratio of St. Louis newspaper circulation to population in its region was found to be 0.54 within a 25-mile radius of the heart of the city, 0.25 in the zone that lies from 25 to 50 miles out, 0.14 in the 50- to 100-mile zone, and 0.08 in the 100- to 150-mile zone.[11] McKenzie got similar results from a study of circulation in the Detroit region,[12] and Gist found the same thing in the territory surrounding Kansas City.[13]

Other methods of identifying the limits of metropolitan regions and various socioeconomic gradients may be described more briefly. One is an enumeration of telephone calls between the central city and various outlying places. When these were combined for successive 25-mile zones of the Detroit region, and their ratios to the population were computed, they showed a steady decrease from the center outward—1.48, 0.26, 0.07, 0.05.[14] Traffic counts have been made by state highway departments. As we proceed outward from a large city, the traffic count drops fairly steadily. After reaching a "low" it rises again until another city is reached. The point at which the low count was taken may be regarded as a sort of watershed between two metropolitan regions. Another method utilizes the distribution of country bank services of metropolitan banks. In addition to the devices already suggested, attention may well be paid to the sale of railroad and bus tickets, the radio stations to which listeners tune in, the institutions of higher learning which young people attend, the cities which hinterlanders visit for shopping, recreation, or other purposes. Enough of these and other data might be secured by sampling the population along what appears to be the outer edge of an urban region to establish the limits more accurately than could be done with a single index such as newspaper circulation.

A slightly different method of getting at the pattern of a metropolitan region was used by Brunner and Kolb in a study of rural social trends.[15] Instead of sketching concentric circles and going through some rather tedious calculations and estimates, they simply reported their findings

[11] From a study by Mary E. Graf in 1946 under our direction.
[12] McKenzie, *op. cit.*, p. 83.
[13] Noel P. Gist and L. A. Halbert, *Urban Society,* pp. 198–199, 1948.
[14] McKenzie, *op. cit.*, p. 83.
[15] Edmund de S. Brunner and J. H. Kolb, *Rural Social Trends,* Chap. 5, 1933.

Table 14. Social and Economic Patterns in Areas Surrounding 18 Cities, by Tiers of Counties, 1930

	City-County	Tiers of counties			
		1	2	3	4
Birth rate per annum per 1,000 population	15.7	17.8	18.7	19.1	20.1
Ratio of children under 10 to women 20–45	87.2	119.7	120.1	131.9	153.9
Sex ratio (males per 100 females)	98.1	104.8	104.2	106.2	110.4
Proportion of children 7–13 in school	96.5	94.9	94.5	95.0	95.2
Per cent aged 15 and over married:					
Males	61.5	59.8	60.2	60.2	58.2
Females	59.3	62.4	63.1	63.8	65.2
Proportion of farms operated by owners	60.9	60.4	60.3	58.9	56.0
Value per acre of all farm property	$143.60	$94.25	$71.82	$65.93	$61.56
Value per acre of all farm crops	$ 14.44	$12.41	$ 9.92	$ 8.82	$ 7.43

SOURCE: Adapted from Edmund de S. Brunner and J. H. Kolb, *Rural Social Trends*, Chap. 5, 1933.

by "tiers" of counties surrounding 18 cities. Table 14 displays some of their findings. While these data do not assure us of metropolitan dominance as such, they do show progressive differences as one goes from center to periphery of the area. Moreover, since the differences are fairly consistent, we may speak of them as gradients and accept them as well-defined aspects of regional patterns.

Further confirmation of these gradients is found in a study of 67 cities by Bogue. He identified the first 25 miles outside a central city as a "zone of direct participation" (suburbs).

The level of land occupancy is high; dormitory towns are numerous; the cities located there are more deficient in retail trade, wholesale trade, and services than are the cities lying in other parts of the hinterland. Because they provide space and yet are able to participate directly in the advantages of the metropolis, the principal hinterland cities in this zone attain a high degree of manufacturing specialization. . . .

At about 65 miles from the metropolis begins the rise in the retail, service, and wholesale specialization of the principal hinterland cities, indicating the presence of a trade territory for each, and their subdominance over that trade territory. In this zone, the factors favoring manufacturing decline progressively, both for principal cities and "other areas." Beyond 65 miles, the "other areas" attain a plateau in retail, service, and wholesale specialization. They appear to provide locally the more standard commodities which are needed frequently or in large quantity, and to depend upon the metropolis and the hinterland city for the more specialized ones. Since such dependence must take the form of exchange, this zone may be termed the *zone of exchange.*

The functions of collection and distribution characterize its principal cities; agricultural production and extraction characterize its "other areas." Here there is little manufacturing activity.[16]

Between 25 and 65 miles is a rather mixed zone. Here are usually found some large hinterland cities which serve as outlying points of distribution and manufacture.

Because this zone does contain such a mixture, it may be called a zone of interchange, for it mediates between the metropolis and its direct participants and the outlying zone of exchange. From such outlying centers in this zone secondary highways radiate to the more remote portions of the hinterland, and for this reason the cities in this zone may be called "hinterland-access cities."[17]

Table 15 shows some of Bogue's findings. Clearly population density and the four types of "sustenance activities," as he calls them, decline as one proceeds from central city to outlying districts. However, the changes are not uniform. Population drops off sharply in the first two zones and gradually thereafter. Beyond the suburban zone there is little change in retailing. This indicates that persons living in the urban fringe do much buying in the central city, but that people farther out in the hinterland obtain their goods in the zone in which they live. Approximately the same thing is true of services (plumber, garage, barber, etc.). Wholesaling is highly concentrated in the central city, but also appears on a modest scale beyond 45 miles. Manufacturing is spread over parts of the central city and the first two zones, that is, out some 45 miles. Another way of referring to these economic activities is this. Measured by per capita value, central cities are more specialized in retail trade, service,

Table 15. Demographic and Economic Patterns in Concentric Zones Surrounding 67 Large Cities, 1940

	Central city	Distance from central city				
		0–24 miles	25–44 miles	45–64 miles	65–164 miles	165 miles and over
Population per square mile......	9,047	215	75	63	36	10
Per capita dollar value of:						
Retail sales.................	$ 471	$303	$301	$293	$236	$240
Services..................	$ 55	$ 21	$ 17	$ 17	$ 13	$ 13
Wholesale sales.............	$1,172	$175	$146	$161	$157	$156
Values added by manufacture..	$ 284	$273	$224	$178	$ 95	$ 56

SOURCE: Adapted from Bogue, *The Structure of the Metropolitan Community*, p. 35, 1949. By permission of the author and the University of Michigan.

[16] Bogue, *op. cit.* By permission of the author and the University of Michigan.
[17] *Ibid.*, p. 54. By permission of the author and the University of Michigan.

and wholesale trade than is any zone of their hinterlands. Manufacturing is a specialization of the entire metropolitan area, but not of the hinterland.

At this point, it may be well to explain briefly how Bogue plotted the metropolitan regions or "communities," to use his term, and how he subdivided them. First, he drew lines from a given metropolis to each adjacent metropolis. Next, he bisected these lines and drew boundary lines at right angles to the original lines. Each county in the United States he then assigned to the region within which the greater part of its area was found to fall. Finally, he considered each city to lie in the hinterland of the metropolis which claimed the county in which the city is located.

Distance zones were established by studying the actual mileage from the central city via the most direct highway route. The geographic center of each county was determined and the entire county was assigned to the zone in which the center lies. Outlying cities were assigned directly to the zones.

Finally, Bogue divided each region into "sectors," proceeding as follows:

The major intermetropolitan highway routes from each metropolis to its neighboring metropolises were determined. A transparent circular template, divided into twelve 30° sectors, was placed over the map of the metropolitan community. Through rotation of the template, an attempt was made to get each route to fall within a single sector. Each route was "centered" as nearly as possible in its sector.

Those sectors which contained an intermetropolitan highway were then coded as "intermetropolitan" sectors.

Of the remaining sectors, those which contained a city of 25,000 or more inhabitants located at a distance of 10 miles or more from the central city were designated as "subdominant" sectors.

The remaining sectors were classed as "local" sectors, for there was no evidence of intermetropolitan or major metropolis-hinterland city activity in their direction.[18]

Figure 6 displays the division of the Memphis region into sectors. This division was based on the assumption that accessibility to a metropolis involves not only distance and time, but also location with reference to major routes. Accessibility in turn was assumed to be directly associated with the degree of metropolitan dominance. Here is what this scheme of analysis yielded.

Density of population is greatest in the subdominant sectors, with relatively large hinterland cities, and lowest in the local sectors. As to specialization in sustenance activities, the intermetropolitan sectors have a slight lead over the subdominant sectors in retailing, wholesaling, and

[18] *Ibid.*, pp. 22–23. By permission of the author and the University of Michigan.

service activities, while the latter have a slight lead in manufacturing. As might be expected, both intermetropolitan and subdominant sectors are much more highly specialized in all respects studied than are the local sectors. In other words, both population and business tend to locate near arterial highways that link metropolitan centers to each other or to lesser cities of the hinterland. This appears to be primarily a matter

METROPOLITAN DOMINANCE AND METROPOLITAN STRUCTURE

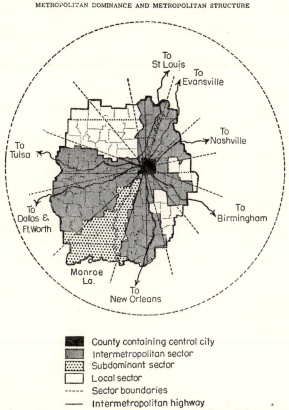

FIG. 6. Sectors of Memphis metropolitan region. (*Adapted by permission of Don J. Bogue and the University of Michigan.*)

of ready access to the metropolis. It further suggests that the outlying units are not independent enterprises competing with business units of the central city. Rather, they appear to be "appendages of an extended metropolis-centered system of production, marketing, and distribution."[19] If hinterland populations were to develop their own commercial and industrial establishments in competition with the central city, they would seem most likely to succeed in sectors least accessible to the me-

[19] *Ibid.*, p. 48.

tropolis. The relative absence of such establishments from these local sectors, therefore, supports the case for regional integration and dominance.

Thus we are led to conclude that the large hinterland cities located in subdominant sectors are intermediary between metropolis and smaller communities, that they specialize in wholesaling and service activities and depend on the central city for certain functions they are not equipped to perform. If this interpretation is correct, these hinterland cities are to be viewed as part of the metropolitan system rather than as "vestiges of a former era."

Bogue's analysis is properly but, from our standpoint, unfortunately limited to population and business activities. We are interested also in such functions as news, entertainment, religion, and education. We suspect that dominance may appear in these fields also, but need more evidence to supplement that presented earlier in this chapter.

Some students may question whether the identification of a recurring pattern of communities, population, and sustenance activities is adequate evidence of dominance. Bogue's reply is this: "If dominance is nonexistent, one should find a random distribution and a random combination of units." If, however, distribution is nonrandom, "if these differences in distribution are directly related to the metropolis, and if nothing else in the environment"—terrain, resources, etc.—"requires this same distribution, then it can be inferred reasonably that the metropolis is exercising dominance over the area."[20]

WHAT IS NEW ABOUT THE METROPOLITAN COMMUNITY?

We have reviewed some of the evidence that there is a set of relationships between central city, suburbs, outlying cities, and rural areas which warrants the use of such terms as metropolitan community, metropolitan region, metropolitan dominance. If the proposition is reasonably well proved, we still have the question: Is there anything new about all this? Unfortunately, reliable statistical data are not at hand, but from the historical materials that are available we seem warranted in saying that such a structure as that which Bogue calls a metropolitan community could not exist without the means of transportation and communication, division of labor, and other modern innovations which were described in Chap. 5. Some relationships indeed developed between city and hinterland in the ancient world, but, as we pointed out earlier, they were limited in space and variety, if not in intensity. The metropolitan community, or, as we prefer to call it, region is not absolutely new, but it differs greatly in degree from anything that appeared in earlier times.

[20] *Ibid.*, p. 14.

SELECTED READINGS

Bogue, Don J.: *The Structure of the Metropolitan Community, A Study of Dominance and Subdominance,* University of Michigan, School of Graduate Studies, 1949. An ecological study of metropolitan regions in the United States in 1940.

Brunner, Edmund de S., and J. H. Kolb: *Rural Social Trends,* McGraw-Hill Book Company, Inc., 1933. A companion volume to McKenzie's. Chapter 5, "Rural and Urban Relationships," contains the analysis of 18 cities and their surrounding tiers of counties.

Dickinson, Robert E.: *City, Region and Regionalism,* Oxford University Press, 1947. Describes metropolitan regions in Great Britain, France, Germany, and the United States.

Hawley, Amos H.: *Human Ecology, A Theory of Community Structure,* The Ronald Press Company, 1950. Chapter 13 deals with metropolitan regions.

McKenzie, R. D.: *The Metropolitan Community,* McGraw-Hill Book Company, Inc., 1933. Part II, "The Rise of the Metropolitan Community," is of special importance at this point.

Quinn, James A.: *Human Ecology,* Prentice-Hall, Inc., 1950. Chapter 8, "The Metropolitan Region," is useful in this connection.

Thompson, Warren S.: *The Growth of Metropolitan Districts in the United States: 1900–1940,* U.S. Bureau of the Census, 1948. An invaluable statistical analysis.

PART 3

Localization of Activity in the City

CHAPTER 8. *Spatial Patterning of the Metropolis*

In Chap. 7 we were concerned with the relation of large cities to their hinterlands, giving special attention to the spatial distribution of population and business activities. In this chapter we will narrow our range of vision to the city itself—more accurately, the metropolitan area as defined in Chap. 2. We will again concentrate on the spatial patterning and seek to discover how this patterning develops and changes. In thus devoting ourselves to large urban centers, we are not ignoring the importance of smaller cities; we are simply limiting the scope of our inquiry as a matter of practical convenience.

When we approach a large city by air, water, rail, or automobile, our first impressions are likely to be of various kinds of structures scattered irregularly over some kind of terrain. We note the presence of hills and valleys, streams, and bodies of water. Presently we observe railways and other transportation facilities in valleys, along water fronts, and in flat, open spaces. Near them we find warehouses, lumber and coalyards, grain elevators, and factories, especially those devoted to heavy industry. Figures 7 and 8 display something of the relation between topography and land use in St. Louis.

Besides these rather obvious surface characteristics of elevation and water, other geographic features enter into the layout of a city. One is the geological structure, whose chief significance lies in the texture and depth of the mantle-rock. If it is deep and can be easily moved, the development of an urban pattern may greatly modify the original surface of the site. For example, a considerable part of the site of St. Louis is underlain by deep, fine-textured loessial clays. With modern grading machinery, the high, rugged slopes can be peeled off and dumped into narrow, shallow ravines, resulting in a gently undulating surface.

At Seattle a major hill composed of glacial sands and gravels obstructed the expansion of the city, but by means of hydraulic flushing the hill was washed away, filling up adjacent marshlands over which Seattle could expand.

95

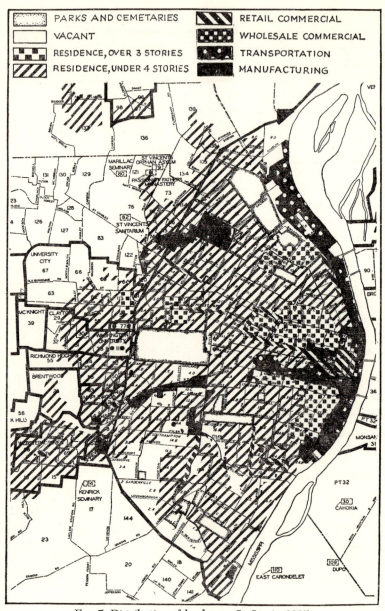

Fig. 7. Distribution of land uses, St. Louis, 1935.

If there is no mantle-rock and the hard bedrock is exposed at the sur-face, great expense is involved in removing hills and knolls which in-terfere with the expansion of the urban pattern. On Manhattan many of the original hard-rock irregularities have been blasted away and the monotonously uniform checkerboard pattern has been extended over the island. The features of the original terrain are somewhat preserved in Central Park. If the bedrock hills and ridges are too large and numerous to be removed, tunnels can pierce them and thus provide access to other valley lands for urban expansion. Such tunnels have been constructed at Pittsburgh and Los Angeles.

Where the bedrock is exposed at the surface or the mantle-rock is ex-ceedingly shallow, the laying of water mains, sewer mains, gas mains, and telephone and electrical conduits is exceedingly expensive, owing to the fact that the ditches must be blasted foot by foot. Also, under such conditions the cost of excavating cellars or basements for buildings is prohibitive and they are set on top of the ground. Large cities which require many subways must spend millions of dollars in construction in such bedrock. New York City is an outstanding example.

The presence of bedrock near the surface is an advantage in the con-struction of tall skyscraper buildings, because the steel skeleton must be firmly keyed. Such keying is essential in regions subject to earthquakes, as has been demonstrated in San Francisco. The buildings which were keyed into the bedrock suffered slight damage from the earthquake, whereas those constructed on "made land" and not keyed into the bed-rock suffered great damage.

Where the mantle-rock is deep and moist, the construction of large, tall buildings is greatly handicapped by the lack of a firm foundation. An outstanding example is found in the Loop district of Chicago, where ex-pensive piling and concrete mats must be constructed as a foundation. Similar conditions prevail in New Orleans. Where the depth of mantle-rock varies markedly in an urban site, this results in localizing the de-velopment of skyscraper districts. Such localization may be noted in the upper and lower Manhattan skyscraper districts, which are built on shallow bedrock, and the intervening space, which is underlain by deep, unconsolidated sands and gravel. Another instance is Minneapolis, where the surface is a smooth glacial plain which buries irregular preglacial rocky surface. Thus it is that a small group of city blocks have shallow mantle-rock and are suitable for skyscrapers. Adjacent to them are many blocks under which the bedrock is so deep that suitable foundations are not found.

Before observing the geological features of an urban site, one becomes aware of the buildings. Sometimes near the geographic center, some-times close to a water front, we find the main business district with its

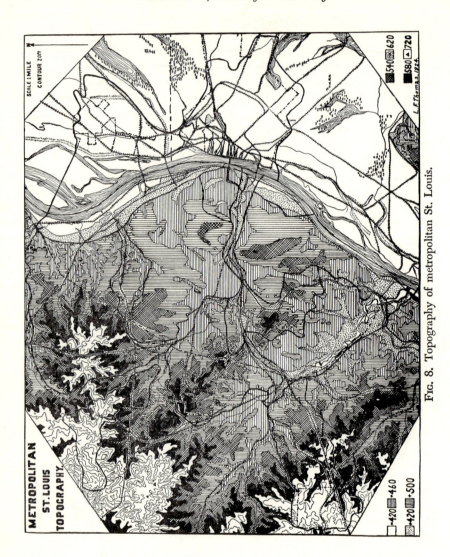

Fig. 8. Topography of metropolitan St. Louis.

skyscrapers containing offices, stores, and banks. Nearby may be found passenger and freight terminals, wholesale houses, light industry, theaters, and municipal buildings. Extending out in several directions are seen "string streets" lined with businesses of many kinds. At outlying intersections are clusters of commercial and service establishments. Scattered between and beyond are all sorts of residential districts. At first glance all this looks like a crazy quilt; after careful study it begins to assume some kind of pattern.

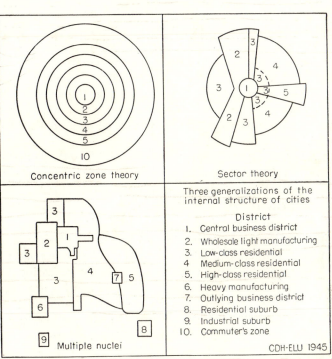

FIG. 9. Generalizations of internal structure of cities. (*By permission of the Amer. Acad. Pol. Soc. Sci.*)

As aids to describing, explaining, and comparing cities, several schemes have been devised. One, the geographic, has already been described. Another is illustrated by the third pattern in Fig. 9. It emphasizes the observation that many phenomena of city life occur in clusters. Centralization, specialization, and segregation are some of the terms we shall presently introduce to symbolize the processes through which these clusters develop. Not only do we find fairly separate areas devoted to commerce, industry, transportation, and residence. We find some areas devoted primarily to wholesaling, others to retailing; some to light industry, others to heavy; some to automobiles, others to women's wear; some to expensive homes, others to cheap tenements; some to native whites, some to foreigners, and others to Negroes.

Harris and Ullman[1] found the distribution of these clusters not to be accidental or random, but to follow a fairly general pattern. They noted that the main business district is "at the focus of intracity transportation facilities," whether at the areal center or not. Within this district financial, legal, and administrative offices are located close together to facilitate communication. Heavy industry is placed along transportation routes and often on the periphery of a metropolitan area, where its need for space may be easily and cheaply met, and where it may offer least annoyance—noise, smoke, ugliness—to householders. The separation of socioeconomic classes is determined largely by ability to pay. The segregation of ethnic groups is due partly to prejudice and partly to the desire of many people to live among those of similar traditions and tastes. Thus for a variety of reasons peoples and functions are scattered over an urban landscape in clusters. The city may be viewed as a collection of "multiple nuclei."

The first pattern of Fig. 9 illustrates Burgess' hypothesis that a metropolitan area tends to resemble a series of concentric zones,[2] At the assumed center is the main business district. Just outside is a zone which Burgess called one of transition, because as the city grows the business district tends to push out into an adjoining area that was earlier residential in character. We prefer to call it a zone of deterioration for reasons which will appear later. The succeeding zones, according to Burgess, are dominated by dwellings of gradually increasing cost until, on the suburban fringe, many different kinds of housing are interspersed with industrial establishments and open spaces. Obviously this sort of scheme fits some cities better than others, and in all cases represents averages which conceal the diversity present in each zone.

In support of the conception of the city as a number of concentric zones Burgess presented several series of data computed for each. He showed that, passing from the center to the periphery of Chicago, home ownership increased steadily; the percentage of foreign born declined; the sex ratio dropped until the fourth zone was reached, after which it remained fairly constant; poverty and divorce rates were highest in the second zone, beyond which they declined steadily; male juvenile delinquency was highest at the center, declining consistently until it practically disappeared in the fourth zone.

[1] Chauncy D. Harris and Edward L. Ullman, "The Nature of Cities," *Annals Amer. Acad. Pol. Soc. Sci.*, November, 1945, pp. 7–17.

[2] Robert E. Park and Ernest W. Burgess, *The City*, Chap. 2, 1925; Ernest W. Burgess, "The Determination of Gradients in the Growth of the City," *Pub. Amer. Sociol. Soc.*, 21 (1927), 178–184.

Some corresponding series have been computed for St. Louis.[3] We found that density of population declined without a break from the second to the seventh mile, while the proportion of single dwellings rose steadily from the second to the seventh mile. Rentals rose only to the fifth mile, after which there was little change. Except for a slight drop in the sixth mile, the percentage of the population that was native white of native parents rose consistently as we passed from the center to the periphery. The sex ratio showed a remarkable drop from the first to the second mile, then a gradual decline to the fifth mile, and thereafter an increase toward equality. The death rates, both crude and corrected, showed a steady decrease from the center to the periphery. The same was true of dependency and of juvenile court cases, except for slight deviations in the sixth and seventh miles. Finally, residential mobility displayed the characteristic direction of change throughout the 7 miles. Now it is admitted without hesitation that not all the other series showed the same progressive changes. Thus the proportion of small children was highest in the second mile, but almost as high in the seventh. The relative number of elderly persons was highest in the first and lowest in the second, rising in the third and fourth, thereafter declining steadily but not greatly. In other words, the wavelike zones in terms of which the city may be viewed do not differ uniformly or in all respects; but there are enough consistent differences to warrant the use of this conventionalized scheme as one device for interpreting the distributive aspects of the great city.

The second conventionalized pattern in Fig. 9 illustrates Hoyt's proposition that a large city can be more appropriately conceived as a number of sectors than as a series of concentric zones.[4] According to Hoyt, there

---

[3] These series are parts of the cooperative research that has been carried on in St. Louis for several years. Net density was computed by Max Colodesch. Data on single dwellings, homeownership, and rentals, as well as population elements and sex ratios, were compiled by the U.S. Bureau of the Census. Vital statistics were secured from the Division of Health, rates being computed by Ralph C. Fletcher, Max Colodesch, and Harry J. Hornback. Dependency data were assembled from the Social Service Exchange. Those from the juvenile court were made available by Ralph Smith. The residential mobility study was made by Donald O. Cowgill. For each of these and more than 20 other series of data, ratios were computed, census tracts were assigned in whole or in part to the appropriate circle or zone, and weighted averages were calculated for each zone. The last steps were checked by Stuart A. Queen, Harry L. Hornback, and—for some of the series—students at Washington University. Despite the care taken, a margin of error remains, but the accuracy is sufficient to establish the hypothesis in question, so far as St. Louis proper is concerned. Unfortunately, data are insufficient to test it for the entire metropolitan district. Many of the data and discussions of methods used may be found in Ralph C. Fletcher, Harry L. Hornback, and Stuart A. Queen, *Social Statistics of St. Louis by Census Tracts*, 1935.

[4] Homer Hoyt, "The Structure of American Cities in the Post-war Era," *Amer. Jour. Sociol.*, 48 (1943), 475–481. See also *The Structure and Growth of Residential Neighborhoods in American Cities*, Chap. 4, 1939.

may early appear on one side of the main business district an expensive residential section. This is likely to expand in the same direction. As fine houses become antiquated or as business approaches, the old residents tend to move farther out, turning their former mansions into multiple dwellings. On another side of the main business district, a collection of cheap houses or tenements may arise. This, like the expensive residential section, is likely to extend outward in the same direction as that in which

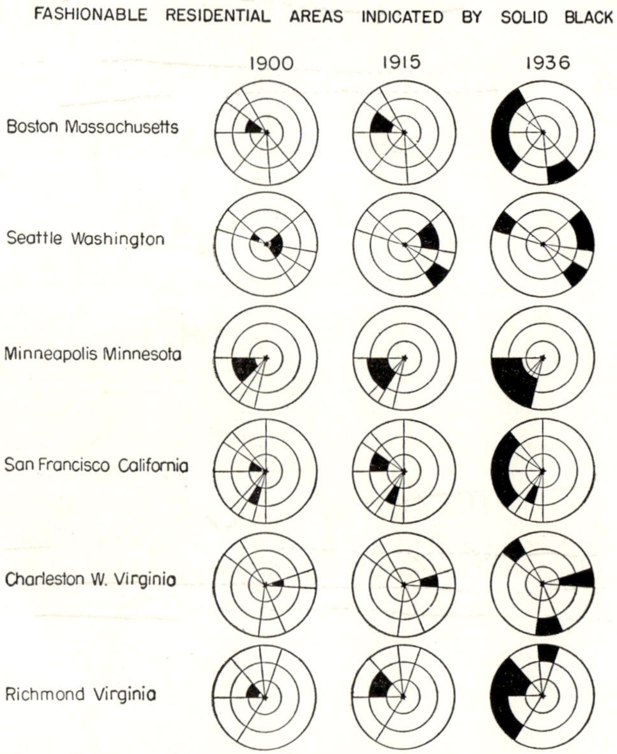

FASHIONABLE RESIDENTIAL AREAS INDICATED BY SOLID BLACK

Fig. 10. Shifts in location of fashionable residential areas. (*By permission of Homer Hoyt and the Federal Housing Administration.*)

it started. Figure 10 displays this mode of interpretation, with special reference to fashionable residential areas. Stated a little differently, people of means move out in axial lines along the fastest transportation routes. Poorer people tend to live near factories and other places of employment, pushing out in different sectors from those occupied by the well to do. Middle-class people locate in between. Thus, whether a given sector of a city develops first as a high-rent or as a low-rent residential area, it is likely to retain that character for a long time and for long distances. The movement of the high-rent area is deemed most important

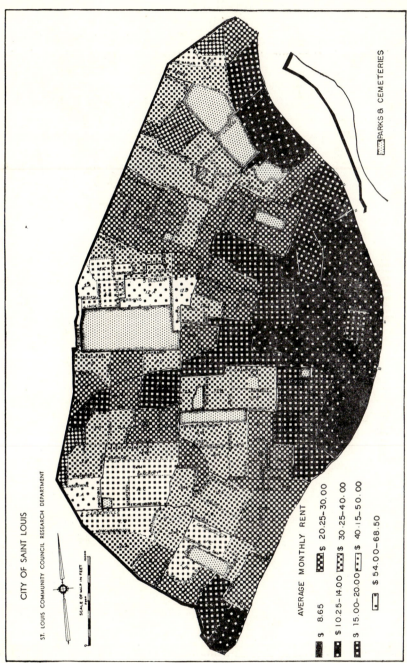

CITY OF SAINT LOUIS

ST. LOUIS COMMUNITY COUNCIL RESEARCH DEPARTMENT

SCALE OF MAP IN FEET

AVERAGE MONTHLY RENT

$ 8.65

$ 10.25–14.00

$ 15.00–20.00

$ 20.25–30.00

$ 30.25–40.00

$ 40.15–50.00

$ 54.00–68.50

PARKS & CEMETERIES

Fig. 11. Average estimated monthly rent, St. Louis, 1940.

on the ground that it tends to pull the growth of the entire city in the same direction. The center of high rent used to move out from the heart of the city along some avenue. But with the increased use of automobiles it has passed over intervening spaces and spread out into exclusive garden communities. New middle-class districts appear just beyond the older middle-class areas or out on the city's edge near the more expensive sections. The people who pay low rents either stay in the heart of the city or move into houses left behind by higher income groups, or erect very poor dwellings on the periphery.

Figure 11 affords the reader an opportunity to utilize all these schemes for analyzing the spatial pattern of a city. It is easy to visualize "sectors," as Hoyt would call them, running from the main business district (right center) north, northwest, southwest, and south. Without difficulty one can pick out such nuclei as the central business district and the "good" residential areas of the west end and southwest. By referring to Fig. 8 one can also identify areas devoted to industry and transportation. With a reasonable use of the imagination, or by actually drawing arcs with a compass, it is possible to visualize concentric zones. In other words, all four devices—topography, sectors, nuclei, concentric zones—are useful schemes for describing, analyzing, and comparing the spatial patterns of large cities.

DEVELOPMENT OF THE METROPOLITAN PATTERN

As has been said several times, every American city began on a small scale. Often it has been merely a subsistence village or a trading post. Gradually there have developed personal services and retail trade for the local inhabitants, presently supplemented by the manufacture of certain articles for local use. Improved means of transportation bring in raw materials from the adjacent territories and distribute finished products through the surrounding region. All these aspects of growth and development are reflected in the changing urban pattern. When the city begins, all these activities are concentrated in a small, compact area; as it grows, they not only occupy more space but also tend to segregate themselves. Presently the retail shopping districts, the warehouses and wholesale establishments, the factories, and the residences become more or less separate each from the others. The major commercial functions are likely to remain near the original site; the manufacturing usually remains nearby for a time and then scatters along transportation routes. The residences tend to occupy most of the periphery of the growing city.

If the place is developing rapidly, stores, shops, etc., are now and again set down in the midst of a district that has been strictly residential. Thereupon some of the inhabitants find this undesirable; they move farther out and establish a new residential section. However, it is not always possible to sell the old house without great loss; hence it frequently happens that the owner retains title to his property, hoping that without too long a delay the land may be needed for commercial or industrial purposes. When this occurs, he expects to sell the lot for a high enough price to recoup the losses due to depreciation of the building and the expense incurred in the interim. Since he does not know how long he may have to wait, he undertakes to rent the old house. Now the people who could afford to pay an economic rent for it as a single dwelling are probably, like the owner, moving to the outskirts of the city. The only ones who are likely to accept the house are those who cannot possibly pay the rent the owner feels that he must receive. Hence he will probably make a few alterations and rent it in small units to several families. The advertisements will read "Light Houskeeping," "Sleeping Rooms," "Apartments," or something of this general character. Thus what was once a residence for a single family of substance is converted into a multiple dwelling occupied by people of small means.

If the period between the first invasion of an old residential district and its complete occupation by commerce and industry is not too long, this general procedure serves a useful purpose for both landlord and tenant. But if the growth of the city is slower than was anticipated, or if the developing subcenters absorb some of the expansion which might otherwise have occurred near the central business district, then the delay may be very great. When the time runs to twenty, thirty, or forty years, deterioration becomes quite marked. Naturally the owner hesitates to spend much money for repairs, since he is still hoping to be relieved of his property. Often the tenants who occupy such houses are careless of the property and hasten its general decline. Thus an area which might have been merely one of transition becomes a zone of deterioration. It is under these circumstances that the city slum characteristically develops.

As the city grows, people and their institutions keep pushing outward, sometimes in one direction, usually in several. These are likely to move out along lines making a map of the built-up area display a star-shaped or octopuslike pattern. Figure 12 illustrates this with the case of Chicago. Hoyt presents similar maps of 13 other cities.[5]

However the details may vary, one result of the centrifugal movement is usually a marked decline of population in the inner city. McKenzie showed that this has been going on for a long time in some cities, notably in Cleveland, Boston, and St. Louis.[6] In the first forty years of the present century that part of St. Louis which lies east of Jefferson Ave. (about 2 miles from the Mississippi River) declined both absolutely and relatively

[5] Hoyt, *The Structure and Growth of Residential Neighborhoods in American Cities,* pp. 157–159.
[6] R. D. McKenzie, *The Metropolitan Community,* p. 192, 1933.

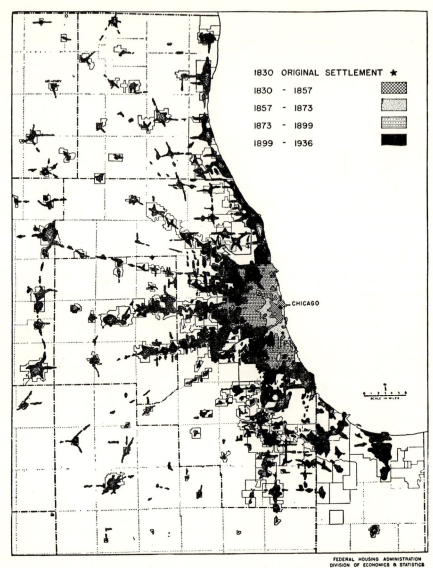

1830　ORIGINAL SETTLEMENT　★

1830　-　1857

1857　-　1873

1873　-　1899

1899　-　1936

CHICAGO

SCALE IN MILES

FEDERAL HOUSING ADMINISTRATION
DIVISION OF ECONOMICS & STATISTICS

FIG. 12. Expansion of the settled area in Chicago and environs. (*By permission of Homer Hoyt and the Federal Housing Administration.*)

in population. In 1900 this section contained 280,000 people, constituting 49 per cent of the city's total. In 1940 the district had only 170,000, who constituted 21 per cent of the total population. Thompson has assembled similar data from 16 cities for the decade 1930 to 1940 (see Table 16) and shows that in 10 of them there was a loss of population in belts ranging from 2 to 5 miles from the center of the city. In the other six

Table 16. Per Cent of Increase in Population in Central Cities and in Satellite Areas, United States, 1900 to 1950

Decade	Number of districts	Per cent of increase				
				Satellite areas		
		Metropolitan districts	Central cities	Total	Urban	Rural
1900–1910	44	34.6	33.6	38.2	35.9	43.2
1910–1920	58	26.9	25.2	32.0	30.7	35.1
1920–1930	97	28.3	22.3	44.0	37.7	56.0
1930–1940	140	8.1	5.1	15.1	7.4	30.0
1940–1950	169	21.2	13.0	34.7		

SOURCE: Adapted from Warren S. Thompson, *The Growth of Metropolitan Districts in the United States, 1900–1940*, p. 5, and Bureau of the Census, 1950 Census of Population, Preliminary Counts, Series PC-3, No. 3.

growth was much less than in more distant zones.[7] However, in cities of both categories there were parts of the zone of deterioration which showed population gains. Often this was due to the in-migration of rural Negroes for whom available housing was restricted. Also there was continued conversion of old residences into tenements and of apartment buildings into rooming houses. Some families "doubled up," and some new multistory apartment houses were erected near the heart of the city. It may be that new programs of slum clearance and urban redevelopment will change the conventional pattern of North American cities. But up to now most cities display deterioration at the center, centrifugal flight, absorption of suburbs, and, in general, growth near the periphery of the metropolitan area.

ECOLOGICAL PROCESSES IN DEVELOPMENT OF THE METROPOLITAN PATTERN

In the efforts to analyze and interpret the development of a large city, a number of semitechnical terms have come into general use. Each of these represents a process or a phase of the inclusive processes of urban growth. First of all, we note *concentration,* the drawing of population into a given area. This is measured by density or the ratio of population to land area. The opposite of concentration is *dispersion,* the scattering of the population, which is similarly measured. For some cities, density maps have been prepared at various points in time, and from these it is possible to see the increasing density of certain parts of the metropolitan district and the concurrent decrease in density of other

[7] Warren S. Thompson, *The Growth of Metropolitan Districts in the United States, 1900–1940,* p. 9, 1947.

sections. In general we find the greatest concentration so far in residential sections close to the central business district. But these areas of greatest density, at least in St. Louis, and apparently in numbers of other cities, are losing population to outlying sections where the density is increasing. A third process is *centralization,* the drawing together of institutions and activities, *i.e.,* the assembling of people to carry on various functions rather than to reside in a given area. This is identified by buildings and other physical equipment, by the prices of land, and by traffic counts. The downtown area is almost always the area of greatest centralization as indicated by these criteria. However, there are subcenters in various parts of every metropolitan district which display the same process, but on a smaller scale. They involve *decentralization* in the sense of scattering functions from the main business district to outlying points. Each of them is itself a new case of centralization.

The most obvious illustration of this is afforded by the chain stores, whose retail outlets are in subcenters and at scattered points but are usually managed from a general office in the main business district. In the *Regional Survey of New York and Its Environs*[8] it was found that banks, brokerage houses, legal firms, commission merchants, and wholesalers are quite consistently located near the heart of the city. Until recently, department stores have been found almost exclusively in the downtown area; of late they have shown a tendency to remove to subcenters. Perhaps it would be more accurate to say that new department stores develop at subcenters rather than in old business districts.

Some of the so-called light industries tend to be drawn toward the center of a city and to remain there after other functions have started to move toward the periphery. Those which are more commonly found near the center are clothing, tobacco, job printing, and others which require relatively little ground space per worker, can operate on a small scale, can utilize obsolete buildings, need to be near their market, or in other ways find time and service important factors. The heavy industries, on the contrary, which demand much space and often have nuisance features and in which the time and service factors are less urgent, seem to find their way toward the outlying parts of the metropolitan district. In recent years decentralization of industry has extended far out into the metropolitan region, apparently as a consequence of employers' efforts to secure a cheap and docile labor supply.

A fifth process identified in the study of urban patterns and their changes is called *specialization.* This is really a special case of centralization. By it is meant the clustering of particular types of institutions and activities. Thus we sometimes find a "bright light" area occupied by

[8] R. M. Haig and R. C. McCrea, "Major Economic Factors in Metropolitan Growth and Arrangement," *Regional Survey of New York and Its Environs,* Vol. 1, 1927.

numbers of theaters, dance halls, and other places of amusement. "Automobile rows," "petticoat lanes," Wall Streets, and medical centers are other examples of specialization.

The drawing together of particular types of people is called *segregation*. This may occur as a result either of external pressure, such as that exerted upon the Negroes, or of relatively free choice, as in the case of upper-class residential districts. In Chap. 10 will be found a map illustrating the segregation of various ethnic groups in St. Louis at a particular time. The process of *invasion* is a convenient name for what happens when a new type of people, institution, or activity enters an area previously occupied by a different type. Thus when Negroes begin to come into a district previously occupied by whites or when business places appear in an area that had been exclusively residential, invasion may be said to be taking place. That is to say, it is a case either of group displacement or of change in land use. Finally, when an invasion has gone so far that the new population or new function dominates an area and the original occupants have moved out, we speak of *succession* as having occurred.

Two other terms will be employed from time to time, although the activities to which they refer may be covered in whole or in part by terms already discussed. As the central city expands and as outlying towns grow toward the city, they come to exchange personnel and services to such a degree that ultimately the smaller community may be said to be absorbed into the larger. When this *absorption* involves political action, we speak of *annexation*. However, it should be plain from earlier discussion that absorption may occur without annexation and that annexation might be forced without the smaller community's becoming fully identified with the larger in its economic and social life. Thus some years ago Los Angeles annexed almost the whole of the San Fernando Valley. In it were a number of small communities which gave up their political independence but remained economically and socially as separate from the central city as did other towns which were not annexed. The important thing to bear in mind throughout this discussion is not the names of particular ecological processes but the fact that changes such as we have described are constantly going on in our cities. There are superficial evidences of stability and permanence, but underneath the surface change is never ending. Many of the changes that take place in our cities are unplanned, unanticipated, and little noticed even after they have occurred; others are surprising and disturbing; still others are unquestionably the result of deliberate planning. It is our belief that much of the confusion in city life results from failure to recognize these processes of change and to deal with them in accordance with some well-defined program of action.

INTERRELATION OF FACTORS IN URBAN AREAS

Whether the pattern identified or utilized in a given city most resembles concentric circles, sectors, or multiple nuclei, we find that certain kinds of events and conditions tend to appear together. To get at this relation more precisely, some of our associates have computed coefficients of rank correlation between various series of data. The method involved ranking census tracts according to various indices and comparing a tract's rank in one series with its rank in another. Using a variation of the Spearman formula,[9] we determined the extent to which the ranking of all tracts in any series corresponded to the ranking in any other series. For example, in St. Louis the age of housing was found to display a high positive correlation with death rates, dependency, illiteracy, the employment of women, juvenile court cases, multiple dwellings, and Negroes. It showed a marked negative correlation with the size of family, homeownership, value of homes, and rentals paid.[10] This means that tracts in which houses were very old had high death rates and many families on relief, illiterates, employed women, delinquents, Negroes, and tenements. They had small families, few homeowners, cheap houses, and low rents. In another study, residential mobility was found to have a high correlation with relief and other social services, juvenile court cases, venereal disease, deaths from tuberculosis, employment of women, Negroes, multiple dwellings, and vacancies in residential property. It showed a marked negative correlation with size of family, percentage of males married, rentals, and the American-born children of immigrants.[11] A third group of correlations undertook to measure the relation between the percentage of males married and various other socioeconomic factors. It showed married men to be most common in areas of homeownership, and relatively fewer where there were Negroes, density of population, illiteracy, relief and other social services, multiple dwellings, employment of women, venereal diseases among men, and tuberculosis deaths.[12]

Numerous other relations have been established, but these should be sufficient to demonstrate not merely that particular aspects of a city's life are different from section to section, but that certain changes seem to occur together. Thus mobility, obsolescence, poverty, disease, delinquency, illiteracy, and several other factors occur regularly together in parts of the inner city, whereas a higher economic status, newer housing, lower density, lower death rates, and more stability are found together in certain outlying parts of the city. Howard Green found similar rela-

[9] $\rho = 1 - [6\,\Sigma d^2]/[n(n^2 - 1)]$.

[10] These correlations were computed by J. Bertram Black in connection with the Assessor's Survey, which was a 1936 WPA project.

[11] This study was made by Donald O. Cowgill in 1935.

[12] Ralph C. Fletcher, Harry L. Hornback, and Stuart A. Queen, *Social Statistics of St. Louis by Census Tracts, 1935*.

tionships in the city of Cleveland.[13] On the basis of rentals paid and values assigned to homes occupied by owners, he divided the Cleveland metropolitan district into 14 types of economic areas. In the higher economic areas he found most single dwellings, home ownership, radios, increase in population, and births in hospitals. In the lower economic areas he found the highest density of population, most unemployment, illiteracy, juvenile delinquency, infant mortality, highest birth rates, and the largest percentage of males single. Since the lower economic areas are more frequently found near the heart of the city and the higher areas more frequently near the periphery, Green's findings and our own support the same general conclusions.

In a study of social areas in Los Angeles, Shevky and Williams[14] obtained similar—though by no means identical—results, handling census tract data by different procedures. They developed three indices and then sought to discover their interrelations. These were indices of social rank, urbanization, and segregation. The index of social rank was based on occupation, education, and income. Occupational status of a tract was determined by computing the number of craftsmen, operatives, and laborers per 1,000 employed persons; the lower the ratio, the higher the status. Educational status was determined by computing the number of persons who had completed eight grades or less per 1,000 persons aged twenty-five and over; again the lower the ratio, the higher the status. Income status was rated on the basis of average rent (paid or estimated) per capita. These three items were reduced to percentiles; the percentiles were added and the sum divided by 3. The result for each census tract was its index of social rank.

In similar fashion an index of urbanization was devised using fertility, employment of women, and single dwellings. Fertility was determined by dividing the number of children under five by the number of women fifteen to forty-four and multiplying by 1,000; the lower the ratio, the higher the urbanization. The second part of the index was the number of women in the labor force per 1,000 women fourteen years old and over. The third variable was the percentage of occupied dwelling units which were single-family, detached; the lower the ratio, the higher the urbanization.

Next Shevky and Williams computed an index of segregation. The percentage of the population in each tract that belonged to a given category or group (*e.g.*, Negro) was multiplied by the number of this group's members in the tract. Then the sum of these products for all tracts was divided by the total number of the group in the county. This average percentage was then divided by the percentage the group con-

[13] Howard Green, *Population Characteristics by Census Tracts, Cleveland, Ohio, 1930*, pp. 64*ff.*, 1931.
[14] Eshref Shevky and Marilyn Williams, *The Social Areas of Los Angeles*, 1949.

stituted of the total county population. Shevky and Williams found five groups[15] with indices exceeding 3; *i.e.*, their average concentration was three or more times what it would have been if they were distributed at random throughout the county. These groups also were found to be closely associated with one another in their spatial distribution. Hence an index of segregation was computed for the five groups taken together, using the same procedure as for the individual groups.

The interrelation of urbanization and social rank was computed in terms of the usual coefficient of linear correlation and displayed as a line of regression (the dotted line in Fig. 13). Census tracts falling within a range of one standard error of the line of regression (between the heavy lines parallel to the dotted line in Fig. 13) were classed as average.

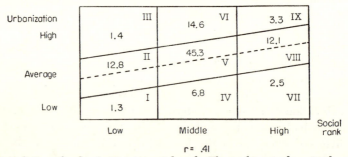

r = .41

Fig. 13. Relation of urbanization to social rank. The arabic numbers in the cells indicate the percentage of the total population in each area or category. (*Adapted from Eshref Shevky and Marilyn Williams, The Social Areas of Los Angeles. By permission of the University of California Press and the Haynes Foundation.*)

Those outside this range were classed as high and low. The base of the figure was divided into three intervals, each representing approximately one-third of the range. Finally census tracts in each of the nine "areas" were divided into two sets according to their indices of segregation. From this classificatory device it was possible to display relationships among the three major indices and between each of them and other statistical series.

Urbanization and social rank were positively related to each other. Segregation varied directly with urbanization when social rank was low, but otherwise showed little relationship to it. Sex ratio (males per 100 females) varied inversely with social rank; directly with urbanization when social rank was low, and inversely with urbanization when social rank was middle or high. The number of older persons (fifty and over) varied directly with urbanization and social rank. Number of women in the labor force varied directly, while fertility varied inversely with both urbanization and social rank. Restated, census tracts in Area IX had few children, many employed women, few single dwellings, few laborers,

---

[15] These groups were Negroes, Orientals, Russians, Mexicans, and Italians.

high rent per capita, high level of schooling, low sex ratio. At the other extreme, in Area I census tracts had many children, few working women, many single dwellings, many laborers, low rent per capita, low level of schooling, high sex ratio. Thus the scheme devised by Shevky and Williams serves to classify census tracts into groups which represent distinctive combinations of socioeconomic and demographic traits.

One more plan for studying the interrelations of factors in the spatial pattern of a city is that of Calvin Schmid.[16] Schmid used 10 series of data by census tracts in 20 medium-sized cities, 2 smaller cities, and 1 very large city. He found, as others before him, that certain factors tend to occur together with considerable regularity. Using the Pearsonian coefficient, he found that the best indicator of a cluster of socioeconomic factors was educational status, as measured by median school grade completed by persons twenty-five years and over. Next to educational status was economic status as measured by mean rental.

With the Cornell technique of scale analysis described in Chap. 3, Schmid made a special examination of the census tracts in Providence. He computed quartile rankings for each of 10 selected indices for all the census tracts. He ranked the tracts from high to low with reference to all 10 indices. This yielded 16 scale types which he later combined into 7. Figure 14 shows how these types differed according to their quartile rankings with reference to each of the 10 indices. Pattern type 1 was characterized by being in the highest quartile with respect to college graduates, professional workers, mechanical refrigeration, mean rental, proprietors, and managers. It was in the lowest quartile with respect to children under fifteen, laborers, unemployed persons seeking work, males, and ratio of children to women of childbearing age. Pattern type 16 (combined type 7) showed exactly the reverse, while the others fell in between.

Finally Schmid developed ecological pattern types based on simple ranking of indices. Using New Orleans data, he ranked each census tract on each of 11 indices. He totaled the respective tract rankings and divided by 11. Tracts were then sorted into seven categories according to mean scores and the results were displayed on a map. Incidentally, the pattern which appears on the map suggests the Harris and Ullman multinuclear hypothesis rather than the Hoyt sector theory or the Burgess interpretation in terms of concentric circles.

The most general conclusions that can be drawn from these various studies of metropolitan patterns and their development are these. Great cities in the United States have quite varied districts in which distinctive combinations of factors appear. These types of districts can be identified by several different methods, which yield comparable results. In detail,

[16] Calvin F. Schmid, "Generalizations Concerning the Ecology of the American City," *Amer. Sociol. Rev.*, 15 (1950), 264–281.

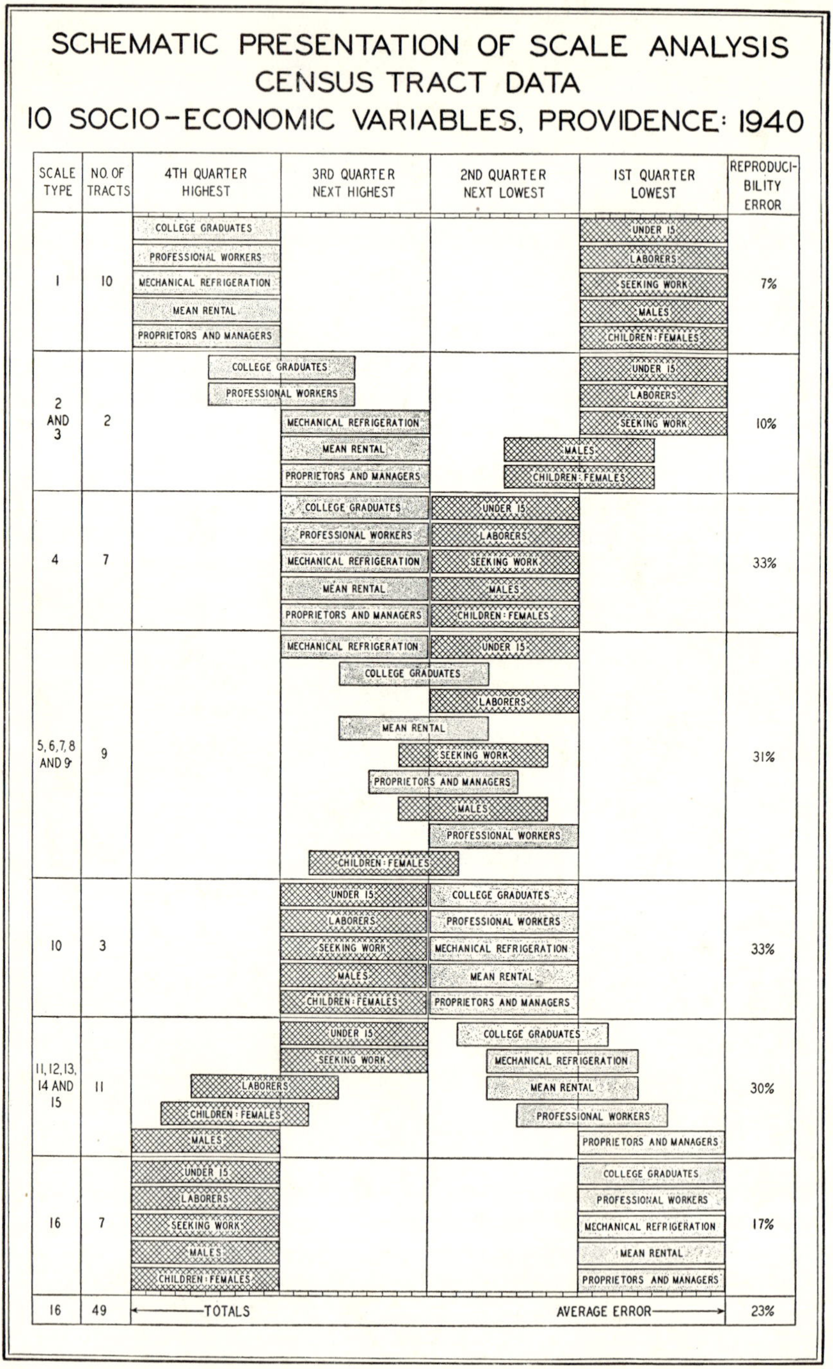

SCHEMATIC PRESENTATION OF SCALE ANALYSIS CENSUS TRACT DATA
10 SOCIO-ECONOMIC VARIABLES, PROVIDENCE: 1940

SCALE TYPE	NO. OF TRACTS	4TH QUARTER HIGHEST	3RD QUARTER NEXT HIGHEST	2ND QUARTER NEXT LOWEST	1ST QUARTER LOWEST	REPRODUCI-BILITY ERROR
1	10	COLLEGE GRADUATES / PROFESSIONAL WORKERS / MECHANICAL REFRIGERATION / MEAN RENTAL / PROPRIETORS AND MANAGERS			UNDER 15 / LABORERS / SEEKING WORK / MALES / CHILDREN-FEMALES	7%
2 AND 3	2	COLLEGE GRADUATES / PROFESSIONAL WORKERS	MECHANICAL REFRIGERATION / MEAN RENTAL / PROPRIETORS AND MANAGERS	MALES / CHILDREN-FEMALES	UNDER 15 / LABORERS / SEEKING WORK	10%
4	7		COLLEGE GRADUATES / PROFESSIONAL WORKERS / MECHANICAL REFRIGERATION / MEAN RENTAL / PROPRIETORS AND MANAGERS	UNDER 15 / LABORERS / SEEKING WORK / MALES / CHILDREN-FEMALES		33%
5,6,7,8 AND 9	9		MECHANICAL REFRIGERATION / COLLEGE GRADUATES / MEAN RENTAL / SEEKING WORK / PROPRIETORS AND MANAGERS / MALES / PROFESSIONAL WORKERS / CHILDREN-FEMALES	UNDER 15 / LABORERS		31%
10	3		UNDER 15 / LABORERS / SEEKING WORK / MALES / CHILDREN-FEMALES	COLLEGE GRADUATES / PROFESSIONAL WORKERS / MECHANICAL REFRIGERATION / MEAN RENTAL / PROPRIETORS AND MANAGERS		33%
11,12,13,14 AND 15	11	LABORERS / CHILDREN-FEMALES / MALES	UNDER 15 / SEEKING WORK	COLLEGE GRADUATES / MECHANICAL REFRIGERATION / MEAN RENTAL / PROFESSIONAL WORKERS / PROPRIETORS AND MANAGERS		30%
16	7	UNDER 15 / LABORERS / SEEKING WORK / MALES / CHILDREN-FEMALES			COLLEGE GRADUATES / PROFESSIONAL WORKERS / MECHANICAL REFRIGERATION / MEAN RENTAL / PROPRIETORS AND MANAGERS	17%
16	49	←——TOTALS			AVERAGE ERROR——→	23%

FIG. 14. (*By permission of Calvin F. Schmid and the American Sociological Review.*)

the spatial patterns of great cities vary considerably, but the few studies referred to indicate similarities as well as differences.

Regrettably our data are almost exclusively from the United States. So far as we know, very few studies of this sort have been made of cities in other parts of the world. Among the exceptions are limited studies of three Latin-American cities and one of Paris, France.[17] We believe that some of the methods we have described could be used in studying cities of other lands, provided reliable statistical data could be obtained for small areas corresponding to our census tracts. But we venture no guesses as to similarities or differences in the patterns which might emerge.

SELECTED READINGS

✗ BURGESS, ERNEST W.: "Urban Areas," pp. 113–138 in *Chicago, An Experiment in Social Science Research*, edited by T. V. Smith and L. D. White, University of Chicago Press, 1929. Probably the best available statement of the hypothesis of concentric circles and gradients.

DAVIE, MAURICE R.: "The Pattern of Urban Growth," pp. 133–162 in *The Science of Society*, edited by George P. Murdock, Yale University Press, 1937. Undertakes to refute the Burgess hypothesis.

FIREY, WALTER: *Land Use in Central Boston*, Harvard University Press, 1947. Emphasizes the importance of noneconomic factors in the determination of a city's spatial pattern.

HARRIS, CHAUNCEY D., and EDWARD L. ULLMAN: "The Nature of Cities," *Annals Amer. Acad. Pol. Soc. Sci.*, November, 1945, pp. 7–17. Clear and brief critique of three theories of urban patterns.

✗ HOYT, HOMER: *The Structure and Growth of Residential Neighborhoods in American Cities*, Federal Housing Administration, 1939. Probably the most comprehensive study of its kind ever published. Based on real property inventories of about 200 cities during the 1930's.

McKENZIE, R. D.: *The Metropolitan Community*, McGraw-Hill Book Company, Inc., 1933. Part IV, "The Process of Metropolitan Expansion," is especially useful in this connection.

QUINN, JAMES A.: *Human Ecology*, Prentice-Hall, Inc., 1950. Chapters 5–7, 13–16, and 18 are especially helpful in analyzing the internal structure of a metropolitan area.

SCHMID, CALVIN F.: "Generalizations Concerning the Ecology of the American City," *Amer. Sociol. Rev.*, 15 (1950), 264–281. A striking analysis of the relations between factors in local districts within cities.

SHEVKY, ESHREF, and MARILYN WILLIAMS: *The Social Areas of Los Angeles*, University of California Press, 1949. Introduces a unique method of characterizing the local districts within a metropolitan area.

[17] Norman S. Hayner, "Mexico City: Its Growth and Configuration," *Amer. Jour. Sociol.*, 50 (1945), 295–304; "Oaxaca, City of Old Mexico," *Sociol. Soc. Res.*, 29 (1944), 87–95; Theodore Caplow, "The Social Ecology of Guatemala City," *Social Forces*, 28 (1949), 113–133; Kathren McKinney, *An Ecological Study of Paris, France, 1911, 1921, 1931*, unpublished master's thesis, Washington University, 1939.

CHAPTER 9. *Communities within the Metropolitan Area*

As we drive about a modern North American city or view it from the air, we at first get the impression of a hodgepodge. Even when we look a little more closely, we seem to see a grand disarray of buildings, people, and activities. But when we utilize one of the schematic devices described in the preceding chapter, we find that the distribution is not really random. Some kind of pattern emerges, and further search reveals something of how the pattern came into existence.

In this chapter we are concerned not with the pattern as a whole, but with the nuclei which appear to be scattered over any metropolitan area. First, we are likely to identify business subcenters, clusters of stores, amusement houses (movies, bowling alleys, dance halls), service establishments (shoe repair, barber and beauty shops, cleaners, laundries, filling stations), and often others. Sometimes a cluster of this sort is the business center of a formerly separate town; sometimes it has developed within the city to serve and be supported by the people who happen to live nearby; sometimes it seems to be a miniature downtown located at the junction of two main thoroughfares and drawing customers who pass by en route from one part of the metropolitan area to another.

Sometimes we find that such a subcenter has a name and a distinctive history. The people who live or work in the vicinity may refer to it as a community or a neighborhood. We are interested in these local aggregations of buildings, agencies, activities, persons, and groups. We shall attempt to classify them on the basis of certain characteristics and to discover whether there are uniformities in the manner of their development.

A study of the subcenters in Baltimore was made in 1930.[1] In it 54 clusters were identified in addition to the central business district, 11 public markets, and several string streets. These clusters differed considerably in the number and variety of retail establishments, varying

[1] Inez K. Ralph, "Nucleation; The Pattern of Retail Marketing," Chap. 9 of R. D. McKenzie, *The Metropolitan Community*, 1933.

116

with population density, average income, topography, transportation facilities, and segregation of ethnic groups. In 1941 a similar study in St. Louis and St. Louis County resulted in the identification of 57 sub-centers. But neither of these studies indicated that the clusters of retail outlets served primarily the people of the immediate vicinity, or that these people depended more on the local establishments than on those in other parts of the city.

In order to shed some light on these questions, we conducted limited surveys in 13 parts of the St. Louis metropolitan area between 1939 and 1946. We used a simple schedule on which interviewers entered the answers to such questions as: Where do you do most of your shopping for groceries, dry goods and clothing, drugs and tobacco? Where do you attend church? Where do your children attend school? Where do you usually attend movies? Club meetings? Where do members of the family work or carry on their business or profession? Where do you usually go for medical attention? Dental care? For each activity engaged in chiefly in the immediate district one point was scored. For an activity fairly evenly divided between that district and others one-half point was given. If an activity was carried on outside the district, the score was zero. Then the points were totaled and divided by the number of activities indicated. The result was a crude index of localization for a given family. The indices for all respondents in a district were then tabulated, and the median was treated as a rough index of localization for the district. The results showed a wide variation from about .30 in one overflow residential suburb to about .80 in a working class district near the heart of the city. In a suburb that was formerly an entirely separate town the index was about .70. In a new residential district near the edge of the central city it was .30. Note that the agencies and activities studied included not only those of retail trade but of religion, education, recreation, and health. The conclusion drawn from the surveys is that in some sections of the city people are served almost exclusively by local facilities, in others very little; while in most cases there is divided patronage.

A more thorough study of a carefully selected sample was made by Foley in 1947.[2] In his study of 400 St. Louis families, Foley showed that shopping for food and attendance at church, elementary school, and movies were predominantly within the immediate district. Employment, club meetings, purchase of clothing and furniture, consultation with physicians, and outdoor sports were mostly outside the district. Of all activities reported for all members of the families interviewed, 41 per cent were carried on within the district and 12 per cent adjacent to the

[2] Donald L. Foley, *Urban Neighborhood Facilities, A Study of a Residential District in Northwest St. Louis,* unpublished doctoral dissertation, Washington University, 1948; summarized in "The Use of Local Facilities in a Metropolis," *Amer. Jour. Sociol.,* 56 (1950), 238–246.

district. Thirty per cent of the facilities used were within half a mile of home, 47 per cent were within 1 mile. Thirty-six per cent were reached by walking. Local facilities were used most by women, by persons under twelve and over sixty-five, by those of limited schooling, by families of low income, and by those not owning automobiles. All this supports these propositions: (1) there is considerable diversity in the degree of localization of interest and activities within a city and (2) there is a greater dependence on local facilities than many observers realize. It does not disprove the proposition that, as we proceed along our hypothetical continuum from folk society to urban society, there is a characteristic change from general sharing of the same facilities and activities by people in a local area to a scattering of interests and activities over a wider territory and among various local communities.

TYPES OF COMMUNITIES WITHIN A METROPOLITAN AREA

As already pointed out, the nuclei or clusters we have described differ as to number and variety of local facilities and as to the use of them by the local population (institutional self-sufficiency). Further study shows them to differ as to marks of local separateness, such as surrounding open spaces, physical boundaries (hills, streams, railroads, parks, etc.), distinctive types of buildings (apartments, cottages), physical identification of the population (Negro, Oriental), cultural identification (Polish, Italian, Chinese, Mexican), the use of a locality name. These local aggregations also differ in some other respects, *e.g.,* mobility-stability. In some the average period of residence is so short that acquaintance, participation in local organizations, and demonstration of local loyalty are quite limited. In others there are many old residents who have many acquaintances in the district, are regular customers of local stores, and belong to local associations. Still other differences have to do with homogeneity-heterogeneity, ethnic, religious, and economic. Where the local people are much like each other and different from those in surrounding districts, there are often verbal expressions and other demonstrations of "belonging." Finally, we note that these districts differ in the number and proportion of persons who receive the attention of formal agencies such as police, courts, clinics, relief offices, etc. These differences symbolize not only variations in economic status, health, and deviant behavior, but also in self-help, mutual aid, and informal social controls.

By utilizing these and other variables, it may some day be possible to develop a scale for measuring degrees of community. Even now we are inclined to speak of degrees rather than presence or absence of community, in spite of the fact that we do not yet have a quantitative device for measurement but have to treat the differences descriptively. However, to avoid the circumlocution of "situations involving varied degrees of community" we will speak of types of communities.

It is our thesis that the great majority of communities within our metropolitan districts are or have been suburbs. The principal exceptions are ethnic groups that have established themselves well inside the city. These will be discussed in Chap. 10. The present chapter will be devoted to suburbs present and past, the stages and the processes involved in their absorption into the metropolis.

Suburbs are roughly defined as communities immediately surrounding a central city. They are characterized by less density of population than is found in the inner city but greater density than is characteristic of rural areas. They differ from independent towns of equal size because the city performs many functions for them. Also, they usually lack hinterlands or outlying trade areas of their own. Suburbs have close connections with the inner city through various means of transportation, whereby many of their inhabitants are enabled to be employed, to shop, and to carry on other activities outside the immediate community. They have many of the benefits of city life without the disadvantages of congestion, noise, and smoke. They belong to the city and yet they are separate from it.

For convenience, suburban communities are usually identified with outlying municipalities, yet they may not be incorporated and they may even be found inside the limits of a major city. The corporate limits of Detroit completely surround Highland Park and Hamtramck, which are independent municipalities; and the city of Los Angeles has annexed several communities that are still suburban in character, *e.g.*, Van Nuys, Canoga Park, Chatsworth, Wilmington. It is plain, therefore, that suburbs may be incorporated or unincorporated and may lie inside or outside the boundaries of a central city. Unfortunately for our purpose, statistical data are usually compiled for political units rather than for communities. This handicap will be recognized in the discussion which follows.

We present seven types of communities which are or have been suburbs and three series of stages through which they may be expected to pass. (1) The first type includes outlying communities whose social and economic life are relatively independent of the rest of the metropolitan area. Extreme isolation is rare, although some of these communities are really "cultural islands," little touched by the busy life about them. Usually they are separated in space from each other and from the central city. Often they are incorporated municipalities, but many of them are not. Their economic level is likely to be rather low. (2) In our second class are outlying communities with a measure of self-sufficiency but also with definite relations to the inner city. A significant number of men carry on their business or professional activities "in town." Economically they belong to the middle and upper classes. Usually such a community has its own government to provide necessary local services and to ward off the encroachments of undesirable elements. (3) Less sharply defined are those parts of the continuous, built-up portion of the metropolitan area with local institutions and names. When set apart by natural or artificial barriers, they are easily identified, but many times there are no distinguishing physical marks. Such a section may once have been like the first or second type described above; but with the increase of its own population and with the centrifugal drift from the inner city, suburb and central city have coalesced or grown together. These suburbs are sometimes independent municipalities and sometimes unincorporated. When they lack a local government of their own, they usually have limited social organization generally. (4) Another type of suburb adjacent to the major city is that which was created to attract or provide for the overflow of urban population. It too may or may not be incorporated. In fact, it may be established in otherwise unoccupied areas within the central city's limits. Because from the outset its inhabitants live an important part of their lives in the urban center, such a suburb may never develop into a well-integrated local community. (5) Quite different from the residential suburbs so far identified are industrial communities, or satellite cities. These are usually built around one or a group of large manufacturing establishments. Frequently marked physiographic features cut them off from the rest of the metropolitan area. Sometimes they are larger, and usually they are more congested, than other suburbs. Satellite cities live more to themselves because their people dwell, shop, worship, play, educate their children, earn their living, and spend most of their time within their own communities. Their people read the metropolitan newspapers less than do the residents of other suburbs. However, the industries of the satellite city are dependent on the central city for financing, managing, sale of products, and extra labor supply, and the inhabitants go to the central city for some forms of recreation and for specialized shopping.

Types, one, four, and five represent different ways in which a suburb may be started. Types two and three represent stages that tend to follow type one. Types six and seven are outgrowths of type three, four, or five. (6) As suburbs are drawn more and more into the orbit of the metropolis, they tend to lose their identity. Through annexation they become politically a part of the central city. Their schools, libraries, playgrounds, police, fire, and health departments, each become part of a city-wide system. Many of their citizens hold membership in metropolitan churches and clubs. The decline of local community life may be slow, but eventual absorption appears to be inevitable. (7) Last of all, then, comes a stage which represents the almost complete disappearance of local unity and of separateness from surrounding groups. What was once the territory occupied by a distinct community is now merely a segment of a great city.

We offer now illustrations of each of the foregoing types of urban community, drawing upon metropolitan St. Louis as our source. While each account describes a particular stage in the development of a particular community, it also represents a point in the general process through which separate communities merge their life with that of a great city.

1. *An Isolated Community in a Metropolitan Area.* In the northwest part of the St. Louis metropolitan area lies the little municipality of St. Ferdinand. Twenty years ago this was a village of 1,000 inhabitants, 7 miles from the St. Louis city limits, surrounded by open fields. An electric line, later replaced by bus service, provided a slow and indirect means of travel between St. Ferdinand and St. Louis. Most of the people went rather infrequently to the central city. In the 1930's very few were employed outside the village and its adjacent farming district. There were several grocery stores, drugstores, saloons, garage, etc., which seemed to provide fairly adequately for the residents' needs along these lines. Some of the people, however, shopped in Wellston, a much larger suburb about 7 miles away.

St. Ferdinand was settled late in the eighteenth century by the French. After the War between the States, many Germans came in, later a few Irish and a scattering of other nationalities. At first the French and the Germans were hostile, as was indicated by their maintaining separate Catholic churches and carrying on Saturday night saloon brawls. In later years there was much intermarriage and the community became very closely knit. A study in 1935 showed over one-half of the population to have been born in St. Ferdinand and one-third in other places in Missouri. Two-thirds were Catholic. Thus there were high degrees of stability and homogeneity. The localization of life was further emphasized by the fact that less than one-third owned either cars or radios; only a little over one-third of the families subscribed for a newspaper.

In 1950 a limited survey showed a large increase in population, chiefly of people who had moved out from St. Louis. Much of the space between the village and the central city had been filled with new houses. A large part of the gainfully employed had jobs in St. Louis, at the airport, or at new factories in the northwest part of the county. Shopping was no longer confined to St. Ferdinand. The population was neither so homogeneous nor so stable as fifteen years before. St. Ferdinand had ceased to represent type one.

2. *A Relatively Independent Community.* About 15 miles from the heart of St. Louis is Kirkwood, a municipality of 18,000 inhabitants. Between it and the St. Louis city limits lies another suburb, Webster

Groves. But there is no real break in the built-up area until we go west of Kirkwood. This municipality has its own police and fire departments, water system, distribution of electric light and power, schools, churches, and 70 different kinds of retail and service establishments ranging from a laundromat to a hatchery. There are food stores, variety and general merchandise stores, hardware, jewelry, automotive establishments, theaters, bowling alleys, tourist courts, etc. It is alleged that 60 per cent of the material needs of Kirkwood residents are supplied by establishments in their own community. A sample interviewed in 1950 indicated that 80 per cent of all families bought their groceries in Kirkwood. For other goods and services much use is made of nearby communities and of the central city. Shopping for clothing and furniture, attendance at concerts, theatrical performances, professional sports, consultation with physicians, dentists, and lawyers often take Kirkwood people to St. Louis. The most marked dependence of the suburb on the metropolitan area as a whole is in the field of employment. The 1950 survey indicated that five-sixths of the gainfully employed had their jobs, businesses, and professional activities outside Kirkwood.

Not only are Kirkwood residents partially dependent on economic facilities of the metropolis as a whole; their own local facilities in turn serve people outside of Kirkwood. Farmers to the west and residents of nearby incorporated districts do some shopping in Kirkwood and sometimes send their children in to school. The junction of U.S. Highway 66 with the by-pass for Highways 40 and 61 is the center of tourist camps, restaurants, and filling stations for the service of transients.

The stability of Kirkwood's population is indicated by a high percentage of home ownership (57 per cent in 1940). Homogeneity is indicated by the small number of Negroes and foreign born, large percentage of professional, managerial, and sales people (54 per cent in 1940), high percentage of single dwellings (84 per cent), and homes with mechanical refrigeration (79 per cent). There is a variety of churches—Catholic, Presbyterian, Episcopal, Baptist, Lutheran—but practically all could be described as middle-class congregations. Very few people receive public assistance, and an unusually high proportion of teen-agers belong to Boy and Girl Scouts.

There are numerous expressions of that intangible something called community spirit. Persons interviewed nearly all said they liked Kirkwood, its hometown atmosphere, and friendly spirit. Most of them said they would rather live here than anywhere else. Local loyalty is exhibited by attendance at high school football and basketball games. Each year elaborate plans are made for a homecoming. There is a parade with floats, bands, and organized bodies marching. There are contests, street dancing, and a fashion show. During the holiday season there is a Christmas program with decorations, Santa Claus, and music. Throughout the year a "welcome wagon" calls on new residents. These expressions of hospitality may be assumed to have some economic motivation, but they seem also to be associated with some local solidarity and independence.

This history of Kirkwood is about what might be expected. Until 1850 there was no town, only farms, one church, and a stagecoach station. During the 1850's a railroad was built out from St. Louis, a town was laid out, and in 1865 it was incorporated. At first the only transportation was by steam train, and only a few people made regular trips to the city. Much later came an electric line and finally busses. Today most coming and going appear to be by private automobile. A majority of Kirkwood business and professional men and wage earners leave in the morning and return at night. Many people go to Maplewood, Clayton, or St. Louis for shopping. Much recreation is sought outside of the local community. Two telephone exchanges serve Kirkwood, one providing local connections with toll charges for calls to the city, the other providing direct connections with St. Louis and the principal western suburbs. Thus, while Kirkwood has been drawn into the orbit of the metropolis, it still retains a measure of local autonomy and group solidarity.

3. *A Suburb Coalescing with the Central City.* Just west of the St. Louis city limits, midway between north and south, lies the municipality of Clayton. There are 16,000 people within its corporate boundaries, but they are not marked off from their neighbors in any direction except by political lines. Clayton has its own municipal government with police and fire protection, library, schools, parks, etc. In recent years it has developed a large shopping center which attracts customers from other suburbs and from the west end of St. Louis proper. It has 10 churches of which 3 are properly described as metropolitan. A survey made in 1944 indicated that 85 per cent of Clayton families bought groceries and drugs locally but did most of their other shopping elsewhere. This has probably changed since many new shops and a large department store have been established. About half attended church outside of Clayton; nearly a fourth sent their children outside to schools (presumably private); the attendance at movies and club meetings was about evenly divided between the local community and other parts of the metropolitan area. Business, professions, and employment were 84 per cent outside; consultation with physicians and dentists was about the same. Clearly Clayton is not an independent, self-sufficient community.

Homogeneity is about as great as in Kirkwood. Although only 3 per cent of the 1940 population was Negro and only 6 per cent foreign born, there is diversity of religion (Catholic, Christian Science, Congregational, Baptist, Lutheran, *et al.*), of education (elementary, secondary, college, professional), of incomes (as indicated by dwellings occupied—

elaborate mansions, humble cottages, apartments of varied rentals). Central heating was reported in 1940 for 96 per cent of the homes and mechanical refrigeration for 94 per cent. As to occupation, professions, proprietors, and managers predominate. In general, Clayton may be called upper middle class. Relief rates are low; participation in Boy and Girl Scouts is high. As to stability-mobility, home ownership is 15 per cent less than in Kirkwood; the 1944 survey showed one-third living at the same address two years or less, but two-fifths five years or more.

The history of Clayton displays the expected transition from a formerly separate, relatively self-sufficient community to a slightly differentiated part of a metropolitan area. In 1875, by act of the Missouri legislature, St. Louis city and St. Louis County were legally separated. After some delay a committee of prominent citizens selected 104 acres, donated by Mr. Clayton and Mrs. Hanley, to be their county seat. Previous to this, no town existed where Clayton now is. Trees, brush, and stumps had to be removed to make room for the new county buildings. By 1883 it was reported that "Clayton now includes twenty dwellings, three hotels, one grocery, three printing offices, three attorneys, one singing hall, and the County buildings." Up to 1892, the trip between the new town and St. Louis was slow and inconvenient. One might take a hack from the courthouse to Wells Station and from there a narrow-gauge steam railroad to Grand Avenue. Otherwise he might spend half a day traveling on horseback or by carriage. Not until 1904 was there a paved road connecting the two places. However, in 1892 an electric car line was extended out to Clayton. Although agitation for telephone connections began in 1881, service was not established until 1900. As late as 1905 there were less than 50 telephones in Clayton, but by 1930 the number had grown to nearly 3,000.

Today Clayton is to the eye merely a part of Greater St. Louis. It now has an impressive commercial subcenter, new and expensive apartment houses, fine old residences, and modest houses occupying separate districts, but Clayton as a whole is not marked off from other municipalities on all sides except for wide and busy streets to the south and west. Institutional self-sufficiency, homogeneity, and stability might be described as intermediate.

4. *An Overflow Suburb: Residential.* We turn now from the suburbs which grew up as independent towns and were gradually drawn into the orbit of the metropolis to a suburb created *de novo* to provide for surplus population of the inner city or at least to attract people from the center to an outlying section. Representative of this type in the St. Louis area is University City, a municipality of nearly 40,000 inhabitants, originated through a series of real estate subdivisions which began in 1904. It is like Clayton in having no natural boundaries. From the outset it was built up

continuously with St. Louis and with other suburbs. But unlike all the suburbs previously discussed, it was settled almost entirely by people who were already established in the central city with business or professional activities, membership in churches, clubs, etc., friends and acquaintances, most of whom did not follow them to the new suburb. Eventually some of their churches did move out to University City, so that at least three draw their membership and attendance from the metropolitan area as a whole; one is frankly known as the First Presbyterian Church of St. Louis.

As to institutional self-sufficiency, University City has a municipal government with all the usual functions. It has a wide variety of retail stores and service facilities plus numerous small industries. Nevertheless, the overwhelming majority of gainfully employed persons are engaged in other parts of the metropolitan area. One survey found this proportion to be nine-tenths. The localization study of the 1940's yielded an average score of .40, which means that inhabitants of University City utilized outside facilities more than those of their own community.

As to mobility-stability, 42 per cent of homes were owner-occupied in 1940. In 1942 three-eighths of the families interviewed had lived not more than two years at their present address, but two-fifths had lived there five years or more. One-fifth had lived not more than two years in University City, but two-fifths had lived there ten years or more. Thus University City is very much like Clayton, but has a less stable population than Kirkwood.

As to homogeneity-heterogeneity, there are practically no Negroes. About 10 per cent are foreign born and perhaps one-fourth are the children of immigrants, mostly Jews from eastern Europe. Religiously there is great diversity—Roman Catholic, Lutheran, Christian Science, Presbyterian, Methodist, and Jewish are the principal faiths reported. The Jews are divided among orthodox, conservative, and reformed. Different parts of University City are identified as Jewish apartment house districts, Catholic parishes, and Protestant neighborhoods. Economically this is predominantly upper middle class, but there is a working class district in the northeast quarter where people of small incomes live in modest cottages and duplexes. The southwest quarter is occupied mainly by brick residences that would sell at $20,000 to $40,000. Along the main thoroughfare are apartments renting from $65 to $250 a month. Professional, managerial, and salespeople constitute two-thirds of the gainfully occupied. In 1940, 96 per cent of all homes had central heat and mechanical refrigeration.

There is a local newspaper so-called, which appears once a week with advertisements of University City businessmen, some political gossip, and occasional personal items. There is a civic organization called the

Charter Committee, which was formed to bring about the adoption of a new city charter with city manager form of government. It continues to study local issues, to put pressure on public officials, and to support candidates for office. However, many people have difficulty informing themselves about local issues and persons, for the weekly paper is very inadequate and the metropolitan papers have little news about the suburbs. A few years ago there was a bitter struggle over the tax rate for public schools. Religion and real estate interests became involved in ways which showed how little united the people of this suburb were. However, that particular tension has subsided, and there is at least superficial evidence of growing community spirit.

5. *Overflow Suburbs: Industrial.* In Greater St. Louis, as in many other metropolitan areas, there are satellite cities or towns each dominated by one or a few industries. Here a working class population lives, works, shops, finds entertainment, goes to church, and engages in politics. On the east side of the Mississippi River, within a few minutes car ride of downtown St. Louis, is a cluster of three such industrial suburbs—Granite City, Madison, and Venice. Iron and steel mills, railroad yards and shops, and meat-packing plants are the major industries. These satellite towns are quite separate from the other parts of the metropolitan area, but they do not live entirely to themselves. While they are well supplied with many kinds of stores and service facilities, their residents go to St. Louis for some shopping and entertainment. This seems to be especially true of Madison.

The heterogeneity of Madison's population is indicated by the list of churches. These include Bulgarian Orthodox, Roman Catholic, Independent Polish Catholic, Russian Orthodox, Greek Catholic, Christian Apostolic, Presbyterian, Methodist, Baptist, and Free Methodist institutions. It appears that most of the present inhabitants are the second generation of migrants from Indiana, the Ozarks, and southeastern Europe. Such a varied lot of folk cannot easily be assimilated into a united community. Neither does independent local life develop readily when the people are so dependent upon employment in various east-side industries and the shopping facilities of the central city. This limited community life manifests itself in the lack of civic organizations. To be sure, there are a Boosters' Club and a Rotary Club, but several attempts to establish and maintain a commercial club and a community council have failed. Perhaps the most popular local institution is the public library.

From the foregoing description it is evident that Madison is not altogether typical of industrial suburbs. Gary, in metropolitan Chicago, and Argentine, in metropolitan Kansas City, appear to be much more complete local communities. Their self-sufficiency and the relatively limited coming and going of their inhabitants make them quite different from Madison.

6. *A Partially Absorbed Community.* In the extreme southern part of St. Louis city is a district called Carondelet. Bounded on two sides by the Des Peres and Mississippi Rivers it blends with the rest of the city on the other two. Once a quite separate community, it is now losing its identity through absorption into the life of the metropolitan area.

Founded a little before St. Louis, several miles to the south, Carondelet was for a long time merely another French village. From the beginning trade was centered in St. Louis, so that Carondelet grew very slowly. As late as 1865 it had less than 5,000 inhabitants, while St. Louis had grown to 200,000. In 1845 Germans began to settle in Carondelet, changing its dominant language and institutions as well as its physical appearance. They opened stores, factories, and banks. About the same time Irish immigrants came to join the French and the German. With the opening of iron and zinc works in the sixties came Italians, Poles, Spaniards, and Negroes.

In the early days the trip between Carondelet and St. Louis was arduous and time-consuming. One of the first German settlers started a bus line, but even then a full day was required for the round trip. Thus the two places remained quite separate. About 1875 a horsecar line was established. Now electric cars, busses, and private automobiles carry people back and forth easily and quickly. In 1870, on the initiative of its own citizens, Carondelet was annexed to St. Louis. The motivation seems to have been related to an empty treasury, rough streets, inadequate water supply and fire protection, and a chaotic school system. In respect to its early annexation to the central city, Carondelet appears to be somewhat unusual. It is common to find more economic and social ties and less physical separation preceding political union.

Industrially Carondelet developed iron foundries, railroad shops, quarries, brickyards, and breweries. It also had its own commercial and financial institutions. But by the turn of the century Missouri's iron ore had played out, and the furnaces and some of the foundries closed. Some of the people moved away, while others found employment in different parts of St. Louis. Improved means of transportation facilitated not only scattered employment but downtown shopping as well. Thus Carondelet has become economically a part of St. Louis, although it still has local stores handling food, drugs, and clothing. Much the same trend of events may be identified in other institutions. The first schools were maintained by Catholic sisters. Today, along with the Catholic and Lutheran parochial schools, there are several public schools, integral parts of the St. Louis system. At first there was only one church, and sermons were preached in French. About 1850 a German priest arrived. By 1875 there were half a dozen Protestant churches, each more closely associated with other St. Louis churches of its own faith than with those of different denominations in Carondelet. Thus in religion, as in education and in business, we find increasing local diversity and ever closer ties with the city as a whole.

The story of leisure time agencies and activities is not very different. Up to 1840 there were cockfights, dances, drinking bouts, and card parties. During the next two decades, Germans founded a lyceum, a debating club, a singing society, and a *Turnverein*. Until World War I this last was popular and influential. More recently have come the YMCA, the YWCA, Boy and Girl Scouts, and a public library, all of them parts of city-wide agencies. From the coming of the Germans until the 1929 depression, the Republican party was dominant in Carondelet, but in 1932 the Democrats carried this ward along with the rest of St. Louis.

In general we find Carondelet becoming more like the rest of the city, but more diversified within itself. As to occupations the 1940 census showed a wide spread: professional 6 per cent, proprietors and managers 10 per cent, clerical and sales 25 per cent, semiskilled 24 per cent, laborers 8 per cent. As to housing, 53 per cent of dwelling units were single family homes, 41 per cent were in two to four family buildings. Median monthly rentals ranged from $13.00 in one tract to $48.50 in another. Central heating was found in 68 per cent and mechanical refrigeration in 75 per cent of all homes. The population was predominantly native white with only 6 per cent foreign born and less than 1 per cent Negro. However, the sex ratio varied from 83 in one tract to 108 in another, and in 1930 the percentage of males married ranged from 58 to 76. Mobility might be described as intermediate. Home ownership in 1940 was 41 per cent. We have made no detailed study of local facilities and their use but have a strong impression of a trend toward the scattering of patronage. Thus through increasing heterogeneity, mobility, and interdependence, Carondelet has been gradually changing from a distinctive community into a section of St. Louis. However, the symbols of its identity are by no means gone. The name persists; people still mention with pride their German or French ancestry; there is considerable localization of facilities and their use. The process of absorption is far advanced but not yet complete.

7. *A Case of Complete Absorption.* There is another section of St. Louis, Cheltenham,[3] which could by no stretch of the imagination be called a community today. It has run the whole gamut from pioneer conditions, through farming and village stages, to suburban mining and

[3] L. F. Thomas, "The Sequence of Areal Occupation in a Section of St. Louis, Missouri," *Annals Assn. Amer. Geog.*, 21 (1931), 75–90.

urban manufacturing. While its social life was apparently never so well integrated as that of Carondelet, there was a village community in the second quarter of the nineteenth century, and there is still an Italian colony.

In 1785 Charles Gratiot secured a grant of land about 3 miles square lying about 5 miles southwest of the village of St. Louis along the River Des Peres. During the next forty-five years there was little tilling of the soil, the owners apparently concerning themselves only with firewood, lumber, and game. But between 1830 and 1839, as far as can be judged, the whole tract was gradually brought under cultivation. By 1840 the original area, called the Gratiot League, had been subdivided into 264 parcels. From that date to 1852 many subdivisions were platted, some for small farming and others for suburban residences. Village life developed.

In 1852 the Pacific Railroad (now Missouri Pacific) was built through the district. This gave a needed stimulus to the manufacture of clay products. Fire clay had been discovered in Cheltenham in 1844, but for eight years lack of adequate transportation made fuel expensive and the distribution of products difficult. Now there was a steady increase in the output of firebrick, building brick, sewer pipe, and terra cotta. The clays were dug from shafts 60 to 100 feet deep, in drifts along the valley walls or in open pits on the hills and slopes. Factory buildings four and five stories high were erected and equipped with many kinds of clay-shaping machinery. Alongside were kilns and extensive acreages covered with piles of bricks and sewer pipe. Industrial development was further stimulated by the Frisco Railroad in 1883, street railway service, and improved highways. The city was growing out this way, and in 1876 Cheltenham became a part of St. Louis.

Because valley locations were damp, the villagers who could afford it had long ago moved to more healthful sites. But wage earners and others of small means continued to live in the lower parts of the district. Population grew with industry. In the 1850's came a French communistic society, which, however, disbanded within a few years. Later came Italians, who established a community on the heights to the south, sometimes called "Dago Hill." Some Negroes were employed, but none of them resided in the district. There were obstacles to the further increase of population. Subsurface workings in the clay beds created a hazard for dwellings, since the surface might sink or settle at any time. Smoke and dust were unattractive, to say the least. Hence many of the subdivisions laid out during previous stages were withdrawn from sale, and streets created on paper never took form on the ground. The surface of the greater part of the clay properties today lies idle, is covered with weeds, or is occupied by scattered squatters.

About 1925, signs of another set of changes began to appear. Because some of the clay beds were exhausted and others had become expensive to work, some companies dismantled their plants and sold their land. Others changed from firebrick to sewer pipe, suitable shales still being available; still others opened pits or mines elsewhere and brought their clay to Cheltenham by rail. In 1928 storm sewers eliminated the flood hazard. With modern excavating machinery it became feasible to create extensive terraces in the valley wall. New industries began to enter the district, and a promising new era seemed to be under way when the depression of 1929 interrupted the development.

Cheltenham has not been a community since the early mining stage of its evolution. Today it is just a part of a great city, occupied by railroad tracks, factories, mine properties, and the homes of wage earners and some middle-class folk. Many of the men who work in Cheltenham live elsewhere, and many of those who live in the district are employed in other parts of St. Louis.

THE LIFE CYCLE OF COMMUNITIES

We have now described several different types of communities that are or have been suburbs, drawing most of our illustrations from a single metropolitan area. We have noted some of their differences in physical appearance, population, institutional life, origin and development, self-sufficiency, and relation to the central city. In general it may be said that the natural history of suburbs is a series of characteristic changes through which they become more completely parts of the city. The typical sequence, however, varies somewhat for the several kinds of suburbs.

An outlying town that later becomes a suburb may at first seem quite as important as the town which eventually becomes the central city. In any event, new means of transportation enable families with business or work in the city to live in what thus becomes a residential suburb. Also, dwellers in the outlying town work and shop in the city. Then intervening land is built up. Eventually annexation may take place, though some suburbs resist this for a long time. Finally there is complete absorption into the metropolis, with heterogeneity, mobility, scattering of activities and affiliations, and interdependence with the rest of the city.

An overflow suburb, on the contrary, may never have an independent existence. A subdivision is laid out, lots are sold, and houses are built. The section is occupied by a growing number of families of the same social class, often *nouveaux riches,* but sometimes old-established families, white-collar folk, or even Negroes. Local institutions appear—stores, churches, schools—which often fail to unite the people because they are from the start partly in and of the city, partly separate from it.

An industrial suburb more commonly has its origin in the erection of a factory, the opening of a mine, or the establishment of some other industrial project. Company houses may be erected. Subdividers and builders bring into being a residential district of shoddy dwellings. Stores, schools, churches, and other institutions develop. Transportation brings laborers from other parts of the metropolitan district to work in the satellite city and carries local folk elsewhere to work, shop, play, etc. Gradually there is economic and social absorption into the larger city, though political independence may continue for a long time.

We have dwelt thus at length upon suburbs because it appears that a large number of the communities that may be found in American cities are or have been suburbs. However, there are some communities that arise inside the central city. Frequently these are immigrant colonies or Negro communities. Such ethnic groups will be discussed in Chap. 10.

SELECTED READINGS

DINWIDDIE, COURTENAY: *Community Responsibility, A Review of the Cincinnati Social Unit Experiment,* New York School of Social Work, 1921. The story of an attempt to develop community life in the heart of a city.

FOLEY, DONALD L.: "The Use of Local Facilities in a Metropolis," *Amer. Jour. Sociol.,* 56 (1950), 238–246. A study of service areas in the northwest part of St. Louis.

GORDON, W. R.: *Satellite Acres,* Rhode Island State College, Agricultural Experiment Station, Bulletin No. 282, 1942. A study of 1,100 households combining agricultural production and nonagricultural employment.

HILLMAN, ARTHUR: *Community Organization and Planning,* The Macmillan Company, 1950. Outlines programs and procedures for community organization.

KOOS, EARL L., and EDMUND DE S. BRUNNER: *Suburbanization in Webster, New York,* University of Rochester, 1945. A study of a community in metropolitan Rochester.

OGBURN, WILLIAM F.: *Social Characteristics of Cities,* International City Managers' Association, 1937. Chapters 10 to 12 describe types of suburbs and how they differ from central cities, with supporting statistical data.

STEINER, JESSE F.: *The American Community in Action,* Henry Holt and Company, 1928. Chapter 5, "From Village Homogeneity to Urban Heterogeneity," depicts the evolution of Roxbury in Greater Boston.

VOSS, J. ELLIS: *Ocean City, An Ecological Analysis of a Satellite Community,* University of Pennsylvania, 1941. A study of a suburb of Philadelphia devoted to recreation.

WARE, CAROLINE F.: *Greenwich Village,* Houghton Mifflin Company, 1935. The story of an independent village that became part of New York.

ZORBAUGH, HARVEY W.: *Gold Coast and Slum,* University of Chicago Press, 1929. Chapters 9 to 12 in particular point out the difficulties of trying to develop community life in the heart of a great city.

CHAPTER 10.   *Ethnic Groups in Cities of the United States*

In the preceding chapter we discussed communities without much reference to their ethnic composition. We noted that most of them had native white populations. But there are in every city local groupings of ethnically distinct peoples. Sometimes their physical appearance, more often their culture, marks them off from people who live around them. Their separate neighborhoods and communities are maintained in part from choice and in part because of pressure from outside. Quantitatively these ethnic groups are important in cities of the United States. Preliminary reports of the 1950 census show that of 96 million city dwellers 10 million are foreign born and 9 million are Negro. Over 80 per cent of all foreign-born persons and over 60 per cent of all Negroes live in cities. Qualitatively, too, these ethnic groups are important. They introduce new culture traits; their lack of assimilation presents problems of social control; the diversity of their folkways and mores is a source of conflict. But what concerns us principally in this chapter is the extent to which these groups are segregated in distinct neighborhoods or communities, the character of these local groups, and their relations with the rest of the population.

IMMIGRANT COLONIES

The history of immigration to the United States, and primarily to our cities, shows continued growth until World War I, since which time there have not been enough newcomers to replace those who died or left the country. The actual number of foreigners in the United States remained about the same from 1910 to 1930, since which time it has steadily declined. At all times there has been a heavy concentration of immigrants in cities of the Northeast. Preliminary figures for 1950 indicate that more than half of the foreign born in the United States still live in the northeastern states and that nine-tenths of these live in cities. They constitute about one-seventh of the urban population of this region.

Table 17 indicates the numerical importance of immigrants in our cities. But it also indicates that the situation varies from one part of the country to another. From city to city, it varies even more. In 1940 the foreign born constituted only 1.5 per cent of the population of Oklahoma City, while they were 23.6 per cent of the population of Newark. The situation also varies with reference to the number of nationalities represented in any given city. In New York, Cleveland, and San Francisco the foreign born are divided among many different nationalities. In San Antonio and El Paso one single group (Mexican) dominates the scene. However, the typical situation is one of heterogeneity.

Never before in the history of the world have great groups of people so diverse in social backgrounds been thrown together in such close contacts as in the cities of America. The typical American city, therefore, does not consist of a homogeneous body of citizens, but of human beings with the most diverse cultural backgrounds, often speaking different languages, following a great variety of customs, habituated to different modes and standards of living, and sharing only in varying degrees the tastes, the beliefs, and the ideals of their native fellow city dwellers.[1]

In most of our large cities we not only find people of many different national origins, but we find some of them segregated in distinctive colonies. These more or less separate communities are identified superficially

Table 17. Urban Foreign-born White Population by Regions, 1950

Region	Population urban foreign-born white	Per cent of urban that was foreign-born white	Per cent of foreign-born white that was urban
Northeast.............	4,665,000	13	90
North Central.........	2,083,000	6	80
West................	1,237,000	8	78
South...............	517,000	2	70
Total United States.....	10,147,000	9	81

SOURCE: Adapted from Bureau of the Census, Preliminary Reports, Series PC-7, No. 3, Apr. 30, 1951.

by foreign signs on stores, the Old World dress of people on the streets, and the sound of strange tongues. A more intimate view reveals distinctive goods in the shops, menus in restaurants, services in church and synagogue, and marriage customs, as well as the celebration of holidays not listed in any American calendar and foreign language newspapers. All these are symbols of the social distance that lies between the newcomers and those whose ancestors arrived long ago.

Comparing and contrasting three cities—Boston, Cleveland, and St.

[1] *Our Cities: Their Role in the National Economy*, National Resources Committee, p. 10, 1937.

Louis[2]—we find some ethnic groups living pretty much apart while others are scattered over the metropolitan area. In general, representatives of the "old" immigration; *i.e.*, British and German, are mixed with the rest of the people. In St. Louis, where in 1930 one-fourth of the foreign born were natives of Germany and one-seventh of the total population was German (born in Germany or the children of German parents), there were two areas in which people of German stock predominated. Nevertheless, there was not a single census tract in which more than one-third of the population was German, as we are using the term. On the other hand, only 2 out of 128 census tracts were less than 1 per cent German. In Cleveland the English-speaking and German-speaking groups (including Austrians) were fairly evenly distributed throughout the city. In Boston substantially the same condition obtained. There natives of the Irish Free State comprised the largest group of foreigners. They were so widely distributed that they constituted one of the four most numerous national groups in 12 of the 14 census areas.

Turning to the non-English-speaking, "new" immigrants, we find Italians markedly segregated in all three cities. Other foreign colonies in Boston and St. Louis were small except for groups of Russian Jews.[3] But in Cleveland there were several fairly large and well-defined areas occupied predominantly by Poles, Jugoslavs, Slovaks (natives of Czechoslovakia), Hungarians, and Jews (natives of Russia), as well as Italians. When data for other cities are examined, details are found to vary, but the general situation is much the same. In the Pacific coast cities Japanese and Chinese have well-established colonies; in those of the Southwest this is true of Mexicans. On the whole we may say that immigrant groups from northwestern Europe, who have had three or more generations in America, have practically ceased to be separate communities, but newer groups from southeastern Europe, the Orient, and Latin America tend to be segregated in rather well-defined colonies. The newcomers are usually found near commercial and industrial districts; the older immigrants and their children are more commonly located in what Burgess calls the zone of workingmen's homes. Figure 15 shows approximately the parts of St. Louis occupied by the largest and most easily identified ethnic groups.

Polish Communities. In selecting ethnic groups for special consideration we have chosen first the Poles, partly because of their large num-

---

[2] *Social Statistics by Census Tracts in Boston,* Boston Council of Social Agencies, 1933; Howard W. Green, *Population Characteristics by Census Tracts, Cleveland, Ohio, 1930,* 1931; Ralph C. Fletcher, Harry L. Hornback, and Stuart A. Queen, *Social Statistics of St. Louis by Census Tracts,* 1935.

[3] Incidentally the census data leave much to be desired, for they indicate country of birth but not language or cultural group. It is from other sources that we know a majority of the Russian and Polish born in Boston and St. Louis to be Jewish.

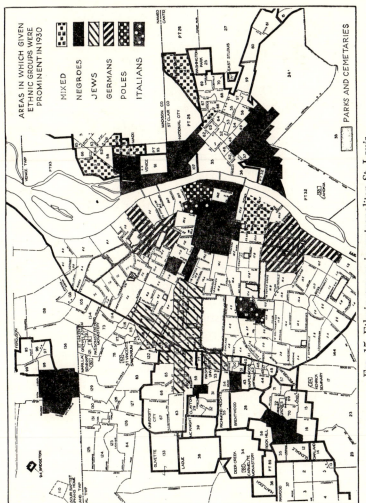

Fig. 15. Ethnic groups in metropolitan St. Louis.

bers and seemingly well-defined communities, partly because during the period of greatest influx they were studied very thoroughly by Thomas and Znaniecki.[4] The characteristic sequence of events which they identified in Polish-American communities was somewhat as follows. First, a Pole (or a small number of Poles) found employment that promised to be permanent; very soon he sent for friends and relatives in other parts of the United States. If they did not come, he either left or became assimilated into the particular American community. But most frequently enough people came to form a small group of Polish workingmen. One of their first efforts was to establish a boarding house so that they might get their accustomed food, save money, and have congenial associates. It was natural that men should want to see familiar faces in a strange land, hear their mother tongue, and enjoy the companionship of their own kind. A married man would send for his wife or a bachelor for his fiancée. Perhaps a house would be rented and furnished on a cooperative basis. If employment proved to be fairly continuous, more invited and some independent arrivals added to the colony. Sometimes work did not last, sometimes the newcomers were restless fellows, and sometimes factional disputes arose; but in general growth in numbers was accompanied by progress in unity and cohesion.

Often the first step in the institutionalization of the colony was the establishment of a "society." Its original purpose was commonly mutual aid in such emergencies as sickness, death, and unemployment. The isolation of the Poles from kinsmen in the old country and citizens of the new land, together with their economic insecurity, made this a natural step. To them public charity was a disgrace and the private charity of their own people was limited; hence cooperation was the more necessary. But such a mutual aid society was more than an economic institution. It brought the often scattered members of the colony together from time to time; it arranged dances and picnics, gave theatrical performances, invited lecturers, subscribed to periodicals, and arranged religious services. It was a center of information for newcomers and for the newspapers. It represented the colony in dealings with Polish nationalist societies and with American agencies—governmental, civic, philanthropic.

The second institution was commonly a church. Even though some of the immigrants were not devout Catholics, they felt the necessity of a minimum of religious ceremonies, such as christenings, weddings, and

---

[4] William I. Thomas and Florian Znaniecki, *The Polish Peasant in Europe and America*. This monograph was first published in 1918 in five volumes. Our own references are to the 1927 edition in two volumes. This is the classic study of an immigrant group. It occupied most of the time of Thomas, an American, and Znaniecki, a Pole, for several years. Each of them shared the research in both countries and in both languages. Data used by permission of the authors and the Social Science Research Council.

funerals. To be sure, they might have joined in Irish-American parishes, but these would not have been community centers, not really their own. The coming of a Polish priest brought new leadership to the group and a stimulus to develop the community in numbers, wealth, multiplicity of activities, and cohesion. In relation to the parish there appeared religious fraternities and lay associations. Presently a parochial school was established, using both the Polish and the English language. This last contributed vitally to the integration of the Polish-American community. First of all, it brought the folk physically near together; they found it desirable to be near the school which small children had to attend daily. Second, it acquainted the children with the language, religion, national history, traditions, and moral values of their parents. It fostered the understanding and respect between the generations which were so easily lost when the children attended American public schools.

Despite the conventional teaching of the Catholic Church, the Polish-American communities developed relatively few charities, and these few were devoted largely to the care of orphans, the aged, and the infirm. In contrast to Jewish communities, they have showed little interest in or provision for inefficient, disabled, maladjusted, and demoralized fellow countrymen. Thomas and Znaniecki attribute this to the difference between the Polish community in Europe and in America. In Poland the peasant community was a stable group of families, united by ties to the land, by kinship, and by long association. Over here it has been a collection of migrant individuals who associated themselves together more or less voluntarily. Hence if a person expected to reap the benefits of membership in the community, he must participate in its activities and contribute financially to its purposes. If he refused or was unable to do his share, he either was not accepted or was cut adrift; the local group assumed no responsibility for him. To some this may seem strange, but it was not very different from the behavior of New England colonists in the seventeenth century.[5]

Such elimination of burdensome individuals did not mean that the community was uninterested in extending its social control. It did this in other ways. First, it sought to engage as many persons as possible in public and semipublic activities. This was facilitated by the fact that some parishes had as many as 70 organizations, and each of these had from 6 to 20 officials. Thus everyone had some chance of recognition, and being chosen for some committee or office, he was then in the public eye and subject to general comment. The second mode of social control was the complement of the first, namely, the widespread institutionalization of activities. Thus public entertainments under the auspices of local asso-

[5] Robert W. Kelso, *The History of Public Poor Relief in Massachusetts, 1620–1920,* Chaps. 2, 3, 1922.

ciations or parish committees played a large part in the local life. The hours required for rehearsals and making arrangements were so many that the individual had a minimum of time for himself. This dual technique of social control—drawing individuals into group activities and institutionalizing these activities—was manifest especially in the immigrant press. There were commemorative pamphlets, published reports, programs of meetings, and ultimately a local Polish newspaper. This might be started by some political machine, by an advertiser, by an idealistic nationalist, or by someone seeking personal recognition. In any case it was likely to promote the unity and cohesion of the community.

Thomas and Znaniecki hold that the order of development in a Polish-American community tended to be unique in this respect, that social organization preceded and stimulated territorial concentration. However, when a large number of Poles occupied a limited, compact area, their proximity furthered their social integration. Recognizing the reciprocal influence of physical nearness and social organization, priests took care to locate their churches as near as possible to places where Poles were employed, giving attention also to low rents and cheap real estate. The Poles did not wait for the original inhabitants of such districts to retire before their invasion, but systematically promoted the occupancy of houses by their own people. Polish real estate agencies, building and loan associations, and loan banks actively hastened the transition. When at last to church, school, and societies of various kinds were added Polish merchants and professional men, the occupation or succession was complete; the Polish-American community had reached its zenith. The story of its decline has not yet been so thoroughly studied. The period that Thomas and Znaniecki covered was essentially one of community building. While we have access to no recent study comparable to that of Thomas and Znaniecki, we know that Polish colonies still preserve their distinctive characteristics in several large cities. However, we suspect that the process of absorption into the life of the metropolis is going on continuously. Factors which suggest this possibility include the practical stopping of immigration, the achieving of Polish independence, the aging and death of the first settlers, the Americanization of their children.

In certain respects we find the life cycle of a Polish immigrant community representative of all ethnic groups in American cities. In other respects we find it different. To bring out similarities and differences we shall describe two other kinds of immigrant colonies, Jewish and Puerto Rican.

Jewish Communities. The Jews, like the Poles, came to America in greatest numbers at the end of the nineteenth and the beginning of the twentieth century. But unlike the Poles, the Jews came with a long background of urban experience, training in business, a distinctive religion, a history of persecution, and an interest in learning. Also, as we shall see, the Jews are noted for their philanthropic work on behalf of the unfortunate members of their group. Fortunately for our purposes a sociologist, who is himself a Jew, has prepared an objective account of the development of Jewish communities in European and American cities.[6] We take the liberty of summarizing and commenting on his narrative and interpretation.

After the Roman conquest of Palestine, the Jews were scattered through the Mediterranean world, forced to be mobile and adaptable. Although they led a precarious existence, their lot was not so bad as it was in later centuries. With the opening of the Crusades, they were widely abused and frequently subjected to mob violence. Amid the general excitement, the crusading spirit, and the thwarting of remote and vague ideals, the Jewish people were regarded first as strangers, then as enemies; they were scapegoats. Against these new outbursts, the Jews turned to popes and emperors for protection and status of a semifeudal sort. This was granted in return for financial contributions, and emperors often sold the privilege of "protecting," *i.e.*, taxing, the Jews.

Now there had already developed a kind of voluntary segregation. For the sake of religious practices, dietary laws, general customs and traditions, the use of their own language, neighborliness, and self-defense, Jews had begun to live apart in distinctive sections of medieval towns. Here they constituted a community within a community. This arrangement was congenial to them and convenient to their gentile rulers. As a united group, they purchased the privilege of residing in a given city and carrying on business. But by the fifteenth century the ghetto, as the Jewish community was called, had become quite generally compulsory. It was commonly situated in an undesirable part of town, usually quite limited in area and surrounded by a wall. At night its gates were locked, and all Jews had to be in by sundown or suffer severe penalties. Its boundaries were rarely extended, even though the Jewish population might increase greatly. Thus the ghetto became overcrowded; its buildings deteriorated; sometimes houses of prostitution (not Jewish) were moved into the ghetto; and in general it tended to become a slum. What the Christians most feared in the Jews is hard to tell; they mentioned heresy, "escape," and "nefarious practices." Thus voluntary gave way to compulsory segregation and tolerance to persecution. But even so the Christians needed and used the Jews—as traders, moneylenders, taxpayers.

Within the ghetto there grew up a vigorous community life. Family ties were strong; religious loyalty was marked; outstanding personalities appeared; self-reliance and mutial aid were highly developed. The most

---

[6] Louis Wirth, *The Ghetto*, 1928. Data used by permission of the University of Chicago Press.

important institution in the ghetto was the synagogue, which was a house of prayer, house of study, and house of assembly, *i.e.*, a center of religious, educational, philanthropic, and recreational life. Indeed, it may be said to have been the administrative center of the ghetto, for the Jewish community was essentially self-governing, within the limits set by outside rulers. It was responsible as a unit for the behavior of its members; it was taxed as a unit. Thus the rabbis were not only religious functionaries but community leaders and officials. Besides the synagogue there were other communal institutions, such as a house for the poor and the sick, a public bath, a ritual bathhouse, a bakehouse, a slaughtering place, sometimes a guest house or a dance house. There was an elementary school (Cheder) and more advanced school (Yeshiba). "In the close life within ghetto walls, almost nothing was left to the devices of individuals. Life was well organized . . . "[7]

Of course the reality was not so simple and uniform as this brief description may suggest. In western Europe the Jews gained citizenship under Napoleon, lost it after his fall, regained it in 1848, lost it again after 1850, received it again in the latter part of the nineteenth century, only to lose it once more in certain totalitarian states. In Russia the Jews lived "within the Pale;" *i.e.*, they were permitted to reside only in certain districts, and within these districts they were restricted to specified places. Thus they had "a ghetto within a ghetto." They were culturally more isolated than were the Jews of western Europe.

Out of such backgrounds as we have just sketched, Jews began coming to America very early in small numbers. Some of the first were Sephardic Jews expelled from Spain. A few German Jews came after Napoleon went into exile. Following the revolutions of 1848, large numbers came from Germany and other central European countries; these were city people who belonged to "Reformed" congregations. But about the same time Russian Jews started coming to escape conscription. They were poverty-stricken villagers, Yiddish-speaking, and very orthodox. In the eighties many more Russian Jews came to escape pogroms, and after that their numbers increased rapidly. No accurate count has ever been made of the Jewish population in the United States, but it has been estimated that there were 1 million by 1900 and about 5 million by 1950.[8] Of these about 2 million live in New York City, 325,000 in Chicago, 245,-000 in Philadelphia, 250,000 in Los Angeles, and smaller numbers in other cities. As we note in the chapter on religious institutions, they are found almost entirely in urban centers.

Representative of Jewish communities in American cities is that of

[7] *Ibid.*, p. 61. By permission of the University of Chicago Press.
[8] *The World Almanac*, 1951, pp. 433–434. *American Jewish Yearbook*, 1951, pp. 4*ff.*

Chicago. First came an itinerant peddler, then a few merchants who lived over their stores. These early arrivals were from Bavaria. They founded a burial society, a synagogue, and a benevolent society. Later others came and founded their separate organizations. Even before 1860 Chicago Jews were engaged in bitter controversy over reform of the ritual. As the number of immigrants from eastern Europe increased, the community became more and more divided. These newcomers were inclined to settle by village groups and to cling to their old customs; they kept splitting off into "store front" congregations. But the real gulf was between the older, Reformed German Jews, who had acquired some wealth and status in the city, and the Latvian, Polish, and Russian Jews, who were poor, ignorant, rural, orthodox, and Yiddish-speaking newcomers. This breach in what might have been a united community was much in evidence during the efforts to raise money for the benefit of those who suffered from the fires of 1871 and 1874. Also after these disastrous fires the physical separation of the two main groups became more marked, the eastern Jews moving across the river toward Halsted Street, the western Jews invading the fashionable South Side residential district. The Reformed group began to substitute Sunday for Saturday services; it sought rabbis who were doctors of philosophy. The orthodox group drew apart and established a new (voluntary) ghetto. In the eighties, when more Russian Jews flocked into Chicago with their beards, long coats, and boots, the German Jews feared that the gentile public would associate them with the newcomers, that all would lose status, and that ground gained in breaking down racial barriers would be lost. So they were active in philanthropic measures for the Russian refugees, but their condescending ways made it plain that the newcomers were to keep their place. This proved an added stimulus to the eastern Jews to develop their own institutions and form a community apart.

In Chicago, as in other cities, the term ghetto has been commonly applied to the Jewish community or that part of it which was found in the zone of deterioration near the heart of the city. The district has been zoned for light manufacturing; no new dwellings have been erected for years; but land values have been rising in anticipation of the displacement of residences by factories. Meanwhile, however, rents for individual families remained low, and the district was near to places of employment. Now the Jews of this ghetto were poor and were accustomed to living under crowded conditions; hence, being hemmed in by commercial and industrial establishments, the section became quite congested. Being an area of "first settlement," *i.e.*, of newly arrived immigrants, the ghetto was sharply distinguished from surrounding districts and from those occupied by Americanized Jews who were the children of immigrants. Particularly it tended to preserve the folkways, mores, and institutions of the European ghetto. Besides synagogues, kosher butcher shops, and outdoor markets, it had its own theater, bookstores, cafés, and newspapers. Despite conflict between village and national groups of Jews, the ghetto presented a united front to the gentile world. Wirth described it as rich in tradition and sentiment but "the slave of forms" and out of touch with the world.

So far as possible it was a closed community. But children attended public schools, grownups worked for American employers, and other contacts were made with outsiders. With the increasing use of English, improved economic status, and stimulation of new wants, the younger generation began to chafe under the restraints of the ghetto. So certain families moved away, seeking freedom, recognition, and pleasanter surroundings. But others followed, and presently the new district became Jewish; some moved again into an area of "third settlement." This movement was not along continuous lines, but in jumps over considerable distances. It was a case of fleeing from the ghetto and being followed by the ghetto. Those who were succeeding in business or professional life wanted to be recognized as persons, not merely as Jews. They moved into residential hotels, they shifted from orthodox, to conservative, to Reformed synagogues, and sometimes to Christian Science or Ethical Culture, if indeed they did not give up all connection with organized religion.

But physical escape from the ghetto did not necessarily bring acceptance into the American community. Rebuffs and exclusion from certain districts and organizations wounded the Jew's pride. He had gained physical comfort at the expense of emotional peace. Within the ghetto, life had been narrow but warm. Outside it was broad but cold. The hostility of gentiles plus the sensitivity of Jews caused some to return to the ghetto. However, others made places for themselves in the larger life of the city, in business, in professions, in civic organizations, even in politics.

We have probably overemphasized the divisive elements in the Jewish community. It is important for the non-Jew especially to realize that there is considerable cohesion within this group. Wirth considers the fact that outsiders treat the Jews as members of a community to be one of the strongest unifying forces. The centralization of fund raising and the development of communal institutions, such as the YMHA, have also doubtless added to their solidarity. But the greatest incentives to group integrity of recent years have apparently been the Nazi persecutions and the establishment of the independent state of Israel. In any case, it may be anticipated that the Jews, having a long experience as city dwellers, having a well-developed set of institutions, considering themselves and being viewed by others as a community, will continue for many years to offer one of the best examples of local community life in our metropolitan areas.

Puerto Ricans in New York. In marked contrast to the Poles and the Jews are the Puerto Ricans. In addition to being less numerous and having come more recently, the Puerto Ricans, at least in New York City, constitute a very undeveloped community. However, their numbers are by no means insignificant. In 1948 it was estimated that there were 200,000 of them in this one city, of whom the majority were segregated in two small areas. The first was between 100th and 125th St. and between Third and Fifth Ave., a district known as Spanish Harlem. In most blocks 50 to 75 per cent of the households were Puerto Rican. The second was the Morrisania section of the lower east side of the Bronx, where 25 to 50 per cent of the households were Puerto Rican. In addition there were other scattered pockets. Over one-fourth of the migrants had arrived after the end of World War II, one-fifth during the war, and one-half between World Wars I and II.

Their "general migration pattern" has been described somewhat as follows.[9] Discouraged by poverty in the Island and lured by hope of a better job in New York, the ablest member of a family makes the move. He hunts up a relative or friend in one of the Puerto Rican colonies in the metropolis and looks around for work. If he gets along fairly well, he may send for others of his family and presently set up another immigrant household. We have used the pronoun "he" in a generic sense, for most of the migrants are women. In fact, the sex ratio among Puerto Ricans studied in New York was 63 males per 100 females. This is almost the opposite of the situation in most immigrant colonies, where men come first and for a long time outnumber the women. Other differences also appear. The Puerto Ricans' ancestry is a mixture of Spanish, Indian, and Negro. In physical appearance, the migrants range from those classed as "white," through "indios" (with copper-colored skin) and "grifos" (with light complexion but kinky hair), to others who are unhesitatingly classed as Negroes. Legally these immigrants are Americans, eligible to vote and subject to the draft. But culturally they are more nearly Spanish. As a matter of fact, they are colonials who have a background of both Spanish and Anglo-Saxon influences, but whose cultural heritages from Africa and aboriginal America have largely disappeared. Thus they are unlike other peoples referred to as Latin Americans.

Contrary to popular impression, the Puerto Ricans in New York City are not *campesinos* (peasants), but come from the cities and towns of the Island. This has given them some familiarity with urban life, but coming to New York was nevertheless a very great change for them.

[9] C. Wright Mills, Clarence Senior, and Rose K. Golden, *The Puerto Rican Journey,* pp. 22–23, 95, 1950. By permission of Harper & Brothers.

Here they have found themselves looked down upon as foreigners (speaking a strange tongue) and as colored (having dark skins or kinky hair). Many of them express strong feelings of being rejected by other groups in the metropolitan population. They respond by calling the Italians "no good," the Irish "drunks," the Latin Americans "jealous," Jews "exploiters," Negroes "ruffians," and white North Americans "dollar chasers."

The Puerto Ricans of New York are huddled together by reason of friendship, poverty, and prejudice; but they are not a united group with strong community feeling. They lack the proud traditions and strong communal institutions of the Jews. They have never been a nation like the Poles. They have not yet developed strong leadership in the metropolis. The center of their social organization is the household; yet family life is fragile and often broken up. In fact, many come to the United States as divorced or separated persons. In New York wives often rebel against their husbands' domination, and children "declare their independence" of their island-born parents. The many detached females face especially difficult problems. Because of the sex ratio they must seek male companionship outside the Puerto Rican colony. Even if she is a "grifa" or "india," a Puerto Rican woman in New York is likely to consider herself above American Negroes. Hence her range of choice may be very limited and her behavior may elicit comments about loose morals.

The households that share an apartment building often engage in considerable neighboring. Cliques may be formed among those who frequent some bar or grocery. Those from the same Puerto Rican town may continue friendly relations in the great city. But there are few formal associations of Puerto Ricans in New York. Thus there is not much to bind them together except the fact of a common origin.

The assimilation of Puerto Ricans into the metropolitan population might be expected to go forward rapidly and, in truth, this does happen in the case of some. Many join trade-unions (especially the International Ladies Garment Workers Union and the National Maritime Union), some become identified with political groups. A good many listen to the radio, some read newspapers, more in English than in Spanish. Those who are most successful economically seem to disappear from the colony. But this perhaps leaves the rest more frustrated than ever. In any case here is a body of new immigrants whose status is very unclear and insecure. They are at the same time Americans and foreigners, white and colored, urban and colonial.

The Life Cycle and the Functions of Immigrant Communities. From the foregoing accounts there can be identified certain recurring events and sequences which justify us in seeking for generalized history of immigrant communities in American cities. They usually begin with the settling of a few individuals or families near the heart of a city or close to some outlying industrial section. If successful, these settlers send for relatives and friends; a neighborhood comes into being; local institutions are established. After a time the invasion of business or of newer immigrants drives them out; or possibly financial advancement and new ideas lure them into a somewhat better district. As numbers grow and status rises, the immigrant institutions develop; a community comes into being. But eventually the colony loses some of its members. The original settlers die out; second- and third-generation folk become partially Americanized and seek to escape the limitations of the ethnic community. In the zone of workingmen's homes, or perhaps in a middle-class area, the colony may disappear and merge into the general population. On the other hand, an area of third settlement, still noticeably foreign, may develop. Disappointed aspirants for Americanism, together with older and more conservative members of the group, plus newcomers, who have acquired few American ways, unite to preserve the folkways, mores, ceremonials, institutions, and general integrity of the colony. Ultimately the original immigrants and their children pass from the scene. If there is no racial hallmark and if prejudice is not too intense, the community will disintegrate. Especially with the stoppage of immigration, with education in American schools, employment in American industries, mobility, and intermarriage, the immigrant community seems doomed to disappear.

But during the period of its existence the colony serves a useful purpose in bridging the gap between the Old World and the New. It provides a place where the newcomer can be at least somewhat at home with people of his own kind. It enables him to adjust himself gradually to the strange life of America. It offers him assistance in time of trouble. It encourages and helps him to preserve culture traits which may enrich the life of his adopted country. Its premature disruption would be a misfortune; but its perpetuation seems neither necessary nor probable.

NEGRO COMMUNITIES

During the first half of our national history cities grew largely through drawing in native white people from farms and villages. Between the War between the States and World War I the largest part of our urban increase came through the immigration of Europeans—at first British, Irish, German, and Scandinavian, later Italian, Polish, and other peoples from southern and eastern Europe. But since then a very significant increment has been of Negroes from our own southern states. However, from the earliest census there have been Negroes in some of our cities. During the period of slavery, free Negroes were concentrated in cities and after Emancipation many more turned cityward. After 1870 this movement slowed down, and in 1890 four out of five Negroes still lived in rural areas. Those who had left the country had gone mainly to southern cities. As late as 1910, seven-tenths of all urban Negroes lived in the South. During World War I the great demand for unskilled labor in northern factories attracted many Negroes into cities of the North Central region. This movement continued during the prosperous 1920's, when the Negro population of northern cities increased over 70 per cent. During the depression of the 1930's, the northward migration was slowed down. But World War II drew Negroes in great numbers to the North and to the West. Tables 18 and 19 indicate some changes of the past decade and the situation obtaining in 1950. Since its beginning this city-ward movement has been related to a variety of factors, which include discrimination in the South, agricultural changes involving mechanization, crop limitation, dispossession of share croppers, unusual demand for industrial workers due to the two world wars and the restriction of immigration, the hope of better income, housing, education, and in general desire to escape "second-class citizenship."

Table 18. Negroes in Cities of the United States, 1950

Region	Urban Negroes	Per cent of Negroes urban
South.....................	4,788,000	46
North Central.............	1,956,000	92
Northeast.................	1,845,000	93
West.....................	530,000	91
United States.............	9,120,000	61

SOURCE: Adapted from Bureau of the Census, Preliminary Reports, Series PC-7, No. 3, Apr. 30, 1951.

This rapid shift of Negroes from rural to urban living is most striking in the case of some of our largest cities. In New York City the Negro population rose from 60,000 in 1900 to 750,000 in 1950. The same fifty years showed the following increases in other cities; Detroit 4,000 to 350,000, Chicago 30,000 to 500,000, Philadelphia 60,000 to 400,000, Washington 85,000 to 300,000, St. Louis 35,000 to 130,000, Birmingham 15,000 to 140,000. In one single decade, 1920 to 1930, the Negro population of New York City increased by 175,000 (115 per cent). During the same decade the Negro population of Detroit increased by 80,000 (almost 200 per cent). So great an influx of newcomers from a different region, often from rural districts and marked by a "racial uniform," could not help having serious repercussions in the cities to which they came.

Community Organization: Strengths and Weaknesses. Merely to provide physical accommodations—houses, transportation, schools, etc.—for
so many newcomers was a problem of considerable magnitude. It was,
of course, made more difficult by the usual attempts to keep Negroes
within narrowly restricted boundaries. The result was that rents went up,
houses were crowded, and new districts were invaded. As colored people

Table 19. Negro Population by Regions of the United States, 1950

Region	Per cent of population that was Negro	Per cent increase of Negroes, 1940 to 1950
South...............	21.6	3.1
North Central........	4.8	50.2
Northeast...........	5.0	44.2
West...............	2.9	237.4
United States........	9.9	15.8

SOURCE: Adapted from Bureau of the Census, Preliminary Reports, Series PC-7, No. 3,
Apr. 30, 1951.

spread out, they often encountered strong opposition. White homeowners
resented the approach of the dark-skinned folk. The latter looked
strange, were considered inferior, usually had different habits and
less money. White people did not want to be disturbed, and they feared
a lowering of property values. When they saw the invasion in their
direction, they often entered into agreements neither to sell nor to rent
to Negroes. When surprised by the unexpected appearance of colored
nigh-dwellers, they sometimes resorted to sterner measures—placing signs
telling Negroes how unwelcome they were, bringing lawsuits, throw-
ing bricks through windows, sending warnings through the mail, starting
fires, bombing houses, and the like. About the time of World War I
segregation ordinances were passed by a number of city councils, but
these have been declared unconstitutional. Resort was then had to
restrictive convenants binding property owners not to sell or rent to non-
Caucasians. It has since been held that these cannot be enforced by court
action. What remains is a variety of informal agreements and contracts
not binding at law. In any case, it seems inevitable that the increasing
number of Negroes and the centrifugal drift of the white population
should be accompanied or followed by expansion of the Negro districts
in most cities of the United States.

In order to get further insight into the significance of numbers and
rate of migration, a study was made in St. Louis of four census tracts into
which Negroes were moving at different rates during the decade 1930 to
1940.[10] One was marked by a large numerical increase (3,600), a large

[10] Lois F. Godown, *Social and Economic Changes That Occur When Negroes
Invade White Areas,* unpublished master's thesis, Washington University, 1946.

percentage increase (217), and a large increase in the percentage of the total population that was Negro (33). At the other extreme was a tract with a small numerical increase (115), small percentage increase (9), and small increase in the percentage of the population that was Negro (2). Samples of both Negroes and whites were interviewed in the four districts. They were asked questions about what happened as Negroes moved into the districts, particularly about efforts to keep them out, changes in the general character of the areas, personal contacts, mutual aid, and conflict. The returns from white residents indicated quite clearly that there was more conflict when the invasion went on at a rapid rate than when it was slower. Curiously, at the same time, the most friendly relations between the races were found in the same areas. Where fewer Negroes were moving in, there was less conflict, but also less neighboring. The responses from Negroes showed little difference between the four districts. Whether this means that Negroes were less troubled than whites by the new contacts or were less willing to discuss conflicts we do not know. But the history of the area of most rapid invasion includes a very bitter struggle over the proposed transfer of a public school from white to Negro use, and no similar conflict in any of the other districts.

Besides housing and schools, controversy has often centered on admission to recreational facilities (especially theaters and swimming pools), eating places, use of transportation, and jobs (restriction to menial tasks, limited up-grading, exclusion from trade-unions). Negroes have sometimes been imported as strikebreakers. The 1917 race riot in East St. Louis grew in part out of this economic issue. Even those who came to fill vacancies in wartime were regarded as interlopers. In general, it appears that these open conflicts—together with the more continuous, though less dramatic, pressures of racial discrimination—promote unity and cohesion within the Negro community.

On the positive side, Negro leaders preach group integrity, pride of race, mutual aid, and insistence upon rights; and yet those agencies founded for the specific purpose of advancing Negro interests do not always work together effectively. The National Association for the Advancement of Colored People is a militant organization demanding the immediate granting of rights to Negroes, utilizing propaganda, lobbying, and law suits. The Urban League has a program of self-improvement and cooperation with white citizens, maintaining an employment service, promoting neighborhood clubs, and interpreting the needs of Negroes to municipal officials, employers, and the public generally. Some Negroes belong to both organizations and regard their programs as complementary. But others consider them as rivals and engage in lively controversy over the relative merits of belligerence and of cooperation. In large cities there will be found Negro newspapers which "race angle" the news. Always there will be Negro churches, lodges, recreational agencies, and small business establishments. In St. Louis City 130,000 Negroes maintain approximately 150 churches and possibly 1,000 businesses. Most of these are very small. Food shops are by far the most numerous; a directory calls them "refreshments and culinary establishments." Personal service comes next—barber and beauty shops, cleaners and dyers. Less numerous, but significant as indicating the economic development of the Negro community, are hotels, garages, laundries, hospitals, florist shops, and insurance companies. But even in 1950 St. Louis Negroes owned no real clothing store, only two small shoe stores handling "factory rejects," no bank, and no pawnshop. In this city, public education is segregated; there are 30 elementary schools and branches, 12 special schools, 3 high schools, and 1 college for Negroes. As in other large communities, there are professional men—clergymen, physicians, dentists, attorneys, teachers, and musicians—but there is a tendency for colored people to pass by their own lawyers and physicians, patronizing white men instead. The greatest economic weakness of the urban Negroes is their dependence on white folk for their employment and their restriction in the main to unskilled, unpleasant, and poorly paid occupations.

We have already referred to the fact that civic organizations in the Negro community do not always work effectively together. Sometimes this is associated with lack of leadership. To be sure, there are some able persons in every large group, but leaders who find acceptance throughout the community are rare. This is sometimes attributed to "displaced aggression"—Negroes who do not find it feasible to express their resentment against whites may develop jealousy of their own folks who are gaining prestige or power. Another possible explanation is in terms of division of the community involving stratification and factional rivalry. There is evidence of barriers between economic levels, between educated and illiterate persons, between old residents of the city and newcomers from the country, between religious sects and denominations, as well as between those who seek cooperation with whites and those who want to fight for their rights. But in general factional rivalry seems less serious than mass indifference and rapid increase of population. To be sure, the migrants have come to our cities hoping to better their condition, but without a pattern of joint effort. Moreover, the bringing together in a short time of thousands of rural Negroes unacquainted with each other, with city life, or with habits of cooperation creates a state of social disorganization. As in the case of the Jews, the old city dwellers fear that the hord of unsophisticated newcomers may drag them all down together. They offer help, but often in the form of charity rather than of comradeship. The net result is that instead of forming a well-knit community, the Negroes in a large city are divided among a number of neighborhoods, perhaps two or three communities; but otherwise they constitute an unorganized mass of disadvantaged folk.

Spatial Patterns of Negro Communities. Four major patterns of racial separation or segregation have been identified in the cities of the United States. These were first demonstrated by Woofter in the 1920's[11] and substantially confirmed by Frazier in the 1940's.[12] (1) In most northern cities the concentration of Negroes is very marked, but it involves a small part of the whole urban area; that is, most of the Negroes are found in a very limited section devoted almost entirely to their own race and relatively few of them are found in districts predominantly white. This is true, *e.g.*, of New York, Chicago, and Detroit. (2) In certain southern cities, such as Richmond, Memphis, and Atlanta, Negroes are highly concentrated in several large parts of the city besides being lightly scattered in other sections. Of the large border cities, Washington conforms to the second pattern, while Baltimore, Louisville, and St. Louis conform to the first. (3) In some of the older cities in the deep South, like Charleston, S.C., the large Negro population is scattered throughout the city. This is due to the large number of servant houses and alley dwellings. (4) In a number of northern cities with rather few Negroes, these people are usually found in a small part of the city and somewhat scattered even within this area. Such is the case in Minneapolis, Gary, Akron, and Des Moines.

When 1950 data are available by census tracts, these spatial patterns should be rechecked graphically by mapping the distribution of Negroes in representative metropolitan areas. Those who wish to engage in more precise analyses may use the method developed by Shevky and Williams and already decribed in Chap. 8, or they may use the formula developed by the Cowgills at the University of Wichita.[13]

Within the districts occupied largely by Negroes, interesting ecological patterns are displayed. Thus Frazier has shown that in Chicago characteristics of the Negro population correspond with those of whites in the same zones. But in New York the Negro community of Harlem has a pattern of its own which corresponds to that of the city as a whole.[14] In Chicago, Frazier found the principal Negro district to be a segment reaching from the heart of the city to the south through seven fairly distinct zones. Proceeding from the Loop toward 73th St., certain characteristic changes occurred progressively and consistently. First of all, the percentage of family heads who were born in the South decreased. Second, the percentage of adults who were mulattoes increased. The

[11] T. J. Woofter, Jr., *Negro Problems in Cities*, Chap. 3, 1928.
[12] E. Franklin Frazier, *The Negro in the United States*, Chap. 11, 1949.
[13] Donald O. Cowgill and Mary S. Cowgill, "An Index of Segregation Based on Block Statistics," *Amer. Sociol. Rev.*, 16 (1951), 825–831.
[14] Frazier, *op. cit.*, pp. 256–266.

relative number of illiterates decreased; the relative number of persons engaged in professional and white-collar occupations and skilled trades increased; while the proportion in semiskilled trades, domestic service, and unskilled labor decreased. The percentage of women gainfully employed decreased; the percentage of men married increased, but the relative number of married women remained about the same. In the succession of all seven zones, home ownership increased strikingly and the number of families and persons per dwelling decreased. The relative number of small children increased. The percentage of families on relief and receiving care from family welfare agencies decreased, as did the incidence of family desertion. There was likewise a decrease in illegitimacy and in juvenile delinquency. All in all, therefore, Frazier found the Negro community of Chicago, if such it may be called, conforming in its several zones to the characteristics displayed by the entire city. Close to the central business district, he found a section in which houses were dilapidated and occupied in the main by impoverished newcomers from the South. Next came the "bright light" area of the black belt, with its theaters, cabarets, gambling places, and houses of prostitution. These were followed by districts of progressively better social and economic status.

In Harlem, Frazier discovered quite a different pattern. Centering about 125th St. and Seventh Ave., he found a Negro community with its own system of concentric circles. This community had grown up first about the indicated center and then pushed out in all directions until it could be described as a series of five zones. The percentage of the population that was Negro was highest in the first, or central, zone, and lowest in the fifth. Buildings not devoted to residential uses were most numerous in the first zone and fewest in the fifth. There was a similar decline from the center to the periphery in the relative number of rooming houses and lodginghouses. The relative number of children increased from the first to the fifth zone, as did the percentage of adults who were married. In the first zone deaths exceeded births in number; in the second they were about equal; and in the next three zones there was a steady increase in the ratio of births to deaths. Delinquency showed an uneven distribution, but dependency declined consistently from the center to the outer edge of this Negro community. Thus the developments in Chicago and New York have been rather different so far as the spatial distribution is concerned. The reasons for this are not altogether clear, but they are perhaps related to the fact that in Chicago, Negroes pushed out from the heart of the city, along with other ethnic groups, while in New York they were concentrated in a district at some distance from the center of the city as this is ordinarily conceived.

Social Patterns: Stratification. We have already indicated that Negro communities are often far from united and that there are frequently divisions along economic, religious, color, and other lines. Sometimes these involve not only separation, but also stratification, *i.e.*, attitudes of superiority and inferiority.

Even under slavery there was evidence of social distinctions, house servants being commonly rated above field hands. Among free Negroes before the War between the States, importance was attached to differences in education, occupational skill, and sometimes complexion. Following emancipation, these same traits continued to be criteria of social status. But, according to Frazier,[15] it is in the twentieth century in northern cities that stratification has been most in evidence. While it would be more accurate to think in terms of a continuum than of sharply drawn class lines, nevertheless, it is clear that within the Negro community various categories of persons have varied status in their own estimation and in that of their fellow citizens.

For convenience we may speak of three classes. The Negro upper class in northern cities includes most professional men—physicians, dentists, lawyers, some clergymen, teachers, and social workers—the more successful businessmen, some public officials, and civil servants. A study in St. Louis in the 1930's[16] indicated that church membership (preferably a large church with a "decorous" form of worship), residential district, and length of residence in the city were also considered important. Frazier found that, in contrast to upper-class white women, Negro wives on this level are often gainfully employed, probably to help maintain the "front" considered essential. As in white society, the "social ritual" is important. Frazier tells of "lavish entertainment in expensively equipped homes," membership in Greek letter fraternities, and "organizations for the uplift of the race." In general it appears that most upper-class Negroes, if integrated into the larger community, would be rated middle class. Perhaps it is for this reason that they are somewhat ambivalent about breaking down all the barriers of racial discrimination.

The Negro middle class in a northern city of the United States includes clerical workers, skilled artisans, firemen, policemen, hairdressers, and the like. They have incomes large enough to enable them to live respectably, they often have gone to high school, they try to buy homes but are often thwarted. They belong to lodges, churches, and other institutions of the Negro community. They take their religion seriously and regard it as inseparable from morality.

The lower class—or classes, for the St. Louis study distinguished two— includes unskilled laborers, domestic servants, people most recently from the South, living in slum areas and leading a rather unstable and insecure existence. These folks attend "store front" churches, if any, and

[15] *Ibid.*, pp. 289*ff.*
[16] Edna Taborn, *Social Stratification among Negroes in St. Louis*, unpublished master's thesis, Washington University, 1937.

indulge in highly emotional forms of worship. At the bottom of the social levels are found gamblers, prostitutes, and others whose behavior flaunts middle-class standards of decency and decorum.

As indicated before, these classes are not really separate. They ✶ represent degrees of prestige, based on varied criteria concerning which there is only partial agreement in the community. However, the facts of social distance, of looking up and looking down, are very real.

CONTRAST OF IMMIGRANT AND NEGRO COMMUNITIES

In the discussion that has just preceded, there have been evident a number of interesting differences between Negro and immigrant communities in American cities. The immigrants, having come recently from distant lands, have to adjust themselves to a new cultural situation with different language, laws, customs, and traditions of many sorts. The Negroes on the contrary, come to the city with a knowledge of English, some familiarity with American legal, political, religious, and other institutions. Their chief adjustment is one that they share with the im- ✶ migrants, namely, that involved in the transition from rural to urban and from agricultural to industrial life. Both groups tend to settle near the heart of a city, but their outward movement is quite different. Immigrants frequently jump over intervening spaces, while the Negroes usually push along a continuous line. With immigrant communities, segregation is largely voluntary, while with the Negroes it is largely compulsory. Members of immigrant communities tend, especially in the second and third generation, to withdraw from the ethnic group and lose themselves in the general population. Negroes occasionally "go white," but on the whole they have little escape from their own group. Some immigrant communities display marked solidarity; usually this is less developed among Negroes. Hence, while the communal institutions of some immigrant communities are well supported, most of the Negro institutions are relatively weak. The outlook is for the gradual disappearance of ethnic groups whose skin is light and against whom prejudice is not particularly marked. But it seems likely that the Negro populations will continue for an indefinite time as communities relatively distinct and yet very dependent upon the city as a whole, and particularly upon its white institutions and leaders.

SELECTED READINGS

Immigrant Colonies

CHILD, IRVIN L.: *Italian or American? The Second Generation in Conflict,* Yale University Press, 1943. A social psychological study of acculturation in New Haven.

MILLS, C. WRIGHT, CLARENCE SENIOR, and ROSE K. GOLDSEN: *The Puerto Rican Journey,* Harper & Brothers, 1950. An account of the Puerto Ricans in New York City.

SMITH, WILLIAM C.: *Americans in Process: A Study of Our Citizens of Oriental Ancestry,* Edwards Bros., Inc., 1937. Presents an interesting contrast between oriental-occidental relations in cities of our Pacific coast and of Hawaii.

THOMAS, WILLIAM I., and FLORIAN ZNANIECKI: *The Polish Peasant in Europe and America,* Alfred A. Knopf, Inc., 2d ed., 1927. Volume 2, pp. 1511–1574, deals with the Polish-American community.

TUCK, RUTH: *Not with the Fist: Mexican Americans in a Southwestern City,* Harcourt, Brace and Company, Inc., 1948. A study of the Spanish-speaking community in a small city of southwestern United States.

WARNER, W. LLOYD, and LEO SROLE: *The Social Systems of American Ethnic Groups,* Yale University Press, 1945. One of the famous Yankee City Series.

WIRTH, LOUIS: *The Ghetto,* University of Chicago Press, 1928. A study of Jewish communities in Europe and America, especially Frankfort and Chicago.

Negro Communities

DAVIE, MAURICE R.: *Negroes in American Society,* McGraw-Hill Book Company, Inc., 1949. See especially Chap. 4, "The Growth of Industry and Migration to the City," and Chap. 19, "Class and Caste."

DRAKE, ST. CLAIR, and HORACE R. CAYTON: *Black Metropolis,* Harcourt, Brace and Company, Inc., 1945. The story of the Negro community in Chicago from its beginning to World War 11.

FRAZIER, E. FRANKLIN: *The Negro in the United States,* The Macmillan Company, 1949. Chapter 11, "Urban Negro Communities," and Chap. 12, "Social and Economic Stratification," are especially useful for our purpose.

JOHNSON, CHARLES S.: *Patterns of Negro Segregation,* Harper & Brothers, 1943. Chapter 1, "Spatial and Institutional Forms of Racial Segregation," and Chap. 8, "Residential and School Segregation by Law," are especially useful.

CHAPTER 11. *Neighborhoods and Neighboring*

Popularly, the terms community and neighborhood are used without much distinction. Both imply the sharing of some interests and activities. Both imply attachment to a locality. Accepting these notions as a point of departure, we have found it convenient to limit the term community to a relatively stable, homogeneous population occupying a fairly well-defined, compact area and utilizing a distinctly local set of institutions or facilities. We have chosen further to modify popular use of the term by emphasizing the fact that the state of affairs just described varies considerably within every metropolitan area, so that we may speak of more or less community life, degrees of community, or points on a continuum.

In a similar fashion we find it convenient to modify popular use of the term neighborhood. Instead of the area it is the social relations to which our attention is mainly directed. Specifically we have in mind those relations which sociologists call "primary," meaning that lives of the people concerned touch at many points, they know each other very well, see each other frequently, and engage in such activities as informal visiting, borrowing and lending tools, books, and recipes, receiving parcels and messages, care of each other's children, going together to the movies, shopping, on picnics, and the like. With reference to such activities and relationships our studies support common observation in identifying degrees of neighboring and degrees of localization. Thus there are still limited areas in our cities occupied by homogeneous groups of stable families which display all the traits mentioned in this paragraph and in which the practice of neighboring involves practically all members of all the families. They associate intimately with all their nigh-dwellers and their primary relationships are mainly identified with the area in which they live. Then there are areas like the rooming-house district described in Chap. 1, where almost no one knows anyone else by name, personal contacts are few, mutual aid is negligible, mobility and heterogeneity are high, local attachments are almost nil. Still a different situation is that of people who have only a few friends and

155

acquaintances in the immediate vicinity, but do maintain close relationships with individuals and families scattered over the city. Some of the interaction involves whole families, but in other cases different members of a family have close friends who are almost unknown to the others of their household. When our cities were smaller and the means of transportation were slower, it appears that there were many situations of the first type—old-fashioned neighborhoods with close ties between the families of a limited area. Today situations of the third type seem to be more common—interfamily and interpersonal association not localized. Those of the second type represent the extreme of urban anonymity, mobility, and heterogeneity, but we do not know what proportion of the population they involve.

SOME STUDIES OF NEIGHBORING

We ourselves have made no separate study of neighboring and similar interaction involving primary relationships. But we included a section on neighboring in the schedule which we used in a general study of social participation in 1945. This involved interviews with 1,503 adults scattered over the city of St. Louis. The following questions were asked about neighborhood participation.

Neighborhood Participation (Bernard Scale revised)

(For purposes of this study, neighbor means someone living in the same block with you on either side of the street.)

1. How many people in your block do you know well enough to speak to?
   a. Nearly everyone
   b. About half
   c. About a fourth
   d. Only a couple of people
   e. None
2. About how often* do you chat or visit with people in your block?
   a. Once a day or more
   b. At least weekly, but not every day
   c. At least monthly, but not every week
   d. Never
3. How often do you exchange or share items with your neighbors such as tools, books, recipes, food, dishes, suggestions, etc?
   (Intervals same as for No. 2)
   a.   *b.*   *c.*   *d.*
4. How often do you make previously planned visits to the home of your neighbors, for tea, a meal, to stay overnite, to spend the day?
   a.   *b.*   *c.*   *d.*

* The answer desired is the maximum frequency. Thus, under item 2, if every day the respondent chats with *someone* in the block, circle *a*. It makes no difference how many persons may be involved. Corresponding responses are intended for items 3 to 8.

5. How often do your neighbors visit you for the same reasons as No. 4?

   a.   *b.*   *c.*   *d.*

6. How often do you and your neighbors exchange favors, such as taking in parcels, delivering messages, etc?

   a.   *b.*   *c.*   *d.*

7. How often do you and your neighbors do bigger favors for each other, such as shopping, caring for children, "sleeping" extra guests, etc.?

   a.   *b.*   *c.*   *d.*

8. How often do you and your neighbors go together to picnics, parties, movies, etc?

   a.   *b.*   *c.*   *d.*

This schedule was scored as follows: Responses to the first question were assigned 4, 3, 2, 1, 0 points, respectively. Answers to the other questions were assigned 3, 2, 1, 0 points. The sum of these points constituted a respondent's score in neighborhood participation. Table 20 shows the distribution of scores. It was perhaps to be expected that women would engage more than men in neighboring. However, the differences were not great. Likewise the differences between Negroes and whites were found to be small. The neighboring scores were positively related to length of residence and amount of schooling completed, negatively related to age. The first of these three relationships was to be expected; the significance of the other two is not clear. The correlations with other kinds of social participation were all negative and small. Specifically the Pearsonian coefficient of correlation between neighboring and participation in organized groups, such as clubs, unions, churches, was —.18; between neighboring and "cultural participation" (movies, sports, reading, radio) was —.16; between neighboring and informal activities involving persons outside the immediate vicinity was —.35. All this points to the probablity that people who have most to do with their nigh-dwellers participate less in other types of social activity. However, without further studies we offer this only as a possibility, not as an established proposition. Our sample was only approximately representative of one city at one time, and our schedule is in need of further revision.

We did not attempt to relate neighboring and other social participation scores to other features of local districts because our sample was too small—12 per census tract. However, Mrs. Bernard in 1935, with a larger sample per tract, found a positive relationship between neighboring and home ownership, single family dwellings, stability of residence, percentage of adults married, and percentage of the population under age five.[1]

[1] Jessie S. Bernard, *An Instrument for the Measurement of Neighborhood with Experimental Applications*, unpublished doctoral dissertation, Washington University, 1935.

Table 20. Neighboring Scores of 1,503 Adults, St. Louis, 1945

Scores	Total		Men		Women	
	Frequency	Per cent	Frequency	Per cent	Frequency	Per cent
0	49	3.3	35	4.7	14	1.8
1–4	319	21.3	180	24.1	139	18.4
5–9	548	36.5	273	36.5	275	36.4
10–14	402	26.7	194	26.0	208	27.5
15–19	161	10.7	60	8.0	101	13.4
20–24	21	1.3	4	0.5	17	2.2
25–29	3	0.2	1	0.1	2	0.3
Total.........	1,503	100.0	747	100.0	756	100.0

On the first page of this chapter we stated our belief that there are some local situations, neighborhoods in the older meaning of the term, in which nearly everyone interacts with nearly everyone else. But some students of primary relationships question this proposition. In order to shed light on the question, Sweetser made a detailed study of nine-tenths of the residents of a square block in the small city of Bloomington, Ind.[2] He found that none of the 54 persons studied was acquainted with all of his neighbors (nigh-dwellers, as we prefer to call them). The median number of acquaintances (persons recognized by name, sight, or reputation) was about half the number of nigh-dwellers about whom each informant was questioned. The median number of associates (persons with whom an informant at least chatted informally from time to time) was about one-sixth of the number that might have been listed. Sweetser then compared lists of acquaintances and associates of given individuals, summarizing the results by means of a "coefficient of comparative compositional uniqueness."[3] The coefficients could vary between 0 and 1, 0 representing identical lists, 1 representing lists completely different. The actual range of coefficients was, for acquaintance pairs, from .10 to .96, and for associate pairs it was from .27 to 1.00. For acquaintance pairs the median was .44, for associate pairs it was .87. The inference drawn by Sweetser was that "individual residents of urbanized areas are differentiated from each other with respect to the neighbors with whom they are acquainted and with whom they associate."[4]

We turn now from studies of personal relationships between people

[2] Frank L. Sweetser, Jr., "A New Emphasis for Neighborhood Research," *Amer. Sociol. Rev.*, 7 (1942), 525–533; *Neighborhood Acquaintance and Association, A Study of Personal Neighborhoods*, doctoral dissertation, Columbia University, 1941.

[3] The formula for the coefficient is $(b + c)/(a + b + c)$, where $a =$ the number of names on the first list which are also found on the second; $b =$ the number of names on the first list which do not appear on the second; $c =$ the number of names on the second list which do not appear on the first.

[4] *Op. cit.*, p. 531.

living near together to studies of local situations commonly referred to as neighborhoods.

SOME STUDIES OF NEIGHBORHOODS

Well-integrated and Disorganized Neighborhoods in Columbus. About thirty years ago McKenzie studied a number of so-called neighborhoods in the city of Columbus, Ohio.[5] A few of these he found to possess rather highly organized local life. One was rather thoroughly disintegrated. He discovered some immigrant groups located near industrial areas or close to the central business district. In outlying sections of moderately high economic status and usually on high ground, he found what were known as organized streets. These were limited areas, usually along a single street, whose inhabitants had established formal organizations for various purposes. The disintegrated neighborhood McKenzie studied was located on low land near the heart of the city, an area of low economic status.

The organized streets, which seemed to be well-integrated neighborhoods, were, as stated, usually on high ground in relatively new parts of the city. Sometimes the boundaries were marked by granite boulders. Characteristically, the lots were wide and the houses were set uniformly back from the street. There were parkways and other evidences of programs to beautify the section. All houses were single dwellings. There were no apartments and no stores. Some of these organized neighborhoods carried on a variety of activities. They had meetings at various intervals, often at the public elementary school. At these meetings they conducted their business as neighborhood improvement associations; afterward they enjoyed a social hour. The program of street beautification has already been suggested. In addition, they sent floral tributes in cases of severe illness or death, published a local paper, organized a bowling team, conducted celebrations on such occasions as the Fourth of July, and held picnics. Many of the residents were close friends, some of them were kinsmen. Each of the successfully organized neighborhoods has given evidence of the work of competent leaders.

The disorganized neighborhood was in an old part of the city which went into further decline after the floods of 1913. Real estate prices dropped, and there was an influx of poor people, including some Negroes. Thus the population became more and more heterogeneous. At the time of the study, women outnumbered men, and children were quite numerous. Mobility was high, as evidenced by the number of boarders and lodgers, a low percentage of homeownership, and changes in the voting

[5] R. D. McKenzie, *The Neighborhood: A Study of Local Life in the City of Columbus, Ohio,* 1923. By permission of the University of Chicago Press.

lists. The low economic status was indicated by the character of occupations, mostly unskilled, the employment of many married women, and the absence of modern conveniences in the houses. Limited social participation was shown by the small number belonging to voluntary organizations, by the sectarianism in the churches, and by the slight amount of mutual aid extended beyond the kinship group. School attendance was relatively poor, dependency and juvenile delinquency rates were high. Recreational facilities were quite restricted. One mark of the disorganized social life of the district was the "individualization" of leisure time activities. Thus older men tended to gather about nearby saloons. Young men were drawn to the poolrooms, cabarets, or cheap dance halls of the area. Young women more frequently went to the uptown dance halls and movies. Small children attended the neighborhood movies, while their mothers had very little recreational life of any sort except that associated with the churches. Thus economic necessity had forced people of unlike attitudes and tastes to dwell near together. They took little pride in their district, paid little attention to their nighdwellers, united in few joint activities, and in general behaved as individuals rather than as neighbors.

Thus McKenzie indicated in this study the significance for neighborhood life of a favorable site, stability, homogeneity, at least a moderate economic status, common activities, pride in the district, and leadership. He assumed, more than he demonstrated, the basic importance of intimate, face-to-face dealings, which sociologists call primary relationships.

Disintegrating Neighborhoods in Chicago. In the 1930's Roper studied the neighborhoods in the part of Chicago known as Hyde Park.[6] This district is on the lake front, 6 or 7 miles south of the central business district. It is bounded on the north by a wide boulevard, on the west by another main thoroughfare and a park, on the south by that wide parkway and trafficway known as the Midway, on the east by the lake and another park. Being thus well defined by natural and artificial barriers, it might be expected to possess a considerable measure of local community life. As a matter of fact, there is evidence that it was once a rather well-defined community. But today it is an apartment house area occupied by people whose business and other interests are scattered throughout the city. Roper estimated that 85 per cent carried on their business and professional activities outside the Hyde Park area. Economically this was an upper-middle-class section. Nevertheless, it was far from being homogeneous. Roper found one-fourth of the population to be of foreign birth and a small number to be Negroes. Moreover, he found that Jewish people and other groups remained somewhat apart even when they lived

[6] M. W. Roper, *The City and the Primary Group,* 1935. Data used by permission of the author.

in the same residential hotel. Considerable mobility was indicated by a relatively high turnover in the public schools. Rising land values also marked a steady change in the character of the occupants. This much information shall serve to characterize the area as a whole.

We turn now to consider the natural subdivisions which in popular language would doubtless be called neighborhoods. To begin with, these smaller areas were found to have no definite names, and some of them had no well-marked boundaries. However, railroad tracks, a business street, and a university campus served to divide the large area rather naturally into seven smaller districts. They differed somewhat from each other as to the proportion of the population that was native white of native parents, and as to occupation. Only the two small districts close to the university showed any marks of a well-knit local life. In these, Roper found considerable friendliness and social intercourse. People visited back and forth, borrowed from one another, and performed numerous minor services. However, those who were acquainted and carried on these practices which we call neighboring were very small, congenial groups living in a single apartment house or in the dwellings stretched along one block. Larger groups were brought together at some of the churches. Children associated at the schools, but this did not ordinarily bring their parents into direct contact. Sometimes homeowners united to prevent the erection of an apartment house. All in all, these areas near the university presented many earmarks of neighborhood life as we are accustomed to think of it, but in each district the inhabitants were too numerous and their natural contacts too few to make possible more than a rather vague sense of neighborhood.

Along Hyde Park Boulevard and in the hotel area on the lake front, neighboring was very much less in evidence than in the university districts. Such intimate contacts as were found seem to have been made outside this district, through a church or otherwise, and to have developed here when the families moved in. In these sections, moreover, the division between Jew and Gentile was especially marked. One resident stated, "the old type of neighborly intimacies is confined almost entirely to the flat and to the small apartment housing six families or less. Mobility increases with the size of the building."[7]

Two other so-called neighborhoods, each centering more or less about a public school, were identified by Roper between the university districts and the boulevard and hotel areas. They were intermediate not only geographically but also in the character of the local life. There were old residents who complained about the strange people who were coming in, and lamented the passing of neighborliness of bygone days. Parent-teacher associations were difficult to promote because of the

[7] *Ibid.*, p. 62.

heterogeneity of the folk and their unwillingness to accept one another. So far as adults were concerned, it seemed that no neighborly contacts extended over districts larger than a block. Often they were confined to a single building. Children, however, formed contacts over somewhat larger areas and of a more intimate character. They met at school or at play. They made friends and showed themselves to be the most real neighbors in the district. But even they found their associates within quite restricted areas. Sometimes a child would not go more than a couple of blocks to join his little friends. Children of the Kozminski school reported that over half of their best friends lived within a distance of two blocks.

Thus in all the subdivisions of this former community we see a diminution of neighboring and of locally organized activities. Large numbers of people living in close proximity have few personal contacts, know little about one another, and have their own diversified interests scattered throughout the city. Within the residential district, children are likely to do more neighboring than their parents and to go a little farther to meet their friends. But for both young and old the range of primary relations is exceedingly limited. This is probably quite characteristic of apartment areas in the large cities of America.

The Columbus study revealed both well-integrated and almost wholly disorganized neighborhoods. The Chicago study shows the dissolution of neighborhood ties far advanced but not yet complete.

Exclusive Neighborhoods in St. Louis. In metropolitan St. Louis there are many subdivisions in which not only the building lots but the streets themselves are, or have been, owned and controlled by the residents. They are usually referred to as private streets or private places. Some of these date back to an earlier period. A few of the older ones have passed out of existence or at least gone into decline, but most of them appear to be thriving ventures in a certain kind of neighborliness. The characteristic sequence of events in the establishment, conduct, and decline of one of these private streets is somewhat as follows. An area which promises to be a desirable residential district is chosen, subdivided, and restricted. The restrictions, which are written into the deeds of the individual lots as sold, usually forbid the erection of any but single family residences, excluding all types of business, even boarding houses and physicians' offices. Often they stipulate minimum cost of building, materials, type of architecture, size of lot, distance from the street, etc. Commonly, ownership is restricted to the Caucasian race. The purposes of all these restrictions, indeed of the venture as a whole, are to maintain property values, ensure a certain exclusiveness, and make possible a kind of neighborhood protected from the encroachment of business or unwelcome types of people.

Whether the venture is promoted by a realtor or by a group of people already associated, it presently comes to be occupied by a homogeneous group of more or less congenial families. They are organized into an association for control of the area and its residents. Usually they elect a small board of trustees who carry on the business of the association. Their powers and duties include the collection of assessments which range from 50 cents per front foot to a flat rate of $400 per year for each lot owner. They make contracts with public utilities and with individuals to supply water, gas, and electricity, to collect garbage, and to afford police protection. Sometimes the members of the association hold annual or special meetings at which they vote on matters of importance. But in most instances no formal meetings are held at all. The law requires that gates to private streets be kept closed at least thirty days in the year lest the streets automatically become public property.

Gradually the surrounding area is filled with family residences. In time these begin to give way to apartment and business houses. Property values decline. For a time all this may have little effect upon the private place, but eventually its occupants are displeased with their surroundings and with the fact that many of their friends have moved much farther toward the periphery of the metropolitan district. From time to time, old families die out or suffer financial loss. Unable to maintain expensive establishments as these usually are, owners wish to sell, rent, or remodel. Forbidden to do this, they may leave the house vacant or tear it down. Discussion of changing or dropping restrictions divides the occupants of the street and marks its decline as a neighborhood. Eventually the streets, *i.e.*, the actual pavements and sidewalks, are voluntarily dedicated to the city, and restrictions are withdrawn. Perhaps a court may set them aside on the ground that the area and its relation to surrounding districts are so changed that the restrictions are no longer valid.

Because some of these places have been in existence for three-quarters of a century and because some of them have ceased to exist, it is possible not only to identify their life cycle as we have just done, but also to consider some of the advantages and disadvantages to the residents. In the first place these folks have succeeded in maintaining property values over long periods of time. In the end, however, they suffer great losses because of the inflexibility of their plan, which impedes their adjustment to changes in the district about them. Also they are successful from the standpoint of exclusiveness, stability, and homogeneity of life. They make possible the escape from noise and traffic.

Like St. Louis's private streets in some respects is Chicago's Gold Coast.[8] Both represent high economic levels and social exclusiveness, both "go in" for philanthropy, civic reform, art, and music. However, the

[8] Harvey W. Zorbaugh, *Gold Coast and Slum*, Chap. 3, 1929.

Gold Coast includes hotels and displays much more mobility than is characteristic of the private streets. One gets the impression of more conspicuous consumption, greater snobbery, and more social climbing on the Gold Coast, although this is obviously difficult to measure. But the greatest difference appears to be in the practice of neighboring. Zorbaugh's account emphasizes the absence of neighborly contacts on the Gold Coast despite the "localization of society," with its self-consciousness and common traditions. But in some of the private streets we have found much informal visiting as well as other previously mentioned marks of the true neighborhood.

From these two studies we are warranted in the inference that high economic status and superior physical conditions may facilitate, but do not guarantee, neighboring. Neighborhoods are essentially matters of folkways and traditions rather than of economics and architecture. The illustrations which follow indicate that neighborhoods may develop on any economic level, provided nigh-dwellers have the willingness and the desire to share their experience and actually behave as a group.

Block Units of the Urban League. Ever since the founding of the first social settlements in the late nineteenth century there have been social workers whose principal efforts have been directed toward the organization of neighborhood activities. Residents of the settlements have often referred to themselves as neighborhood workers. During World War I Cincinnati was the scene of what was known as a social unit experiment. People were organized by blocks and by larger districts to give expression to their felt needs and to develop programs for their satisfaction. Somewhat after the same fashion, the Urban League of St. Louis maintains a department whose principal function is the promotion of neighborhood clubs and block units in the Negro community.

While the purposes of these organizations have been stated chiefly in terms of material objectives, an additional goal and sometimes a consequence is the bringing together of people who live in a limited area for the stimulation of friendly relations, development of leadership, and cultivation of teamwork in attainment of common ends. The purpose as stated in the 1938 report of the St. Louis Urban League is "to improve the physical appearance of homes, lawns, side walks and alleys; abating nuisances which destroy the beauty and peace of a residential area; obtaining group action in expressing approval or disapproval of any city or state legislation which would tend to harm property values in that area." Membership in the block units is open to all adults who live in a given block. Meetings are held once a month with an average attendance of 10 to 15, chiefly women. Besides a friendly gathering for sociability, each meeting also includes a business session. The order of business usually runs something as follows: reciting of the Lord's Prayer, reading of the minutes, report of the Sick Committee, presentation of general issues by a worker from the Urban League, discussion of local problems by the membership. The local problems and projects include cleaning of alleys, improvement of lawns, provision of vacant lot playgrounds, complaints about bus service and crowding in nearby movie houses, protesting the presence of prostitution and gambling houses, arrangement of co-operative buying, boycotting stores which refuse to employ Negro clerks, holding of parties, and raising money. As a result of this movement, there is no doubt that people in the organized blocks are better acquainted, engage in some common activities, and achieve some tangible objectives. But by no means all the residents take part, especially in blocks whose population covers a considerable range of social and economic levels.

Rise and Decline of a Neighborhood in Los Angeles. About 1875 a woman named Mary Newman secured a Federal land grant near the little town of Los Angeles.[9] After farming it for several years, she began to sell tracts. These too were cultivated, until, in 1887, their owners began to subdivide them into building lots. By 1903 this subdivision was completed. By this time the area had, moreover, become a part of the city. It was covered with bungalows and other single dwellings for middle-class homeowners. In the beginning it appears that everyone knew everyone else and "all were on an equal footing." In the years that followed, there was a steady increase in population of the original type. Fields and orchards disappeared; more houses were built. Ultimately the numbers and varieties of inhabitants became too great for wide-spread acquaintance.

About 1914 some rear houses were built and others were remodeled to accommodate more than one family. After the World War, the housing shortage and high rentals gave further impetus to the erection of multiple dwellings. But it was not until 1927 that the first real apartment house was built. During this period, as the population became more numerous, it also became more heterogeneous and more mobile. Homeownership declined and tenancy increased. Some old homes were turned into rooming houses. The character of the area was rapidly being changed. Presently, one street became a business thoroughfare with a growing number and variety of stores and populations. Soon divergent racial types invaded the area. Not only Europeans, but Negroes and Japanese, found their way here and there into the district. By this time the old residents were disappearing. Some had died, but others moved away. Some found opportunities to sell their property to advantage. Others left because they feared depreciation of property values or a loss of social status. As the

[9] Bessie A. McClenahan, *The Changing Urban Neighborhood*, 1929. Data used by permission of the University of Southern California Press.

homogeneous group of old residents departed and the heterogeneous types of newcomers established themselves in the district, the practices of neighboring showed marked decline. There was less and less participation in localized activities; there were fewer and fewer personal contacts. Interests were scattered over the city. Many persons displayed attitudes of superiority toward the district and apologized for having to live there. Conflicts developed between the residents. What was once a well-knit neighborhood had become just another part of the city.

CHANGES IN URBAN NEIGHBORHOODS

From the numerous studies that have been made and from the illustrations offered in this chapter it is possible to identify, tentatively at least, a typical life history or expected sequence of events in urban neighborhoods. (1) The first stage is the occupying of a district by homeseekers who wish pleasant, healthy, and otherwise acceptable surroundings in which to rear a family. They want congenial nigh-dwellers who will become neighbors in the sense of people who visit back and forth, go shopping together, care for each other's children, and engage in the other practices associated with neighboring. (2) As time passes, the number of residents increases and personal acquaintance declines. The neighborhood is surrounded by various sorts of people and perhaps by business houses. It may be divided by a new thoroughfare. Some of the earlier settlers die or move away. Some of the newcomers are tenants instead of owners. Neighboring and neighborliness decline. (3) In a third stage, there may be invasion of the neighborhood area itself by business or by strange ethnic groups. As single dwellings give way to converted tenements, apartments, and rooming houses, occupied increasingly by racial or other groups regarded as inferior, neighborhood pride and loyalty decline still further. (4) Finally, personal contacts practically disappear, neighboring ceases, and the district loses its identity in the general life of the city. It may continue as part of a respectable residential section; it may be taken over by business or industry; or it may deteriorate slowly while vice and crime get a foothold. In any case the life of a neighborhood has been completed.

Now these events do not occur in identical sequence. Some of them may be absent from particular cases. But in general the shifts follow the approximate order that we have indicated: from residential home-ownership, to tenancy, to business, to heterogeneity of inhabitants, sometimes to disorder, and to the final displacement of residents by other uses of the land.

From the foregoing discussion it is plain that we do not have to be content with casual observations and descriptive accounts in order to identify urban neighborhoods and discover trends in the practice of neighboring. From graphic displays of significant facts, it is possible to locate quickly areas in which neighboring is most likely to occur and others from which it is almost certain to be absent. By correlating various series of data, it is possible to identify rather definitely a number of social, economic, and demographic factors with the presence or absence of neighborhood life. From our own studies in St. Louis we have concluded that among the important criteria of neighborhoods are stability, homogeneity, standard age and sex distribution, family life, land use, and absence of the so-called pathologies.

First of all, it is apparent that unless the local population remains in the same vicinity for a reasonable length of time there cannot be personal acquaintance, familiarity with local traditions, behavior in accordance with local customs, or pride in local institutions. We shall see in a later chapter how stability and mobility may be measured. Second, it is believed that the integration of neighborhoods and communities requires a certain homogeneity of the population. We have not attempted to construct any index of homogeneity as such, but we do have rather definite indications of this in census data concerning color, nativity, and economic status. We ought to have data concerning religious affiliations as a further check on homogeneity or heterogeneity. In the third place, we assume that neighborhood and community life is most likely to be found in districts where the population pyramid conforms to that of a static or slow-growing population; that is, the sex ratio will approximate 100 and the number and percentage of persons in each age group will decrease steadily from youngest to oldest.[10] Fourth, it appears that family life and neighboring bear some relation to each other; that is, neighborhood and community organization may be expected in areas where a large percentage of the adult population is married, where families are above the city average in size, and where most of the residential units are single dwellings. A fifth criterion is land use. As just mentioned, when an area is occupied almost exclusively by single dwellings, neighborhood life seems more likely to develop, although its existence cannot be taken for granted. Multiple dwellings indicate that local organization is likely to be absent, although we know there is real neighboring in some apartment houses. A large number of rooming houses, hotels, or converted tenements almost guarantee the nonexistence of neighborhood and community. A mixture of residential with commercial and industrial property seems to interfere with the organization of local life.

Negatively, such items as juvenile delinquency, adult crime, vice, poverty, and disease are related to the integration or disintegration of local groups or institutions. For example, the occurrence of a relatively

[10] R. D. McKenzie, *The Metropolitan Community*, pp. 181, 246, 1933.

large amount of juvenile delinquency indicates that informal controls are breaking down or do not exist. If a small boy in a real neighborhood breaks a window, the chances are good that he will receive parental discipline and that some financial adjustment will be made with the owner of the damaged property. But in an area where people neither know nor trust one another such an event is more likely to be followed by a complaint to the police or the juvenile court. Thus a high juvenile court rate may indicate neighborhood disorganization rather than excessive delinquency; however, the latter may also occur.

As yet, it is too early to say with assurance that neighborhood groups and practices are disappearing from American cities, but such evidence as we possess indicates that they have been declining and may be expected to diminish further. Among the factors related to this apparent disintegration of neighborhood life is, first of all, mobility, which we shall discuss more fully in Chap. 13. Another aspect of the same phase of city life is the continuing invasions of residential districts. Few years pass without some new kinds of occupants or some new land use. The occurrence of these is doubtless related to immigration from rural America as well as from abroad, the centrifugal flight, obsolescence, and changing methods and routes of transportation. A third factor, related to the first two, is the dispersion of contacts and centers of activities. Many city dwellers have personal friends scattered over a metropolitan district rather than concentrated in a limited area. Their recreational and religious activities are carried on elsewhere. In the fourth place, it appears that special interest groups are increasing in number and in their demands on time, energy, and money, leaving less and less for local groups.

The significance of changes in urban neighborhoods for the persons who live in them has been the object of an inquiry of Deutschberger.[11] He studied census tracts in Pittsburgh and New York. Two in each city were undergoing marked changes; one in each city was relatively stable. In Pittsburgh Italian and Russian Jewish districts were being invaded by Negroes. In New York an Italian district was losing population rapidly and a Jewish district (occupied by Jews from Russia and Poland) was being invaded by Negroes and Latin Americans. The stable tracts were occupied predominantly by Russian Jews and Italians.

Deutschberger had questionnaires filled out by 480 boys and girls, aged nine to sixteen, on two occasions six months apart. They listed their best friends, indicated how much of their free time was spent with each friend, which of their friends went with one another, where each friend lived, and his religious affiliation. He analyzed these data by the use of

[11] Paul Deutschberger, "Interaction Patterns in Changing Neighborhoods: New York and Pittsburgh," *Sociometry*, 9 (1946), 303–315.

some simple formulas and arrived at the following conclusions. In the changing districts the range of friends was narrower, there were fewer friends of different races and religions, and fewer friends who lived in other districts. Those over the age of thirteen sought more group attachments in the changing districts than in the stable areas. The friendship range involved both the number of friends and the amount of time spent with them. This was not only lower in changing neighborhoods but tended further to contract. This meant that these boys and girls not only lost old friends of their own race and religion, but failed to replace them with new friends among the "invaders." "The findings suggest that members of the residual portion of the moving-out group in changing neighborhoods develop a growing sense of social isolation."[12]

Deutschberger's study is limited in that it deals only with three minority groups in two eastern cities, and by the fact that we have little evidence that the statistical areas employed (census tracts) correspond to what we have been calling neighborhoods. Nevertheless, his findings are rather challenging. His study should be repeated in other situations in order to see whether the results he found are unique or are common to changing neighborhoods of North American cities.

SELECTED READINGS

DAHIR, JAMES: *The Neighborhood Unit Plan: Its Spread and Acceptance,* Russell Sage Foundation, 1947. History and description of projects in the United States and abroad.

DEUTSCHBERGER, PAUL: "Interaction Patterns in Changing Neighborhoods: New York and Pittsburgh," *Sociometry,* 9 (1946), 303–315. A comparison of social relations in stable and changing districts.

DEWEY, RICHARD: "The Neighborhood, Urban Ecology and City Planners," *Amer. Sociol. Rev.,* 15 (1950), 502–507. Raises important questions about the practicability and possible consequences of establishing neighborhood units.

McCLENAHAN, BESSIE A.: *The Changing Urban Neighborhood,* University of Southern California Press, 1929. The rise and decline of a neighborhood in Los Angeles.

McKENZIE, R. D.: *The Neighborhood: A Study of Local Life in the City of Columbus, Ohio,* University of Chicago Press, 1923. A comparison of organized and disorganized neighborhoods.

ROPER, M. W.: *The City and the Primary Group,* University of Chicago Libraries, 1935. A study of neighborhoods in the Hyde Park section of Chicago.

SWEETSER, FRANK L., JR.: "A New Emphasis for Neighborhood Research," *Amer. Sociol. Rev.,* 7 (1942), 525–533. Proposes the hypothesis that primary contacts of persons in a local district are highly diversified.

[12] *Ibid.,* p. 314.

CHAPTER 12. *Blighted Areas and Social Disorganization*

In several of the preceding chapters we have commented on the variation in degrees of social organization in different parts of metropolitan areas. In particular we have noted the mobility, heterogeneity, and anonymity often found in the blighted areas that surround the central business districts. In this chapter we propose to review more systematically the characteristics of these zones of deterioration—physical, economic, demographic, and sociological—and to consider ways of determining how much of a liability they are.

CHARACTERISTICS OF BLIGHTED AREAS

Surrounding the central business district of the typical American city is a zone of deterioration. Its existence is due primarily to the expansion of commerce and industry and secondarily to the slowing down of this expansion. What we mean is this: As a town grows into a city, its stores, shops, warehouses, and factories spread into the residence sections. But they do not push out evenly or in a straight line. Instead, we see here and there small shops established in old dwellings and other structures. Some of them develop into successful businesses and take over additional space. Still other shops are set up apparently at random—though not actually so—until the old residential section is dotted with light manufacturing and commercial establishments. Naturally, old residents move out as they are able, leaving their houses vacant or converting them into tenements, as described in Chap. 8. Now if the city is growing rapidly, business will probably occupy nearby residential sections within a few years. Houses will not have had time to deteriorate excessively, and slums will not develop. But the expansion of commerce and industry may slow down, because the city ceases to grow so fast, because vertical expansion in tall buildings displaces horizontal expansion into new blocks, or because subcenters absorb new business which might otherwise flow downtown. When that happens, property is held a long time awaiting the

170

delayed rise in land values supposed to accompany commercial and industrial demands. Over the years, houses deteriorate excessively and come to be occupied by new sorts of people and groups with new folkways and institutions. Figure 16 is adapted from Henry Wright's graphic presentation of the changes that may be expected to occur in the near downtown sections of any large city of the United States.

The most obvious physical traits of a blighted area are usually near-

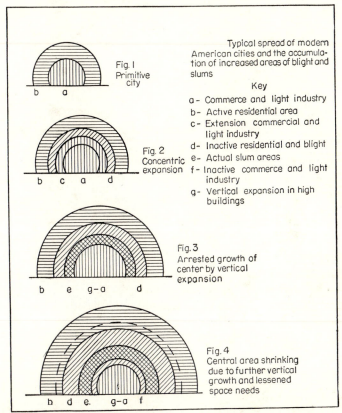

Fig. I
Primitive city
b   a

Typical spread of modern American cities and the accumulation of increased areas of blight and slums

Key

a- Commerce and light industry
b- Active residential area
c- Extension commercial and light industry
d- Inactive residential and blight
e- Actual slum areas
f- Inactive commerce and light industry
g- Vertical expansion in high buildings

Fig. 2
Concentric expansion
b   c   a   d

Fig. 3
Arrested growth of center by vertical expansion
b   e   g-a   d

Fig. 4
Central area shrinking due to further vertical growth and lessened space needs
b   d   e.   g-a   f

Fɪɢ. 16. Blighted area–pattern of development. (*Adapted by permission of Henry Wright.*)

ness to the business center and deteriorated buildings. Figure 17 shows the concentration of old houses in this part of the city. Parenthetically, it should be remembered that blighted areas may also be found in outlying parts of a metropolitan district, near industries, and along transportation routes. Their history and appearance are rather different from those of areas near the center. But both display a mixture of residential, commercial, and industrial land use. The dwellings are largely converted tenements, rooming houses, and alley dwellings. Visitors are impressed

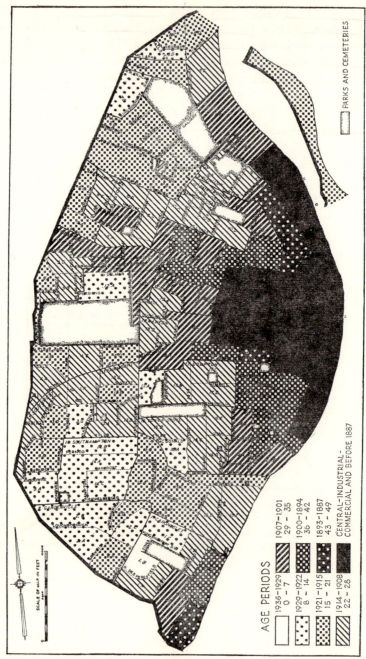

Fig. 17. Median age of dwellings, St. Louis, 1936.

with dirt, smoke, rubbish, noise, odors, and other marks of confusion and disorder. Those with more intimate knowledge report a scarcity of gas, electricity, telephones, running water, mechanical refrigeration, and central heating. They can tell of basement apartments, stove heat, kerosene lamps, faucets in the hall, toilets in the yard, broken stairs and windows. Parts of such a blighted area may be cut off from the rest of the city, the narrow streets poorly paved and poorly lighted being little used except by those who live or work in the district. Other parts may have widened streets that carry a large volume of traffic which has no relation to the district except to pass through.

Turning from the physical appearance to economic aspects of the blighted area, we find property held at high prices but bringing low returns. The high holding values are based in part on previous but principally on expected demand for commercial and industrial uses. The relatively low rents are due to the fact that few people live in such districts from choice. Most of those who dwell there are not able to pay much for their housing. They are people of low and irregular incomes. They are largely unskilled laborers, though some are ill-paid white-collar workers and others make their livings by unconventional means. These include "bookies," "policy" sellers, "dope" peddlers, prostitutes, pickpockets, gangsters, and racketeers. Some of these may have good-sized incomes and pay fairly high rents, while others lead a precarious existence. Employed women and unemployed men are relatively more numerous than in most parts of the city. In general, dependency rates are high (see Fig. 18). Many families and single individuals are on relief; many children are receiving foster care; large numbers attend free clinics. A little later we shall show that this is an area from which the city receives a small income (taxes collected) but in which it spends very large sums.

Demographically this is an area of declining population, partly because some dwellings are demolished but chiefly because of the centrifugal flight. This evacuation is going on so steadily that some owners of slum property and some realtors are seriously worried. Downtown merchants too might well be concerned. However, despite the falling off in actual numbers, the density of population is still relatively high. Both lots and rooms are more crowded than in other sections. Heterogeneity also marks the blighted area. Zorbaugh found 29 nationalities on the Near North Side of Chicago. In such a section are found the stragglers from ethnic groups that have passed on and the vanguard of new invaders, as well as any larger bodies that may be having their day. Marooned old families and newcomers, members of dominant groups, and stray individuals jostle one another on the street. Mingled with the others are those whose past or present lives render anonymity an asset.

Such a population is highly mobile. There is constant movement, some of it in and out of the district, some of it within the area: a perpetual search for a better house that does not exist, flight from collectors or from the law. In the Chicago rooming-house section which he studied, Zorbaugh found the turnover to be about 300 per cent a year. Other features that characterize the population of the blighted area as a whole are a high sex ratio (many more males than females); a small per-

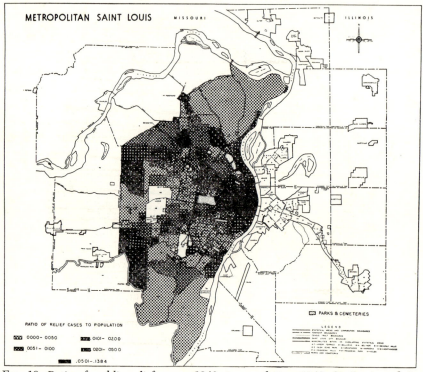

Fig. 18. Ratio of public relief cases, 1942, to population, 1940, St. Louis and St. Louis County.

centage of children; many old men but a predominance of young unmarried adults; high morbidity and mortality rates (see Fig. 19), especially high incidence of tuberculosis, venereal diseases, and suicide. In general it is an unbalanced population that is not perpetuating itself. However, different parts of the area vary considerably. An immigrant colony may have a normal population pyramid, which means approximately equal numbers of males and females and a fairly high birth rate.

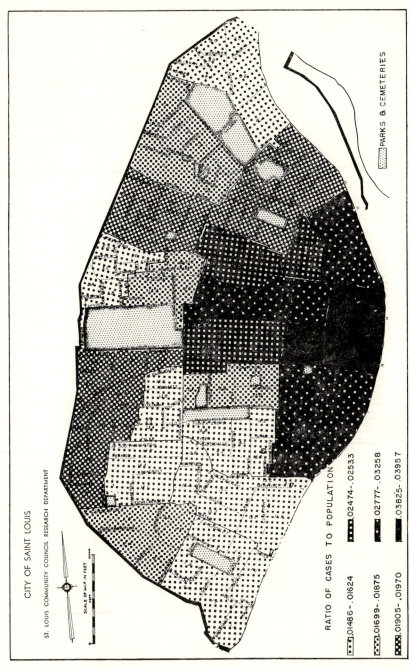

Fig. 19. Ratio of reported cases of communicable diseases to estimated population, St. Louis, 1943 to 1945.

Sociologically the blighted area is characterized by large numbers of detached individuals. Whether from choice or from necessity, the inhabitants have few acquaintances and fewer friends. Some of them are very lonesome, while others seem to be quite satisfied with their isolation. Social distance (mingling with other people yet keeping them at arm's length), anonymity (telling no one your past or your business), and mobility ("here today and gone tomorrow") pretty well characterize the life of many people who dwell in the blighted area of an American city. On the other hand, an ethnic community in the slum may display close social relations, warmth, and stability.

The human types represented in the blighted area have been suggested in naming some of the occupations. They include day laborers, domestic servants, clerks, waitresses, artists, young men and women who are just starting out for themselves, perennial failures, those who have seen better days, hoboes (men who wander and work), bums (men who neither wander nor work), Bohemians (people who "like to wear bow ties and expose themselves to temptation"), prostitutes, drug addicts, homosexuals, "ward heelers," old residents in the city, and recent arrivals from rural America or Europe. Such terms as these suggest the variety of personalities to be found in the near downtown sections of a city, but they do not constitute in any sense a classification.

The threats to personality that exist in rooming-house and other transient districts have been revealed in several studies of mental disorders.[1] Leaving to one side organic conditions and physical environments which may be associated with psychoses, let us consider cultural setting, group membership and participation, and person-to-person relationship. Faris and Dunham posit the hypothesis that schizophrenia is associated with personal isolation, that such isolation is most marked near the heart of a city, in blighted areas where rooming houses and converted tenements abound, where residential mobility and the sex ratio are high. Further evidence in support of Faris and Dunham's hyphothesis lies in their discovery that the incidence of schizophrenia in any district was highest among whatever population element was in the minority. Thus in a predominantly Negro district, schizophrenia occurred most frequently among the whites. The next problem was to discover whether the blighted area "produced" mental patients or "attracted" them. The findings of Faris and Dunham indicated that both things happened, but that most of the cases of mental breakdown occurred among persons who had lived for some time in the district. Figure 20 shows the spotty distribution of schizophrenics in one city. However,

---

[1] Robt. E. L. Faris and H. Warren Dunham, *Mental Disorders in Urban Areas,* 1939; Stuart A. Queen, "The Ecological Study of Mental Disorders," *Amer. Sociol. Rev.,* 5 (1940), 201–209.

comparison with other maps of St. Louis makes it apparent that this type of mental breakdown occurs most frequently in areas of high mobility and low economic status.

As to social groups, families are relatively few, often small, and quite varied. Immigrant families are apt to be patriarchal in character, above the city average in size, but frequently broken by desertion. Negro

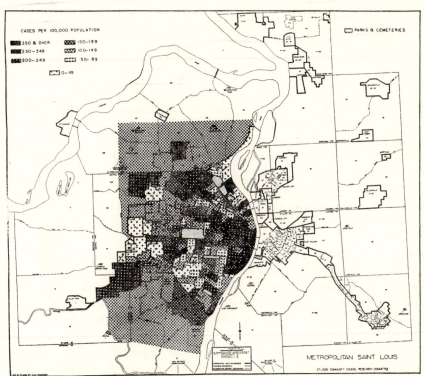

Fig. 20. Residential distribution of schizophrenic cases in public and private hospitals, St. Louis, 1931 to 1935. (*Based on Wm. L. J. Dee, An Ecological Study of Mental Disorders in Metropolitan St. Louis, unpublished master's thesis, Washington University, 1939.*)

families are sometimes large, but usually small, and often broken. Native white families are of the kind that Mowrer called "emancipated", *i.e.*, husband and wife both work, there are few children or none, divorce and desertion are common. Thrasher and Whyte have shown that gangs thrive in the blighted area, as in other districts described as "interstitial" (in between well-defined sections of the city).[2] Some of these gangs are

[2] Frederic M. Thrasher, *The Gang*, 1927; William F. Whyte, *Street Corner Society*, 1943.

fairly harmless play groups, others are definitely criminal in character; some are much like athletic clubs, others are deeply involved in politics. They represent the most vigorous groups in the blighted area, yet even they do not have a long life cycle. In general, neighboring is at a low ebb in the blighted area, though neighborhoods may be found in the midst of immigrant colonies. An ethnic group may maintain a local community here for some time, but it too seems doomed to pass away.

In a blighted area may be found three types of local institutions: those left over from an earlier day, those that develop spontaneously in a slum, and those brought in to overcome some aspects of the blight. By way of analogy, and semifacetiously, they might be called, respectively, vestigial, indigenous, and exotic. Those inherited from a more prosperous and more respectable past include metropolitan churches and public schools. The institutions that seem indigenous to the blighted area include secondhand stores, pawnshops, lodginghouses, cheap restaurants, shabby motion picture theaters, burlesque shows, "store front" churches, poolrooms, barber "colleges," taxi-dance halls, and houses of prostitution. Institutions of another sort are imported usually for the purpose of "uplifting" or "saving" the local inhabitants; these include missions and social settlements. The public schools gather in the children of the district, but they are controlled from the office of the board of education and seem hardly to belong to the area. The functioning of relief agency, police department, and juvenile court seems likewise depersonalized and remote. The mores of various groups are in conflict, detached individuals are little affected by any moral code, vice and crime are prevalent, social control is mechanical and weak.

The data pertaining to isolation, mobility, heterogeneity, broken homes, gangs, and low degrees of neighborhood and community life represent what is sometimes referred to as "social disorganization." In spite of individuals who have friends, families that hold together and live long at the same address, compact neighborhoods of fellow countrymen, youths who obey the law, and adults who earn their living by honest labor—in spite of all these, the blighted area is one of many social problems. The essence of the disorganization is that there is no "consensus," the people do not have common goals nor have they learned to work together.

MEASURING THE COST OF BLIGHT

In the 1930's there were some interesting attempts to determine what blighted areas cost the city. In part these grew out of a characteristic American desire to reduce things to a dollars and cents statement; in part they were an effort to determine what slum clearance and social reform will actually cost. If these can be projected as self-liquidating business ventures, this is one thing; but if they must be subsidized, either through governmental bounty or private philanthropy, that is another. Without in any wise belittling the role of humanitarians, it can safely be asserted that, if it can be shown that slum clearance will pay in dollars and cents, this will be a great advantage. In the first place, it will be easier to secure adherents to such a program. In the second place, it is hard to see how, in the long run, cities can afford projects which are not worth what they cost. This reduces our problem to one of method. How can we discover whether a city can afford slums or slum clearance? Before answering, we must find out as nearly as possible just what a slum area costs, over and above what it contributes to the maintenance of a city.

The first effort in this direction, so far as we are aware, was made in Cleveland by Rev. R. B. Navin and associates with the counsel of Howard W. Green.[3] They selected a slum area of some 300 acres, with 22,000 inhabitants, including 5,200 families. The area contained 2.5 per cent of the city's population and 0.75 per cent of its land area in 1930. In it were committed, over a twelve-year period, 21 per cent of all the murders. Eight undercover surveys located 26 per cent of all known houses of prostitution within its boundaries. During four years 7 per cent of all boys brought into juvenile court lived in this section. Ten per cent of reported unmarried mothers, 8 per cent of families on relief, 6 per cent of jobless workers were identified within this district. It was the home of one-eighth of all Clevelanders who died from tuberculosis. Thus it was clearly a slum area. In general it was a liability to the city, but how could this be determined more precisely?

The investigators first enumerated the costs to the county of direct services rendered in this district in 1932. These included mothers' pensions, juvenile court cases, tuberculosis cases, child welfare, soldiers' and sailors' relief. The figure arrived at was $176,000. This evidently did not include administrative costs, but only care given directly to persons living in the area. Next the investigators calculated the costs of direct services rendered by the city in the same year. These items included fire department, police department, ash and rubbish collection, garbage collection, street cleaning, street lighting, sewer maintenance, library, bathhouse, playgrounds, milk fund, and health department. The estimated total was $818,000.

The report of this study does not set forth the details of cost accounting which would enable us to know just how this part of the work was done. However, we are told that in computing the cost of fire protection, for example, there was a count of calls for fires, false alarms, unnecessary

[3] R. B. Navin, *et al.*, *An Analysis of a Slum Area in Cleveland*, prepared for the Cleveland Metropolitan Housing Authority, 1934.

calls of other sorts, grass fires, emergency calls (presumably not for fires), rubbish fires, dumps, and some others. The cost per call was computed (apparently for the whole city), and then the cost of all calls in this section. The layman can hardly expect to understand all the steps that must have been taken by the accountants, but the results may be accepted as approximately correct.

The third major item in this study was the cost of direct services from the board of education. Presumably this was computed by adding to the cost of maintaining schools that served only this district, shares of the cost of other schools in proportion to the number of children from this area, and shares of the attendance and school health services on a per capita basis. Again it appears that general administrative costs were omitted. This item of education came to $362,000 bringing the total for tax-supported services to $1,357,000.

From this figure there should, of course, be deducted the taxes paid by residents of the district or on property located in the district. The investigators chose to consider only taxes on real estate in the area. They found the assessed value of land and buildings to be $8,153,000. The tax rates per $1,000 of assessed value for the following tax authorities were added together: state, county, city, school board, library board. Perhaps the state was included on the ground that it was furnishing considerable sums for relief. The tax rate for 1931 and 1932 was $27.60. On this basis the tax-rate income was easily found to be $225,000. That was the amount of tax receipts which would have come in, had all real estate taxes levied been actually collected. But they were not all collected. Indeed, in 1932 the delinquent taxes had accumulated to the amount of $369,000, which is 164 per cent of the expected tax income for one year. This should be contrasted with a 97 per cent delinquency for the city as a whole. Green holds that "the tax-rate income is better than the actual income from taxes, since even though taxes become delinquent, they will have to be paid some time with accumulated interest."[4] Hence, if the district be credited with the tax-rate income of $225,000, the operating loss was $1,132,000.

But this was really not the whole cost of public service in the district, for various semiprivate agencies carried on several kinds of social work among its residents. Omitting all except community fund agencies—which included neighborhood centers, visiting nurses, the Associated Charities, and other family welfare societies—all together these rendered direct services estimated to have cost $362,000. This brings the total operating deficit for this district to approximately $1,500,000. This may be restated as a subsidy of $333 per family per year. In still another form, the net deficit, not counting community fund agencies, was 21 per cent of the

[4] From a personal letter to one of the authors.

appraised value of taxable land and buildings in the area. (Public and semipublic tax-exempt structures and land were omitted from the calculations.) This means that, if 1932 was a typical year, the governmental operating losses in and for the district would amount in five years to the total value of all privately owned property. This does not prove that the city could afford to buy and clear the area, but it brings us one step nearer to the question: What can the city best afford to do? As a matter of fact, Cleveland did decide to enter upon a program of slum clearance and rehousing, but this decision may have been affected by the possibility of securing Federal funds.

In commenting on their own work the investigators say:

> After so careful an analysis of a section of the Slum Area it might have been well to have analyzed another section of the city far removed from such conditions. Lacking such an analysis, rates have been calculated for the more important elements of cost and compared with rates similarly calculated for some of the nearby suburbs.[5]

Thus were computed the cost of fire and police protection per capita, per family, per $1,000 appraised value of land and buildings, per $1,000 appraised value of buildings, per capita per square mile. As an example of what these calculations revealed, fire protection cost, per $1,000 appraised value of real estate, $49.81 in the slum district, but only $2.59 for the city as a whole, and only $0.63 for a residential suburb. Police protection cost, per family, $57.60 in the slum district, $18.12 for the whole city, but only $3.63 in one of the suburbs. Surely no municipal government can afford to ignore such wide variations as these. The Cleveland study has been described as fully as it has because it was a pioneer undertaking and because it illustrates many of the problems and methods that must be considered.

A St. Louis study[6] profited by the preceding work in Cleveland. Funds were made available whereby 13 separate districts of St. Louis were examined in a manner similar to that described. Three districts were in the blighted area just outside the downtown section; two were well-established mid-town residential districts; one was still in process of development; one included apartments, hotels, and rather expensive single dwellings; five were representative industrial districts with rather small populations; and the last was the central business district. Thus it is possible from the St. Louis data to compare various sorts of areas.

In computing costs, the St. Louis City Plan Commission counted everything that enters into the municipality's budget, including general adminstration, debt service, courts, water department, art museum, zoo,

---

[5] Navin, *op. cit.*, p. 15.
[6] *Urban Land Policy*, St. Louis City Plan Commission, 1936; *A Year of City Planning*, St. Louis City Plan Commission, 1937.

and public schools. The inclusion or exclusion of some of these items would not affect the relative status of districts, but by taking account of them the commission was considering the total cost of local government. (The city of St. Louis is independent of St. Louis County.)

In regard to income, the St. Louis study differed from that in Cleveland not only by taking a five-year average (1930 to 1935), but also by including taxes on personal property (money, notes, vehicles, household goods, locally assessed public utilities), water rates, and miscellaneous sources of income such as license fees, hospital and golf course charges. Perhaps this accounts for the fact that the deficits of St. Louis slum areas were much less than those computed in Cleveland. In none of the St. Louis districts studied were the costs of government, as computed, more than 250 per cent of the tax income credited to the district.

In the report of the first Boston study, which covered six districts, the point is made that "as the districts vary considerably in size comparisons should be made, not by the total cost or income but by the ratios 'per capita' or 'per acre of gross area' or 'per acre of net area'."[7] Since the true business and industrial districts contain few residents, their costs were reported per acre and not per capita, which seems to us altogether sound. But the residential areas were reported both per acre and per capita. Incidentally, the business, industrial, high-rent residential, and miscellaneous residential districts showed favorable balances, while the suburban and low-rent residential districts showed deficits.

In 1936 the Boston City Planning Board reported an analysis of income and cost for all 127 census tracts which go to make up the city proper. The general findings of this more complete survey were forecast by the first study, except that for the whole city industrial districts show a net loss instead of a favorable balance. However, industrial districts differ from each other.

There remain several important questions to consider: Are we to concern ourselves with the various districts of a city as such or with their inhabitants? If we center attention on physical areas, is it legitimate to charge them with the expense of schools for children who would have to be educated no matter where they live, with pensions for handicapped persons who would be dependents no matter what their residence, with relief for unemployed men who might have difficulty in finding work anywhere, with prostitutes whose patrons come from "nice" districts, etc.? On the other hand, if we center attention on the people, is it fair to credit an area with the tax income from business properties or to debit it with the fire protection required by obsolete buildings? It must be confessed that the issue is very puzzling. All that seems clear is that

[7] *Report on the Income and Cost of Six Districts in the City of Boston,* Boston City Planning Board, p. 16, 1934.

industrial areas should be compared with other industrial areas as to costs per acre or per $1,000 assessed valuation, while residential districts should be compared with other residential districts as to costs per capita.

The second question is this: How great a deficit shall be considered excessive? It is unlikely that variations in income and standard of living will vanish. People will probably continue to group themselves somewhat according to economic levels; hence some areas will present great assets with few liabilities, while others will present great liabilities and few assets. In other words, some deviations in extent of needs and in capacity to pay for services may be considered normal. Furthermore, it seems to be generally accepted in America that the more fortunate should bear a large share of the costs of public and semipublic services. The question may be put in this form: How great a deviation (negative in capacity to pay, positive in services needed) shall be considered normal, and beyond what point shall it be regarded as pathological? That is, at what point does a deficit become great enough to warrant a given program of reorganization or reconstruction? Perhaps we might consider the second and third quartiles normal, the first pathological, and the fourth superior.

This brings us to the third question: How can we determine the possible financial benefits of a given program? If present assets and liabilities, or costs and contributions, have been computed, the next step is to estimate the probable initial outlay for renovation. If this is to include demolition, rehousing, revision of street plan, provision of open spaces, in whole or in part, there is a task primarily for engineers, architects, and accountants. The next step is to estimate the probable costs of public services over varying periods of time, contrasting how much they would probably be if the proposal were carried into effect and how much if it were not undertaken. Doubtless these can at best be only rough approximations and hence should be estimated conservatively. Then there must be an estimate of the relative costs of maintenance and depreciation, with and without the new program. Next is the calculation of probable changes in tax receipts.

Is this group of problems capable of solution as it has been stated? Perhaps not. It may well be that a census tract or even a large section of a city is too small a unit of area and population. For schools and roads and relief we have deliberately enlarged units of taxation and administration from township to county, to state, and even to nation. The principle has been that of equalization. It has rested on the assumption that need and capacity to pay are very unlikely to be evenly distributed or to show a high correlation. In the light of this experience and of the difficulties inherent in the major problem of this chapter, the issue may have to be completely restated or even abandoned.

Perhaps all we can profitably do about social needs on an ecological basis is to discover their distribution and thus locate the areas in which effort may wisely be concentrated, without any assumptions as to the size of units that may be expected to pay their own way. An even more difficult problem is that of determining the human costs of blighted areas. We may never reduce human deprivation, suffering, frustration, and conflict to dollars and cents. But there is plenty of evidence that all of these are heavily concentrated in the slums. Human lives as well as houses are blighted. Poverty, disease, vice, and crime are identified with far greater frequency in these areas than in other parts of the city.[8]

SELECTED READINGS

DEAN, JOHN P.: "The Myths of Housing Reform," *Amer. Sociol. Rev.*, 14 (1949), 281–288. Reports that "anticipated improvements in social welfare have failed to materialize" from new housing, thus questioning certain assumptions about causal relationships.

GALLION, ARTHUR B.: *The Urban Pattern*, D. Van Nostrand Company, Inc., 1950. Chapters 12 and 26 deal with the development and control of blighted areas.

NAVIN, ROBERT B.: *Analysis of a Slum Area*, Catholic University of America, 1934. Presents the methods and findings of the Cleveland study described in this chapter.

SCHULMAN, HARRY M.: *Slums of New York*, Albert & Charles Boni, Inc., 1938. Description of four slum areas in prosperity and depression.

WOOD, EDITH E.: *Slums and Blighted Areas in the United States*, U.S. Housing Authority, 1938. Deals primarily with physical and economic problems.

[8] This statement is well supported, but it needs to be qualified in two or three ways. First of all, it takes no cognizance of "white-collar crime" (mink coats, "outside activities" of tax collectors, etc.) nor of the fact that many patrons of prostitutes come from "nice" parts of town, nor of the broken windows and stolen fruits in suburban homes.

CHAPTER 13. *Physical Movement and Its Social Significance*

At various points in preceding chapters we have had occasion to discuss the physical movement of people and something of its social significance. In the present chapter we shall deal more systematically with movement of three kinds: (1) migration to and from cities, (2) change of residence within cities, and (3) daily coming and going within cities. As previously noted, immigration and rural-urban migration involve providing housing and other facilities for newcomers, require adjustments on their part, and sometimes precipitate conflict between old residents and new arrivals. Change of residence within a city is associated with centrifugal flight, search for more satisfactory living quarters, and limitations on local neighborhood and community life. Daily coming and going further restricts participation in local neighborhoods and communities; it involves the strain, confusion, and expense of traffic congestion, parking, and transit systems; it implies freedom to utilize facilities and associate with persons scattered over a metropolitan area.

MIGRATION TO AND FROM CITIES

In Part 2 of this book we pointed out that cities in general, and those of the United States in particular, have grown mainly by migration. The extent to which this is true has been effectively presented by the National Resources Committee.

It is safe to say that, with the exception of a few southern cities, a large share of the 1930 population of all large cities (ranging from 30 to 80 per cent for the individual cities) was born elsewhere. . . .
In general, the cities east of the Mississippi have a large fraction of their population (usually at least half of the total) born in the State of residence. Many of the cities north of the Mason-Dixon Line have also large proportions of foreign-born immigrants. In most of the south-eastern cities (except those in Florida) the population has grown chiefly by natural increases and by migra-

185

tion from within the State where the city is located. The population of the cities west of the Mississippi River, on the other hand, is largely native-born, but has been drawn from other States than the one in which the present city of residence is located. Without its population born outside California, Los Angeles would in 1930 have been a city of 250,000, instead of the fifth largest city in the United States with a total population of 1,238,000.[1]

This migration, which has contributed so heavily to the growth of our cities, has been of three main types: rural white, rural Negro, and foreign. All three types have appeared at all times in American history, but each of them has been most conspicuous during a particular period. The foreign-born immigrants came in greatest numbers from 1840 to 1915, starting with the potato famine in Ireland and the revolutions of continental Europe and ending with World War I. The Negroes have come to our cities in greatest numbers since 1915, supplying new industrial labor no longer provided by immigrants. In addition to migration *to* our cities, there have also been migration *from* cities to rural areas and migration *between* cities—not to mention change of residence *within* cities which will be discussed in the next section of this chapter.

Briefly to recapitulate the changes that have taken place since 1900, there was heavy migration into North American cities from southern and eastern Europe from the turn of the century to World War I. During the war there was much moving about (for which no reliable statistics are available), including a noticeable influx of southern Negroes into northern cities. In the 1920's there was a large net movement of farm people into urban areas. During the early years of the depression there was a back-to-the-farm movement; but only in 1932 was there a net shift away from cities. In the late 1930's the cityward trend was revived. (This is the period for which we have most adequate data.) During and after World War II, there was much moving about, with cities receiving most of the migrants, but many of them moving from one city to another.

Most of the data at our disposal indicate *net* movement and give little notion of the total number of moves made during a given period. But Hawley has made some estimates which are very helpful.[2] According to his calculations, the net migration of 6.3 million into cities of the United States between 1920 and 1930 involved a total of 31 million moves, and the net cityward migration of 2.2 million in the 1930's involved a total of 22 million moves.

Here are some further indications of the contribution to city growth made by migrants from various sources. In 1940, the United States

[1] National Resources Committee, *The Problems of a Changing Population*, pp. 99, 101, 1938. All this may be restated in terms of differential rates of net reproduction. Cities in general do not produce enough offspring to replace those who die. Rural districts in general produce enough offspring to maintain their own population and to send large numbers to the cities.

[2] Amos H. Hawley, *Human Ecology*, p. 331, 1950.

census reported, 8.3 million persons, constituting 11.1 per cent of the urban population, had been living in other counties, states, or countries in 1935.[3] Somewhat surprisingly this was more marked in the case of cities under 100,000 than in those over this size. In 1947, the census reported, one-fifth (19.7 per cent) of the urban population had moved from other counties since 1940.[4] In 1950, the census reported, 6 per cent of the urban population had been living in another county, state, or

Table 21. Residence in 1935 and 1940 of Migrants, Percentage Distribution

Residence in 1935	Residence in 1940			
	Cities of 100,000 or more	Smaller cities	Rural-nonfarm	Rural-farm
Total migrants................	100.0	100.0	100.0	100.0
Total urban:	70.2	67.9	54.1	26.8
Cities of 100,000 or more.......	32.3	33.0	28.7	12.1
Smaller cities................	37.9	34.9	25.4	14.8
Rural-nonfarm	16.6	18.7	25.6	12.0
Rural-farm	9.2	9.4	14.5	52.8
Inadequate reports............	3.9	3.9	5.9	8.4

SOURCE: Adapted from Bureau of the Census, *Population: Internal Migration, 1935 to 1940*, p. 4.

Table 22. Type of Migration by 1940 Residence of Migrants, Percentage Distribution

Type of migration	Residence in 1940			
	Cities of 100,000 or more	Smaller cities	Rural-nonfarm	Rural-farm
Total migrants................	100.0	100.0	100.0	100.0
Within a state................	39.5	58.9	64.5	70.2
Between contiguous states........	23.1	20.6	18.1	18.4
Between noncontiguous states.....	37.4	20.5	17.4	11.4

SOURCE: Adapted from Bureau of the Census, *Population: Internal Migration, 1935 to 1940*, p. 4.

country in 1949.[5] This means that, while a majority of our population is fairly stable, there is an enormous amount of moving about. But contrary to some impressions, more people move from city to city than from rural to urban areas—at least this is true for the period 1935 to 1940, for which we have most satisfactory data.[6]

Tables 21 and 22 support some of the foregoing propositions. Table 22

[3] Bureau of the Census, *Population: Internal Migration, 1935 to 1940*, p. 2.
[4] Bureau of the Census, *Current Population Reports*, Series P-20, No. 14, Apr. 15, 1948. This figure includes only those born on or before Apr. 1, 1940.
[5] Bureau of the Census, *Preliminary Reports*, Series PC-7, No. 1, Feb. 25, 1951.
[6] Bureau of the Census, *Population: Internal Migration, 1935 to 1940*, pp. 4, 7.

also shows that, at least for the period under study, cities drew more migrants from a distance than did rural areas, and large cities drew more migrants from a distance than did smaller cities. This corresponds to the findings of a study of migration to and from British cities published in 1885.[7] Another finding of the 1885 British study is supported by United States data for 1935 to 1940, namely, that more women than men migrate to cities.[8] This was true in the United States regardless of the size of community from which the migrants came; but women most outnumbered men among those who moved from rural areas to cities. Only in the matter of distance was the sex ratio reversed; among migrants into cities from noncontiguous states men slightly outnumbered women. However, most of the migrants proceeded only a short distance, again confirming the British study. Propositions two and three are further supported by United States census data for the period 1940 to 1947, previously cited. A fourth proposition, well established by data from many sources, is that migrants to cities are predominantly young adults.[9] The statements just made pertain specifically to cities in the sense of incorporated municipalities. But a special study of two states in 1947 indicates that some of them apply to metropolitan areas and that others probably do.[10] Using data for employed persons covered by Old Age and Survivor's Insurance in Ohio, Bogue found that both out-migration rates and in-migration rates were higher in metropolitan than in nonmetropolitan areas. Rates of migration were highest for workers between twenty and twenty-four years of age; they were definitely higher for men than for women.

Concerning the quality of people who move to cities, especially the rural-urban migrants, conflicting data compel us to suspend judgment. Thus a Virginia study indicated that it was the superior countryfolk who were going to the city.[11] Of the samples studied, 46 per cent of the persons considered upper class moved to the cities, 41 per cent of the middle class, and 38 per cent of the lower class. The three classes were identified with educational levels—college, high school, and elementary school, respectively. In contrast to the Virginia study, one made in Minnesota appeared "to show that children of successful farm families stay

[7] Noel P. Gist and L. A. Halbert, *Urban Society*, pp. 263–266, 2d ed., 1941, summarizes and discusses the study by Ravenstein originally published in *Jour. Royal Stat. Soc.*, 48 (1885), 167–235. By permission of The Thomas Y. Crowell Company.

[8] *Internal Migration, op. cit.*, pp. 5ff.

[9] Bureau of the Census, Current Population Reports, Series P-20, No. 36, p. 7, Dec. 9, 1951.

[10] Donald J. Bogue, *An Exploratory Study of Migration and Labor Mobility Using Social Security Data*, Scripps Foundation Studies in Population Distribution, No. 1, June, 1950.

[11] W. Gee and D. Runk, "Qualitative Selection in Cityward Migration," *Amer. Jour. Sociol.*, 37 (1931), 254–265.

on the farms more often, while those of the less successful families migrated to large industrial cities."[12] An Arkansas study contained within itself somewhat conflicting evidence.[13] It showed that, comparing different educational levels, the percentage of rural-urban migrants increased with the amount of schooling, but in absolute numbers persons with eighth-grade education or less constituted three-fifths of all those who moved to cities.

A study by Gist and Clark[14] involved one of the most promising methods yet applied to the problem of the quality of rural-urban migrants. In 1922–1923, psychological tests were given to pupils in certain rural and village schools in Kansas. Starting with records of these tests, Gist and Clark undertook to discover the present residence of as many of the subjects as possible. They succeeded in locating 2,544, of whom 964 had moved to cities. Then the urban migrants were compared with those who remained in the country. The results showed a mean intelligence quotient of 98.26 for those who had gone to the city and 94.78 for those who continued to be rural dwellers. At first glance the difference between the two seems slight, but it is statistically significant. Gist and Clark also found that the mean IQ of their subjects was higher in large than in small cities—99.31 in cities over 100,000, contrasted with 97.02 in cities under 10,000. Again the difference is small but statistically significant.

In another study, Gist, Pihlblad, and Gregory[15] used somewhat different methods but obtained very similar results. They gathered data concerning 5,461 persons who had been students in high school in 97 rural Missouri communities between 1920 and 1930. These persons were then classified according to their average grades in high school—actually each individual's average was divided by the average for the whole school, in order to correct for possible differences in standards of grading—according to the size of community in which they were living in 1938, distance from the community of origin, and occupation. The analysis showed that there was a direct association between the school grades and the size of community in which the former students were living in 1938; that is, the scholastic averages were highest in large cities, descending regularly through small cities and villages to lowest scholastic averages among those living on farms. There was a corresponding association with the range of migration or distance covered.

[12] C. C. Zimmerman, "The Migration to Towns and Cities," *Amer. Jour. Sociol.*, 33 (1927), 105–109.

[13] T. C. McCormick, "Urban Migration and Educational Selection," *Amer. Jour. Sociol.*, 39 (1933), 355–359.

[14] Noel P. Gist and Carroll D. Clark, "Intelligence as a Selective Factor in Rural-Urban Migration," *Amer. Jour. Sociol.*, 44 (1938), 36–58.

[15] Noel P. Gist, C. T. Pihlblad, and C. L. Gregory, *Selective Factors in Migration and Occupation*, 1943.

The average scholastic index increased regularly from the home community, through outlying parts of the home county, adjoining counties,
and other counties in the state; but the increase did not continue beyond
the boundaries of Missouri. The pattern of distribution was about the
same for both sexes. However, there were other differences; men
tended to leave the home community less frequently than women, but
when they did migrate they were inclined to travel greater distances.
Cities over 50,000 attracted more men, cities of 10,000 to 50,000 attracted more women, and those under 10,000 attracted the two sexes
in about equal proportions.

So far the bulk of the available data indicates that cities tend to draw
in the ablest young people from rural districts. But the samples may not
be representative, the criteria may be subject to question, and the rural-
urban differences are not great. Perhaps it is the extremes that migrate.

One additional study is cited, because it raises more questions than it
answers. It is a study of 1,100 eighth-grade school children in Knoxville
made by Mauldin in 1939.[16] Children born in Knoxville were compared
with those who moved in from rural, small urban, and metropolitan
districts. The average scholastic ratings were: natives 2.22, rural 2.19,
small urban 2.50, metropolitan 2.39. Thus, except for those from the open
country, migrant children did better than those born in Knoxville, but
those from small cities did better than children from the metropolitan
areas. We suspect that these data reflect the character of the various
schools rather than the native capacities of the pupils. Still more puzzling
is the finding that the longer children had lived in Knoxville, the poorer
their grades were. We would suspect that perhaps city life had proved to
be a demoralizing experience, were it not for the fact that the same
deterioration in schoolwork appeared among those who came from other
cities as among the rural-urban migrants. Clearly there is more work to
be done on this problem.

In earlier chapters we have stated that newcomers to a city are likely
to settle first in the zone of deterioration surrounding the central business
district. Historically this has been true both of immigrants from abroad
and of migrants from rural America. But there are indications that this
pattern of settlement is changing. Freedman's study of migrant population in Chicago, 1935 to 1940,[17] shows that while migrants of widely
different origins tend to be concentrated in limited parts of the city,
"these areas are not exclusively near the center of the city; they do not
follow the settlement pattern of older foreign migrants; and the
migrant populations are not distributed in a gradient pattern with

[16] W. Parker Mauldin, "A Sample Study of Migration to Knoxville, Tennessee,"
Social Forces, 18 (1940), 360–364.
[17] Ronald Freedman, *Recent Migration to Chicago*, 1950; "Distribution of Migrant
Population in Chicago," *Amer. Sociol. Rev.*, 13 (1948), 304–309.

reference to the center of the city."[18] These apparent changes are evidently associated with several other facts: there are more intercity than rural-urban migrants; intercity migration involves persons on a wide range of economic levels; immigration from abroad is both limited in numbers and highly selected, many migrants being professional people in the categories of refugees and displaced persons. Under these conditions we would not expect the entire "migrant zone," as Freedman called it, to be located in the area of deterioration, but rather in those parts of the city designated as most typically urban. That is, the newcomers tended to settle in districts characterized by rented living quarters, small dwelling units, large apartment buildings, rooming houses, and vacancies, where there is apt to be "a maximum of freedom from family or neighborhood social controls and a minimum of responsibility tying the individual to his home."[19] What all this will mean in terms of human personality and family and other groups is yet to be determined. But at least in Chicago, in 1940, the newcomers were not primarily slum dwellers. Many of them were on higher economic levels and already accustomed to living in cities. If the same things are going on in other cities, we may in the future be less concerned with adjustment of farm people to urban ways of life than with the relations among racial, religious, and economic groups. This, however, remains to be seen.

RESIDENTIAL MOBILITY WITHIN CITIES

In several of the preceding chapters we have called attention to the general fact of intracity mobility and its relation to. neighborhood and community organization. But until very recently we have had no inclusive data which might indicate how general are changes of residence within individual cities. In 1948 the U.S. Bureau of the Census issued one of its current population reports[20] which indicated that out of 79 million persons born on or before Apr. 1, 1940, and living in cities Apr. 1, 1947, nearly 27 million had changed houses within the same county during the seven-year period indicated. The number who remained in the same house was 31.4 million. Thus 46 per cent of the urban nonmigrants (persons remaining in the same county) had changed houses at least once during the seven years. This is about 6.6 per cent per year. Preliminary reports of the 1950 census show that of 94 million city dwellers one year old and over, 10.8 million had changed houses within the same county during the preceding year. This was 11.4 per cent of

[18] *Amer. Sociol. Rev.*, 13 (1948), 304. By permission of the University of Chicago Press.

[19] *Ibid.*, pp. 308–309. By permission of the University of Chicago Press.

[20] Bureau of the Census, Current Population Reports, Series P-20, No. 14, **Apr.** 15, 1948.

the total under consideration, or 12.4 per cent of the nonmigrants.[21] For separate metropolitan areas the corresponding rates of residential mobility ranged from 7 in Johnstown, Pa., to 23 in Miami, Fla.[22] These rates are lower than those derived from earlier studies. Perhaps the individual cities previously studied were not representative; perhaps during and since World War II the housing shortage has caused people to hold on to whatever quarters they occupied instead of moving as often as they had in the past. We are inclined to the latter interpretation.

One of the early studies of residential mobility was made in Columbus, Ohio, by McKenzie.[23] His attention had been called to the weakness of churches, trade-unions, and other voluntary associations when their local membership did not remain in a given area. He had observed the difficulty of creating interest in municipal affairs among people who move about a great deal. Hence he undertook to measure the residential mobility rates in different parts of the city and to discover their relation to various other social data.

The method he employed was the study of changes in lists of registered voters by precincts over a period of one year. Thus the 1917 list was checked against the 1918 list for each precinct. The percentage of names from the 1917 list that reappeared in 1918 was taken to represent the relative stability of one precinct as compared with another. This device obviously took no account of moves from house to house within a given precinct. Perhaps they are less important than changes covering a greater distance; nevertheless they may signify instability and lack of vital social connections. Furthermore, McKenzie's study took no account of persons ineligible to vote at all, or negligent about reregistering. There may have been many persons in both categories. Another possible criticism is that one year may not afford a fair test. Obviously the way to settle this issue is to study the changes in voters' lists for another year or for several years.

In Columbus, mobility, as identified, was high in sections surrounding the central business district and low in outlying parts of the city. Its correlation with economic status was decisive and negative, economic status being measured by the ratio of tax returns on household furniture to the number of registered voters. In other words, where houses were well furnished, mobility was low, and vice versa. Residential mobility showed a high positive correlation with dependency and delinquency.

---

[21] Bureau of the Census, 1950 Census of Population, Preliminary Reports, Series PC-7, No. 1, Feb. 25, 1951.

[22] Bureau of the Census, 1950 Census of Population, Preliminary Reports, Series PC-5.

[23] R. D. McKenzie, *The Neighborhood: A Study of Local Life in the City of Columbus, Ohio,* 1923. Data used by permission of the University of Chicago Press.

Where there was much moving about, there were many people on relief or in court.

A quite different procedure was employed by Lind in his study of residential mobility in Seattle.[24] He used school records, autobiographical material, and, to a limited extent, addresses of newspaper subscribers and patrons of the telephone company and municipal light department. From the school records he calculated the percentage of the annual enrollment that was in a given school at the end of the year. Thus in a mobile district he found that only 44 per cent of all the children who had been in the school at some time during the year were enrolled there in June; whereas in a stable district the percentage was 87. In general, districts with the highest mobility were near the downtown section and those of low mobility were outlying. However, there were some exceptions. One school near the center of the city and attended by Chinese and Japanese children showed little change in enrollment, while some schools in outlying districts where real estate was active showed a large number of transfers. It may be objected that this method of measuring mobility does not include single adults or families without children of school age. Nevertheless, it does cover a large part of the population.

An inquiry on a much smaller scale was made in Kansas City and Topeka.[25] Three pairs of precincts were studied to determine whether there was any relation between mobility and services requested of social work and public health agencies. In Kansas City, Mo., Kansas City, Kans., and Topeka, pairs of precincts were chosen so that in each city one precinct was the residence of many clients of agencies, while the other contained very few. Their selection also involved the attempt to eliminate such variables as race, nationality, education, and economic status. This effort was not wholly successful, but the inhabitants of all six precincts were white and overwhelmingly native born. There were no Negroes at all, and the few foreigners had been long in this country and were naturalized. In two pairs of precincts the family incomes were approximately the same. The lists of occupations were similar except for a slightly larger percentage of white-collar jobs in the A precincts (those with few clients of social agencies). Also there were more employed women and children in the B precincts (those receiving many services from agencies). As to education, there was little difference either in the average age of leaving school or in the grade attained. However, among children still in school there was somewhat more retardation and less acceleration in the B precincts. These data, together with facts concern-

[24] A. W. Lind, *A Study of Mobility of Population in Seattle*, 1925. Data used by permission of the University of Washington Press.

[25] Stuart A. Queen, "Segregation of Population Types in the Kansas City Area," *Pub. Amer. Sociol. Soc.*, 32 (1926), 230–232.

ing mobility, were secured by a house-to-house canvass and are important because of the definite effort to reduce the number of variables in the situation.

Residential mobility was measured in terms of length of residence in house, precinct, and city, and reregistration of voters; it was negatively correlated with ownership of homes and furniture, and continuity of employment. In general, the people who lived in the A districts had lived longer in the same house, precinct, and city than had those who lived in B districts. The percentages that had lived in the same place less than one year were distinctly greater in the B districts. These results seem decisive, provided length of residence is really a good index of mobility. The criticism has been made that length of past residence in one place is not a measure of future prospects or of habits of moving about. The objection would be valid if other indices of mobility did not yield the same results. In Kansas City, Mo., it was possible to check this in terms of the reregistration of voters in two successive years. In the A precinct 90 per cent of the 1924 voters were reregistered there in 1925, while in the B precinct the percentage was only 68. In the A precinct only 16 per cent of the 1925 voters were new to the district, while in the B precinct the percentage was 29. In all three pairs of districts, the ownership of homes and of furniture was greater in the A precincts. These are indirect measures of mobility, for we know that people who own their furniture are less likely to move than those who live in furnished rooms, and homeowners are less likely to move than are tenants.[26] Hence it seems to be established that residential mobility was greater in B districts than in A districts.

Occupational mobility corresponded rather closely to residential. Length of time in job and in type of work was markedly and consistently greater in A than in B precincts. Membership in local organizations differed in the same general fashion; that is, a larger percentage in the A precincts than in the B precincts belonged to church, lodge, or trade-union. Especially was there a larger percentage of those who were members of two or more organizations in the A districts. These items seem to us of even more significance than residential mobility, to which they are related. People who belong to local groups are believed to find in these organizations both material and moral support in time of trouble. Hence they do not have to turn so early or so frequently to the impersonal agencies of the city. This is as yet an unverified hypothesis, but we offer it as an important clue to the intimate relation between mobility and the services of social work and public health agencies.

---

[26] Whether this is a case of "a rolling stone gathers no moss" or of "a moss-covered stone does not roll," we are unable to say.

In 1933 Howard W. Green made a detailed study of residential mobility in metropolitan Cleveland on the basis of public utility records.[27] Specifically he identified moves by the turning on or off of gas and electric meters. This had the advantage of counting all moves of families that changed their address more than once during the year, but it had the disadvantage of missing rooming-house and hotel families, for which individual meters were not provided, and those too poor to pay for gas or electricity. We do not know how many Cleveland families in 1933 were cooking on wood or coal stoves and lighting their quarters with kerosene lamps, but we suspect that many of the unemployed and underemployed were without modern conveniences. Nevertheless, this study must have identified the great majority of changes of residence. Furthermore, it reported for the entire mertopolitan district families leaving and entering each census tract and civil division and families moving around within the tract.

With these and some additional data, Green devised several indices of instability. These included the percentage of increase or decrease in population 1920 to 1930, the percentage of change in number of families from April, 1930, to October, 1932, the percentage of change in number of families during 1933, the percentage of families owning their own homes, the percentage of residential units that were vacant in October, 1932. Finally he constructed an "instability ratio," which was the sum of a year's moves from a location within a tract plus moves to a location within the same tract, divided by the number of families living in the tract at a given date.

The most important findings of Green's study were these. Twenty-eight per cent of all families in metropolitan Cleveland moved somewhere during the year 1933. Almost nine-tenths of these moved from one place to another within the metropolitan area. Instability ratios for the 321 census tracts showed that there was a definite segregation of mobile families in certain districts and of stable families in others. Ratios varied from 106 to 19, but tracts with high ratios were not concentrated in any one section. Nevertheless, it does appear from Green's maps that tracts near the central business district tended to have higher instability ratios than tracts near the periphery of the metropolitan area.

In St. Louis a number of different kinds of data have been used in the effort to measure residential mobility. These included school transfers, "For Rent" advertisements in the newspapers, reports of bonded movers, and the city directory of householders. All but the last proved unsatisfactory. School data were confusing because of the segregation and

[27] Howard W. Green, *Movements of Families within the Cleveland Metropolitan District,* 1933. Data used by permission of the Real Property Inventory of Metropolitan Cleveland.

geographic overlapping of white and colored districts, plus the large number of parochial schools. Moreover, they gave no information about families without children in school. Newspaper advertisements obviously did not cover all vacancies. The records of bonded movers were also inadequate for our purpose; it is well known that many poor families move in a suitcase, wheelbarrow, or peddler's truck.

The method finally adopted by Cowgill[28] for a city-wide study over a one-year period was that of comparing directories for 1931 and 1932, classifying changes of address by census tracts, and computing the ratio of changes to the number of families enumerated in 1930. The principal limitation of this procedure is that no family was counted more than once, even though it may have moved several times during the year. In other words, it reports the number of mobile families, not the number of moves. However, it was deemed the most accurate method available. Furthermore, its validity was partially tested in two ways. The ratings of certain middle-class tracts (*i.e.*, near the city median as to rentals paid and values of homes owned) on three scales were compared. The three scales were those based on newspaper advertisements, movers' reports, and the directories. The comparison showed that the relative standing of given tracts was the same or very nearly the same no matter what measure was used. The second test was based on a house-to-house survey directed by Dr. H. I. Spector, assistant health commissioner of St. Louis. In addition to questions about health matters his schedule included these: How many times have you moved within the last two years? How long have you lived at the present address? This survey was made in a low economic area inhabited largely by Negroes. The total number of moves reported by 2,700 families was divided by the total number of families, and that quotient was divided by 2 in order to get an annual rate. The result was 0.471, which is surprisingly close to the ratio 0.460 arrived at by the directory method for the same district. From answers to the second question—How long have you lived at the present address? —a weighted average was computed. Assuming a constant turnover, or 100 per cent mobility in the 2.25 years indicated as the average length of residence, we arrive at a mobility rate for one year of 0.445. This again is close to the ratio computed by the directory method.

Figure 21 shows graphically the results of Cowgill's study. Observe that most of the tracts with high mobility were near the central business district and that the ratios tend to decline as we proceed toward the periphery. In addition to this graphic display, Cowgill computed rank correlations of mobility with several other series of data that have been assembled for St. Louis. These showed that mobility was high in areas

---

[28] Donald O. Cowgill, *Residential Mobility of an Urban Population*, unpublished master's thesis, Washington University, 1935.

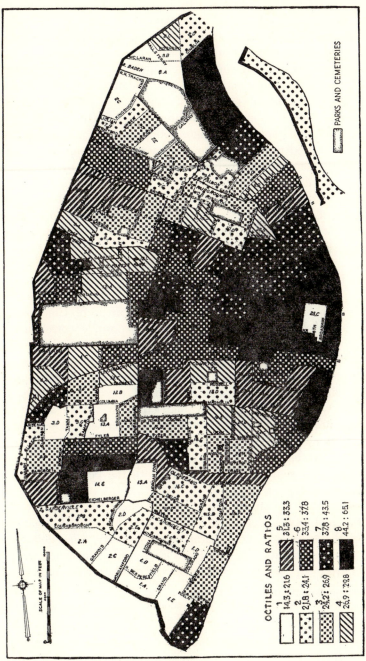

FIG. 21. Residential mobility, St. Louis, 1931–1932.

of low economic status, measured by home ownership, value of homes, rentals, families on relief, and employment of women. They demonstrated that mobility was low in areas of well-established family life, indicated by percentage of males married, size of family, numerical equality of the sexes, and single dwellings. They displayed a positive relation between mobility and death rates, tuberculosis, veneral disease, suicide, illiteracy, and the presence of Negroes.

In the preceding section of this chapter, we commented on Freedman's study of recent migrants to Chicago, noting that the newcomers tended to settle in limited portions of the city, marked by small dwelling units in large apartment buildings, by rooming houses, and by other distinctively urban features. These were spread from the central business district north and south along Lake Michigan; they were not concentrated in the zone of transition. Now we note that the districts into which newcomers moved also housed the more mobile elements of the nonmigrant population. In other words people who had recently come to the city and those who had changed residence within the city lived in the same districts. Referring to these as "inter-city migrants" and "intra-city migrants," Freedman computed rank correlations of the percentage of each with various characteristics of 75 community areas of Chicago.[29] The percentages of both categories showed high positive correlation with per cent of tenant-occupied dwelling units rented furnished, per cent of tenant-occupied dwelling units of one or two rooms, per cent of all dwelling units in apartment buildings with more than five units, per cent of all dwelling units vacant, and per cent of population (fifteen years and over) widowed, divorced, or married with spouse absent. Both categories showed significant negative correlation with households per lodger and per cent of population foreign-born white. "Average equivalent rental" showed a positive correlation with the per cent of intercity migrants, but no significant relationship with the per cent of intracity migrants.

From several of the studies cited it seems clear that, on an area basis, residential mobility is definitely associated with social disorganization and with the so-called "social pathologies"—poverty, vice, delinquency, disease, and deterioration of housing. Other studies to which we might have referred support this conclusion.[30] Together they indicate that

[29] Freedman, *Recent Migration to Chicago*, p. 165.

[30] Examples of ecological studies of residential mobility in relation to other features of urban life are the following: T. Earl Sullenger, "The Social Significance of Mobility: An Omaha Study," *Amer. Jour. Sociol.*, 55 (1950), 559–564; Elsa S. Longmoor and Erle F. Young, "Ecological Interrelationships of Juvenile Delinquency, Dependency and Population Mobility," *Amer. Jour. Sociol.*, 41 (1936), 598–610; Christopher Tietze, *et al.*, "Personality Disorder and Spatial Mobility," *Amer. Jour. Sociol.*, 48 (1942), 29–39; Stuart A. Queen, "The Ecological Study of Mental Disorders," *Amer. Sociol. Rev.*, 5 (1940), 201–209; Clarence W. Schroeder, "Mental Disorders in Cities," *Amer. Jour. Sociol.*, 48 (1942), 40–47.

much moving about often means lack of stable relationships with other people, which, in turn, means more frequent involvement in personal difficulties, less informal assistance, and more frequent appearance on the records of such formal agencies as juvenile courts, departments of public welfare, medical and psychiatric clinics, and hospitals. However, Freedman's study of Chicago suggests that we may be getting a new sort of mobile population whose life organization involves scattered contacts and frequent changes of base without maladjustment. Only further research can reveal whether or not this is true. Even if such is the case, we will almost certainly continue to have in our cities areas of high mobility which are also zones of deterioration, social disorganization, and personal maladjustment.

DAILY COMING AND GOING WITHIN CITIES

In addition to the kinds of movement referred to as migration (change of residence which involves entering or leaving a city) and residential mobility (change of residence within a city or metropolitan area), there is a third which consumes much time and energy of urban dwellers. It is the daily coming and going between home, work, recreation, and other activities variously designated as traffic or "fluidity." It has been said—not altogether facetiously—that millions of city people wear themselves out "shuttling back and forth daily between a place they would rather not live and a place they would rather not work." A hundred fifty years ago our cities were small, distances were short, and a little time sufficed to reach any point. The paths and narrow streets were often unpaved, sidewalks were crude or nonexistent. Nevertheless, afoot or in a horse-drawn vehicle, citizens got where they wanted to go without much delay. As numbers increased and areas expanded, some streets were widened and a few boulevards were laid out; much later came express highways. Streetcar lines developed with horse, cable, and electric power; first on the surface, later on elevated and subway tracks. In the twentieth century busses have been supplanting streetcars. Finally, we have a steady increase in the number of private automobiles. Not only is there traffic within the central city, but also much movement between the center and the suburbs. At first, commuters' trains were powered by steam, then they were electrified; now some are giving way to motor coaches and private automobiles.

In order to guide the planning of facilities for the masses of people who move about the city every day, traffic counts are taken from time to time. For our purposes, it will perhaps be enough to consider those pertaining to the central business district. Table 23 indicates for one city both the growth of traffic and changes in the means of transportation over a thirty-year period. During this time the total volume more than doubled, the use of streetcars declined, bus travel increased steadily, and the number of persons going downtown by private automobile multiplied fivefold. An analysis of the movement of persons in and out of the central business district of Chicago shows a similar trend.[31] Since the traffic structure of Chicago is rather different from that of St. Louis, we are including Table 24. The distinguishing feature is the number

Table 23. Persons Entering St. Louis Central Business District, 7A.M. to 7 P.M. Daily, 1916 to 1946, in Thousands

Year	Total	Means of transportation used			
		Private automobile	Streetcar	Bus	Miscellaneous*
1916	180	31	149		
1926	275	71	158	18	28
1937	310	140	84	37	49
1941	335	150	90	45	50
1946	375	160	110	65	40

SOURCE: St. Louis City Plan Commission, *Comprehensive City Plan*, p. 59, 1947.
* Includes trains and service cars but not pedestrians.

Table 24. Persons Entering Chicago Central Business District, Weekday in May, 1940

Means of Transportation	Persons
Chicago surface lines....................	213,000
Elevated, including interurban............	192,000
Busses, including out-of-town.............	63,000
Automobile and taxi.....................	256,000
Railroads, suburban and through..........	103,000
Pedestrian.............................	152,000
Total.............................	979,000

SOURCE: Gerald W. Breese, *The Daytime Population of the Central Business District of Chicago,* adapted from Table 15, pp. 106–109, 1949. By permission of the University of Chicago Press.

of commuters' trains which carried nearly 100,000 of the million people (979,000 to be exact) who daily entered the Loop.

Now the increasing numbers of passengers, especially the increasing number of automobiles, have created a traffic jam which is alleged to cause an economic loss of $2 billion a year.[32] For example, 50 persons may go downtown in 25 or 30 automobiles or in a single bus or streetcar. A street which can handle 2,500 persons an hour in private cars can probably transport 10,000 persons in busses and streetcars. The mone-

[31] Gerald W. Breese, *The Daytime Population of the Central Business District of Chicago,* Table 16, pp. 114–115, 1949.
[32] *Amer. Mercury,* 66 (1948), 151.

tary waste referred to involves the value of time lost in waiting for signals, the cost of time and money for parking, property damage, and personal injuries in traffic accidents. In the heart of the city, automobiles are definitely a liability; they do not even save time. For example, the Southern California Automobile Club estimated that in 1890 a horse and buggy on Broadway could go from 1st to 10th St. in 10 minutes and 21 seconds; in 1940 an automobile could cover the same distance in 14 minutes and 12 seconds.[33] In the face of these facts, one may well wonder why people continue to drive their own cars downtown. Perhaps it does something to one's sense of self-importance, perhaps it gives some independence of movement, but a more likely reason is that many persons are so badly served by the streetcars and busses or are so far from public transportation that they have little choice. Moreover, suppose that a suburbanite or even a resident of the inner city gives up his automobile. He risks the discontinuance of car lines or the change of bus routes which may leave him quite without public transportation or at least cause him great inconvenience. On the bus or streetcar, he may have to listen to radio advertising while he stands hanging to a strap, packed against other riders, jolted about, and breathing stale air. Despite all these inconveniences and hazards, more and more people crowd into our cities, and doubtless will continue to do so, unless the atom bomb destroys them or frightens them into decentralization.

SELECTED READINGS

Migration to and from Cities

BOGUE, DONALD J.: *An Exploratory Study of Migration and Labor Mobility Using Social Security Data,* Scripps Foundation Studies in Population Distribution, No. 1, June, 1950. Migration in and out of metropolitan and nonmetropolitan areas of Ohio and Michigan in 1947.

FREEDMAN, RONALD: *Recent Migration to Chicago,* University of Chicago Press, 1950. A unique study of intercity and intracity migration by local communities within the metropolitan area between 1935 and 1940.

GIST, NOEL P., C. T. PIHLBLAD, and CECIL L. GREGORY: *Selective Factors in Migration and Occupation,* University of Missouri, 1943. A study of rural-urban migration in relation to high school grades.

Population: Internal Migration, 1935 to 1940, U.S. Bureau of the Census, 1943. The most adequate data so far available on a nationwide basis.

The Problem of a Changing Population, Report of the Committee on Population Problems to the National Resources Committee, May, 1938. Note especially Chap. 3, "Trends in Population Distribution." Maps graphically depict population movements in different periods.

[33] Arthur B. Gallion, *The Urban Pattern,* p. 193, 1950.

Residential Mobility within Cities

QUEEN, STUART A.: "The Ecological Study of Mental Disorders," *Amer. Sociol. Rev.,* 5 (1940), 201–209. Discusses the relations between status and locus, mobility, and mental health.

QUINN, JAMES A.: *Human Ecology,* Prentice-Hall, Inc., 1950. A good discussion of intracity mobility is found in pp. 381–393.

STOUFFER, SAMUEL A.: "Intervening Opportunities: A Theory Relating Mobility and Distance," *Amer. Sociol. Rev.,* 5 (1940), 845–867. An unusual study testing a significant hypothesis.

SULLENGER, T. EARL: "The Social Significance of Mobility: An Omaha Study," *Amer. Jour. Sociol.,* 55 (1950), 559–564.

Daily Coming and Going: Traffic

BREESE, GERALD W.: *The Daytime Population of the Central Business District of Chicago with Particular Reference to the Factor of Transportation,* University of Chicago Press, 1949. Reports trends for the period 1926–1946.

GALLION, ARTHUR B.: *The Urban Pattern,* D. Van Nostrand Company, Inc., 1950. Chapters 14 and 23 deal with traffic, transportation, and parking.

New York's Commuters, Trends of Commuter Transportation in the New York Metropolitan Region, 1930–1950, Regional Plan Association, Bulletin No. 77, July, 1951.

PART 4

The Social Life of the City Dweller

CHAPTER 14

Making a Living

The making of a living poses a problem which must be met in every human community which survives. Industrialization and urbanization have at once enormously increased man's ability to produce the means of his sustenance and sharply reduced the individual's self-sufficiency. City dwellers would shortly die were it not for vastly complex economic organization based upon an intricate division of labor within the city, between ,cities, and between city and country. But the city dweller's job is not only the ticket of admission to sustenance for himself and his family; it is crucial in the determination of his way of life, his attitudes and values, his pattern of social participation, and his status in the city's hierarchy of prestige and power.

THE ECONOMIC ROLE OF THE CITY

As McKenzie has pointed out, the activities required to sustain any society involve two kinds of labor:

(1) the field work at the sources from which the basic materials are procured from nature; and (2) the center work where the raw materials are processed for consumption and where group services are performed.[1]

As industrialization has brought vast increase in wealth and complexity, two general tendencies are observable with regard to the production of goods and services:

(1) the proportion of labor required to obtain the original materials from nature is becoming relatively less than that required to fabricate them and to effect the various services demanded by a population with a rising standard of living; and (2) modern communications have so shrunken space that these center activities may be performed over wider areas than formerly.[2]

Whereas in 1820, 28 per cent of the labor force was employed in non-agricultural pursuits, by 1940, 81 per cent was so employed, and in 1950

[1] R. D. McKenzie, *The Metropolitan Community*, p. 50, 1933.
[2] *Ibid.*, pp. 50–51.

205

all but 13 per cent was nonagriculturally employed.[3] Mechanization of field industries, elaboration of transportation and communication, and intricate organization of trade and processing facilities have enabled well over 80 per cent of the labor force to be freed from field activities and to become integrated into the center work which is urbanism's economic function.

In Chap. 7 we considered the role of the metropolis as the effective center of dominance over the hinterland upon which it reciprocally depends for existence. Contemporary United States can be viewed as a closely articulated composite of metropolitan communities, each a functionally integrated unity of metropolis, subdominant cities and towns, and rural hinterland. While each metropolitan community is a kind of independent empire, internally self-sufficient in important measure, each also is integrated into a scheme of national and international division of labor and specialization of function. While Detroit services its hinterland and is enabled to exist by its reciprocal trade of goods and services with its hinterland, it exports to other metropolitan regions and nations its motor vehicles and imports from outside its region needed goods and services. Interregional imports and exports of goods and services generally flow through the metropolis which acts as principal middleman for the region as a whole.

The 138 principal cities, defined in terms of metropolitan areas,[4] had, in 1940, 51 per cent of the total population of the continental United States, 53 per cent of the population aged fourteen years and over, and 55 per cent of the population fourteen years and over in the labor force. In these 138 metropolitan areas were located 53 per cent of all retail establishments (1939), 61 per cent of all service establishments (1939), 60 per cent of all wholesale establishments, and 67 per cent of all manufacturing establishments (1939). The same 138 metropolitan areas accounted for 64 per cent of all retail sales (1939), 77 per cent of all the receipts of all service establishments (1939), 85 per cent of all wholesale sales (1939), 76 per cent of all bank deposits (1944), 65 per cent of all E bond sales (1944), 74 per cent of all value added by manufacture (1939), 65 per cent of all major war facilities projects (June, 1940 to

---

[3] Bureau of the Census, Series P-9, No. 11, *Trends in Proportion of the Nation's Labor Force Engaged in Agriculture: 1820–1940;* Series PC-7, No. 2, *Employment and Income in the United States, by Regions: 1950.*

[4] "The term 'metropolitan area' as used in this volume is a concept which includes entire counties. However, a county is included in a metropolitan area only when 50 per cent or more of its population was within the limits of a metropolitan *district* in 1940. The metropolitan *district* as defined for the 1940 Census of Population consisted of a *central city or cities having a population of 50,000 or more* and certain adjacent minor civil divisions or incorporated places. Ordinarily the adjacent places included only those *having a population of 150 or more per square mile.*" Bureau of the Census, *County Data Book,* p. v, 1947.

June, 1945), 88 per cent of all major war supply contracts for combat equipment (June, 1940 to September, 1945), and 77 per cent of all major war supply contracts for other than combat equipment (June, 1940 to September, 1945).[5] It is clear that (1) heavy industry and (2) wholesale trade are most sharply centralized in the metropolis, followed in order by (3) service facilities, (4) light and medium manufacturing, and (5) retail trade. It is clear also that the volume of production or sales per establishment is greater on the average in the metropolis than in smaller places.

Table 25. Retail Sales, by Type of Store, United States and 32 Standard Metropolitan Areas of 500,000 or More Population, 1948

Type of store	Retail sales in $1,000's		Metropolitan sales as per cent of U.S. total
	United States total	32 standard metropolitan areas	
Total, all retail stores.............	$130,520,548	$56,502,747	43.3
Food group......................	30,965,674	13,783,630	44.5
Automotive group...............	20,104,054	7,607,118	37.8
General merchandise group........	15,975,357	8,551,090	53.5
Lumber, building, hardware group..	11,151,470	2,844,111	25.5
Eating and drinking places........	10,683,324	5,464,264	51.1
Apparel group..................	9,803,218	5,230,197	53.4
Furniture, furnishings, appliances...	6,914,179	3,148,575	45.5
Gasoline service stations..........	6,483,301	2,141,319	33.0
Drugs and proprietary stores.......	4,013,231	1,828,786	45.6
Liquor stores...................	2,579,507	1,317,276	51.1
General stores..................	1,159,361	73,943	6.4
Secondhand stores...............	304,654	160,582	52.7
All other retail stores............	10,383,218	4,251,874	40.9

SOURCE: Data from Bureau of the Census, Bulletin No. I-R-O, *U.S. Census of Business, Retail Trade, U.S. Summary, 1948.* Population is according to preliminary figures from the 1950 Census of Population.

The 32 cities of half a million or more population, defined in terms of standard metropolitan areas,[6] had, in 1950, 37 per cent of the total population of the continental United States. As shown in Table 25, these 32

[5] Bureau of the Census, *County Data Book,* pp. 8–13, 1947.

[6] "Each standard metropolitan area contains at least one city of 50,000 or more. In general, each comprises an entire county or group of two or more contiguous counties that are economically and socially integrated. The outlying counties must meet several qualifications regarding population density and the volume of non-agricultural employment. In New England, standard metropolitan areas comprise groups of contiguous cities and towns." Bureau of the Census, Series PC-5, No. 1, *Characteristics of the Population of Akron, Ohio, Standard Metropolitan Area: April 1, 1950,* p. 3.

standard metropolitan areas accounted in 1948 for 43 per cent of the country's total retail sales, or one-sixth more than would be expected on the basis of their population. Of the 13 type groups of stores, the metropolitan areas dominated in 10, in relation to population. Only in three did the metropolitan areas account for less than 37 per cent of the sales: (1) lumber, building, hardware group, (2) gasoline service stations, (3) general stores. That the general store is rare in the metropolis is well known, although its function is in part served by the urban neighborhood drugstore, selling a variety of nondrug items. The dominance of gasoline service stations outside the metropolis is clearly a function of hinterland service to tourists, travelers, and truckers. The unexpected weakness of the metropolis in the retail lumber, building, and hardware group appears to reflect the greater use in the metropolis of wholesale channels of supply by builders and contractors. It is clear that it is in the speciality shops and services, apparel group, general merchandise group, liquor stores, and eating and drinking places that the metropolis draws retail trade most strongly from adjoining areas of its hinterland.

Although the 32 standard metropolitan districts of half a million or more population had in 1950 a little more than one-third of the total United States population, they accounted for nearly two-thirds of wholesale trade in 1948, as shown in Table 26. In none of 17 type groups of merchant wholesalers did they account for less than half of the volume of trade. The dominance of the city over the marketing of farm produce is clearly shown. In general, however, it is in the wholesale distribution of manufactured products that the 32 areas dominate most completely.

The 28 standard metropolitan areas of half a million or more population, for which manufacturing data were available, had, in 1950, 35 per cent of the total United States population. In 1947 these 28 areas accounted for 51 per cent of all manufacturing establishments and 52 per cent of the total value added by manufacturing. In 1939 the same areas accounted for 50 per cent of all manufacturing establishments and 54 per cent of the total value added by manufacturing.[7]

The direct dominance of the metropolis is postwar, as it was prewar, most marked in service and wholesaling functions, less in manufacturing, and least in retail trade. In all functions, save the field and extractive ones, the large city exercises a direct role out of proportion to the numbers of its population. Even with regard to field enterprises, the crucial marketing and financing functions are dominantly exercised by the metropolis.

[7] The four standard metropolitan areas of half a million or more population for which manufacturing data were not available were Dallas, Denver, San Diego, and Washington. Data are from Bureau of the Census, MC-201, *Census of Manufactures, 1947.*

Table 26. Wholesale Trade, by Type of Establishment, United States and 32 Standard Metropolitan Areas of 100,000 or More Population, 1948

Type of establishment	Wholesale sales in $1,000's		Metropolitan sales as per cent of U.S.total
	United States total	32 standard metropolitan areas	
Total, all merchant wholesalers......	$79,766,589	$52,346,116	65.6
Groceries, confectioneries, meats.....	11,356,738	6,168,181	54.3
Edible farm products..............	7,500,941	4,800,552	64.0
Farm products (raw materials)......	6,903,993	4,405,659	63.8
Machinery, equipment, supplies.....	6,731,372	4,122,077	61.2
Dry goods, apparel...............	5,727,719	5,300,040	92.5
Electrical goods..................	4,424,566	2,849,121	64.4
Automotive......................	4,091,589	2,108,129	51.5
Beer, wines, distilled spirits........	4,069,729	2,207,397	54.2
Lumber, construction materials......	3,934,736	2,521,564	64.1
Hardware, plumbing, heating.......	3,326,957	2,172,800	56.8
Waste materials..................	2,699,300	1,752,975	64.9
Tobacco and products (exc. leaf).....	2,529,576	1,306,541	51.7
Drugs, chemicals, allied products.....	2,282,226	1,641,640	71.9
Metals, metal work (exc. scrap)......	2,056,715	1,815,739	88.3
Paper and its products.............	1,901,747	1,439,322	75.7
Furniture, home furnishings.........	1,314,945	1,117,287	85.0
All other merchant wholesalers......	8,413,740	6,617,092	78.6

SOURCE: Data from Bureau of the Census, *U.S. Census of Business, Wholesale Trade, 1948.* Population is according to preliminary figures from the 1950 Census of Population.

OCCUPATIONS

Of the 150,697,000 persons tabulated as residents of the continental United States on Apr. 1, 1950, 64 per cent were classified as urban,[8] 21 per cent as rural-nonfarm, and 16 per cent as rural-farm. Among the urban population are a larger proportion aged fourteen and over than among rural-nonfarm and rural-farm population, as shown in Table 27. Rural-farm males fourteen and over have a higher proportion in the labor force and fewer unemployed than either urban or rural-nonfarm, a result, probably, of the lower rural percentage in school and the flexibility of family farms in absorbing otherwise unemployed family mem-

[8] "According to the new definition, the urban population comprises all persons living in (a) places of 2,500 inhabitants or more incorporated as cities, boroughs, and villages; (b) the densely settled suburban area, or urban fringe, incorporated or unincorporated, around cities of 50,000 or more; (c) unincorporated places of 2,500 inhabitants or more outside of any urban fringe; and (d) places of 2,500 inhabitants or more incorporated as towns except in New England, New York, and Wisconsin, where "towns" are simply minor civil divisions of counties. The remaining population is classified as rural" Bureau of the Census, Series PC-7, No. 1, *General Characteristics of the United States: April 1, 1950* (preliminary data), p. 3.

bers. The sharpest contrast between urban and rural is exhibited by the employment status of women. Percentages of female population aged fourteen years and over in the labor force drop from 33 per cent for urban to 23 per cent for rural-nonfarm to 16 per cent for rural-farm. Corresponding percentages keeping house rise from 53 to 61 to 67.

Table 27. Employment Status of the Population, by Sex, for the United States, Urban and Rural, 1950

Employment status	U.S. total	Urban	Rural-nonfarm	Rural-farm
Total population................	150,697,000	96,028,000	31,092,000	23,577,000
Total, 14 years and over........	111,915,000	73,730,000	21,970,000	16,215,000
Male, 14 years and over........	54,923,000	35,291,000	11,079,000	8,554,000
Female, 14 years and over.......	56,991,000	38,439,000	10,891,000	7,662,000
Per Cent Distribution				
Male, 14 years and over........	100.0	100.0	100.0	100.0
Total labor force...............	78.8	79.2	74.0	83.2
Civilian labor force...........	77.3	78.1	70.4	82.9
Employed.................	73.4	73.5	66.7	81.6
Unemployed..............	3.9	4.6	3.7	1.4
Not in labor force..............	21.2	20.8	26.0	16.8
Unable to work..............	.5.1	4.6	7.0	4.8
Inmate of institution.........	1.8	1.5	4.1	0.0
School, other, not reported....	14.3	14.7	14.9	12.1
Female, 14 years and over.......	100.0	100.0	100.0	100.0
Total labor force...............	28.6	32.6	23.3	16.4
Civilian labor force..........	28.6	32.6	23.2	16.3
Employed.................	27.2	31.0	22.0	15.9
Unemployed..............	1.3	1.6	1.1	0.4
Not in labor force..............	71.4	67.4	76.7	83.6
Keeping house..............	56.1	52.6	61.1	66.6
Unable to work..............	3.2	3.1	3.4	3.6
Inmate of institution.........	1.1	1.2	1.5	0.0

SOURCE: Data from Bureau of the Census, Series PC-7, No. 2, *Employment and Income in the United States, by Regions: 1950* (preliminary).

Of all employed workers in the United States in 1950, 71 per cent were private wage and salary workers, 10 per cent government workers, 17 per cent self-employed, and 2 per cent unpaid family workers. The corresponding 1940 percentages were, respectively, 67, 8, 22, and 3. There has been a continuation of the long-term trend in the United States toward decrease in self-employment and in employment in family enterprises. In the 57 largest standard metropolitan areas the percentages employed at each of the four work categories ranged, respectively, for private wage and salary workers from 55 to 86, for government workers from 5 to 39, for self-employed workers from 7 to 15, and for unpaid family workers from 0 to 1. In every case the metropolis had a smaller percentage than the United States total of unpaid family workers and self-employed workers, and a greater percentage of employed working for wages or salary. Between 1940 and 1950 the amount of this disparity between metropolis and nonmetropolis was reduced. It seems clear that the self-employed worker and unpaid family worker are primarily nonmetropolitan and nonurban phenomena, and are rapidly being reduced in both metropolitan and nonmetropolitan areas. Less than one out of

Table 28. Major Occupation Group of Employed Persons, United States, 1950 and 1940, and 57 Most Populous Standard Metropolitan Areas, 1950

Occupation group	United States, per cent		57 standard metropolitan areas,* 1950, per cent	
	1950	1940	Median	Range
Total employed, all occupations...............	100	100	100	100–100
Professional, technical, and kindred workers.....	9	8	10	6–15
Managers, officials, and proprietors, including farm.......................................	17	20	10	8–15
Clerical and kindred workers..................	12	10	15	9–27
Sales workers................................	7	7	8	6–11
Craftsmen, foremen, and kindred workers.......	14	11	16	12–20
Operatives and kindred workers...............	20	18	21	10–44
Private household workers.....................	3	5	2	1–6
Service workers, except private household......	7	7	9	5–14
Laborers, except mine........................	11	14	7	4–12
Occupation not reported......................	1	1	1	1–2

SOURCE: Data from Bureau of the Census, Series PC-7, No. 2 *Employment and Income in the United States, by Regions: 1950;* Series PC-7, No. 4, *Summary of Characteristics of Standard Metropolitan Areas: April 1, 1950.*

* The 57 standard metropolitan areas are those which in 1940 had populations of 250,000 or more.

eight wage and salary workers was in 1950 employed by local or national government, a ratio that approximately obtained in most metropolitan areas except for such centers of public administration as Washington. It is of interest that in Washington less than 40 per cent of workers were employed by government, the balance being employed in private trade, service, and manufacturing enterprises.[9]

In Table 28 are shown major occupation group data for the employed population of the United States and of the 57 most populous standard

[9] Bureau of the Census, Series PC-7, No. 2, *Employment and Income in the United States, by Regions: 1950;* Series PC-7, No. 4, *Summary of Characteristics of Standard Metropolitan Areas: April 1, 1950.*

metropolitan areas. In both metropolis and nonmetropolis, there were increases between 1940 and 1950 in the percentages employed as "professional, technical, and kindred workers," "clerical and kindred workers," "craftsmen, foremen, and kindred workers," and "operatives and kindred workers"; and decreases in the percentages employed as "managers, officials, and proprietors, including farm," "private household workers," and "laborers, except mine." There was between 1940 and 1950 an increase in both metropolis and nonmetropolis in percentages employed as "managers, officials, and proprietors, including farm." The trend away from agricultural, domestic, and unskilled labor characterized not only the metropolis but also the nonmetropolis, as the characteristically urban specialization in center occupations diffused outward from the metropolis. Women were employed more frequently than men, both in and out of the metropolis, as "professional, technical, and kindred workers," "clerical and kindred workers," "sales workers," "private household workers," and "service workers." Women between 1940 and 1950 were increasingly employed as "clerical and kindred workers," "sales workers," "craftsmen, foremen, and kindred workers," "operatives and kindred workers," and "service workers, except private household." There was in the ten-year period a sharp decline in the employment of women in domestic service and a sharp increase in employment of women in clerical and sales positions. The employment of women in operative, craftsmen, and foreman positions has shown a small but significant increase. In general, both in and out of the metropolis, the increases in employment of women, like those of men, have been in urban types of occupations.

In Table 29 are shown major industry group data for the employed population of the United States and for the 57 most populous metropolitan areas. The metropolitan areas contrast most sharply with the United States total with regard to the greater city percentages in such center industries as manufacturing, trade (particularly wholesale), and service enterprises. Between 1940 and 1950 there was an increase both in the United States total and in the 57 metropolitan areas in the percentage employed in construction, manufacturing, and trade; and a decrease in the percentage employed in service and other (primarily field) industries. Variability between cities was most marked in manufacturing, ranging from 7 per cent in Washington to 50 per cent in the Allentown-Bethlehem area. The high metropolitan percentage in "other industries" was primarily accounted for by employment in public administration in Washington. In both metropolis and nonmetropolis, women are employed disproportionately often in trade and service industries. Between 1940 and 1950 there was a sharp percentage decrease of female employment in service industries and small percentage increases in female employment in other industries, especially trade. There were small increases in the percentage of men employed in all industries except the field industries, where there was a marked decline.

Table 29. Major Industry Group of Employed Persons, United States, 1950 and 1940, and 57 Most Populous Standard Metropolitan Areas, 1950

Industry group	United States, per cent		57 standard metropolitan areas,* 1950, per cent	
	1950	1940	Median	Range
Total employed, all industry groups...........	100	100	100	100–100
Construction..............................	6	5	6	4–11
Manufacturing.............................	25	24	27	7–50
Durable goods...........................	13	11	13	2–45
Nondurable goods........................	12	12	12	4–36
Transportation, communication, and other public utilities.................................	8	7	9	5–16
Wholesale and retail trade..................	19	17	20	15–29
Service industries..........................	22	23	23	15–34
All other industries, including agriculture and mining.................................	19	24	7	4–30
Industry not reported......................	2	2	1	1–3

SOURCE: Data from Bureau of the Census, Series PC-7, No. 2, *Employment and Income in the United States, by Regions: 1950;* Series PC-7, No. 4, *Summary of Characteristics of Standard Metropolitan Areas: April 1, 1950.*
* The 57 standard metropolitan areas are those which in 1940 had populations of 250,000 or more.

To summarize, nearly two-thirds of the United States population reside in towns and cities of 2,500 and over, more than one-third live in great cities of half a million population or more, while less than one-sixth live on farms. Over three-fourths of males fourteen and over are gainfully employed, while more than one-quarter of women are so employed. Around one-third of urban women and one-sixth of rural women age fourteen and over are gainfully employed outside the home. Employment for wages and salary is more common in the city than in rural areas, but is increasingly characteristic of work in both areas. Self-employed workers and unpaid family workers are much commoner in rural areas than in cities but are sharply declining in both areas. Employment in the city is, much more frequently than in rural areas, at specialized jobs and much less frequently in proprietor or unskilled labor categories. Trends in both urban and rural areas are in the direction of larger percentages employed at specialized jobs other than proprietor or unskilled labor. In general, in both city and country, there is a shift of men away from agriculture and other field industries and a shift of women away from domestic service positions. In both city and country, there is a steady rise in the percentage of women gainfully employed. The occupation trends in both city and country appear to be in the direction of increasing specialization of labor, employment by others in larger and more complexly organized enterprises, and increasing impersonality of relationship between owner, manager, worker, and customer.

INCOMES AND PLANES OF LIVING

During 1949 the median family in the United States as a whole had an income of $3,068, while the median nonfarm family had an income of $3,245. In the highly urbanized Northeast, the median family income was $3,362, while in the less urbanized South, the median family income was $2,248. Incomes under $2,000 were reported for 30 per cent of all United States families and 26 per cent of nonfarm families. Incomes of $5,000 or more were reported for 20 per cent of all United States families and 22 per cent of nonfarm families. In the more urbanized Northeast, incomes under $2,000 were reported for 21 per cent of families and incomes of $5,000 or more were reported for 23 per cent of families. In the

Table 30. Income in 1949 of Families, United States and 57 Most Populous Standard Metropolitan Areas

	United States	57 standard metropolitan areas*	
		Median	Range
Median family income.....................	$3,068	$3,396	$2,395–$4,130
Per cent of families reporting 1949 incomes of:			
Less than $2,000........................	30	20	11–40
$2,000–$4,999..........................	50	56	45–63
$5,000 and over........................	20	23	12–38

Source: Data from Bureau of the Census, Series PC-7, No. 2, *Employment and Income in the United States, by Regions: 1950;* Series PC-7, No. 4, *Summary of Characteristics of Standard Metropolitan Areas: April 1, 1950.*
* The 57 standard metropolitan areas are those which in 1940 had populations of 250,000 or more.

less urbanized South, incomes under $2,000 were reported for 45 per cent of families and incomes of $5,000 or more were reported for 14 per cent of families.[10]

In Table 30 are shown 1949 family incomes in the United States and 57 most populous metropolitan areas. On the average, the metropolitan medians were well above the national median. Only in the southern cities

[10] Bureau of the Census, Series PC-7, No. 2, *Employment and Income in the United States, by Regions: 1950.*

did the percentage of families with incomes under $2,000 approach the national figure of 30 per cent. The marked variability in median family incomes among great cities appears to be primarily related to (1) region and (2) pattern of industry. Median family incomes of nonfarm families were in 1949 in the four major regions of the United States: West $3,499, North Central $3,407, Northeast $3,391, and South $2,622.[11] Regional variations for the 57 great cities show similar patterns, with cities of the West having the highest median family incomes, North Central cities next, Northeast cities third, and cities of the South low. In general, manufacturing cities, other than those characterized by heavy industry, appear to have lowest median family incomes. It is of interest that the national capital has the largest percentage of families with incomes of $5,000 or more. In general, it is clear that median family incomes in cities are on the average higher than in rural areas, and that the cities have a smaller percentage of families with incomes under $2,000 and a larger percentage of families with incomes over $5,000. Although differentials in cost of living and the underreporting by rural families of nonmoney income probably reduce somewhat the contrast in real income, there appears nevertheless to be a significant differential which has acted in all years except those of extreme depression to make rural-to-urban migration exceed the urban-to-rural movement. In general, the steady rise of urbanism and the city in the United States has been made possible by the more attractive incomes and planes of living of the city, which have acted as a constant magnet to rural residents. The low net reproduction rates of the city in contrast to rural areas would have made for decreasing percentages of population in the city were it not for the constant net migration toward the city, drawn primarily by economic advantage, real and imagined.

The higher plane of living of the city is not merely a function of higher average incomes. It is more economical to provide many of the goods and services demanded in present-day America in the densely settled city than in sparsely settled rural areas. Provision of electricity, water, education, telephone, delivery service, transportation, mail, protection, medical and dental care, and many other services is more difficult and more expensive in sparsely settled areas than in cities. Moreover, with the larger scale enterprises which cities can support, more elaborate and professionalized services are feasible than in rural areas. In 1940, 76 per cent of metropolitan dwelling units had private bathtub or shower in contrast to 33 per cent of nonmetropolitan dwelling units; 95 per cent of metropolitan and 61 per cent of nonmetropolitan units had electric lighting; 57 per cent of metropolitan and 30 per cent of nonmetropolitan occupied dwelling units had mechanical refrigeration. On Jan. 1, 1945, there were

[11] *Ibid.*

on the average, for every 100 occupied dwelling units, 59 residence tele-phones in metropolitan areas and 35 residence telephones in nonmetro-politan areas.[12]

In Table 31 are presented plane-of-living items for the United States, urban, rural-nonfarm, and farm for 1950, and for the United States for 1940. Although consistent increases in plane of living occurred between 1940 and 1950, the sharp disparity between urban and rural remains. Rural-nonfarm families occupy a position midway between the more privileged urban and the less privileged rural-farm families, as is ex-pected under the hypothesis of a rural-urban continuum. Urban occupied dwelling units are consistently less overcrowded, less dilapidated, much more often equipped with modern sanitary facilities, are more expensive to rent, and have a greater value. Substandard, dilapidated, overcrowded, outdoor-privy-equipped dwelling units are much more characteristic of rural areas than of cities. From the point of view of deteriorated, over-crowded, unsanitary housing, the slum is much more a rural character-istic than an urban one; much more a characteristic of farm than of nonfarm communities.

ECONOMIC CORRELATES OF THE RURAL-URBAN CONTINUUM

In Chap. 3, we presented evidence supporting the hypotheses (1) that there is a continuous gradation in United States communities from rural to urban and (2) that, as human communities are arrayed along this rural-urban continuum, consistent variations occur in patterns of be-havior. In testing our hypotheses we developed, utilizing a randomly representative sample of 100 United States counties and 1940 census data, an Index of Urbanism as a quantitative measure of ecological urbanism. We are now proposing to use our Index in further study of behavior variations which may be consistently associated with position on the rural-urban continuum.

In Fig. 22 are presented the scatter diagram and one of the lines of regression for each of six economic measures in relation to the Index of Urbanism. In Table 32 are shown eight correlation coefficients, including the six charted in Fig. 22 and two which were charted in Fig. 2. Most highly correlated with urbanism are nonfield employment, nonfarm resi-dence, and possession of private bath or shower, followed by possession of electricity. Nonfield employment, nonfarm residence, and electricity evidence similiar patterns of relationship, with geometric progression in urbanism associated with arithmetic progression in the economic meas-ure. Geometric progression in urbanism is associated with geometric progression in per cent of dwelling units possessing private bath or shower. Retail sales per capita (1948) and percentage employed in trade

[12] Bureau of the Census, *County Data Book*, pp. 8–13, 1947.

(1950) show approximately identical coefficients of correlation and patterns of relation with urbanism—geometric progression in urbanism is associated with arithmetic progression in each of the measures of trade. Straight-line arithmetic relationships obtain between urbanism and both employment of women and employment in manufacturing.

Reference was made in Chap. 3 to the study carried on by one of the authors in Grays Harbor County, Washington, in which 116 neighborhoods were scored with regard to position on the rural-urban continuum

Table 31. Selected Plane-of-living Items, for the United States, Urban and Rural, 1950 and 1940

Item	1950				1940 total
	Total	Urban	Rural-nonfarm	Rural-farm	
Per cent of occupied dwelling units with					
0.75 or less persons per room........	60	61	58	58	55
1.00 or less persons per room........	84	87	81	78	80
1.50 or less persons per room........	94	95	92	90	91
Nondilapidated condition...........	91	94	88	82	*
Private toilet and bath, and hot running water.....................	66	81	49	24	*
Hot and cold piped running water inside structure...................	71	85	53	29	*
Running water inside structure......	84	96	69	45	*
Private flush toilet inside structure....	73	87	56	29	60
Private bathtub or shower..........	71	84	55	31	57
Renter-occupied dwelling units:					
Mean contract rent per month......	*	$41	$28	*	*
Median contract rent per month.....	*	37	24	*	*
Owner-occupied dwelling units:					
Mean value.....................	*	$12,200	$7,200	*	*
Median value...................	*	8,400	4,900	*	*

Source: Data from Bureau of the Census, Series HC-5, No. 1, *Housing Characteristics of the United States: April 1, 1950.*
* Data not available.

Table 32. Correlations between the Index of Urbanism and Selected Economic Measures, 100 Randomly Representative United States Counties

Economic Measure	Coefficient of Correlation of Measure with Index of Urbanism
Percentage of employed in industries other than agriculture, mining, fishing, forestry, or logging (1940)............................	+.84
Percentage of population with nonfarm residence (1940)..........	+.82
Percentage of dwelling units with private bath or shower (1940)....	+.80
Percentage of dwelling units with electricity (1940)..............	+.73
Retail sales (in dollars) per capita (1948).......................	+.63
Percentage of employed in wholesale and retail trade (1940).......	+.61
Percentage of females 14 years and over in labor force (1940)......	+.58
Percentage of employed in manufacturing (1940).................	+.52

Source: Figures 2 and 22.

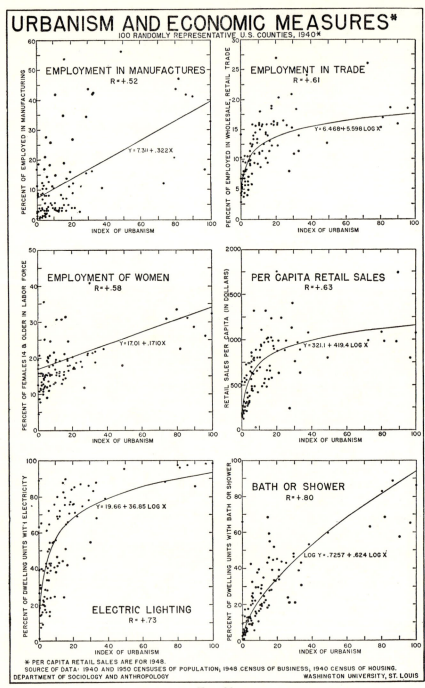

URBANISM AND ECONOMIC MEASURES*
100 RANDOMLY REPRESENTATIVE U.S. COUNTIES, 1940*

EMPLOYMENT IN MANUFACTURES
R = +.52
Y = 7.311 + .322X
PERCENT OF EMPLOYED IN MANUFACTURING
INDEX OF URBANISM

EMPLOYMENT IN TRADE
R = +.61
Y = 6.468 + 5.598 LOG X
PERCENT OF EMPLOYED IN WHOLESALE, RETAIL TRADE
INDEX OF URBANISM

EMPLOYMENT OF WOMEN
R = +.58
Y = 17.01 + .1710X
PERCENT OF FEMALES 14 & OLDER IN LABOR FORCE
INDEX OF URBANISM

PER CAPITA RETAIL SALES
R = +.63
Y = 321.1 + 419.4 LOG X
RETAIL SALES PER CAPITA (IN DOLLARS)
INDEX OF URBANISM

Y = 19.66 + 36.85 LOG X
ELECTRIC LIGHTING
R = +.73
PERCENT OF DWELLING UNITS WITH ELECTRICITY
INDEX OF URBANISM

BATH OR SHOWER
R = +.80
LOG Y = .7257 + .624 LOG X
PERCENT OF DWELLING UNITS WITH BATH OR SHOWER
INDEX OF URBANISM

* PER CAPITA RETAIL SALES ARE FOR 1948.
SOURCE OF DATA: 1940 AND 1950 CENSUSES OF POPULATION; 1948 CENSUS OF BUSINESS; 1940 CENSUS OF HOUSING.
DEPARTMENT OF SOCIOLOGY AND ANTHROPOLOGY   WASHINGTON UNIVERSITY, ST. LOUIS

FIG. 22.

as measured by an internally consistent scale made up of 24 component measures. In Table 33 are presented coefficients of linear correlation between rurality scores and scores on four internally consistent scales measuring aspects of economic status. It is clear that, in the study area, urbanism is positively associated with plane of living and occupational status and negatively associated with satisfaction and continuity of residence and job. The data suggest that, as one moves along the rural-urban continuum, one finds rising plane of living and occupational status, and declining stability and satisfaction with status.

Table 33. Correlations between Rurality and Selected Economic Measures, 116 Neighborhoods, Grays Harbor County, Washington, 1940

Scaled Continuum	Linear Coefficient of Correlation with Rurality
Satisfaction with residence and job	+.78
Continuity of residence and job	+.35
Occupational status	−.17
Plane of living	−.31

Source: Table 4.

As shown in Table 34 Fenton Keyes found a consistent increase in the availability of specialized services and stores associated with size of community. Of the 30 types of stores listed, all were present in all cities of 500,000 or more; 28 types in all cities of 250,000 and over; 21 types in all cities of 100,000 and over; 13 types in all cities of 50,000 and over; 8 types in all cities of 25,000 and over; 1 type in all cities of 10,000 and over. Only in the 100,000 and over classes did a majority of cities possess all 30 types of stores. These data illustrate the consistent rise in service and occupational specialization as communities are arrayed along the rural-urban continuum.

William F. Ogburn found associated with increase in United States city size in 1930: consistent increase in (1) annual earnings in manufacturing establishments; (2) annual earnings in retail stores, (3) values of homes owned, (4) median rents paid by families not owning their homes, (5) percentage of families owning or paying installments on radios, and (6) income taxpayers per 1,000 adult inhabitants.[13] Ogburn's findings corroborate more recent evidence of consistent increase in income and plane of living as one moves from more rural to more urban.

Available evidence confirms the existence of consistent variation in the United States in economic activity and status as one moves along a continuum from sparse settlement to dense settlement. In general as communities are arrayed along this rural-urban continuum, there appears to be consistent shift from family self-sufficiency to specialization of labor and economic interdependence; from extractive, field-type occupations to center-type occupations involving processing, distributive, and

[13] William F. Ogburn, *Social Characteristics of Cities*, The International City Managers' Association, Chicago, 1937.

Table 34. Percentage of Cities of Different Size Groups Possessing Specified Types of Stores, 1930

	Population, in thousands									
	2.0–2.5	2.5–5.0	5–10	10–25	25–50	50–100	100–250	250–500	500–1,000	1,000 and over
Number of cities studied...	580	1,440	880	614	185	98	56	24	8	5
Grocery store............	96	100	99	99	100	100	100	100	100	100
Drugstore...............	95	96	99	100	100	100	100	100	100	100
Filling station...........	93	96	99	99	100	100	100	100	100	100
Restaurant..............	91	91	97	99	100	100	100	100	100	100
Garage.................	83	89	95	96	100	99	100	100	100	100
Furniture store..........	74	80	87	93	98	99	100	100	100	100
Lumberyard.............	73	80	87	90	94	99	100	100	100	100
Farmer's supply store.....	69	73	79	87	95	93	100	100	100	100
Jewelry store............	66	76	85	93	99	100	100	100	100	100
Candy store.............	66	77	89	100	100	100	100	100	100	100
Dry goods store..........	66	73	85	91	88	95	100	100	100	100
Variety store............	63	70	81	93	95	96	100	100	100	100
General merchandise store.	60	51	64	85	83	86	92	100	100	100
Meat store..............	60	69	81	91	99	100	100	100	100	100
Men's store.............	54	68	96	93	98	99	100	100	100	100
Radio store.............	48	58	79	94	100	100	100	100	100	100
Household appliance store.	45	60	88	85	89	95	100	100	100	100
Heating and plumbing....	44	56	74	86	94	92	100	100	100	100
Coal distributor..........	43	56	70	84	94	99	92	99	100	100
Automobile sales.........	41	55	79	95	99	100	100	100	100	100
Shoe store..............	39	53	80	99	100	100	100	100	100	100
Women's ready-to-wear...	39	43	83	91	98	100	100	100	100	100
Women's accessories......	39	43	71	92	94	98	99	100	100	100
Cigar store.............	39	45	65	84	97	100	100	100	100	100
Hardware store..........	23	60	87	95	99	100	100	100	100	100
Electrical store..........	15	27	45	64	63	68	93	100	100	100
Paint store..............	15	26	47	79	90	96	100	100	100	100
Department store........	10	21	45	68	78	78	98	100	100	100
Book store.............	7	25	25	37	61	75	96	100	100	100
Floor covering store.....	1	2	6	24	36	43	86	88	100	100

SOURCE: Adapted from Fenton Keyes, *The Correlation of Social Phenomena with Community Size*, unpublished doctoral dissertation, Yale University, p. 6, 1942. By permission of the author and Yale University.

service enterprises; from self-employment and family-sized enterprises to wage employment in complex enterprises in which formal relationships between worker, management, and ownership obtain; from community-wide economic associations to segmental economic associations which represent specialized occupational categories, such as Barbers' Union,

Restaurant Owners' Association, Real Estate Board, or Bar Association; from continuity of employment to occupational mobility; from lower income and plane of living to higher income and plane of living; from informal economic relations between friends and neighbors to formalized economic relations between strangers. In general, the secular trend at all points on the continuum appears to have been, and to continue to be, in the direction of the urban types of economic relationships.

ECONOMIC VARIABILITY WITHIN THE CITY

In previous chapters we have examined the patterns of facility and residential localization in the metropolis and the processes of invasion and succession by which the spatial organization of the city constantly mirrors changes in population, economy, and institutional values. As shown in Table 35, Calvin F. Schmid has systematically studied inter-

Table 35. Highest, Mid-rank, and Lowest Rectilinear Coefficients of Correlation between Mean Rent and 11 Other Indices for Census Tracts of 23 Cities, 1940

Index	Coefficient of correlation with mean rent		
	Highest	Mid-rank	Lowest
Percentage of labor force classified as proprietors, managers, and officials..............................	+.98	+.90	+.80
Percentage of population 25 years of age and over classified as college graduates........................	+.95	+.90	+.79
Percentage of labor force classified as professional workers.......................................	+.91	+.90	+.79
Percentage of total population 60 years of age or over	+.89	+.23	−.46
Percentage of total population classified foreign-born white..	−.64	−.60	−.15
Ratio of children under 5 to females 15 to 44 years of age	−.71	−.51	−.04
Percentage of labor force classified as laborers........	−.75	−.66	−.50
Percentage of total population classified as males......	−.75	−.50	−.07
Percentage of total population under 15 years of age...	−.77	−.41	+.24
Percentage of total population classified as Negro......	−.78	−.39	−.18
Percentage of labor force seeking work (unemployed)..	−.93	−.77	−.67

SOURCE: Adapted from Calvin F. Schmid, "Generalizations concerning the Ecology of the American City," *Amer. Sociol. Rev.*, 15 (1950), 264–281. Only cities with 10 per cent or more foreign-born white or 9 per cent or more Negro were included among those analyzed for those indices. Cities analyzed included 20 in the population class of Seattle together with Detroit, Berkeley, and Macon. By permission of the *American Sociological Review*.

correlations between mean rent and other variables by census tracts for 23 United States cities, utilizing 1940 census data. In 1940, rent controls had not yet destroyed the value of mean rent as an index of plane of living and economic status, as evidenced by the consistently high positive intercorrelations between mean rent and percentages of (1) proprietors, managers, and officials, (2) college graduates, and (3) professional workers; and the consistently high negative correlation between mean rent and percentages (1) seeking work and (2) laborers.

As we shall develop much more fully in the following chapter, the metropolis is a mosaic of economically and socially distinct groupings and natural areas, functionally integrated but socially separated. In contrast to the folk community, the metropolis has achieved closely articulated division of labor without breaching sharp social distance between groups distinct in their respective economic status, religion, national tradition, and values. And of all characteristics which play roles in this urban segmentation, none appears to be more important than the job of the chief breadwinner of the urban family. The intricate occupational specialization of labor of the city is paralleled by an intricate pattern of status assignments and a complex hierarchy of social groupings, within which lie subtle systems of social attraction and repulsion, acceptance and rejection, accommodation and conflict.

SELECTED READINGS

Bogue, Don J.: *The Structure of the Metropolitan Community*, University of Michigan, Ann Arbor, 1949. Analyzes the functional interrelationship of the parts of the metropolitan region with special reference to population and four major sustenance activities: retail trade, services, wholesale trade, and manufactures.

Lynd, Robert S., and Helen M. Lynd: *Middletown in Transition*, Harcourt, Brace and Company, Inc., 1937. A study of the impact of the depression on the social structure of a small Middle Western city. Particularly pertinent are Chap. II "Getting a Living"; Chap. III "The X Family: A Pattern of Business-class Control"; Chap. XII "The Middletown Spirit"; Chap. XIII "Middletown Faces Both Ways."

McKenzie, R. D.: *The Metropolitan Community*, McGraw-Hill Book Company, Inc., 1933. One of the monographs in the series sponsored by President Hoover's Committee on Recent Social Trends, McKenzie's work has emerged as the classic study of the structure of the metropolitan region. The emphasis of the work is economic and ecological.

Ogburn, William F.: *Social Characteristics of Cities*, The International City Managers' Association, Chicago, 1937. Ogburn, utilizing primarily 1930 census data, attempts to account for the variability between cities by comparison of cities of various sizes, several regions, different economic bases, increasing and decreasing, size, etc.

Bureau of the Census, Series PC-7, No. 2, *Employment and Income in the United States, by Regions: 1950*, Washington, 1951. Presents preliminary 1950 data by region, color, and sex for employment status, class of worker, major occupation group, major industry group, and income. Some 1940 data are presented for comparative purposes.

CHAPTER 15. *Achieving Status*

According to the Bible, "Unto every one that hath shall be given, and he shall have abundance; but from him that hath not shall be taken away even that which he hath."[1] It has elsewhere been observed that those persons who possess most bountifully the desiderata of any society in one regard tend to possess more frequently than can be accounted for by chance the desiderata of that society in other regards. While students of social anthropology and comparative sociology have documented the very great variability of value and goal systems among human societies, prestige and influence appear to occupy high positions in the effective value hierarchies of all known human social systems.

Within any system of interaction between human beings, rarely, if ever, do all participants exercise equal power or influence or receive equal deference. It appears, moreover, that the hierarchies of prestige and influence positions within the groups in any community or society are overlapping. "Interlocking directorships" appear to characterize not only corporate organization in the contemporary United States, but human groupings more generally. Students of the community have tended to find a hierarchy of prestige and influence for the community as a whole—possession of high prestige in one group tends to be positively associated with possession of high prestige in other groups in the community; possession of much influence in one group tends to be positively associated with possession of much influence in other groups in the community. This observed clustering of prestige and influence statuses forms the focus of much of the literature of social stratification.

It has further been observed that the amount of interaction between the members of any society tends to be directly associated with the degree of proximity of members with regard to prestige and influence positions. This "birds of a feather flock together" concept forms the basis of class identification in important recent research in the field of strati-

[1] Matt. 25: 29; Mark 4: 25.

fication. It appears, however, that what have been identified in the United States have been prestige and influence *continua* rather than social classes in any substantive sense.

Hatt and Reiss have recently argued that as one moves from rural to urban, personal reputation of the individual becomes less important, and such objective characteristics as occupation, plane of living, and formal authority position become more important in a community's system of composite status assignment. They also argue that as one approaches the urban end of the rural-urban continuum vertical social mobility increases.

This difference in stratification [between the small community and the large urban settlement or still larger mass society] can be traced to two fundamental differences between the small local community and the urban center. These are the degree to which the division of labor is elaborated and the amount of anonymity present. As the community decreases in size, there is less and less division of labor actually present in the locality. This relative homogeneity in conjunction with the smaller number of people involved and the effect of sheer propinquity, serves to increase the amount and depth of interpersonal knowledge and interaction. This then makes possible the development of a rating system within the community which employs, not only the more "objective statuses," but also the personal reputation of the individual.

As the locality increases in size, the opposite characteristics appear. Increased heterogeneity associated with a more complex division of labor, greater cultural diversity, and increased numbers of persons and distance, all decrease the possibility and, indeed, the relevance of interpersonal knowledge. The segmented quality of urban interaction therefore emphasizes the importance of the more "objective statuses" for individual identification. There is thus a greater tendency to think of urban stratification in terms of impersonal statuses or institutional niches rather than as a system of rated individuals. In larger cities stratification tends to be analyzed in terms of typical groups of statuses usually associated with economic, political or other advantages.

. . . In modern stratified urban communities the tendency to change one's social position is more marked than in small-scale societies. Individuals seek to improve their statuses by moving to communities where opportunities are prevalent and by changing their occupation for one which provides increased economic power or confers more prestige. Concomitantly, the risk involved in holding one's position is likewise greater and individuals often surrender or lose their position in status struggle. Such changes in position are due to a number of factors, viz., changes in the size and composition of the class and status structure, changes in the relative prestige accorded positions in the structure and by manipulation of specific technical and social skills within an established structure. . . .[2]

[2] Paul K. Hatt and Albert J. Reiss, Jr., "The Status Structure and Processes," in Paul K. Hatt and Albert J. Reiss, Jr., Editors, *Reader in Urban Sociology*, pp. 344–345, 1951. By permission of The Free Press, Glencoe, Ill.

In order to see how status systems and the community position of given types of persons vary on the rural-urban continuum, a series of empirical studies will be summarized and the pattern of their findings analyzed.

REPRESENTATIVE STUDIES OF LOCAL STATUS SYSTEMS

The 12 studies summarized have been selected to provide maximum heterogeneity with regard to size of community, region of location, conceptual framework, and methodology. The studies are arranged in ascending order of the size of the most populous settlement in the subject area.

Plainville, Missouri (275).[3] This is a study of a small trade center and its hinterland of approximately 200 farms, located at the border of the corn belt and Ozarks, made originally by its anthropologist author as an acculturation study of the impact on an isolated agricultural community of urbanizing influences. The author was drawn through his research experience to focus on the problems of stratification and socialization. Plainville had originally been selected as a community lacking social classes, a characteristic confirmed by all of West's early informants. Utilizing participant-observation, paid and unpaid informants, informal interviewing, life histories, and available documentary sources, West sought to identify the enormously complex system of discrimination, which he discovered early in his field work.

West found a class system which provided for every member of the 300 households of Plainville and its trade area

. . . a master pattern for arranging according to relative rank every other individual, and every family, clique, lodge, club, church, and other organization or association in Plainville society. It provides also a set of patterns for expected behavior according to class, and a way of judging all norms and deviations from these norms in individual behavior.[4]

West identified three classes: upper class, good lower-class people, and lower element. Criteria found to be utilized by West's informants and interviewees in ranking their fellows were: (1) prairie or hill location, (2) degree of utilization of farm machinery, (3) lineage, (4) worth or wealth, (5) morals, and (6) manners. Manners were found to be of most importance in separation of the upper class from the lower class. The lower class was subdivided by informants primarily on the basis of morality. West found that those of higher status spoke more clearly and frankly about the class system than their inferiors, and that leaders

[3] James West, *Plainville, U.S.A.*, 1945. The author's and town's names are pseudonyms. By permission of Columbia University Press.
[4] *Ibid.*, p. 115. By permission of Columbia University Press.

understood the system better than did others, since they had to know and use it in the successful manipulation of people.

In spite of Plainville's credo that "anybody can rise," practically, the two main classes formed rigidly exclusive systems, with mobility from lower class to upper class virtually impossible without leaving the community. Social mobility between the two sectors of the lower class was found to be relatively easy in Plainville, a matter most commonly of religious conversion. Vertical mobility from lower to upper class via migration was found to be generally illusory. According to West, the youthful migrant to the city from Plainville was under the erroneous conception that there was only one kind of urban prestige, which was based on money. This misconception he found to account in part for the limited status achievements of most Plainville youth of all classes who sought opportunity in the city. West observed that urban social classes equated poorly with rural social classes, and that city people tended to class all rural migrants as countrified or as "hicks." In general, it was found that Plainvillers identified with the city working classes, but with a greater valuation of individualism and property, and less sympathy toward organized labor.

Vermont Village (1,000).[5] The interest in this study was the identification of the intricate network of informal relationships in the study community, popularity and power position in that system of relationships, and factors associated with position in the informal social structure. Ninety-four per cent of the 272 families of the village and its immediately adjacent hinterland were successfully studied, interviews most frequently being with the housewife. In the course of each interview, data were collected regarding each family, including the names of the interviewee's most intimate friends in the community.[6] These names provided the data utilized in charting informal relationships. The charting technique consisted in taking as nuclei those persons most frequently named; charting in full those choosing, and those chosen by, each of the nuclei; charting in full those choosing, and those chosen by, the satellites of the nuclei; etc. Mutual and nonreciprocated choices were suitably differentiated.

Eight constellations or networks of interaction were identified in the

[5] George A. Lundberg and Margaret Lawsing, "The Sociography of Some Community Relations," *Amer. Sociol. Rev.*, 2 (1937), 318–335; George A. Lundberg and Mary Steele, "Social Attraction Patterns in a Village," *Sociometry*, 1 (1938), 375–419.

[6] Other data included: (1) socioeconomic status according to the Chapin Living Room Scale, (2) cultural content of periodicals taken, according to the Morgan-Leahy Scale, (3) occupation (of the husband in the case of a housewife) classified according to the Goodenough-Anderson grouping, (4) relatives by blood or marriage, up to and including first cousins, (5) church membership, (6) club memberships, (7) home location.

community. At the core of these networks were popular persons (those most frequently named) and powerful persons (those named as a best friend by popular persons or other powerful persons). Popularity was thus measured by number of direct choices received. Power was measured by number of direct and indirect choices received.

Lundberg found a high direct association between both popularity and power and (1) socioeconomic status, (2) occupational status, (3) "cultural content" of periodicals taken, and (4) church membership. He found some tendency for persons to choose as best friends individuals of higher socioeconomic status. He found that kinship ties did not dominate the informal groupings of the village, although such ties were of some importance.

Elma, Washington (1,500).[7] In this study of a community served by a small trade center located 20 miles west of Olympia, the state capitol of Washington, the focus of interest was the influence position of each of the households in the organized group life of the community. Information was collected in connection with a community planning project[8] from 1,190 of the 1,800 households residing in the town and its hinterland of mixed farming, logging, and lumber milling settlements. An internally validated 15-point scale was developed for the measurement of household influence position in the associational structure of the community. Component measures utilized participation and leadership data in such a way as to reflect the influence positions of the associations in the community's social structure.[9]

The distribution of the households of the area according to influence position scores was sharply skewed in the direction of high scores, with most households getting low scores. In Table 36 are presented selected relationships discovered in the sample between household influence position in the local associational structure and other variables. Confirmation was indicated for the study hypothesis: "Influence position in the associational structure of the Elma Community is positively associated with possession of those desiderata valued most highly in the Elma Community." It would appear from Table 36 that the most influential households were maximumly differentiated from other households in the study area in (1) plane of living, (2) professional, managerial, and other white-collar employment, and (3) college educa-

---

[7] David B. Carpenter, *Some Factors Associated with Influence Position in the Associational Structure of a Rural Community*, unpublished doctoral dissertation, University of Washington, 1951.

[8] See Chap. 3 for additional information on this study.

[9] The Influence Position Scale had a reproducibility of 97.0 per cent and a predictability of 88.3 per cent. Perfect internal consistency would be indicated by 100.0 per cent on each of the validity criteria. For an explanation of these criteria of internal consistency, see Table 3 and the accompanying text in Chap. 3.

Table 36. Relation of Selected Characteristics to Influence Position
in the Associational Structure, 1,190 Households,
Elma Community, Washington, 1940

Household characteristic	Household influence position score		Coefficient of association between (1) and (3)	Value of chi-square	Probability of the null hypothesis, * less than
	Modal or below	Above modal			
(1)	(2)	(3)	(4)	(5)	(6)
Percentage of households possessing:					
Furnace..................	2.3	9.9	+.65	50.21	.001
Indoor toilet..............	38.8	67.4	+.53	82.45	.001
Telephone................	14.8	35.4	+.52	62.84	.001
Fifty or more books........	23.0	46.5	+.49	53.44	.001
Piano....................	19.3	38.3	+.44	47.80	.001
Income $1,500 or more......	15.0	30.1	+.42	31.77	.001
Savings..................	18.4	33.9	+.39	33.42	.001
Percentage of employed heads of households:					
Professional..............	1.0	6.5	+.75	24.52	.001
Professional and managerial..	4.3	18.5	+.67	61.23	.001
White collar..............	7.7	25.3	+.61	64.66	.001
Not factory worker........	58.0	72.5	+.31	20.98	.001
Percentage of population no longer in school who completed:					
College: 3 or more years.....	1.9	7.3	+.60	33.04	.001
College: 1 or more years.....	7.0	17.5	+.47	60.73	.001
High school: 3 or more years.	31.7	45.8	+.29	26.25	.001
Percentage of heads of households employed in the same industry as:					
Ten years before...........	43.3	68.1	+.47	63.37	.001
Five years before...........	51.9	71.9	+.41	40.77	.001
Percentage of heads of households resident in the same:					
Community 5 years before....	65.0	80.5	+.38	29.44	.001
County 10 years before......	68.0	80.6	+.32	20.18	.001
Percentage of heads of households whose preference and realization coincide in:					
Occupation...............	50.7	65.1	+.25	10.58	.01
Industry of employment.....	49.7	62.0	+.25	10.20	.01
Farm-town residence........	63.9	70.5	+.15	4.33	.05
Community of residence.....	68.0	72.0	+.09	1.41	.3
Percentage of households:					
Visiting Seattle, previous week	2.7	7.7	+.51	15.93	.001
Not living in open country...	47.6	56.7	+.27	20.56	.001
Not living on a farm........	52.3	60.3	+.16	6.68	.01

SOURCE: Adapted from David B. Carpenter, *Some Factors Associated with Influence Position in the Associational Structure of a Rural Community*, unpublished doctoral dissertation, University of Washington, 1951.

* Probability that the apparent relationship is fortuitous.

tion. Other less sharp, but statistically significant, differentials indicated that "influentiality" was directly associated with (1) direct use of Seattle metropolitan services, (2) continuity of employment, (3) continuity of residence in a single community, (4) high school education, and (5) town rather than farm residence. Least sharp was the contrast between influential and other households with regard to degree of satisfaction with job and residence. The materially advantaged influentials indicated little more satisfaction than the otherwise less advantaged noninfluentials. The degree of contrast between influentials and noninfluentials on each characteristic appeared to reflect the position of it in the effective value hierarchy of the Elma Community.

Valley View, Great Plains (3,300).[10] Wheeler selected this agricultural trade and processing center for his study of social stratification in part because he was born and reared in it. His primary purpose, identification of the local pattern of social stratification, was associated with two secondary objectives: (1) determination of the validity of lay judgments with regard to the number and boundaries of social classes and (2) identification of the indices of social status in Valley View.

A sample of 190 families was chosen as representing the range of status variation within the study community. From this sample 25 persons were selected as judges of the prestige rank of each of the families, except his own. Judges were selected who were (1) cooperative, (2) long-time residents, (3) well acquainted locally, and (4) had rapport with the investigator as a result of some months of informal research prior to the systematic interview stage of the study. Each of the judges was given the family names on cards and asked to sort those cards which named families of his acquaintance or knowledge into groups of families who "belong together," "hold the same prestige in the community," "belong to the same social class," or "have the same social standing or social rank." The rankers were then asked to rank the piles of cards from highest to lowest, and to explain why each of the families was grouped and ranked as it was.

The majority of Wheeler's judges delineated seven classes. There appeared to be some tendency for the judges, by building from the top down and from the bottom up, to identify two upper and two lower classes rather easily, but to hesitate with regard to subdivision of the "sort of dead space between." The 190 ranked families numbered by class from high to low: 12, 20, 18, 28, 18, 75, and 19. The families of the judges numbered by class from high to low: 3, 5, 6, 1, 6, 6, and 0. Criteria reported by the judges as important in their allocation of families by class were (1) wealth and its use (2) education and its use, (3) community leadership, (4) association membership and activity, (5) religious

[10] Wayne Wheeler, *Social Stratification in a Plains Community*, 1949.

affiliation and religious activity, (6) occupation, (7) behavior and personal appearance , (8) ethnic background and "ethnicity," (9) kinship affiliation and family reputation, and (10) place of residence.

Wheeler also constructed an interview schedule composed of objective status indicators which in general corresponded to components of the 10 criteria used by the judges in their ranking of the sample families. These separate items were integrated into a composite score for each family through a system of item weighting in which a panel of Valley View citizens participated. The final scores of the families interviewed clustered into three groups, which were identified as the three major social classes: upper, middle, and lower. The upper and lower classes were subdivided into two groups each, while the middle class was subdivided into three groups. The resultant seven classes were then compared to the seven classes identified by the judges. Wheeler found a correlation coefficient of $r = +.92$ between the classes as determined by prestige judges and classes as defined in terms of social status scores.

Elmtown, Middle West (6,000).[11] In this study, Hollingshead has identified and characterized the social classes of a small, all-white, Middle Western trade and industrial center and its immediately adjacent hinterland. His methodology consisted in class placement of the families of 735 adolescents by a panel of 31 raters, and scheduled interviews with members of each of the families. The five classes he identified and the number of families falling in each class were: I, 4; II, 31; III, 158; IV, 312; V, 230. His tentative conclusions were:

> First, each of the five strata, as delimited by the procedures used, has a distinct subculture. Second, identification with a given class or stratum is dependent upon the possession of a constellation of appropriate traits. Third, the members of each class participate in community activities in significantly different ways from the members of other classes.[12]

Class II families were found half to have achieved their positions and half to have inherited them. Further ascent was deemed virtually impossible for the half whose positions had been achieved, because of common knowledge of their lower origins of such recent date. Although well aware of the prestige differentials between themselves and Class I members, they attempted to identify with Class I and exaggerated differences between themselves and Class III.

Class III adults recognized the I's as superior in prestige because of their wealth, lineage, and way of life. They identified the superior position of the II's as resting on different bases than the I's: dignified occupations, income, education, and leadership in prestigeful activities. Their

---

[11] August B. Hollingshead, "Selected Characteristics of Classes in a Middle Western Community," *Amer. Sociol. Rev.,* 12 (1947), 385–395.

[12] *Ibid.,* p. 395. By permission of the *American Sociological Review.*

view of the IV's as "the common man" was not found to be scornful, since many III's traced their immediate background to this class. Upward mobility was found to be particularly present in Class III.

Class IV people considered themselves to be "the backbone of the community." They viewed the III's as socially ambitious and as persons who unwarrantedly "put on airs." They were convinced that the V's were inferior because of their poverty, dirtiness, immorality, and lack of ambition, and avoided contact with the V's whenever possible. The upper classes did not expect leadership from the IV's but did expect "them to work, produce, pay taxes, vote right, pay their bills, and buy the things they need locally while the higher classes provide the direction and reap the profits from their efforts."[13]

Class V members were looked upon by other classes as the "scum of the city." It was believed that nothing beyond charity could be done for them, and only a minimum of charity was justified for such shiftless people. This class appeared to exist apart from much of the organized life of the community, with an intraclass social life of neighboring, gossip, petty gambling, drinking, etc.

Southtown (6,000).[14] Stewart studied the pattern of influence among the white, permanent-resident families of a southern town. He interviewed 163 adults, who represented approximately 25 per cent of these families; and 55 persons found in his 163 interviews to be the 55 most influential in the town. He measured influence by the number of times subjects were named in answer to a series of 14 questions of the following sort: Who around here knows the most about political matters? Who is the all-around best-informed person you know? Who would you say are the important people in town? Other items covered in the interviews included self-evaluations as leaders and advisors, magazine reading interests, income and plane of living, education, activities in the community, etc.

Fifty-five persons were named 10 times or more in the list of 3,401 names mentioned by 163 Southtowners in answer to the 14 "Who is the most influential?" type questions. The distribution of the 3,401 names showed extreme skewness, with only a few persons getting very high scores. He found women to be virtually absent from the upper reaches of the town's influence structure. His 55 top influentials displayed a significantly greater than average tendency of (1) holding office in civic activities, (2) being mentioned in a nonroutine way in the local newspaper, (3) being sought out as advisers, (4) getting a high "cultural" score on magazine reading, (5) being in the forty to forty-nine age

[13] *Ibid.*, p. 391. By permission of the *American Sociological Review.*
[14] Frank A. Stewart, "A Sociometric Study of Influence in Southtown," *Sociometry,* 10 (1947), 11–31, 273–286.

bracket, (6) having a high income and plane of living, (7) being college graduates, (8) having long residence in the community, (9) being widely acquainted in the community, and (10) satisfaction. He concluded, in contrast to some students of stratification, that "influentiality is nothing if not a highly individualized characteristic. While its incidence is a little greater in certain socio-economic classes, *the fact is that finding centers of influence is a matter of identification of individuals, not of classes.*"[15]

Old City, Deep South (10,000).[16] This is a study of life in a small city which served as trade center for a cotton plantation hinterland in the heart of the Old South. Over half of the city residents and about 80 per cent of the hinterland residents were Negro. The field work of the study was done by four investigators, a white man and wife and a Negro man and wife, who had lived in Old City for two years. Their research was carried on primarily as participant observers and as conforming members of their respective castes, white and Negro. Their interviews were "free associative," with a minimum of formal questioning and of interview guidance by the investigators. Field findings with regard to Negro-white relations were continuously cross-checked by Negro and white field workers. Effort was made to participate in both formal and informal behavior at all class levels. In addition to 5,000 pages of recorded overt behavior and verbalization, available statistical and newspaper records of social behavior were collected.

The fundamental division in the social organization of Old City was found to be between Negro caste and white caste. Marriage between castes was absolutely forbidden, and any offspring of extralegal sex relations was automatically assigned to the subordinate Negro group. Mobility between castes was absolutely prohibited. In all social interaction between white and Negro, superordinate-subordinate statuses were enforced by a strongly sanctioned system of behavior norms by which every individual knew how he should act and what he could expect in his relations with members of his own and the other caste. Within each of the castes, the investigators identified social classes. A social class was thought of by the authors as "the largest group of people whose members have intimate access to one another." An individual was identified as a member of that social class within which most of his informal and intimate interaction took place. The authors argued that an important factor in modifying caste behavior was the class structure of each of the two castes, and the important changes observed in them. Before the War between the States, the caste and class structures were

[15] *Ibid.*, p. 273.

[16] Allison Davis, Burleigh B. Gardner, and Mary R. Gardner, *Deep South, A Social Anthropological Study of Caste and Class*, 1941. The study was directed by W. Lloyd Warner.

closely articulated. The white caste, it was observed, occupied the upper- and middle-class positions; the Negro caste comprised the lower class. Subsequently, an emergent lower class was observed in the white caste, and a middle and upper class developed in the Negro caste. Implicit recognition was noted in the white caste of the fact that upper-class Negroes had a higher class position than the lower-class whites. The

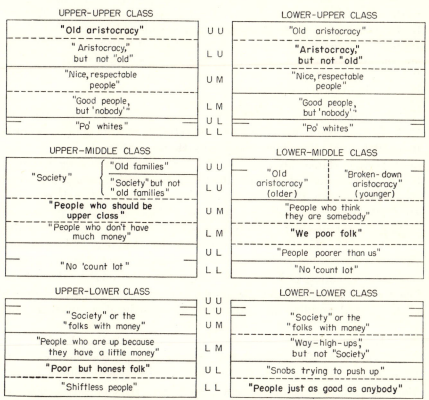

Fig. 23. The social class system of the Old City white caste as viewed from the perspective of members of each of the six classes. (*Adapted from Allison Davis, Burleigh B. Gardner, and Mary R. Gardner, Deep South. By permission of The University of Chicago Press.*)

position of the upper-class Negro was thus found to be paradoxical. He was at once the social superior of the "poor white" classwise and his social inferior castewise.

In Fig. 23 is presented the system of social classes of the white caste of Old City from the social perspective of each of the six social classes identified in the study. In each of the six diagrams, the group doing the viewing is presented in boldface type. It can be noted that to the upper-uppers there was no subdivision of "po' whites" into upper-lower and lower-lower, and to the lower-lowers there was no subdivision of "folks with money" into upper-upper, lower-upper, and upper-middle. In short, sharpest differentiation was made of persons of adjoining status groups; while persons of much higher or much lower social status tended to be lumped into large classes, in which fine status gradations were not sharply discerned. According to the authors,

> The classes may be characterized by general patterns of behavior. The past is of prime importance to the upper class. Wealth and "morality" mark the aspirations of the middle class, as well as concern with making themselves and the community "better." Poverty, lack of formal organization, and isolation from the other classes distinguish the lower class, and the "job" and area of residence serve to differentiate segments within it.[17]

Davis and his associates found that class lines were less sharply drawn in the Negro caste than in the white, reflecting in part the limited occupational differentiation which the caste system permitted to Negroes. The most explicit statements concerning stratification were made by those in the Negro upper class, who identified three social classes. They emphasized, however, the weakness of class sanctions and their own dissatisfaction with the lack of sharper class differentiation in patterns of participation. Questions tacitly asked of those seeking upper-class status related to (1) education, (2) occupation, (3) language, (4) manners, (5) dress, (6) color, and (for women) (7) sexual relations with white men. Three-quarters of Negroes were found by their own standards to be lower class. In general, the Negro lower class contrasted to the upper-class oriented middle class most markedly in education, manners, and morals.

Yankee City, Massachusetts (17,000).[18] This small New England city was the scene of one of the most ambitious attempts ever undertaken to study *in toto* the social life of a modern industrial city. Informal interviewing and partipant-observation were the principal techniques of data collection. Only limited use was made of schedules and questionnaires. Information collected included personal data on almost 17,000 men, women, and children. Early in their field work, Warner and his associates concluded that Yankee City's intricate social structure operated in terms of a hierarchy of rank and class, in which economic considerations did not play a determining role. Six classes were identified through observation of which persons interacted with which other persons as equals, and through analysis of deference behavior. These classes, and the percentage of the population falling within each, were:

[17] *Ibid.*, p. 83. By permission of the University of Chicago Press.
[18] Lloyd Warner and Paul S. Lunt, *The Social Life of a Modern Community,* 1941. This is the summary volume of the six-volume Yankee City Series.

upper-upper, 1.4; lower-upper, 1.6; upper-middle, 10.2; lower-middle, 28.1; upper-lower, 32.6; lower-lower, 25.2; unknown, 0.8.

In Table 37 are presented selected findings with regard to the characteristics of each of the Yankee City classes. It appears clear that status and class were highly correlated with occupation, wealth, plane of living, ethnic background, length of local residence, participation in formally organized associations, and freedom from arrest. In general, the hierarchy of values of Yankee City residents was sharply reflected in the social class structure as identified. It was in those characteristics most sought after in the community that the contrast between uppers and lowers appeared to be most pronounced.

Middletown, Indiana (50,000).[19] This classic study and restudy pioneered in transferring to the study of a contemporary United States urban community the dispassionate and "wholistic" approach of the cultural anthropologist, and his heavy research emphasis on participant-observation and free-associative interviewing. The original study focused on the institutional change associated with the thirty-five-year development of a 1925 manufacturing city from a placid 1890 county seat town. The 1935 restudy of Middletown had as its focus the crisis impact of "boom and bust" on the local social structure. In both studies, social structure was primarily interpreted in terms of the division of the population into business class and working class.

The Lynds concluded that

> One's job is the watershed down which the rest of one's life tends to flow in Middletown. Who one is, whom one knows, how one lives, what one aspires to be,—these and many other urgent realities of living are patterned for one by what one does to get a living and the amount of living this allows one to buy.[20]

Further, they concluded that the two-class system which they identified was becoming more sharply crystallized as mobility between classes sharply decreased during the period of their study:

> . . . Andrew Carnegie's advice to enterprising young men to begin at the bottom appears no longer to be sound advice. Men of his type are advising young men today to get a toe hold in one of the managerial or technical departments halfway up the ladder. What appears increasingly in Middletown industries is not one unbroken ladder but two: the one becoming shorter, harder to climb, and leading nowhere in particular; the other a long and repaying one but beginning a long jump above the plant floor. Middletown's industries consist more than ever before of a large, crowded floor of little-

---

[19] Robert S. Lynd and Helen Merrell Lynd, *Middletown*, 1929; *Middletown in Transition*, 1937.

[20] Lynd, *Middletown in Transition*, p. 7. By permission of Harcourt, Brace and Company, Inc.

Table 37. Comparison of the Six Social Classes with Regard to Selected Characteristics, Yankee City

Characteristic	Upper-upper	Lower-upper	Upper-middle	Lower-middle	Upper-lower	Lower-lower
Percentage of class members:						
Male.	40	49	45	49	49	53
Age under 21 years.	11	15	14	18	23	28
Age 60 years and over.	32	24	25	18	17	9
Born in Yankee City.	52	50	48	49	41	31
Foreign born.	0	1	6	14	30	30
Percentage of class members locally identified as:						
Yankee.	100	95	83	67	38	43
Irish.	0	5	13	23	38	11
French.	0	0	1	4	11	16
Jewish.	0	0	1	4	3	1
Italian.	0	0	0	1	2	3
Armenian.	0	0	0	1	3	2
Greek.	0	0	1	0	3	5
Polish.	0	0	0	0	1	12
Russian.	0	0	0	0	1	2
Negro.	0	0	0	0	0	2
Percentage of class members living in:						
"Large and good" houses.	56	39	10	2	1	0
"Small and bad" houses.	0	1	2	12	25	46
Percentage of gainfully employed members of the class:						
Professionals and proprietors.	83	86	62	14	3	1
Wholesale and retail dealers.	0	7	15	11	6	3
Clerks and kindred workers.	17	7	15	29	9	4
Skilled workers.	0	0	5	17	13	5
Semiskilled workers.	0	0	2	27	62	79
Unskilled workers.	0	0	0	2	8	9
Percentage of the budget of each class spent on:						
Food.	12	14	24	31	37	45
Rent and shelter.	10	13	17	17	20	21
Clothing.	11	9	10	10	9	9
Formal education.	10	1	3	2	1	0
Medical.	5	3	4	4	3	5
Percentage of class members belonging to:						
One or more associations.	72	71	64	49	39	22
Two or more associations.	49	48	40	21	14	5
Five or more associations.	21	19	9	2	1	0
Percentage of class members with:						
Police records of arrest.	1	1	1	1	3	11

SOURCE: Adapted from various tables and charts in W. Lloyd Warner and Paul S. Lunt, *The Social Life of a Modern Community*, 1941. By permission of Yale University Press.

differentiated "hands," and a different class of individuals (businessmen and engineers) doing all the "going up" in a world of their own largely beyond the reach of the working class. . . . Our American culture has founded its exuberant boast of a classless society upon the two facts of universal suffrage and of vertical mobility up the pecuniary ladder. . . . As symbol and reality draw thus apart, the scene would seem to be set for the emergence of class consciousness and possible eventual conflict.[21]

Central City, Middle West (60,000).[22] On the basis of 36 statistical series, this middle-sized city was selected as the most typical of all Middle Western cities of 50,000 to 80,000 population. In this study Mills was concerned with the relation between objective economic criteria of class and attitudinal evidences of class consciousness, particularly with regard to the middle classes. When the occupations of a sample of Central City married men were coded in 24 groups and ranked according to family income, natural breaks occurred between five occupational strata. The strata and average weekly income for each as of August, 1945, were: (1) big business and executives, $137, (2) small business and free (nonsalaried) professionals, $102, (3) higher white-collar, $83, (4) lower white-collar, $72, (5) wage workers, $59. The three middle classes, located between the sharply defined upper and lower strata, were found to occupy the most ambiguous and least clearly defined social position of the social structure.

Although small business and free professionals fell together in the second class in terms of income, they contrasted sharply in other respects. The small business group included retail, service, wholesale, and industrial proprietors employing less than 100 workers—usually less than 10 workers. To lower-class observers, the small business group was generally identified with the upper-class business group. To upper-class observers, the small business group was placed far below the upper class, both because the weak power position of the small businessman was recognized and because of the background, limited education, and manners of the small business group. In general, the small business group was found to be an insecure, ascendant group, quite in contrast to the free professionals, who resembled the big business owners and executives with regard to family, occupational, and educational background.

The higher white-collar strata included salaried professionals and semi-professionals, salesmen, government officials, and minor managerial employees, with a weekly income range from $80 to $87. The lower white-collar class included government protection and service workers, clerks, stenographers, bookkeepers, and foremen, with a weekly income range

[21] *Ibid.*, pp. 71–72. By permission of Harcourt, Brace and Company, Inc.
[22] Wright Mills, "The Middle Classes in Middle-sized Cities," *Amer. Sociol. Rev.*, 11 (1946), 520–529.

from $71 to $76. The upper and lower white-collar strata were found to be sharply contrasted not only with regard to income, but also extraction, job history, and education.

Mills found that the centers of organizational life for the upper class were the Chamber of Commerce and the service clubs, and for the lower class, the labor unions. In the general polarization of the stratification system, the top and bottom were becoming more rigid and self-conscious. Least unified, least self-conscious, and least powerful were the three middle strata. Though the middle classes frequently identified with the upper class, they were found to have little effective power in the organizations in which they participated and in the community at large.

Black Metropolis, Chicago (300,000 *Negro Population*).[23] Drake and Cayton have studied here the social structure of the second largest Negro city in the world (Harlem in New York City is largest), a Negro city within a white-dominated metropolis. Continuities in methodology and personnel made this study in many ways a sequitur to the study of Old City, the Deep South city which we have already considered. Despite the contrast of Black Metropolis to Old City, particularly with reference to the heightened status of the Negro in Chicago, the authors found that the caste system remained, keeping the Negro in an inferior position. Although legally cross-caste marriage was permitted, actually it was rare. The children of such marriages were defined as Negro and suffered with their parents caste deprivations. The authors found that everyone in Black Metropolis recognized, explicitly or implicitly, the existence of social classes, although the white community appeared less aware of the Negro class structure.

The upper class, making up 5 per cent of the Negro population, consisted of

. . . an articulate social world of doctors, lawyers, schoolteachers, executives, successful business people, and the frugal and fortunate of other occupational groups who have climbed with difficulty and now cling precariously to a social position consonant with what money, education, and power the city and the castelike controls allow them. They are challenged at every point, however, by the same forces that condemn the vast majority of the people to poverty and restricted opportunities.[24]

In general, the standards of behavior of the upper-class Negroes approximated those of the white middle class. The upper-class attitudes toward the lower class were found to be ambivalent. They resented the

---

[23] St. Clair Drake and Horace R. Cayton, *Black Metropolis, A Study of Negro Life in a Northern City*, 1945.
[24] *Ibid.*, p. 522. By permission of Harcourt, Brace and Company, Inc.

tendency of outsiders to "judge us all by what ignorant Negroes do." Though they emphasized their differentness, as race leaders upper-class members had to identify psychologically with "the Race," even though it included a majority of persons who weren't accepted socially. Upper-class Negroes, moreover, depended upon mass Negro support for their businesses, professions, and other enterprises. "The whole orientation of the Negro upper class thus becomes one of trying to speed up the processes by which the lower class can be transformed from a poverty-stricken group, isolated from the general stream of American life, into a counterpart of middle-class America."[25]

The lower class, representing two-thirds of the Negro population, comprised the bulk of the working class world of Black Metropolis. To the Negro working class fell a large share of the least desirable work of the Chicago metropolitan area, and during the depression, the least opportunity of nonrelief employment. The bulk of the Negro working class was identified as lower class in terms of manners, morals, and ambition. Restraints of convention were here less marked, and there was not a consuming drive for the symbols of higher social position. Desertion, illegitimacy, delinquency, fighting, and roistering were common. Lower class in Black Metropolis was found to be a world apart from both whites and other Negroes.

The 30 per cent of the population who made up the middle class of Black Metropolis were found to be in an amorphous position, sandwiched between uppers and lowers. Ambitious for acceptance into the upper-class population, whose manners and morals they attempted to imitate, they were continually beset by fear of falling into the lower-class group, with whom they were frequently identified occupationally. Primarily working class, they had been released somewhat from the restraints of poverty, had achieved some stability and order in their lives, and were free of the lower-class extremes of religious or recreational behavior. Their church and associational participation were not handicapped by poverty, inadequate clothing, or lack of formal or informal education.

Within the tripartite class structure was found, proportionately least in the upper class and most in the lower class, a group known as "shadies," whose income was earned in pursuits not generally recognized as respectable. The marginal position of the Negro in the total economy, and the traditional role of the Negro community in supplying to the city certain illegal and semilegal services, have brought into being a complex of "protected" business, composed of "policy" and betting enterprises, prostitution, and allied pursuits. Important portions of each class are more or less involved in such enterprises. More mobile individuals have

[25] *Ibid.*, p. 563. By permission of Harcourt, Brace and Company, Inc.

been able to rise to upper-class positions through success in such shady enterprises and have secured from the upper "respectables" some measure of social recognition. The upper shadies have been sensitive to the opinions of the upper respectables and have sought prestige by adapting much of their behavior to respectable upper-class norms and by supporting upper- and middle-class organizations and causes.

Mid City, Middle West (2,000,000).[26] This study is concerned with the stratification within the 0.3 per cent of the population listed in the 1947 *Social Register* of a Middle Western metropolis. A list was made up of the 1,473 names (generally of couples) listed first at each address which was within, or within 20 miles of, the limits of Mid City. From this list a sample of 210 was taken, by selecting every seventh name. Twenty judges, themselves generally of *Social Register* status, were then asked individually to rank as many of the 210 as they were able. The resultant ratings appeared to form three clusters. The 10 couples falling closest to each of the three modal scores were selected for further analysis and comparison. Table 38 presents in summary form Miss Faust's principal findings, based primarily on the indirect evidence of informants who were acquainted with members of her sample. Her evidence clearly points to important status differentials within the upper segment of what Warner would probably designate as the upper-upper class.

SOCIAL STATUS AND THE RURAL-URBAN CONTINUUM

In the 12 community studies just reviewed, prestige and influence, variously defined and measured, were found to be directly correlated with each other and with other characteristics highly valued in the communities investigated. Composite status indices, made up of measures of a variety of objectively defined desiderata, were found to be highly correlated with subjective evaluations by judges, of the rank, standing, or influence position of community members. Apparently subjective evaluations of the standing of individuals or families represented judgments based on a kind of subjective composite index, in which weights were accorded component characteristics in rough relation to the position of such characteristics in the community hierarchy of values, as interpreted by each of the rankers. Such subjective evaluations appear to be an unconscious part of social interaction generally—each member evaluating on the basis of available evidence the composite status of fellow participants in relation to his own self-evaluated status.

Although there appeared to be a large degree of similarity among the 12 communities with regard to the weighting of various items—influ-

---

[26] Ann Faust, *A Study of Stratification*, unpublished master's thesis, Washington University, St. Louis, 1949.

Table 38. Selected Characteristics of a Sample of Social Register Couples, by Status Assignment, Mid City, 1948

Characteristic	Status assignment		
	I	II	III
Number of couples in sample..............................	10	10	10
Percentage of persons aged over 60........................	60	30	40
Percentage of men major business executives................	60	40	50
Percentage of couples with annual income over $50,000........	50	10	20
Percentage of men college graduates........................	100	50	70
Percentage of men graduates of Harvard, Yale, or Princeton....	90	30	30
Percentage of couples Episcopalian..........................	80	10	10
Percentage of couples with both persons listed in *Social Register* at time of marriage..	100	50	0
Percentage of non-out-of-towners in families listed in *Social Register* continuously since 1903.................................	88	44	13
Percentage of couples related to Queen or special Maids of Honor at one or more harvest festivals..........................	50	30	0
Percentage of couples who reside, or have resided, on one of the three most prestigious private streets in Mid City............	100	50	10
Percentage of couples with membership in:			
Chamber of Commerce...............................	50	40	60
Civic League......................................	40	60	20
Brookfield Country Club.............................	90	70	10
Meadowside Country Club............................	0	0	30
Gourmet Club (men's luncheon).......................	60	30	30
Midday Club (men's luncheon)........................	20	30	0
Union Club (men's luncheon and sport).................	50	60	30
College Club (men's luncheon and sport)...............	50	10	20
Longfellow Club (women's)...........................	0	0	20
Acorn Club (women's)...............................	0	0	20
Forefather's Society................................	30	30	20
National patriotic societies such as Colonial Dames..........	0	0	30
Symphony Boards..................................	10	10	10
Community Chest Boards.............................	90	50	30
University Board of Trustees..........................	20	0	0
Community Chest Board Memberships per couple............	2.1	0.6	0.5

SOURCE: Adapted from Ann Faust, *A Study of Stratification,* unpublished master's thesis, Washington University, 1949.

ence, occupation, wealth, participation, and reputation, components of this informally calculated index of status—there appeared also to be important dissimilarities. It seems clear that, as communities vary with regard to the characteristics most highly valued, the relative weights given such characteristics in composite status evaluations will also vary. And, when as in the metropolis, interaction becomes increasingly impersonal and secondary, more reliance on status assignments will likely be made on the immediately visible valued characteristics such as occupation, house, car, dress, speech, and manners.

Among the objective criteria of status in our society, the occupation of the family head has been found to be particularly important.[27] Yet we have already noted the sharp variation of dominant occupation types and occupational differentiation as communities are arrayed along the rural-urban continuum. It would appear that the status connotations of occupation would be both much less important and quite different in occupationally undifferentiated subsistence farming areas than in the intricately differentiated metropolis. Fortunately, there is available research bearing on rural-urban differentials with regard to prestige positions of a sample of contemporary United States occupations. In 1947, National Opinion Research Center interviewers approached a nationwide United States sample with regard to their personal opinions of the general standing of 90 specified occupations.[28] North and Hatt found that, as the size of place of residence decreased, the average ratings given generally became lower. They found that metropolitan residents gave higher ratings to vocations more frequently found in city than country, such as artist, musician in a symphony orchestra, author of novels, singer in a night club, bartender, radio announcer, newspaper columnist, reporter on a daily newspaper, scientific occupations, and priest. Rural and small-town dwellers gave higher ratings to occupations with whose practitioners they had more immediate contact, such as farm owner and operator, railroad conductor, and mail carrier. To the question of the best occupation for young men to aim toward, 8 per cent of the total sample answered farming, while 33 per cent of farmers answered farming.

In general, the distribution of desiderata scores in the 12 communities appeared to be most frequently unimodal, skewed in the direction of high status, with the mode nearer the lower end of the range. Class consciousness, implicit or explicit, appeared to be most marked in communities of all sizes, at the upper and lower ends of the status continua, with the more numerous middle-scoring individuals or families less self-conscious, and more likely to be split into lower- and upper-oriented groups. Useem and his associates found in the prairie town which they studied, though lowers and uppers both indicated a preference for restricting interaction as far as possible to their own stratum, that the degree of ingroup preference was much greater among uppers than among

[27] Warner and his associates found occupation, of the objective criteria considered, to be most highly predictive of composite status position. They discovered a +.91 linear correlation between occupation score and their evaluated participation status score among old Americans in Jonesville, a small Middle Western city. Between occupation, source of income, house type, and dwelling area scores and their evaluated participation score, they discovered a multiple correlation of .972. See W. Lloyd Warner, Marchia Meeker, and Kenneth Eells, *Social Class in America*, p. 168, 1949.

[28] Cecil C. North and Paul K. Hatt, "Jobs and Occupations: A Popular Evaluation," *Opinion News*, Sept. 1, 1947, pp. 3–13. Also reprinted in Logan Wilson and William L. Kolb, *Sociological Analysis*, pp. 464–473, 1949.

lowers.[29] The evidence available suggests that social classes in the contemporary United States are little more substantive groups, either by objective or subjective definition, than are groups of students designated by such commonly used terms as superior, good, fair, and poor. Actually in both cases there appear to be quantitative continua, divided for convenience into somewhat arbitrarily defined categories to which qualitative designations are applied.

SELECTED READINGS

DAVIS, ALLISON, BURLEIGH B. GARDNER, and MARY R. GARDNER: *Deep South, A Social Anthropological Study of Caste and Class*, The University of Chicago Press, 1941. The study was directed by W. Lloyd Warner and is briefly reviewed in this chapter.

DRAKE, ST. CLAIR, and HORACE R. CAYTON: *Black Metropolis, A Study of Negro Life in a Northern City*, Harcourt, Brace and Company, Inc., 1945. This caste-class oriented study of the Chicago Negro community is reviewed in this chapter.

HATT, PAUL K., and ALBERT J. REISS, JR.: *Reader in Urban Sociology*, The Free Press, 1951. Part VI is devoted to social stratification.

HOLLINGSHEAD, AUGUST B.: *Elmtown's Youth*, John Wiley & Sons, Inc., 1949. The highly readable account of the impact of social class on the life of teen-agers in the same Middle Western town reported on in the Hollingshead study, reviewed in this chapter.

LOOMIS, CHARLES P., and J. ALLAN BEEGLE: *Rural Social Systems*, Prentice-Hall, Inc., 1950. Part III, "Social Strata as Social Systems," represents a systematic treatment of frames of reference and methods of analysis currently being used by students of stratification, as well as a careful review of research done in the United States and abroad on the local status systems of rural and semirural communities.

LYND, ROBERT S., and HELEN MERRELL LYND: *Middletown*, Harcourt, Brace and Company, Inc., 1929; *Middletown in Transition*, Harcourt, Brace and Company, Inc., 1937. The classic studies of a Middle Western city reviewed in this chapter.

WARNER, W. LLOYD, MARCHIA MEEKER, and KENNETH EELLS: *Social Class in America*, Science Research Associates, Inc., 1949. This is a manual of procedure for the measurement of social status, written in the perspective of the authors' experience in pioneering stratification studies of Yankee City, Old City, and Jonesville.

WEST, JAMES: *Plainville, U.S.A.*, Columbia University Press, 1945. This highly readable study of class in a Missouri farming community was reviewed in this chapter.

American Sociological Review, Vol. 15, No. 2, April, 1950. A majority of the articles appearing in this issue relate to social stratification.

[29] John Useem, Pierre Tangent, and Ruth Useem, "Stratification in a Prairie Town," *Amer. Sociol. Rev.*, 7 (1942), 331–342.

CHAPTER 16.   *Making a Home*

In all known societies the family plays an important role in procreation, child rearing, personality development, and the satisfaction of the response needs of human beings. The long period of helplessness of the human child has posed for every society the need for placing responsibility for infant care and training in family or quasi-family groups. Every society has also been under compulsion to protect the solidarity of the family unit by measures such as the control in some form or other of those sexual relations which are viewed as intrafamilial, or incestuous. With respect to other aspects of marriage and family relations, known societies evidence very great variability, as in their definition of that which is right and moral and that which is wrong and immoral.

Contrasts between city and country have commonly been observed with regard to family size, solidarity, functions, control, mores, and receptivity to change. Redfield has argued that the folk society, in contrast to the urban society, tends to be familial, homogeneous in values and norms, traditional, stable, resistant to innovation, and highly solidary; while the urban society tends toward individuated behavior, heterogeneity of values, secularity, receptivity to change, and a greater measure of social disorganization.[1] He thought of the folk society as being composed of families rather than individuals, families which themselves reflect a minimum of variability in organization, norms, roles, authority, and patterns of internal interaction. Becker has developed a similar typology in his sacred-secular dichotomy,[2] as has Tönnies in his *Gemeinschaft-Gesellschaft* types.[3]

Loomis and Beegle have developed preliminary scales for the measurement of the position on the *Gemeinschaft-Gesellschaft* continuum of

[1] Robert Redfield, "The Folk Society," *Amer. Jour. Sociol.*, 52 (1947), 293–308. See Chap. 2 of the present volume for additional discussion of Redfield's hypotheses.
[2] See Harry Elmer Barnes and Howard Becker, *Social Thought from Lore to Science*, Chap. I, 1938.
[3] See Charles P. Loomis, *Fundamental Concepts of Sociology*, 1940, for a translation in edited form of Ferdinand Tönnies, *Gemeinschaft und Gesellschaft*, 1887.

any concrete social system, such as a specific family, association, or government agency.[4] They find, for example, that the typical Amish family of Lancaster County, Pennsylvania, possesses to a high degree "familistic *Gemeinschaft*" characteristics: (1) Interpersonal ties and relationships are highly valued as ends, rather than being viewed primarily as means to ends, (2) the range of activities of family members and the extent of the family head's rights over, and responsibilities to, family members is general and blanket rather than narrowly limited and specific, (3) the family represents a relatively complete community of fate, in that the hardships are borne by all and the pleasures are the pleasures of all, and (4) the family requires that members play no role outside the family which conflicts with roles within. In adding "familistic" to *Gemeinschaft,* and "contractual" to *Gesellschaft,* Loomis and Beegle have been influenced by Sorokin, in whose view rural society is characterized by familism, urban society by contractualism, but with decreasing sharpness of contrast in an age in which rural and urban societies are merging.[5]

In the present chapter we have set for ourselves the task of determining within the limits of available data the degree to which consistent variation in family characteristics of the sort hypothesized does actually occur in the contemporary United States as one moves from the open country and small town to the city and metropolis.

MARITAL STATUS

In comparing the marital status of urban and rural populations, we must first take note of significant contrasts in sex and age distribution. As we move from rural to urban, there is an increase in the proportion of females, a decrease in the proportion of children, and an increase in the proportion of adults. This pattern is the result of higher rural fertility, steady excess of rural-to-urban over urban-to-rural migration, and greater tendency of females than males to migrate from rural areas to the city,[6] as we have already noted in Chap. 13.

"City life may . . . be said to discourage marriage about 10 per cent."[7] This was Ogburn's conclusion after careful analysis of 1920 data on marriage. In Table 39 are presented 1950 data concerning marital status for urban and rural populations. Among females, city living was

[4] Charles P. Loomis and J. Allan Beegle, *Rural Social Systems,* especially pp. 3–36, 789–824, 1950.

[5] Pitirim A. Sorokin, *Social and Cultural Dynamics,* Vol. 3, 1937; Pitirim A. Sorokin, Carle C. Zimmerman, and C. J. Galpin, *Systematic Source Book in Rural Sociology,* 1930.

[6] Bureau of the Census, 1950 Census of Population, Preliminary Reports, Series PC–7, No. 1, Feb. 25, 1951.

[7] E. R. Groves and W. F. Ogburn, *American Marriage and Family Relationships,* p. 440, 1928.

associated with lower percentages married and higher percentages widowed and divorced. In contrast, urban males had the higher, and rural males the lower, percentage married. Only with regard to percentages widowed and divorced did urban males conform to the expected. However, when we examine the marital status of rural and urban populations by age groups, we find that the tentative conclusions reached on the basis of Table 39 are misleading. The excess of young people to be found in rural areas tends to reduce the percentages married, widowed, and divorced, since young people are less likely than adults to be married. When we examine marital status data by age groups, we are able to conclude that, as one moves from the open country to the city, there tends to be an increase at most age levels in the percentages single, widowed, and divorced, and a decrease at most age levels in the percentage married. Further, we can conclude that the marital status contrasts between rural and urban are much more marked for females than for males.[8] These findings tend to confirm the hypothesis of greater urban individuation. The greater rural-urban contrast in marital status of females appears to be associated with stronger rural traditions of marriage and family as the preferred career for women, greater rural prejudice against the divorced woman, and more limited rural occupational opportunity for the unattached woman.

Table 39. Marital Status of the Population Age 14 Years and Over, by Sex, for the United States, Urban and Rural, 1950

Marital status	Male, per cent distribution				Female, per cent distribution			
	Total	Urban	Rural-non-farm	Rural-farm	Total	Urban	Rural-non-farm	Rural-farm
All statuses.......	100.0	100.0	100.0	100.0	100.0	100.0	100.0	100.0
Single.........	26.2	25.0	26.0	31.3	20.4	21.1	17.5	21.1
Married.......	67.8	68.7	67.9	64.0	65.5	63.3	69.8	70.7
Widowed or divorced.....	6.0	6.3	6.1	4.7	14.1	15.6	12.7	8.3

SOURCE: Bureau of the Census, 1950 Census of Population, Preliminary Reports, Series PC-7, No. 1, Feb. 25, 1951.

FAMILY AND HOUSEHOLD COMPOSITION

A family may be defined as "a group of two or more persons related by blood, marriage, or adoption and residing together"; and a household as including "all of the persons, without regard to relationship, who

[8] Bureau of the Census, Current Population Reports, Series P–20, No. 33, Feb. 12, 1951. These data are based on a sample survey conducted in March, 1950.

occupy a house, an apartment or other group of rooms, or a room, that constitutes a dwelling unit."[9] Both family and household are defined in terms of common residence, but family is additionally defined in terms of relationship.

Between 1940 and 1950 the median size of United States households declined from 3.28 to 3.04, continuing the long-time downward trend which has been associated with urbanization. Table 40 shows the consistent 1950 relationship between urbanism and the small household. One-member households are more characteristic of urban areas, while large households are more characteristic of rural areas. When only related persons per household are considered, the pattern remains the same. In 1948 the median number of related persons per household for urban areas was 2.90, rural-nonfarm 3.15, and rural-farm 3.43. The corresponding numbers for 1940 were 3.01, 3.12, and 3.72.[10] It is noteworthy that between 1940 and 1948 the rural-urban differential in median number of related persons per household became less marked, reflecting the continuing urbanization of rural life.

Table 40. Households by Size, for the United States, Urban and Rural, 1950 and 1940

Date and area	Percentage distribution of households by size of household										Median household size
	Total	1	2	3	4	5	6	7	8	9+	
1950, United States	100.0	9.1	28.6	23.0	18.1	10.5	5.3	2.6	1.4	1.5	3.04
Urban...........	100.0	10.3	29.5	23.8	18.0	9.6	4.8	2.0	1.0	1.1	2.93
Rural-nonfarm ...	100.0	7.8	27.9	22.0	18.6	11.9	6.0	2.9	1.4	1.5	3.15
Rural-farm	100.0	5.0	25.5	21.0	17.8	12.5	6.7	5.0	2.9	3.6	3.43
1940, United States..	100.0	7.7	24.8	22.4	18.1	11.5	6.8	3.8	2.2	2.7	3.28

SOURCE: Bureau of the Census, Current Population Reports, Series P-20, No. 33, Feb. 12, 1951. Data based on March, 1950, sample survey.

Table 41 makes it clear that the contrast in both household and family size between rural and urban areas is almost wholly accounted for by the greater number of persons under eighteen years of age in rural households and families.

According to Table 42, of the 1950 population of the United States, 1.9 per cent were living in institutions, hotels, and large rooming houses, while 98.1 per cent were members of households. About 7 per cent of

[9] Bureau of the Census, 1950 Census of Population, Preliminary Reports, Series PC–7, No. 1, Feb. 25, 1951, p. 3. The 1950 definition of a household excludes quasi households, such as institutions, hotels, large rooming houses, and military barracks.

[10] Bureau of the Census, Current Population Reports, Series P–20, No. 21, Dec. 19, 1948. "Related persons per household include the household head and all persons related to the head."

Table 41. Population in Households and Families, by Age, for the United States, Urban and Rural, 1950 and 1940

Year and area	Mean population per household			Mean population per family		
	All ages	Under 18 years	18 years and over	All ages	Under 18 years	18 years and over
1950, United States.....	3.39	1.09	2.30	3.57	1.20	2.36
Urban.............	3.24	0.94	2.30	3.42	1.05	2.37
Rural-nonfarm......	3.51	1.28	2.24	3.69	1.39	2.31
Rural-farm.........	3.90	1.53	2.37	4.02	1.61	2.41
1940, United States.....	3.67	1.14	2.53	*	*	*

SOURCE: Bureau of the Census, Current Population Reports, Series P-20, No. 33, Feb. 12, 1951. Data based on March, 1950, sample survey.

* The change in definition of the family between the 1940 and the 1950 census prevents comparison.

Table 42. Civilian Population in Households, Quasi Households, and Families, for the United States, Urban and Rural, March, 1950

Family and household status	Per cent of population			
	United States	Urban	Rural-nonfarm	Rural-farm
Total population........................	100.0	100.0	100.0	100.0
Living in households.................	98.1	98.4	95.8	100.0
Living in quasi households*...........	1.9	1.6	4.2	0.0
Total population........................	100.0	100.0	100.0	100.0
Living in families....................	93.1	92.2	92.3	97.5
Living in primary families†..........	92.3	91.1	91.9	97.4
Living in secondary families‡.........	0.8	1.1	0.4	0.1
Not living in families.................:........	6.9	7.8	7.7	2.5

SOURCE: Bureau of the Census, Current Population Reports, Series P-20, No. 33, Feb. 12, 1951. Data based on March, 1950, sample survey.

* Institutions, hotels, and large rooming houses.

† The head of the household and all (one or more) other persons in the household related to the head.

‡ Consists of two or more persons, such as guests, lodgers, or resident employees and their relatives, living in a household or quasi household and related to each other but not to the head of the household.

the total population were not members of families; 4.3 per cent were living in families which were doubling up with relatives; 0.8 per cent were living in families which either boarded with nonrelatives or resided in institutions, hotels, or large rooming houses; and 88.0 per cent were living in primary families not doubling up with relatives. Urban population more frequently than rural-farm lived in quasi households, did not live in families, and boarded with nonrelatives. Doubling up with relatives was equally common among urban and rural populations. In general, these data are consistent with the hypothesis of decrease in familism as one moves from rural to urban.

Table 43 presents more detailed information on the composition of rural and urban households. The average (mean) household in 1940

Table 43. Population per 1,000 Households, by Relation to the Household Head, for the United States, Urban and Rural, 1940

Relationship to the head of the household	Population per 1,000 households			
	Total	Urban	Rural-nonfarm	Rural-farm
All relationships......................	3,674	3,506	3,600	4,246
Male head of the household.............	849	819	862	923
Female head of the household...........	151	181	138	77
Wife of head.........................	760	737	769	818
Child of head........................	1,468	1,300	1,468	1,959
Grandchild of head....................	70	55	66	108
Father of head.......................	18	17	16	21
Mother of head.......................	46	49	38	46
Other relatives of head................	157	161	127	174
Lodger..............................	127	161	92	66
Male servant or hired hand.............	9	2	3	37
Female servant or hired hand...........	21	22	20	13

SOURCE: Adapted from data presented in Bureau of the Census, *Statistical Abstract of the United States, 1949*, p. 24.

had 3.7 members, including a head (85 per cent had male heads), a wife of the male head in 76 per cent of households, 1.5 children of the head, 0.1 grandchildren of the head, 0.1 parents of the head, 0.2 other relatives, and 0.1 lodgers. As one moved from rural to urban areas in 1940, he found smaller households, more female household heads, fewer husband-wife households, fewer children and grandchildren, more lodgers, fewer hired male hands, and more female servants. These 1940 rural-urban contrasts are generally consistent with the 1950 comparisons we have been making, and appear to be in line with hypotheses of less urban familism, less fertility, less resistance to household residence of outsiders, and less range in generations within a single household.

THE FAMILY'S HOUSING

Of all contrasts between urban and rural families, none is more visible than in the physical setting of family life. The comparison of the farm homestead or the shaded small-town home on the one hand with the city flat or apartment on the other is obvious. Yet the comparison of the crowded quarters of migrant agricultural workers with the wooded estates of city executives is also pertinent in assessing the housing contrasts of rural and urban residents.

More families owned their own homes, the average size of households was smaller, and fewer homes lacked plumbing facilities in 1950 than ever before reported by a national census. Homeowners exceeded renters for the first time, with a 54 per cent increase in home-ownership over 1940.[11] This shift was due partially to government programs of home-purchase aid and rent control. Out of all dwelling units in 1950, only 1.6 per cent were vacant units offered for rent or sale. As indicated in Table 44, owner occupancy decreased as one moved from rural to urban, as would be expected under the hypothesis of greater rural stability. Nonseasonal, nondilapidated dwelling units were least available for rent or sale in rural-farm areas. Seasonal vacant dwelling units were primarily rural-nonfarm, located principally at resorts.

Table 44. Occupancy and Tenure of Dwelling Units, for the United States, Urban and Rural, 1950

Occupancy and tenure	Per cent distribution			
	Total	Urban	Rural-nonfarm	Rural-farm
All dwelling units......................	100.0	100.0	100.0	100.0
Occupied dwelling units.................	92.7	96.1	84.1	90.9
Owner-occupied......................	51.0	48.5	52.6	59.4
Renter-occupied......................	41.7	47.6	31.4	31.4
Nonresident dwelling units..............	0.2	0.2	0.3	0.1
Vacant dwelling units..................	7.1	3.8	15.6	9.0
Nonseasonal, not dilapidated, for rent or sale...............................	1.6	1.7	1.8	0.7
For rent...........................	1.1	1.2	1.3	0.6
For sale only.......................	0.5	0.6	0.5	0.1
Nonseasonal, not dilapidated, not for rent or sale............................	1.8	1.0	3.2	2.7
Seasonal...........................	2.7	0.6	9.1	2.2

SOURCE: Bureau of the Census, 1950 Census of Housing, Preliminary Reports, Series HC-5, No. 1, Feb. 17, 1951.

Over three-fifths of all United States dwelling units in 1950 were one-dwelling-unit detached structures without business. The proportion of single household structures varied from about one-half for urban dwelling units to 95 per cent for rural-farm units. As one moves from open country to metropolis, one tends to find a sharply increasing proportion of families housed in rented dwellings located in multiple-unit structures,

[11] Bureau of the Census, 1950 Census of Housing, Preliminary Reports, Series HC–5, No. 1, Feb. 17, 1951.

and a sharply decreasing proportion of families housed in owner-occupied single-unit structures. Trailer living presents little rural-urban contrast, accounting for less than 1 per cent of 1950 dwelling units.[12]

Compared with 1940, there were relatively fewer of the smallest and largest dwelling units in 1950. The median number of rooms in occupied units declined slightly from 4.8 to 4.7. On the average, farm dwelling units were larger than nonfarm units, 5.2 compared with 4.6. The sharpest increment between 1940 and 1950 was in four- and five-room units; the sharpest decline was in one- and nine-or-more-room units. Many of the very largest single-family structures were converted to multiple-dwelling units during this period. Trends reflected in part the adaptation of dwelling-unit size to the declining size of households.[13]

Between 1940 and 1950 consistent decrease occurred in room crowding in the United States, as indicated in Table 45. The percentage of

Table 45. Persons per Room in Occupied Dwelling Units, for the United States, Urban and Rural, 1950 and 1940

	Per cent of occupied dwelling units				
Persons per room	1950 total	1950 urban	1950 rural		1940 total
			Non-farm	Farm	
All occupied dwelling units...............	100.0	100.0	100.0	100.0	100.0
0.75 or less persons per room............	60.2	61.4	57.7	58.1	54.9
0.76 to 1.00 persons per room...........	24.1	25.2	23.1	20.2	24.9
1.01 to 1.50 persons per room...........	9.6	8.7	11.0	12.0	11.3
1.51 or more persons per room..........	6.1	4.7	8.2	9.7	9.0
Nonwhite occupied dwelling units.........	100.0	100.0	100.0	100.0	100.0
0.75 or less persons per room............	40.5	43.4	39.5	29.9	34.3
0.76 to 1.00 persons per room...........	24.2	26.4	21.5	18.7	25.7
1.01 to 1.50 persons per room...........	15.1	13.5	15.2	21.2	16.6
1.51 or more persons per room..........	20.2	16.7	23.8	30.1	23.4

SOURCE: Bureau of the Census, 1950 Census of Housing, Preliminary Reports, Series HC-5, No. 1, Feb. 17, 1951.

dwelling units with more than 1.50 persons per room decreased from 9 to 6; among nonwhites from 23 to 20. The percentage of dwelling units with 1.00 person per room or less increased from 79 to 84; among nonwhites from 60 to 65. This change was a function both of decline in household size and of greater rate of increase in new dwelling units than in population. For both the total population and nonwhite population, there was significantly more room crowding in rural than in urban areas. Crowded living is, contrary to popular impression, more characteristic of

[12] *Ibid.*
[13] *Ibid.*

rural than urban households. This rural-urban contrast is in large part a function of the larger size of rural households, since rural-farm dwelling units have on the average more rooms than nonfarm dwelling units.

Out of every 100 occupied dwelling units in the United States, 91 were found in 1950 not to be dilapidated and 65 were found to have private toilet, bath, and hot running water. Among nonwhite occupied dwelling units, 69 per cent were not dilapidated and 31 per cent had private toilet, bath, and hot running water. Between 1940 and 1950 the percentage of all occupied dwelling units with no flush toilet decreased from 35

Table 46. Condition and Plumbing Facilities of Dwelling Units, for the United States, Urban and Rural, 1950

Condition and plumbing facilities	Per cent of dwelling units			
	Total	Urban	Rural-nonfarm	Rural-farm
All occupied dwelling units..............	100.0	100.0	100.0	100.0
Not dilapidated.......................	90.8	94.1	88.3	79.2
With private toilet, bath, and hot running water..........................	63.5	78.5	46.5	22.1
With private toilet, bath, and only cold water..........................	3.3	3.1	4.3	2.5
With running water, lacking private toilet or bath..........................	12.1	10.5	15.0	14.7
No running water...................	11.9	2.1	22.5	39.9
Dilapidated..........................	9.2	5.9	11.7	20.8
With private toilet, bath, and hot running water..........................	1.4	1.8	0.9	0.5
Lacking hot water, private toilet, or private bath.............................	7.8	4.1	10.8	20.3
Nonwhite occupied dwelling units........	100.0	100.0	100.0	100.0
Not dilapidated.......................	68.5	76.1	62.7	47.7
With private toilet, bath, and hot running water..........................	27.3	40.1	5.8	2.3
With private toilet, bath, and only cold water..........................	3.9	5.8	0.2	0.8
With running water, lacking private toilet or bath..........................	15.1	20.9	7.2	2.1
No running water...................	22.1	9.2	49.5	42.7
Dilapidated..........................	31.5	23.9	37.3	52.3
With private toilet, bath, and hot running water..........................	3.2	4.9	*	*
Lacking hot water, private toilet, or private bath........................	28.3	19.0	37.3	52.3

SOURCE: Bureau of the Census, 1950 Census of Housing, Preliminary Reports, Series HC-5, No. 1, Feb. 17, 1951.

* Per cent not shown where base is less than 100,000.

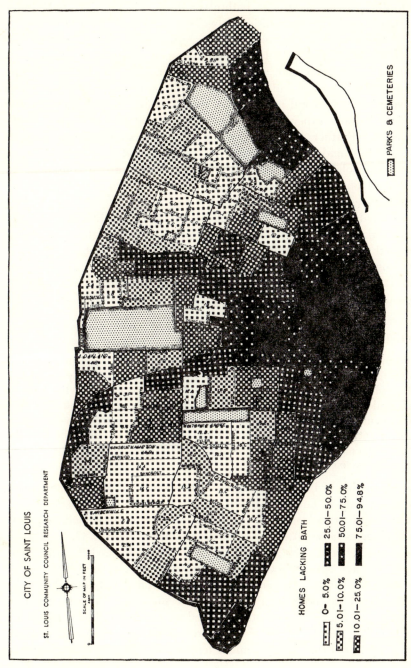

Fig. 24. Per cent of dwelling units lacking private bath, St. Louis, 1940.

to 23; the percentage with no bathtub or shower decreased from 39 to 27. As shown in Table 46 rural-farm dwelling units were most often dilapidated and had least plumbing facilities; urban dwelling units were least often dilapidated and had most plumbing facilities. City dwellers, in contrast to rural residents, are markedly advantaged in rooms per person, condition of housing, and possession of plumbing and other household conveniences. As noted in Chap. 14, the provision of many facilities and services is more expensive in areas of sparse settlement than of dense settlement. Further, sparse settlement is likely to support in its contiguous services and facilities less specialization and professionalization. Physically isolated households are more likely than urban households to be forced both to become more self-sufficient and to do without more conveniences and specialized services.

As noted in Chap. 12, blighted areas in American cities are generally characterized by poor housing, high mobility, and high incidence of personal and social disorganization. Figure 24 presents data on St. Louis dwelling units lacking bath. The area characterized by least adequate bath facilities is one dominantly of old, deteriorated tenements. In it the typical physical and social characteristics of a blighted area are present.

THE LIFE CYCLE OF THE FAMILY

From its formation until its dissolution, a family passes through a series of stages that are subject to demographic analysis. Typically, a family comes into being when a couple is married. The family gains in size with the birth of each child. From the time when the last child is born until the first child leaves home, the family remains stable in size. As the children leave home for employment or marriage, the size of the family shrinks gradually back to the original two persons. Eventually one and then the other of the parents die and the family cycle comes to an end.[14]

During the life of the typical family, Glick points out, important changes occur not only in family composition but in other characteristics.

The rapid urbanization of the United States was reflected in family cycle changes between 1890 and 1940, as shown in Table 47. In general, there was between 1890 and 1940 a trend toward somewhat earlier marriage, less age spread between husband and wife, a shorter period of childbearing, a much longer period together after the children had married and set up their own families, and somewhat briefer period of widowhood. Beegle and Loomis utilized an approach similar to Glick's in comparing the life cycles of farm, rural-nonfarm, and rural-farm families. They found that urban families tended to be smaller throughout the

[14] Paul S. Glick, "The Family Cycle," *Amer. Sociol. Rev.*, 12 (1947), 164. By permission of the *American Sociological Review*.

Table 47. Median Age of Husband and Wife at Each Stage of the Family Cycle, for the United States, 1940 and 1890

Stage of the family cycle	Median age of husband		Median age of wife	
	1940	1890	1940	1890
First marriage.....................	24.3	26.1	21.6	22.0
Birth of first child...............	25.3	27.1	22.6	23.0
Birth of last child................	29.9	36.0	27.2	31.9
Marriage of first child...........	48.3	51.1	45.6	47.0
Marriage of last child...........	52.8	59.4	50.1	55.3
Death of first of spouses.........	63.6	57.4	60.9	53.3
Death of second of spouses.......	69.7	66.4	73.5	67.7

Source: Adapted from Paul S. Glick, "The Family Cycle," *Amer. Sociol. Rev.*, 12 (1947), 165. By permission of the *American Sociological Review*.

Table 48. Characteristics of Husband-and-Wife Families by Age of Husband, for the United States, 1940

Family characteristic	Age of husband in years						
	Under 25	25–29	30–34	35–44	45–54	55–64	Over 64
Per cent of husband-wife families with:							
One or more related children under 18...................	53.5	65.7	74.7	77.0	60.2	35.6	18.1
One or more relatives 18 or over	8.9	11.2	15.8	29.6	54.4	55.8	44.8
Per cent of husband-wife families:							
In same house in 1935 as in 1940	*	*	15.5	36.6	52.2	63.8	*
Owning their homes..........	11.8	18.8	27.1	39.2	52.1	60.6	68.5
Median rental value of home.....	$ 11.41	$15.92	$19.15	$22.48	$24.24	$23.34	$20.89
Median family wage or salary income in 1939...............	$861	$ 1,193	$ 1,393	$ 1,527	$ 1,626	$ 1,467	$ 1,192
Per cent of family heads in labor force.......................	98.1	98.6	98.5	97.6	95.5	88.6	52.2
Per cent of wives of family heads in labor force.................	14.8	16.5	15.4	13.7	10.8	7.6	4.8

Source: Adapted from Paul S. Glick, "The Family Cycle," *Amer. Sociol. Rev.*, 12 (1947), 172. By permission of the *American Sociological Review*.
* Data not available.

family cycle. Although urban females married later than rural, urban males did not differ from rural in age at first marriage. Urban couples ended childbearing at an earlier age, were older when the first child married, were about the same age when the last child married, and lived less long.[15]

[15] Allan Beegle and C. P. Loomis, "Life Cycles of Farm, Rural-nonfarm, and Urban Families in the United States as Derived from Census Materials," *Rural Sociol.*, 13 (1948), 70–74.

Table 48 indicates the considerable variation not only in family composition but also in economic characteristics of families at various stages in their cycle. Although families are at their maximum size when the husband is in the thirty-five to forty-four age bracket, residential stability, homeownership, value of home, and income are maximum when the husband is at a more advanced age. A maximum percentage of husbands and wives are in the labor force in the childbearing period, suggesting economic pressures which are related to family size limitation, particularly in urban areas.

COURTSHIP

It is commonplace to suggest that associated with the rapid urbanization of recent years there has been a decline in familism, a decline in the acceptance of family good as paramount and of individual desires as subordinate. As an integral part of this development, there appears to have been a decline of family authority and control over the processes of courtship and mate selection. Increasingly, adolescents and young adults have appeared to view dating and courtship behavior as an individual prerogative to be carried out for the satisfaction of personal rather than of family goals.

In testing such hypotheses with regard to the changes in courtship behavior in recent years, Koller studied three generations of women living in Columbus, Ohio.[16] The modal ages of the three generation samples were 78, 48, and 23 years. The first generation was primarily educated only in elementary schools, the second generation primarily in high school, and a majority of the third generation sample had attended college. Whereas only three grandmothers had done clerical or sales work before marriage, 62 of the granddaughters had. The older generation was mainly rural in background; the second generation was about equally divided in rural and urban background; and the younger generation was 74 per cent urban.

Koller found that parental disapproval of boys being dated in the respondent's early courtship was greatest in the young generation and least in the old generation. Of the first generation, 23 per cent yielded to their parents' wishes rather than attempting to change their minds when the young ladies faced parental disapproval of the boys they were dating. In contrast, only 9.5 per cent of the third generation had yielded at the suggestion of parental disapproval. Of the daughters, 50 per cent had

---

[16] Marvin R. Koller, "Some Changes in Courtship Behavior in Three Generations of Ohio Women," *Amer. Sociol. Rev.*, 16 (1951), 366–370. Koller used samples of 200 women in each of the three generations.

used argument and persuasion to change parental attitudes, while only 13 per cent of the grandmothers had argued for parental approval. Parental homes, local neighborhoods, and church services had been the chief settings for meeting husbands-to-be for the older generation, while the younger generation women had relied more heavily upon school and secondary-group situations for meeting their prospective mates. Although a majority of women in each generation claimed to have considered seriously only the one man they finally married, the percentage of first generation so claiming was much larger than the percentage of third generation. No significant difference by generations was found in the mean age at first date with the mate-to-be. For all three generations the man primarily financed dating activities. "Home dating" and "parlor dating" were much more characteristic of the older than the younger generation. Formal and informal chaperonage were more characteristic of the older generation. Median dating frequencies per week were one, two, and three for the first, second, and third generation, respectively. The grandmothers gave gifts to their men rarely, the mothers more frequently, and the daughters most frequently. Women in all generations made a point of visiting the homes of both sets of parents in connection with courtship. Serious discussion in advance of marriage of the problems to be encountered was more characteristic of the younger generation than of the older. The mean lengths of engagement were for first, second, and third generation, 8.99, 8.45, and 7.18 months, respectively. The grandmothers had known their husbands-to-be for a longer period prior to marriage than the daughters had known their prospective spouses. The mean age differences of spouses were for the first, second, and third generation, 4.45, 3.78, and 2.74 years, respectively. The total duration of courtship for all three generations averaged a little more than one year. In general, Koller's findings support the hypothesis of increase in individuated and decline in familistic behavior in courtship and mate selection.

Kinsey found significant contrasts in the sexual behavior of rural and urban males.[17] The rural males were found to have fewer "sociosexual contacts," such as premarital petting, premarital and extramarital intercourse, and homosexual relations, and much higher frequencies of animal intercourse. Such differentials would appear to be in part due to differential opportunity for the several forms of sexual behavior. Differences in heterosexual petting and nonmarital intercourse would appear to be related also to strong family and local pressures for conventional behavior in rural areas.

[17] Alfred C. Kinsey, Wardell B. Pomeroy, and Clyde E. Martin, *Sexual Behavior in the Human Male,* p. 464, 1948.

MARRIAGE

It would appear to be reasonable to expect that "like marries like" more commonly in the homogeneous rural community than in the more heterogeneous urban community. By similar reasoning, one would expect that during recent years of rapid urbanization there would have been a rising proportion of marriages which crossed cultural, ethnic, religious, and class lines—in short, a rising proportion of mixed marriages.

Kennedy studied all marriages in New Haven, Conn., in 1870, 1900, 1930, and 1940, in order to identify trends with regard to interethnic and interreligious marriages. She concluded that *"while strict endogamy is loosening, religious endogamy is persisting and the future cleavages will be along religious lines rather than along nationality lines as in the past."*[18] She summarized her findings as follows:

In New Haven a "triple-melting-pot" type of assimilation is occurring through intermarriage, with Catholicism, Protestantism, and Judaism serving as the three fundamental bulwarks. Catholics mostly marry other Catholics; Jews almost always choose Jewish mates; while Protestants prefer non-Catholic Gentiles. Our statistics show a marked adherence to these religious choices. Thus the different nationalities are merging, but within three religious compartments rather than indiscriminately: with Protestant British-Americans, Germans, and Scandinavians intermarrying mutually; Catholic Irish, Italians, and Poles forming a separate intermarrying group; and Jews remaining almost completely endogamous. A triple religious cleavage rather than a multilinear nationality cleavage, therefore, seems likely to characterize American society in the future. When mixed marriage does occur, it would appear that the relative strength of each religion can be gauged by the type of ceremony employed to sanction such unions. In New Haven, Catholics are the most successful in having their marriages to persons of other faiths performed by their own clergymen; Protestants are considerably less insistent on their own type of ceremony in mixed marriages; while Jews show the lowest frequency in this respect.[19]

Thomas found, in contrast to the New Haven situation analyzed by Kennedy, that mixed Catholic–non-Catholic marriages represented 26.2 per cent of all 1950 marriages sanctioned by the Roman Catholic Church.[20] In 132 parishes distributed throughout the East and Middle West, he discovered 29,581 mixed marriages during 1950, of which 39.6 per cent were not sanctioned by Catholic nuptials. His studies revealed three factors which particularly affected the intermarriage rate: (1) the percentage of Catholics in the total population, (2) the presence of co-

[18] Ruby Jo Reeves Kennedy, "Single or Triple Melting-pot? Intermarriage Trends in New Haven, 1870–1940," *Amer. Jour. Sociol.,* 49 (1944), 332.

[19] *Ibid.,* p. 331. By permission of the University of Chicago Press.

[20] John L. Thomas, "The Factor of Religion in the Selection of Marriage Mates," *Amer. Sociol. Rev.,* 16 (1951), 487–491.

hesive ethnic subgroups, and (3) the socioeconomic status of the Catholic population in the community. He found that, where there was a small percentage Catholic in the population, the intermarriage rate was high; where the percentage was high, the intermarriage rate was low. His finding that ethnic subgroups among the Catholics acted as barriers to Catholic–non-Catholic intermarriage developed out of his analysis of Table 49. There the expected increase in intermarriage as one moved from rural to urban reversed itself in cities of 100,000 and over. Intensive comparative study of large-city parishes indicated that major ethnic subgroup concentrations were present in unusually large degree and acted to reduce the intermarriage rate. A third factor operating to discourage intermarriage he found to be the low socioeconomic status of a considerable proportion of the Catholic population. He found in 30 parishes of a large urban center that percentages of mixed marriages for various types of residential areas were: lower, 8.5; mixed lower and middle, 9.1; middle, 12.0; mixed middle and upper, 16.3; upper, 17.9; and suburban, 19.3. Thomas concludes that the trend of gradual increase in the rate of intermarriage will continue into the future, as immigration decreases, acculturation proceeds, and increasingly tolerant attitudes toward intermarriage develop.

Table 49. Percentage of Mixed Marriages (Catholic with Non-Catholic) According to Size of City

Population of city	Number of parishes	Number of families	Percentage of mixed marriages
100,000 and over............	25	36,353	14.9
25,000–100,000.............	25	15,000	24.2
5,000–25,000..............	25	16,624	21.4
5,000 and under............	25	9,431	19.6

Source: John L. Thomas, "The Factor of Religion in the Selection of Marriage Mates," *Amer. Sociol. Rev.*, 16 (1951), 490. By permission of the *American Sociological Review*.

Hollingshead in a recent study of New Haven marriages found strong support for

. . . the proposition that one's subculture, and one's race, age, and class positions in the society effectively determine the kind of a person one will marry, but not the exact individual. In a highly significant number of cases the person one marries is very similar culturally to one's self. . . . [21]

Hollingshead found in 1948 that there were no interracial marriages in New Haven; that there was a corrected coefficient of contingency of

[21] August B. Hollingshead, "Cultural Factors in the Selection of Marriage Mates," *Amer. Sociol. Rev.*, 15 (1950), 627. By permission of the *American Sociological Review*.

0.80 between the ages of husbands and wives, with husbands tending to marry wives no older than themselves; that 91 per cent of marriages involved partners from the same religious group (for Jews the percentage was 97.1, among Catholics 93.8, and for Protestants 74.4); that interethnic marriages occurred primarily within rather than between members of the three religious groups; and that there was a corrected coefficient of contingency of 0.77 between the class positions of husband and wife, as measured by type of residential area.

Centers in a recent study of occupational factors in mate selection analyzed the relation between the occupations of married men and of their wives' fathers, utilizing results of a 1945 nationwide sample survey. He restricted his sample to married couples in which nonfarm occupations were reported for both husband and father-in-law, since farm employment status was not generally reported precisely enough to be an indicator of economic class position. The data were viewed from the position of the male, of the female, and of the parents, with the findings in each case showing a substantial amount of occupational endogamy. Marriage within the person's own or immediately contiguous occupational group was found to be highly typical. As shown in Table 50, females tended to marry at the same level, or up, more frequently

Table 50. Marriage Directions (as Measured by Occupation) of Urban Males and Females in Urban Marriages, 1945

| Occupational status* | Per cent who are married | | | | | |
| | Up | | At own level | | Down | |
	Male	Female	Male	Female	Male	Female
Business executive.........	..	..	15	55	85	45
Professional..............	7	20	25	37	68	43
Small business............	11	24	40	29	49	47
White collar..............	37	24	23	40	40	36
Skilled manual............	24	48	46	30	30	22
Semiskilled...............	49	49	41	38	10	13
Unskilled................	60	63	40	37		

SOURCE: Richard Centers, "Marital Selection and Occupational Strata," *Amer. Jour. Sociol.*, 54 (1949), 530–535. Adapted from Tables 3 and 6. By permission of The University of Chicago Press.

* The occupational stratum of the woman is defined by her father's occupation.

than males, with the sharpest contrast at the business executive level (85 per cent of business executive males and 45 per cent of business executive females married down).

Glick and Landau found that the median age at marriage has declined since 1890, apparently in part because of decline in the proportion of farm operators in the United States and because of decline in need to delay marriage as a means of limiting family size, since there was increased knowledge of alternative birth control measures.[22] The estimated median age at first marriage for men dropped from 26.1 years in 1890 to 24.3 years in 1940 to 22.7 years in 1949. The corresponding figures for women were 22.0, 21.6, and 20.3 years. Glick and Landau found that the age difference between husband and wife was for the median couple married for the first time 2.8 years, and for the median couple with one or both partners married more than once, 4.7 years. In general, they found greater age variability among remarried than first married couples.

Glick and Landau found important differences in age at marriage among various occupational and income groups. Men in occupations requiring capital or specialized training tended to delay their first marriages from one to three years. Consistent with this pattern was the fact that two rural occupations, farmer and farm laborer, had the greatest and least median age at first marriage, respectively.

PROCREATION

We have already noted that rural families tend to be larger than urban families. In large measure, the differential in family size reflects the lower urban birth rate. In Table 51 fertility data are presented for the United States, urban and rural. Between 1940 and 1949 there was a consistent increase in the fertility rates at all age levels, urban and rural. This pattern of increase represents a temporary wartime reversal of the long-term trend of declining birth rates associated with industrialization and urbanization. At all age levels in both 1949 and 1940, there was a sharp increase in the fertility rates as one went from urban to rural-farm, with rural-nonfarm rates consistently intermediate. These data confirm earlier findings that there is an inverse relationship between urbanism and number of children per household.

The known rural-urban differentials in gainful employment of women immediately suggest themselves in explaining the sharp rural-urban differentials in fertility. The 1949 age-standardized fertility rates of women not in the labor force were around three times the rates of women in the labor force in urban and rural-nonfarm areas, and around two times in rural-farm areas. Percentages of women with children under five years old showed a similar pattern. Clearly gainful employment on the one hand and childbearing and child care on the other are heavily

[22] Paul C. Glick and Emanuel Landau, "Age as a Factor in Marriage," *Amer. Sociol. Rev.*, 15 (1950), 517–529.

competitive activities for both urban and rural women. And clearly city women tend to choose working rather than bearing and rearing children much more frequently than do rural women.

High plane of living and income, it has been argued, tend to be competitive with large families, particularly in the city. While children may be an economic asset in the labor of a family enterprise such as a farm, for most urban families children involve costs without immediate economic return. Table 52 indicates an inverse relation between income and fertility. Since money income tends to be somewhat higher in urban

Table 51. Number of Own Children under 5 Years Old per 1,000 Women 15 to 49 Years Old, Married and Husband Present, by Age of Woman, for the United States, Urban and Rural, 1949 and 1940

Age of woman	Children under 5 per 1,000 women 15 to 49							
	1949				1940			
	Total	Urban	Rural-non-farm	Rural-farm	Total	Urban	Rural-non-farm	Rural-farm
15 to 49 years.....	555	503	632	631	452	369	516	618
15 to 24 years.....	815	748	885	936	720	614	796	864
25 to 29 years.....	920	857	993	1,049	736	629	803	980
30 to 39 years.....	568	515	642	664	457	380	486	665
40 to 49 years.....	127	102	130	202	117	80	124	212

Source: Bureau of the Census, Current Population Reports, Series P-20, No. 27, Feb. 3, 1950.

Table 52. Per Cent Distribution of Women 15 to 49 Years Old, Married and Husband Present, by Total Money Income of Family, and Number of Own Children under 5 Years Old per 1,000 of These Women, Standardized for Age of Women, for the United States, 1949

Total money income level	Per cent distribution of women, married and husband present	Children under 5 per 1,000 women	
		Unstandardized	Standardized
All income levels........	100.0	555	550
Under $1,000............	6.2	629	677
$1,000 to $1,999.........	12.5	702	628
$2,000 to $2,999.........	22.6	673	580
$3,000 to $3,999.........	23.3	629	571
$4,000 to $4,999.........	14.8	486	476
$5,000 and over.........	20.5	351	407

Source: Bureau of the Census, Current Population Reports, Series P-20, No. 27, Feb. 3, 1950.

areas, the data suggest that income factors may be of some significance in explaining the rural-urban fertility contrasts.

In Table 53 standardized fertility rates for married men are shown in relation to occupational status. The impact of war and inflation resulted in consistently significant fertility increases in every occupational status category between 1947 and 1949. Members of the armed forces and farm laborers had outstandingly high fertility rates in 1949. Second high in rates among civilian occupational groups was the farmer and farm manager category, reflecting again the high fertility in rural, and

Table 53. Number of Own Children under 5 Years Old per 1,000 Men 20 to 59 Years Old, Married and Wife Present, by Employment Status and Major Occupation Group of Man, Standardized for Age of Man, for United States Civilians, 1949 and 1947

Employment status and occupation of men	Children under 5 per 1,000 men			
	Unstandardized		Standardized	
	1949	1947	1949	1947
Total, 20 to 59 years..........................	493	458	482	458
In labor force..............................	497	463	483	460
Employed................................	492	463	483	462
Unemployed.............................	535	433	517	441
In armed forces..........................	771	549	*	*
Not in labor force..........................	351	284	427	359
Employed, 20 to 59 years....................	492	463	483	462
Professional and semiprofessional workers.........	520	501	459	465
Farmers and farm managers..................	504	485	559	549
Proprietors, managers, and officials, except farm...	401	376	464	412
Clerical and kindred workers..................	455	407	413	389
Salesmen..................................	495	434	453	395
Craftsmen, foremen, and kindred workers........	463	449	462	454
Operatives and kindred workers................	554	516	482	469
Service workers............................	393	361	424	406
Farm laborers and farm foremen...............	785	682	740	634
Laborers, except farm and mine...............	556	511	522	502

SOURCE: Bureau of the Census, Current Population Reports, Series P-20, No. 27, Feb. 3, 1950. Civilian population includes the small number of members of the armed forces living off post or with their families on post but excludes all other members of the armed forces.
  * Rate not shown because there were too few men in some component five-year age groups to permit standardization for age.

particularly farming, areas. The evidence here points to the generalization that children are least competitive with occupational and economic status in farming areas, and most competitive in cities. However, the contrast between the fertility of farm owners and managers on the one hand and farm laborers and foremen on the other suggests that economic status is inversely related to fertility in rural areas.

Table 54 shows the inverse relation between amount of formal education and fertility. It is clear that formal education tends to reduce fertility by delaying marriage and childbearing. The closely corresponding education, occupation, and income statuses tend to converge in reducing the fertility rates of higher status groups, particularly in cities. It is paradoxical in one sense that those who seem most suited by education and income to child rearing have fewest children. Yet those who have achieved such preferred status have in part gained it by delaying marriage and childbearing and by having few children. It is in urban areas, where the struggle for status is particularly in terms of education,

Table 54. Number of Children under 5 Years Old per 1,000 Women 15 to 49 Years Old, Standardized for Age of Women, by Years of School Completed and Marital Status of Woman, for the United States, Civilian Population, 1947, and Total Population, 1940

Years of school completed	Children under 5 per 1,000 women			
	All marital classes		Married, husband present	
	1947	1940	1947	1940*
Less than 5 years of grade school	508	405	718	634
5 and 6 years of grade school	477	405	661	589
7 and 8 years of grade school	422	339	572	505
1 to 3 years of high school	396	292	535	444
4 years of high school	323	218	465	381
1 to 3 years of college	306	197	482	368
4 years or more of college	271	153	446	333

SOURCE: Bureau of the Census, Current Population Reports, Series P-20, No. 18, June 30, 1948.
* Married once, husband present.

occupation, and income, that the incentive to delay and limit fertility is greatest. There is, however, evidence that the contrast between urban and rural fertility rates is lessening as the processes of urbanization extend increasingly to the open country and small towns.

CHILD REARING AND FAMILY RELATIONS

Among the changes taking place in the American family under impact of urbanization, few are of greater importance than the loss of traditional functions. It has been commonly hypothesized that such changes are least present in rural families and most present in urban families. Leevy compared the activities of 1,000 rural and 1,000 urban families in Illinois interviewed during the period 1934 to 1938. As indicated in

Table 55, he found that urbanites consistently proved to be less self-sufficient in the family, and more dependent on outside facilities and organizations, in which participation tended to be more individual and less familial.

Table 55. Activities of 1,000 Rural and 1,000 Urban Illinois Families, 1934 to 1938

Activity	Percentage distribution	
	Urban families	Rural families
Self-sufficient activities:		
Home laundry..............................	32.4	83.6
Home canning.............................	13.2	61.4
Home production of garden vegetables...........	4.2	86.4
Home sewing of garments for family members......	16.4	34.2
Home cleaning and pressing of garments.........	14.3	23.3
Family reading of Bible.......................	19.3	26.4
Use of community facilities:		
Use of bakery products.......................	93.2	62.4
Use of café or restaurant.....................	46.2	13.2
Movie attendance weekly or oftener (men)........	80.5	36.2
Movie attendance weekly or oftener (women)......	91.0	54.3
Lodge membership (men).....................	79.4	36.4
Lodge membership (women)..................	83.2	20.3

SOURCE: Adapted from J. Roy Leevy, "Contrasts in Urban and Rural Family Life," *Amer. Sociol. Rev.*, 5 (1940), 948–953. By permission of the *American Sociological Review*.

In the city, specialization of labor is maximized. A proliferation of specialized services and facilities is easily available to family members. The city family is rarely the economic unit the farming family typically is. Members of city families go their separate ways during a large proportion of their waking hours. Only in the evening is the family likely to be together, and then in competition with the opportunities for individuated participation of members in various age-sex graded associations and recreational activities. Yet as the city family has lost many traditional economic, educational, religious, and recreational functions, it appears to have gained in importance in providing for the primary-group response and affectional needs of its members as relationships outside the family have become increasingly secondary and formalized.

The greater authoritarianism of the rural family and the greater equalitarianism of the urban family have been widely hypothesized. Stott's research findings tend to confirm such hypotheses.[23] However, recent research on child-rearing practices in urban families has indicated

[23] Leland H. Stott, "Parental Attitudes of Farm, Town, and City Parents in Relation to Certain Personality Adjustments in Their Children," *Jour. Soc. Psych.*, 11 (1940), 325–339.

great variability among socioeconomic strata in patterns of family control. Davis and Havighurst studied mothers of young children in Chicago, interviewing samples of 50 each of (1) white middle-class, (2) white lower-class, (3) Negro middle-class, and (4) Negro lower-class mothers. They found greater similarity between the practices of white and Negro mothers of each class than between classes. They concluded that

. . . middle-class parents are more rigorous than lower-class parents in their training of children for feeding and cleanliness habits. They also expect their children to take responsibility for themselves earlier than lower-class parents do. Middle-class parents place their children under a stricter regimen, with more frustration of their impulses, than do lower-class parents.[24]

A recent study of rural and urban families comparatively with regard to marital and family adjustment utilized questionnaire information on 161 college coeds and their mothers, both of whom had been reared in a rural environment, and 146 coeds and their mothers, both of whom had been reared in an urban environment.[25] In general, contrasts between generations appeared to be greater than between urban and rural. This finding suggests that the more important aspect of urbanization relates not so much to rural-urban residence as to the rapid rise of urban dominance through the automobile, radio, movies, and other media of mass communication and contact. However, the daughter generation in this study has been subjected to the secularizing and urbanizing influence of a common college experience, while many of the mothers had no such experience.

Such consistent contrasts between urban and rural samples as do emerge in this study are revealing. Unexpected is the evidence of happier home experience among urban than among rural respondents of both the mother and daughter generation. A similar finding was reported by Nye in a study of adolescent-parent adjustment in high school student families.[26] Such findings seem contrary to the hypothesis of greater rural familism, stability, and *Gemeinschaft*. However, from another point of view these data suggest that the urbanizing impact of recent technological developments may be producing more rapid change in the traditional ways of rural life than in the already more secular city life.

[24] Allison Davis and Robert J. Havighurst, "Social Class and Color Differences in Child Rearing," *Amer. Sociol. Rev.*, 11 (1946), 710. By permission of the *American Sociological Review*.

[25] Arlene Sheeley, Paul H. Landis, and Vernon Davies, *Marital and Family Adjustment in Rural and Urban Families of Two Generations*, Bulletin 506, The State College of Washington, Institute of Agricultural Sciences, Agricultural Experiment Station, May, 1949.

[26] Ivan Nye, "Adolescent-Parent Adjustment—Socio-economic Level as a Variable," *Amer. Sociol. Rev.*, 16 (1951), 341–349.

Various kinds of evidence have already suggested more rapid rate of rural than urban change, *e.g.*, the more rapid recent rural decline in family size. Such greater rural change would seem likely to lead to greater conflict of values between generations in rural than in urban families. And conflict of values is less likely to be accommodated in a more *Gemeinschaftlich* setting.

Consistent with findings elsewhere reported were the beliefs of a greater percentage of rural mothers and daughters that a girl should gear her education toward marriage and a home; the most important problem of women is that of balance between career, home, and social life; and four or more children are an ideal number. A greater percentage of urban respondents believed that a woman should work after she has married until she has children; all families should practice birth control; and children should be disciplined by other means than corporal punishment.

OLD AGE AND THE FAMILY

In 1940 the husband was typically fifty-three and the wife was fifty when the last of the children had married and left the parental home. Subsequently the original marital pair typically had eleven years together before one of the spouses (usually the husband) died. The median period of widowhood was for women thirteen years and for men six years. Industrialization and urbanization have increased the life ex-

Table 56. Place of Residence of the Population 60 Years of Age and Over, by Sex and Age, for the United States, 1940 (Percentage Distribution)

Sex and age	Total	Live outside private household*	Live in private household			
			Head of family	Wife of head	With children, other relatives	Lodger, servant, etc.
Males:						
60–64......	100.0	4.2	83.5	....	6.9	5.4
65–69......	100.0	4.1	81.2	....	9.2	5.5
70–74......	100 0	4.5	77.0	....	13.0	5.5
75 plus....	100.0	5.7	65.1	....	23.3	6.0
Females:						
60–64......	100.0	2.6	24.7	52.7	15.6	4.4
65–69......	100.0	2.7	30.1	41.3	21.3	4.6
70–74......	100.0	3.4	34.5	29.7	27.7	4.7
75 plus.....	100.0	5.1	34.6	14.0	41.2	5.1

SOURCE: 1940 Census data presented in Ruth Shonle Cavan, "Family Life and Family Substitutes in Old Age," *Amer. Sociol. Rev.*, 14 (1949), 71. By permission of the *American Sociological Review*.

* Those outside private households were primarily in boarding or lodginghouses, institutions, and hotels.

pectancy, and thus the period of old age, of our population. But with the decline of familism in the city, the role and status of the increasingly numerous older family members have become confused and often difficult.

Mrs. Cavan found that in 1940 there was associated with increase in age a progressive increase in residence outside private households, and residence with adult children or with nonfamily members, as shown in Table 56. In order to compare the impact on the aged of such alternative housing arrangements, she studied a sample of 498 males and 755 females, aged sixty to one hundred years, typical of United States aged in marital status, percentage unemployed, and the type of living arrangement, but atypical in being primarily an urban, middle-class, native-born, white group. Table 57 presents in summary form Mrs. Cavan's findings with regard to attitudinal aspects of adjustment under four type forms of living arrangement. Males generally showed poorer adjustment in old age than females. Only in their own homes did the morale of men appear to be as high as that of women. Women seemed to be as well adjusted in hotels, rooming houses, and boarding houses as in their own homes; and only slightly less well adjusted in the homes of friends, relatives, or adult children. Although women in institutions felt

Table 57. Favorable Attitudes Expressed by Persons Aged 60 and Over, According to Living Arrangements (Percentage Distribution)

Attitude	Own home		Hotel, rooming, boarding house		Someone else's home		Institution	
	Male	Female	Male	Female	Male	Female	Male	Female
Feels economic security.....	62	62	52	45	46	55	*	62
Feels close family ties......	43	42	24	35	49	45	*	31
Feels close friendship ties...	68	69	49	68	61	60	*	52
Feels satisfied with leisure activities...............	47	43	28	49	33	39	*	26
Feels satisfied with organized activities..............	35	43	25	50	17	36	*	18
Feels satisfied with work activities..............	55	41	55	35	33	32	*	17
Feels life is still useful......	79	79	62	71	55	63	*	46
Feels happy and contented..	42	35	23	21	33	28	*	14
Composite above average on zest...................	24	23	5	26	18	17	*	5
Good adjustment score overall...................	29	30	12	32	11	24	*	10

Source: Ruth Shonle Cavan, "Family Life and Family Substitutes in Old Age," *Amer. Sociol. Rev.*, 14 (1949), 77. By permission of the *American Sociological Review*.
* Too few male cases for dependable comparisons.

economic security, they appeared less well adjusted in other repects. Mrs. Cavan concludes that:

Each type of living arrangement has its advantages and disadvantages. Granting that it is often impossible for the old person to maintain his home until death, what type of living arrangement seems best? Clearly, more institutions of the present type are not the answer; nor do rooming houses meet all the problems; homes with adult children have both advantages and disadvantages. A new type of living arrangement is needed that will combine the economic and physical security provided by the institution, the personal contacts found in the own home or the home of adult children, and the activities and sense of usefulness of the person who is still living independently.[27]

FAMILY DISSOLUTION

All families must face the stage of dissolution. In 1948 there were 31 marital dissolutions per 1,000 married couples, 19 as a result of the death of one or both spouses, and 12 as a result of divorce or annulment. In 1890 the comparable figures were 33, 30, and 3. The reduction in the rate of marital dissolutions as a result of death reflects the upward trend in life expectancy. The fourfold increase in marital dissolution by divorce and annulment appears to reflect the sharp rate at which urbanization has proceeded since 1890. In 1948 the divorce rate was maximum in the fourth year of marriage and in childless marriages. However the divorce rate is now rising more rapidly among families with children than among childless couples.[28]

Urban areas have consistently greater incidence of divorce at all age levels. Available data indicate that rural women whose marriages have been broken by death or divorce are more likely than their male counterparts to move to urban areas. The role of the single, widowed, or divorced female seems to be less satisfying in rural areas than in the city, with its occupational and other opportunities for unattached women.[29]

The rising tide of divorce and separation in American family life appears to be associated with the rise of urbanism in a number of specific ways, among which the shifts in family functions seem particularly important. As the family has lost to other agencies many of its traditional economic, educational, religious, and recreational functions, its role in

[27] Ruth Shonle Cavan, "Family Life and Family Substitutes in Old Age," *Amer. Sociol. Rev.*, 14 (1949), 83. By permission of the *American Sociological Review*.

[28] Paul H. Jacobson, "Differentials in Divorce by Duration of Marriage and Size of Family," *Amer. Sociol. Rev.*, 15 (1950), 235–244.

[29] Bureau of the Census, Current Population Reports, Series P-20, No. 33, Feb. 12, 1951. See also tables and text presented in connection with the discussion of marital status earlier in the present chapter.

satisfying the response and affectional needs of family members has become relatively more important. Many marriages which were not happy in an affectional and response sense were formerly held together because other important functions of the family were being performed in a manner satisfying to the spouses, whereas today such marriages would be less likely to be maintained.

Research findings indicate that factors associated with successful marital adjustment appear in the contemporary United States to include: (1) a background of successful social participation, (2) similarity of cultural backgrounds of spouses, (3) happy parental family experience, and (4) marriage approved by friends and relatives and based on affection developed over a period of time.[30] Stated differently, successful marriages are more likely to be of mates who have been successful in other social relations; who bring to the marriage similar values, attitudes, and expectancies; who have experienced an apprenticeship in a successful and stable parental family; who have given the relationship a pretest period of courtship and engagement before marriage. The higher incidence of family separation and divorce in the city appears to be symptomatic of the greater personal and social disorganization to be found in the more individuated, mobile, and secular life of the urbanite. It is in those areas of the city in which life is most mobile that one finds the greatest incidence of family and personal disorganization.[31]

SELECTED READINGS

BURGESS, ERNEST W., and HARVEY J. LOCKE: *The Family,* American Book Company, 1945. A systematic treatment of the field, which emphasizes the point of view that the family is in transition from an institution to a companionship. Of particular interest in relation to the present chapter are the accounts given of the rural family and the urban family.

CAVAN, RUTH SHONLE: "Family Life and Family Substitutes in Old Age," *Amer. Sociol. Rev.,* 14 (1949), 71–83. The report of a study of the status and adjustment of urban, middle-class aged under alternative household arrangements.

FARIS, ROBERT E. L.: *Social Disorganization,* The Ronald Press Company, 1948. A highly readable documentation of the hypothesis that social and personal disorganization are closely associated with the process of urbanization. The chapter on family disorganization is especially pertinent.

GLICK, PAUL C.: "The Family Cycle," *Amer. Sociol. Rev.,* 12 (1947), 164–174. An analysis of 1940 family characteristics in relation to stages in the life history of the median United States family. The 1890 to 1940

---

[30] See as a pioneer study in this field, Ernest W. Burgess and Leonard S. Cottrell, *Predicting Success or Failure in Marriage,* 1939.

[31] For systematic development of these disorganization hypotheses, see Robert E. L. Faris, *Social Disorganization,* 1948. See also Chap. 12 of this book.

comparisons of ages of the spouses at each of the stages provide insight into the impact of urbanization upon the family.

HOLLINGSHEAD, AUGUST B.: "Cultural Factors in the Selection of Marriage Mates," *Amer. Sociol. Rev.*, 15 (1950), 619–627. A report of the relation to mate selection of ethnic background, race, age, and class position in 1948 marriages in New Haven, Conn.

KOLLER, MARVIN R.: "Some Changes in Courtship Behavior in Three Generations of Ohio Women," *Amer. Sociol. Rev.*, 16 (1951), 366–370. A study of the impact of urbanization on courtship behavior through the comparison of the courtship experience of three generations of Columbus, Ohio, women.

LOOMIS, CHARLES P., and J. ALLAN BEEGLE: *Rural Social Systems*, Prentice-Hall, Inc., 1950. A documentation of the *Gemeinschaft-Gesellschaft* interpretation of rural-urban differences in social behavior. Chapters 2 to 4 are devoted to the family.

CHAPTER 17. *Attending School*

It has been said that among the outstanding characteristics of North American culture are mass schooling and belief in education as a solution for all social problems. The second part of this statement may be somewhat exaggerated, but both the faith and the practice seem to us characteristic of contemporary civilization in the United States. An annual expenditure in 1947 of $7 billion for public and private schools, the employment of 1.2 million teachers, and the instruction of 30 million children and adults are evidence that education is a major complex in our culture. During the period of rapid industrialization and urbanization since 1869, the percentage of children five to seventeen years of age enrolled as full-time day students in public elementary and secondary schools increased from 57 to 79; the percentage of children enrolled in public secondary schools increased from 1 to 24; the percentage of enrolled elementary and secondary students attending each day increased from 59 to 87; the mean number of days per year the schools were in session increased from 132 to 178; and the mean number of days attended by each student enrolled increased from 45 to 123. During this same period there was an enormous expansion of the physical plant of schools, a proliferation of specialized schools and courses, and the development of a complex professionalization and specialization within the teaching and nonteaching staff of formal education.[1]

The educational effect of the very great changes wrought by industrialization and urbanization has been equally great, though different, on city and country. Of the two, the country has appeared to fare less well. Because education is primarily a state and local responsibility, those states which are less wealthy, less industrialized, and largely rural are at a great disadvantage in comparison with their richer and more urban neighbors. Mississippi, for instance, spends only a fifth as much per pupil as New York. Since birth rates are higher in the country than

[1] U.S. Office of Education, *Biennial Survey of Education in the United States, 1946–48*, Chap. 1.

in the city, the poorer states are disadvantaged by having a relatively higher proportion of children to educate. Yet cities, not reproducing themselves, depend on migration from rural areas to maintain and increase their populations. Thus the quality of education in rural areas sharply affects the educational status of city residents.[2]

STATUS OF THE POPULATION WITH REGARD TO SCHOOLING

Between 1940 and 1950 the percentage of the population aged five to twenty-four years enrolled in school rose from 58 to 61, continuing a long-term trend in the United States associated with urbanization. The corresponding percentages for the nonwhite population were 53 and 59,

Table 58. Percentage of the Population in Specified Age Groups Enrolled in School, for the United States, Urban and Rural, 1950 and 1940

Age group and race	United States total		1950		
	1950	1940	Urban	Rural-nonfarm	Rural-farm
Persons 5 to 13 years:					
White and nonwhite..............	81.4	84.1	82.1	79.9	81.3
Nonwhite......................	81.4	79.0	82.4	79.8	80.9
Persons 14 to 17 years:					
White and nonwhite..............	84.4	79.3	87.5	82.4	78.7
Nonwhite......................	75.6	68.2	79.7	71.7	71.4
Persons 18 to 24 years:					
White and nonwhite..............	18.6	13.3	22.0	12.1	12.2
Nonwhite......................	14.6	9.1	15.7	9.1	15.7

SOURCE: Bureau of the Census, 1950 Census of Population, Preliminary Reports, Series PC-7, No. 1, Feb. 25, 1951. "School enrollment is defined as enrollment at any time between February 1 and April 1, 1950, in any school which qualifies as a 'regular' school. 'Regular' schools are those in which a person may be advanced toward an elementary or high school diploma, or a college, university, or professional school degree. Such schools may be public or private; day or night; and enrollment in them may be full or part time. 'Regular' school enrollment does *not* include enrollment in kindergarten or nursery school or, generally, enrollment in vocational, trade, business, or correspondence schools."

representing a sharp reduction in the contrast of school enrollment percentages of white and nonwhite. The sharpest increase over all was in the older years, as shown in Table 58. The decline in percentage enrollment in the age group five to thirteen years may reflect the shiftover to kindergartens in the five- and six-year age groups—kindergarten enrollments are not included in these figures. Table 58 indicates a clear

[2] Paul H. Buck, *et al.*, *General Education in a Free Society*, Report of the Harvard Committee, p. 16, 1945.

pattern of higher proportional urban than rural enrollments, becoming most marked in the older age groups. The hypothesis of positive relationship between urbanism and formal schooling tends to be confirmed by these data. It appears that formal education is most valued in the complex life of the metropolis, where secondary relationships dominate and where upward mobility tends to be carried on primarily in terms of occupation, income, and economic competition.

In Table 59 the pattern of urban-rural contrast with regard to school

Table 59. Per Cents of School Enrollment of Persons 5 to 20 Years Old, by Age, for the United States, Urban and Rural, 1950

Age and school enrollment	United States	Area		
		Urban	Rural-nonfarm	Rural-farm
5 to 20 years old enrolled in school............	72.9	74.0	71.2	71.9
5 and 6 years old enrolled in school...........	37.4	39.3	35.6	34.1
5 and 6 years old enrolled in kindergarten......	16.5	23.3	9.3	6.2
7 to 9 years old enrolled in school.............	94.7	95.1	95.2	93.2
10 to 13 years old enrolled in school...........	96.1	96.8	95.4	95.2
14 to 17 years old enrolled in school...........	84.1	86.9	82.5	78.8
18 to 20 years old enrolled in school...........	28.7	34.2	19.8	19.2

SOURCE: Adapted from Bureau of the Census, Current Population Reports, Series P-20, No. 32, Dec. 4, 1950.

enrollment is clear. At all ages, enrollment percentages are greatest in urban areas, least in rural areas. The contrast is least marked in the seven- to thirteen-year age range, and most marked in kindergarten enrollment and in the eighteen- to twenty-year age range. There is least urban-rural contrast in elementary school enrollments, more contrast in high school enrollment, and sharpest contrast in kindergarten and college enrollments. Specialized educational facilities are most easily available to the city resident and least easily available to the resident of the open country.

In 1940 the median years of school completed for persons twenty-five years old and over was 8.4 for the United States, 8.7 for urban, 8.4 for rural-nonfarm, and 7.7 for rural-farm areas. Between 1940 and 1947 the median for the United States increased from 8.4 to 9.0. In 1947, 2.7 per cent of the population of the United States fourteen years old and over was reported to be illiterate (unable to read or write in any language). The 1947 illiteracy percentages for urban, rural-nonfarm, and rural farm, respectively, were 2.0, 2.4, and 5.3. Among persons fourteen years old and over, age was found to be inversely related to median years of school completed and directly related to percentage of illiteracy, reflecting the steady extension of educational facilities and enrollment at all school-grade levels over the past hundred years.[3]

Table 60 presents data on median years of schooling completed by the

Table 60. Median Years of Schooling Completed by the Population 14 to 20 Years Old, for the United States, by Region, Sex, and Rural-Urban Residence, 1950

Region of residence and sex	United States, total	Area		
		Urban	Rural-nonfarm	Rural-farm
United States:				
Male	9.7	10.2	9.3	7.8
Female	10.2	10.7	9.8	9.1
Northeast:				
Male	10.2	10.3	9.9	8.7
Female	10.6	10.7	9.9	*
North Central:				
Male	10.2	10.5	9.9	9.6
Female	10.6	10.9	10.3	10.1
South:				
Male	7.9	9.4	7.8	6.6
Female	9.4	10.1	9.2	7.6
West:				
Male	10.2	10.5	9.4	9.7
Female	10.6	11.1	9.9	9.8

Source: Adapted from Bureau of the Census, Current Population Reports, Series P-20, No. 32, Dec. 4, 1950. Data based on a preliminary sample.
* Data not available.

population fourteen to twenty years of age according to preliminary findings of the 1950 census. The more limited median schooling of youth in the South, the least urbanized region of the country, is particularly striking. Except among male youth in the West, urban medians are consistently highest, rural-nonfarm are intermediate, and rural-farm are lowest. It is of interest that the exceptional region, the West, is characterized by the most industrialized agriculture in the nation. In every case, female youth have higher medians than male youth. It appears that male youth are more likely than female youth to be under economic pressure to drop out of school and to enter the labor force. However, a greater percentage of males than females go on to college and professional schools. In general, the pattern of these data suggests that formal education is more highly valued in urban than in rural areas.

Table 61 presents data consistent with earlier findings. Of youth

[3] Bureau of the Census, *Statistical Abstract of the United States, 1949*, pp. 111–114.

Table 61. Years of School Completed by Persons 18 to 20 Years Old, for the United States, Urban and Rural, 1950

Highest school year completed	Per cent distribution			
	United States	Urban	Rural-nonfarm	Rural-farm
Persons 18 to 20 years old..............	100.0	100.0	100.0	100.0
Under 1 year of high school............	20.7	13.2	25.9	42.4
1 to 3 years of high school.............	29.6	27.2	36.9	29.8
4 years of high school.................	36.2	41.0	32.2	23.3
1 year or more of college..............	12.2	17.2	4.0	3.6
School years not reported.............	1.2	1.3	1.1	0.8

SOURCE: Adapted from Bureau of the Census, Current Population Reports, Series P-20, No. 32, Dec. 4, 1950. Data based on a preliminary sample.

eighteen to twenty years old, the percentages who had completed less than one year of high school were for urban, rural-nonfarm, and rural-farm, respectively, 13, 26, and 42, while the percentages who had completed four years of high school or more were, respectively, 58, 36, and 27.

CITY SCHOOLS

Thirty-one million persons five to twenty-nine years old were enrolled in the public and private schools of the United States in October, 1950. This number represented an increase of 850,000 over October, 1949, and an increase of 1,625,000 over October, 1948. Of the 1950 total, 3 per cent were enrolled in kindergarten, 68 per cent in elementary schools, 22 per cent in high schools, and 7 per cent in colleges or professional schools. About one-fifth of the kindergarten enrollment was in parochial and other private schools, while the corresponding private school enrollment percentages were for elementary 12, high school 8, and college and professional school 41.[4] Formal education in the United States is overwhelmingly in public-operated schools, except at the college and professional level, where the dominance of public schools is less marked.

Of the approximately 25 million students enrolled in public schools in the academic year 1947–1948, about half were enrolled in the public school systems of cities of 2,500 or more population. The other students were enrolled in schools operated by school districts, cities of less than 2,500, counties, or states. Systems of cities of 2,500 or more population accounted in 1947–1948 for the following percentages of all public school enrollment: 78 per cent in public nurseries and kindergartens, 40 per cent

[4] Bureau of the Census, Current Population Reports, Series P-20, No. 34, July 26, 1951.

in public elementary schools, 76 per cent in public secondary schools, and 14 per cent in public universities, colleges, and normal schools.[5]

When the public school systems of cities of 2,500 and more population are grouped according to city size, results consistent with the urban-rural contrasts already made emerge. It is clear from Table 62 that the

Table 62. Selected Statistics, Public School Systems Operated by Cities of 2,500 Population and Over (1940), by Size of City, 1947–1948 School Year

Item	1940 population of the city				
	100,000 and over	30,000– 99,999	10,000– 29,999	5,000– 9,999	2,500– 4,999
Number of school systems reported.....	89	254	742	917	1,202
Per cent of total full-time enrollment:					
Nursery and kindergarten..........	8.3	5.8	4.9	4.2	3.8
Elementary......................	54.8	56.3	57.3	60.8	61.5
Secondary.......................	34.6	36.1	36.7	34.8	34.6
University, college, and normal......	2.3	1.8	1.1	0.2	0.2
Mean length of school year in days.....	184	181	180	180	179
Value of school property per pupil in average daily attendance..........	$670	$660	$595	$559	$496
Average (mean) annual salary for total instructional staff.................	$3,730	$3,131	$2,803	$2,545 *	
Annual current expenditure per pupil in average daily attendance in full-time public day schools.................	$220	$206	$181	$167 *	
Per cent increase in per-student expenditure 1937–1938 to 1947–1948...	84	109	114	122 *	
Per cent of revenue from:					
Federal government...............	3.5	1.4	1.5	1.9	1.7
State government..................	26.1	25.6	30.0	34.2	37.1
County government................	5.4	6.2	8.5	9.4	10.6
Local government.................	63.7	64.5	57.7	52.3	48.0
Other sources....................	1.3	2.3	2.3	2.2	2.6
Per cent of city systems with:					
Nursery or kindergarten schools......	80.9	63.8	52.4	49.7	45.8
Universities, colleges, or normal schools	23.6	10.6	5.8	2.6	2.1
Adult education, Americanization, night, or continuation schools.....	85.4	58.3	33.4	23.4	15.7
Summer schools..................	57.3	28.7	12.9	4.0	1.7

SOURCE: Adapted from U.S. Office of Education, *Biennial Survey of Education, 1946–48*, Chap. 3. These data do not cover urban schools which are administered as part of a larger unit, such as a county.

* Data are available only for the combined category, 2,500 to 9,999.

larger the city, the more extensive the public school program, the greater the per-student investment and expenditure for school purposes, and the greater the salary level for the instructional staff. It is also clear that, in the ten-year period between 1937–1938 and 1947–1948, this disparity

[5] U.S. Office of Education, *Biennial Survey of Education in the United States, 1946–48.*

was somewhat reduced through heavier nonlocal expenditures aimed at equalizing school facilities of city, town, and rural systems. The consistent variation in public school education along the rural-urban continuum is clearly demonstrated, with maximum diversification of facilities and maximum expenditures per student in the great cities. Table 63

Table 63. Percentage of Cities of Different Size Groups Possessing Specified Educational Facilities, 1930

Facility	Population of the city, in thousands									
	2.0–2.5	2.5–5.0	5–10	10–25	25–50	50–100	100–250	250–500	500–1,000	1,000 and over
Number of cities studied...	580	1,440	880	614	185	98	56	24	8	5
Private school...........	1	3	7	16	35	64	79	100	100	100
Nursery school..........	0	1	1	2	3	11	11	50	63	100
University..............	0	1	1	4	6	11	32	63	100	100
College................	2	4	6	13	17	39	45	79	100	100
Professional school.......	0	2	2	7	10	22	34	79	100	100
Art school.............	1	2	3	8	10	26	45	92	100	100
Teachers' college........	2	2	5	6	6	16	25	42	100	100
School for the deaf.......	0	0	1	4	14	26	52	83	100	100
School for the blind......	0	0	0	1	7	8	11	42	50	100
Classes for exceptional children.................	1	1	2	3	47	76	86	92	100	100
Sight-seeing class........	0	0	0	1	6	14	45	58	88	100

SOURCE: Fenton Keyes, *The Correlation of Social Phenomena with Community Size*, unpublished doctoral dissertation, Yale University, 1942. Adapted from tables on pp. 100 and 114. By permission of the author and Yale University.

indicates similar findings with regard to both public and private educational facilities. These rural-urban contrasts are not only functions of higher urban wealth and of higher urban valuation of formal education but are also inherent in the difficulty of supporting a highly diversified program of education in areas of sparse settlement and limited population.

Among the most notable developments of recent decades has been the rise of the public high school and the tendency to extend the age of compulsory education to include the high school years. It is at the high school level that the impact of urbanization on the social life of youth is particularly dramatic. The Harvard Committee argues cogently that:

. . . the city, with all its familiar complexities and contradictions, its unity yet discord, its efficiency yet waste, its opportunity yet frustration, is after all the characteristic feature of the times, and it is the city high school which puts most neatly the current problems of education. These spring in part from the weakening or loss of precisely those things which the country school can assume: the . . . influence of family, household, chores, animals, countryside, community, church, which had always been taken for granted as the framework of education until they began to disappear. They reflect in part also the growth of entirely new influences, comparative freedom from work, readier access to books, ideas, and music, the indiscriminate presence of the movies, radio, and pulp magazines. Not least important, they reflect the economic and cultural schisms within the seeming unity of the city, schisms which are all the greater if one reckons as part of the city the industrial and residential areas around it. And with everything else they reflect the weight of sheer numbers.[6]

City schools reflect the characteristics of the areas in which they are located and the populations which they serve. The Harvard Committee has, for example, identified and described certain types of high schools:

First there is the very large school of two thousand students or more, situated in the crowded part of the city and drawing mostly from working-class families. The classes are big, averaging at least forty, and an air of regimentation and discipline prevails. Students march from class to class, and it is no accident that men teachers are in the halls between periods and that a patrolman loiters by the entrance. Equipment and objects of art are under lock and key. Teachers, all specialists in their subject, have five classes daily in addition to keeping the "home room." Their material is largely planned for them by the state and local authorities. In the press of faces they have difficulty in knowing or following any one student, a task left to a rarely adequate staff of professional counselors. There are athletic teams, which, however, affect only comparatively few. The building is closed at a certain hour in the afternoon, after which, unless a student has a job, he has little to do except to idle at the street corner or play the juke box or finger magazines in a drugstore. Such a school offers many different kinds of vocational training, and the great majority are enrolled in one of these, having made their choice more or less at random at the age of fourteen or fifteen. Only a few, perhaps a tenth, go on to college. Like this school, though smaller, poorer, less ably taught, harsher in atmosphere, thinner in offering, and usually still more dominated by politics, are high schools in the very heart of industrial areas. Many of these are made up almost wholly of first- or second-generation Americans. Very few of their graduates go to college.

In sharp contrast to either of the foregoing is the high school in some comfortable suburb. Classes are smaller; teachers are better paid; the Parent-Teachers Association is eager and interested; there are many activities such as plays, athletics, and student publications; an atmosphere of concern for education pervades the school and the staff. A cleavage, to be sure, runs between the college-preparatory group and those who are taking vocational and business courses, and this cleavage reflects a difference of means and background.

[6] Paul H. Buck, *et al.*, *General Education in a Free Society*, Report of the Harvard Committee, p. 19, 1945. By permission of Harvard University Press.

But lines are not sharply drawn; many able but less well-to-do pupils, responding to the favorable atmosphere and encouraged by interested teachers, take the college-preparatory course. The activities of the school are also a common bond. About half the graduates of this school go on either to college or to further education of some sort.

Two other schools somewhat resemble it: the private school and the central high school in prosperous small towns, particularly in the Middle West. These are the extremes, so to speak, of which the suburban high school is the mean. All three have in common a sense of solidarity and pride in the school, a more or less personal relationship between teachers and pupils, a fairly thorough-going internal democracy, however unrepresentative the private school may be of the whole community, and a vigorous set of activities surrounding the schoolwork as such. The two extremes differ in that the private school draws from a much more restricted class and sends virtually all its graduates to college. The students are both more sheltered and more forced. The good small-town high school, on the other hand, is a cross-section of the town itself, and its strength is that of a community where everyone goes by his first name. In an academic sense it is perhaps less good than either the suburban high school or the private school, but it always sends a fair proportion of its graduates to college and contributes at least its full share, probably more than its share, of distinguished people.[7]

EDUCATION AND SOCIAL STRATIFICATION

The American public schools are, in the opinion of the people of the United States, basic and necessary parts of our democracy. We are convinced that they must, and we hope that they do, provide equal opportunity for every child. This means that those at the bottom can compete through education for life's prizes with those at the top. All that is needed are brains, a will to do, hard work, and plenty of ambition. In our faith every aspiring student may not have a marshal's baton in his knapsack, but in his public schooling he does have an equal chance with everyone else for the White House.

This basic belief in the democratic functioning of our public schools is only partly true . . . our schools, functioning in a society with basic inequalities, facilitate the rise of a few from lower to higher levels but continue to serve the social system by keeping down many people who try for higher places. The teacher, the school administrator, the school board, as well as the students themselves, play their roles to hold people in their places in our social structure.[8]

Schmid found in his correlation analysis of various indices available by census tracts in a sample of 23 cities that educational level is most highly predictive of the composite socioeconomic status of local areas. His findings are summarized in Table 64. Similar findings for St. Louis

---

[7] *Ibid.*, pp. 19–21. By permission of Harvard University Press.

[8] W. Lloyd Warner, Robert J. Havighurst, and Martin B. Loeb, *Who Shall Be Educated?* p. xi, 1944. By permission of Harper & Brothers.

were reported by Fletcher, Hornback, and Queen in their correlation matrix of 32 social and economic variables including "per cent of population 10 years and over illiterate."[9] Figure 25 indicates, for the St. Louis metropolitan area, the close correspondence of education to other indices of socioeconomic status. The pattern of this map lends support to both the zonal and the sector hypotheses of city spatial structure, as discussed in Chap. 8.

Table 64. Highest, Mid-rank, and Lowest Rectilinear Coefficients of Correlation between Median School Grade Completed and 11 Other Indices by Census Tracts, 23 Cities, 1940

Index	Coefficient of correlation with median school grade completed for population 25 years of age and over		
	Highest	Mid-rank	Lowest
Contract or estimated monthly mean rent.............	+.98	+.87	+.76
Percentage of labor force professional workers........	+.95	+.79	+.55
Percentage of labor force proprietors, managers, and officials..	+.94	+.83	+.70
Percentage of population 60 years of age and over.....	+.85	+.34	−.31
Ratio of children under 5 to females 15 to 44 years of age	−.76	−.53	−.27
Percentage of population male......................	−.79	−.54	+.01
Percentage of population under 15 years of age.......	−.80	−.48	+.01
Percentage of population foreign-born white..........	−.81	−.66	−.40
Percentage of population Negro....................	−.84	−.50	−.35
Percentage of labor force laborers.................	−.89	−.74	−.51
Percentage of labor force seeking work (unemployed)..	−.90	−.76	−.68

SOURCE: Adapted from Calvin F. Schmid, "Generalizations Concerning the Ecology of the American City," *Amer. Sociol. Rev.*, 15 (1950), 264–281. By permission of the *American Sociological Review*.

In attempting to determine the importance of education in social mobility, Centers has utilized data collected in a 1945 nationwide survey of occupations conducted by the Office of Public Opinion Research at Princeton University. He sought an answer to the question: Do sons who are better equipped educationally than their fathers more commonly have better occupational stations than those not so well endowed? Table 65 summarizes his findings, which indicate that the better educated sons tended to get better occupations than their fathers, particularly when the father's occupation was manual worker. It is of interest that most of the sons did complete more formal education than their fathers, suggesting that the educational requirements for many positions are higher today

[9] Ralph Carr Fletcher, Harry L. Hornback, and Stuart A. Queen, *Social Statistics of St. Louis by Census Tracts*, 1935.

than when these fathers were the age of their sons. Although the evidence does not demonstrate that more schooling was responsible for better jobs, it does suggest that formal education plays an important role in upward social mobility.

It is known that those who tend to be eliminated along the educational ladder from primary school to college include disproportionately large numbers of pupils of inferior intelligence and pupils whose parents'

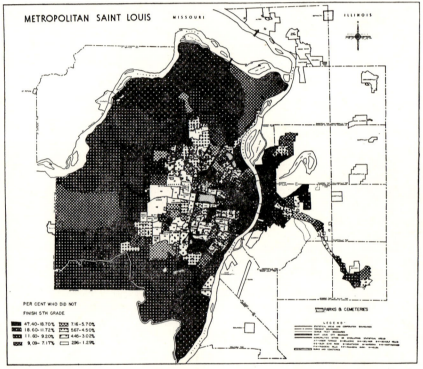

Fig. 25. Per cent of adults with less than five years of schooling, St. Louis, 1940.

socioeconomic status is low. There have developed competing interpreters of these phenomena: those who attribute the failure of poor children to their low intelligence and those who argue that the children of the poor fail because their families are not rich. Sibley has attempted to analyze the relative roles which intelligence and socioeconomic status play in the school progress of children. Table 66 presents his principal findings. Sibley concludes:

At the ninth grade and at the twelfth grade level, father's status has less influence than intelligence on educational opportunity; but at the college level,

Table 65. Occupational Positions of Urban Fathers and Sons of Various Relative Educational Levels, 1945

Education of son in relation to that of father	Number of cases	Per cent of cases where son's position is		
		Better than the father's	The same as the father's	Poorer than the father's
All occupations:				
Son's education better........	291	46	33	21
Son's education same.........	80	29	41	30
Son's education poorer........	45	16	35	49
Father's occupation business, professional, and white collar:				
Son's education better........	135	38	33	29
Son's education same.........	37	14	56	30
Son's education poorer........	28	11	21	68
Father's occupation manual worker:				
Son's education better........	156	53	33	14
Son's education same.........	43	42	28	30
Son's education poorer........	17	23	59	18

Source: Adapted from Richard Centers, "Education and Occupational Mobility," *Amer. Sociol. Rev.*, 14 (1949), 143–144. By permission of the *American Sociological Review*.

the situation is sharply reversed. While the most intelligent boys have only a 4 to 1 advantage over the least intelligent, the sons of men in the highest occupational category enjoy an advantage of more than 10 to 1 over those from the lowest occupational level. A particularly striking feature . . . is the sudden rise of a boy's chances of going beyond high school which takes place near point 10 on the Barr scale—the point which roughly divides white-collar from blue-collar workers.

. . . Although there has been (in Pennsylvania) an approach to the "social-economic democratization" of high-school education, college education and higher vocational training remain to a large extent the special privilege of children of superior social-economic backgrounds. Even on the lower levels, perfect apportionment of educational opportunity to ability as indicated by the I.Q. is not achieved.

As recruitment for the higher-paid and otherwise more desirable occupations tends increasingly to be limited to those who have had higher education, it is evident that the American educational system is far from being as effective as it might be in counteracting tendencies toward social stratification. Increased enrollment on any particular level of the system does not automatically mean progress toward the goal of assorting individuals into positions commensurate with their own abilities. A system of higher education might admit only a small minority of applicants and yet stimulate rather than retard vertical circulation in society, provided that the minority were selected for admission solely on the basis of their abilities; and *vice versa*.[10]

[10] Elbridge Sibley, "Some Demographic Clues to Stratification," *Amer. Sociol Rev.*, 7 (1942), 330. By permission of the *American Sociological Review*.

Table 66. Percentages Completing Specified Grades of School, by Intelligence Quotients and Father's Occupational Status Ratings, 2,158 Boys Entering the Sixth Grade in Pennsylvania Schools in 1926

Barr Scale ratings of fathers' occupations*	Boys' intelligence quotients				
	Under 88	88–99	100–111	112–123	124 and over
Percentage Completing 9 or More Grades					
Under 4.................	53	76	90	93	82
4–7.....................	64	85	92	95	100
8–9.....................	64	82	93	96	97
10–11...................	75	90	95	99	100
12 and over.............	86	90	96	98	100
Percentage Completing 12 or More Grades					
Under 4.................	25	30	63	69	65
4–7.....................	29	61	63	71	87
8–9...	30	46	67	72	79
10–11...................	36	72	72	85	85
12 and over.............	64	67	74	88	85
Percentage Completing 13 or More Grades					
Under 4.................	1	2	2	3	0
4–7.....................	0	5	2	14	10
8–9.....................	0	5	4	15	5
10–11...................	7	12	14	21	18
12 and over.............	14	13	26	35	37
Number of Boys in Sample					
Under 4.................	75	102	89	29	17
4–7.....................	86	173	166	76	39
8–9.....................	61	93	127	89	38
10–11...................	81	151	233	126	76
12 and over.............	14	39	82	66	30

SOURCE: Elbridge Sibley, "Some Demographic Clues to Stratification," *Amer. Sociol. Rev.*, 7 (1942), 328. By permission of the *American Sociological Review*.

* Representative occupations in the class intervals used above are: 0–3, hoboes, day laborers; 4–7, miners, policemen, bakers; 8–9, metalworkers, carpenters, salesmen in stores; 10–11, highly skilled craftsmen, clerks, traveling salesmen; 12 and over, executive and professional workers.

Hollingshead in 1941–1942 collected data on the 735 high school age adolescents of a small Middle Western city of 6,000 population and its adjoining hinterland of 4,000 population. He was interested in analyzing the relationships existing between the behavior patterns of these adolescents and the positions occupied by their families in the class structure of the community. He found that the high school was least oriented toward the needs and interests of lower class adolescents, who were disproportionately likely to drop out of school.[11] Of the lowest class youth Hollingshead concludes:

By way of contrast, the class V child reared "below" or "near" the canal learns very soon that his family is stigmatized in many ways—area of residence, kind of residence, occupation, reputation, number of children—and that he is held in contempt by boys and girls in the higher classes. He learns to resent his family, . . . but he must rely upon it for food, clothes and shelter. However, he has almost unlimited freedom to do as he desires, for his father is generally away from home, at work, or in search of pleasure, many times in jail, and his mother is busy trying to eke out a bare existence for her many children by means of a job outside the home. Since there is little or no room in the severely overcrowded small house where he may play, he plays along the river and the canal, in and near the coal chutes, and along the railroad tracks. His parents admonish him to be a "good" boy (a "little lady" in the case of a girl), but there is little effective control over his play. From the age of 5 or 6 he is faced with the responsibility of looking out for himself in the neighborhood, in school, and around the community. By the time adolescence is reached he has assumed full control of himself and his activities. He earns his own money, makes his own choices, and believes that he is acting as a "free agent." Actually he does what he and his fellows have learned they must do if they are to play the roles appropriate for their age and class statuses. In his thoughts and actions, he is bolstered by his clique mates (and it is not coincidence that almost all are class V's, and the rest are class IV's) as well as by older youths and adults in the social circles in which he moves. He insists upon absolute freedom in the spending of his money. If one tells him he is foolish to spend his money for old cars, flashy clothes, liquor, gambling, and sex one will be told forcibly—we experimented on this point with a few class V's we knew well—"No one can tell me how I am going to spend my money. Did you earn it?" This insistence upon freedom to do what he desires brings him into conflict with the law with significantly greater frequency than the other classes. This situation, however, is accepted by the class V youngster as something he must expect, for he has seen it happen with parents, relatives, and friends.[12]

SELECTED READINGS

Buck, Paul H. *et al.*: *General Education in a Free Society*, Report of the Harvard Committee, Harvard University Press, 1945. A thoughtful appraisal of American education against a background of rapid social change and urbanization.

Hollingshead, August B.: *Elmtown's Youth*, John Wiley & Sons, Inc., 1949. A highly readable account of the study of the impact of social classes on the life in and out of school of the high school age adolescents of a small Middle Western city.

[11] August B. Hollingshead, *Elmtown's Youth*, 1949.
[12] *Ibid.*, pp. 443–444. Reprinted by permission from *Elmtown's Youth* by August B. Hollingshead, published by John Wiley & Sons, Inc., 1949.

LOOMIS, CHARLES P., and J. ALLAN BEEGLE: *Rural Social Systems*, Prentice-Hall, Inc., 1950. Part V is devoted to the analysis of educational groups as social systems, including careful rural-urban comparisons.

SIBLEY, ELBRIDGE: "Some Demographic Clues to Stratification," *Amer. Sociol. Rev.*, 7 (1942), 322–330. A careful study of the relative importance of intelligence and socioeconomic status in educational achievement.

WARNER, W. LLOYD, ROBERT J. HAVIGHURST, and MARTIN B. LOEB: *Who Shall Be Educated?* Harper & Brothers, 1944. An analysis of the roles of caste and class in making American education one of unequal opportunities.

CHAPTER 18. *Engaging in Religious Practices*

Religion is one of the most difficult phases of life to define. Ames has identified it with "the most intimate and vital phase of the social consciousness."[1] But undoubtedly more people think of it as "the complex of man's interrelations with the superhuman forces."[2] For our present purpose we shall consider religion as a culture complex with characteristic activities, such as praying or assembling for the performance of ceremonies; characteristic attitudes, such as reverence, fear, devotion; characteristic symbols, such as cross, altar, hymn; characteristic traditions, beliefs, rules of conduct, and perhaps sacred books; characteristic physical equipment, such as church buildings and their furnishings. By a church we shall mean a fairly permanent local group of men, women, and children who engage in worship and religious instruction and who are usually affiliated with a more inclusive body, which we shall call a denomination or, in some cases, a sect.

Becker[3] has undertaken to classify modern religious bodies into four general types: ecclesia, sect, denomination, and cult. *Ecclesia* refers to an inclusive, dominant religious organization which "attempts to amalgamate itself with the state and dominant classes, and studies to exercise control over every person in the population."[4] Examples of this are the Roman Catholic Church in Spain, and the state churches in 9 of the 13 English colonies which later formed the United States. A *sect* is a small group in rebellion against the established church, appealing to persons who lack security and recognition, making ethical demands, and frequently requiring "some definite type of religious experience as a prerequisite of acceptance." "Denominations are simply sects in an advanced stage of development and adjustment to each other and the secular world."[5] The Methodist, Presbyterian, and Baptist churches started as

[1] E. S. Ames, *The Psychology of Religious Experience*, p. 285, 1910.
[2] *Encyclopaedia of the Social Sciences*, Vol. 13, p. 229.
[3] Leopold von Wiese and Howard Becker, *Systematic Sociology*, Chap. 44, 1932.
[4] *Ibid.*, p. 624. Reprinted by permission from *Systematic Sociology* by Leopold von Wiese and Howard Becker, published by John Wiley & Sons, Inc., 1932.
[5] *Ibid.*, p. 626. By permission of John Wiley & Sons, Inc.

sects and became denominations. Jehovah's Witnesses, the Assemblies of God, the Pentecostal Holiness Church, and the Church of the Nazarene are examples of contemporary sects. Finally, a *cult* is a more loosely integrated body of persons seeking a "personal ecstatic experience, salvation, comfort, and mental or physical healing."[6] Theosophy, Unity, and Spiritualism may be classed as present-day cults. It might be said that one is born into an ecclesia, joins a sect, is confirmed in a denomination, chooses the beliefs and practices peculiar to a cult.

In framing these definitions we have deliberately avoided the mystical in order to confine our study to relatively objective data. We recognize that there is a mystical element in much, if not all, religion, but our concern is with religion as a complex of ideas, attitudes, and activities which can be studied. Moreover, we are not interested here in the validity of beliefs or in the efficacy of ceremonies in dealing with the unknown. We are trying to discover what religious traits have developed or survived in modern cities, particularly in the United States, and how they differ from those of rural districts. We should like to compare urban and rural religion in every aspect, but because of limitations of data we shall have to content ourselves largely with a comparison of city and country churches.

RELIGIOUS DIFFERENCES BETWEEN CITY AND COUNTRY

While there were established churches in nine of the colonies which formed the United States, this nation early developed the policy of separating church and state. Hence we have no true case of an ecclesia in our country. Perhaps the nearest approach is the Church of Jesus Christ of Latter Day Saints in Salt Lake City and its region. The Catholic, Lutheran, and Episcopal churches, which are, or have been, ecclesiae in other lands, function pretty much as denominations in the United States. Now it happens that the Catholics and Episcopalians are overwhelmingly urban (80 and 85 per cent, respectively, according to the latest Census of Religious Bodies), the Lutherans are predominantly urban (about 60 per cent), and the Mormons about equally divided between urban and rural.

Religious bodies which may be called sects or cults or newly developed denominations are found principally in cities, although they are by no means absent from rural areas. The *Denver Post* on July 14, 1951, carried advertisements of the Assembly of God, Nazarene Church, Foursquare Gospel, Religious Science, Spiritual Science, Divine Science, Mental Science, and Christian Science, along with Methodist, Presbyterian, Lutheran, and other established denominations. The 1936

---

[6] *Ibid.*, pp. 626–627. By permission of John Wiley & Sons, Inc.

Census of Religious Bodies, the latest enumeration by the Bureau of the Census, showed the Pentecostal group to be 67 per cent urban and the Holiness group to be 64 per cent urban. These two groups are primarily regional, being concentrated chiefly around Birmingham, Knoxville, Chattanooga, Nashville, southern mill and mining towns, and some parts of Florida.[7] Their members are in the main poorly paid, unskilled workers, many of whom have recently moved in from rural areas. It appears that, being separated from their country churches, they do not feel at home in the town and city churches. Lacking social security and status, they seek compensation in religious groups of their own class. Being accustomed to "fundamentalist" doctrines and emotional evangelism, they respond to the appeal of the unschooled but earnest leaders of these sects.[8]

The religious bodies which Becker would classify as denominations vary considerably in the proportion of urban and rural members. Thus the Northern Baptists are three-fourths urban, while the Southern Baptists are three-fifths rural. The Methodists, since union of the northern and southern groups, are slightly more urban than rural. Lutheran, Congregationalists, Presbyterians, Episcopalians, and Unitarians are overwhelmingly urban, although they have strong rural followings in some regions. Most of the denominations which are predominantly rural are small in numbers, for example, United Brethren, Mennonites, Friends, Churches of Christ.

Other religious bodies, some of which would be difficult to classify according to Becker's scheme, are mainly urban in membership. Jewish synagogues in the United States are all in cities. Christian Science Churches and Ethical Societies are nearly all urban in location. Federated churches, however, are found mostly in small towns and the open country.

Considered from a somewhat different point of view, religions brought over by early settlers predominate in rural areas, while those introduced by more recent immigrants predominate in the city. Thus Protestants took possession of much of the territory which became the United States, but Catholics early occupied Maryland, Florida, Louisiana, and the Southwest. Most Roman Catholic, Greek Orthodox, and Jewish folk have come to America since 1880; they are found chiefly in cities, where they and similar groups consitute a large part of the church membership. But in rural America there is a predominance of Protestants, although many of the older denominations now have more members in cities than in the country. Sorokin and Zimmerman hold that religious

[7] John B. Holt, "Holiness Religion: Culture Shock and Social Reorganization," *Amer. Sociol. Rev.*, 5 (1940), 740–747.
[8] Liston Pope, *Millhands and Preachers*, 1942; Charles S. Braden, "The Sects," *Annals Amer. Acad. Pol. Soc. Sci.*, 256 (1948), 53–62.

innovations and drifting away from established faiths occur first in cities and later spread to the country. Certain it is that Christian Science, Spiritualism, Foursquare Gospel, Theosophy, the Pillar of Fire Church, and many other cults, sects, and denominations originated in cities and are still predominantly urban. As to the falling away from established faiths, it is natural that this should occur more frequently in areas of cultural diffusion and conflict such as our great cities. Perhaps it was with something like this in mind that Park is reported to have said, "In the country the church needs to sophisticate the evangelized, but in the city it must evangelize the sophisticated."[9]

As might be expected, city churches tend to be larger and better financed than country churches; data from the last two Federal enumerations and from other sources confirm this. Some approximate ratios of the average urban church and the average rural church follow:

Mean number of members	3:1
Mean number of Sunday school scholars	3:1
Mean expenditures	6:1
Mean values of church edifice	7:1

As a warning to the student, it should be pointed out that the definition of members differs greatly from denomination to denomination. Hence the data presented must not be accepted too literally. Thus the Roman Catholic Church reports all persons baptized, including small children, while most of the Protestant churches count only those who have formally joined the church, thus omitting nearly all children. However, we may tentatively accept the figures cited as indicating the approximate facts about rural-urban differences.

One of the most important differences to be noted is between rural and urban clergy. Among Protestants four-fifths of the urban white clergy are reported to be graduates of colleges or theological seminaries or both, while in rural districts less than half have had this much training.[10] Catholic clergy on the average have had more formal education than Protestant; since they are located principally in cities, this accentuates the rural-urban difference. Negro clergy on the average have had less formal education than white; since they were mostly country dwellers at the time these data were collected, this emphasizes the rural-urban differences still more. Country ministers often are non-resident circuit riders, irregularly and poorly paid, with relatively short tenure.[11] Very few city pastors serve more than one church, and very few are nonresident. As to salaries, it is impossible to secure satisfactory data, but there seems to be no doubt about the financial advantage of the

---

[9] Samuel C. Kincheloe, *The American City and Its Church*, p. 144, 1938.

[10] *Recent Social Trends*, Vol. 2, p. 1032.

[11] J. H. Kolb and E. de S. Brunner, *A Study of Rural Society*, pp. 527–528, 3d ed., 1946.

urban clergy.[12] The larger city churches have staffs that include not only ordained ministers but also paid secretaries, visitors, musicians, specialists in religious education, recreation, and social casework, and maintenance workers. Thus, on the whole, professional leadership of city churches differs greatly from that of country churches. However, if we were to distinguish between village and open country churches, we should find fewer differences between city and village clergy than between urban and rural in general.

The programs and activities of city and country churches differ in striking fashion. Kolb and Brunner found about seven out of eight village churches having at least one service every Sunday, while less than two-fifths of open country churches reached this goal. The great majority of both groups maintained Sunday schools, usually under the leadership of untrained laymen. Village churches more frequently had subsidiary organizations.[13] Town churches maintained them still more regularly and in greater numbers and variety. In city churches, as we shall see in the next section, diversification and specialization of activities have been carried still further.

Table 67. Frequency of Certain Subsidiary Church Organizations in Town Churches and in Modal Churches of Large Cities

Organizations	Per cent frequency	
	Town church	Modal city church
Some subsidiary organizations besides Sunday school...........	93	100
Women's organization.....................................	87	99
More than one women's organization.......................	44	81
Mixed-sex organizations (usually young people's).............	67	77
More than one mixed-sex organization.....................	37	8
Men's organization..	10	53
Boy's organization..	15	52
Girl's organization..	20	34

Source: H. Paul Douglass and Edmund de S. Brunner, *The Protestant Church as a Social Institution*, p. 137, 1935. By permission of Harper & Brothers.

TYPES OF CITY CHURCHES

We have been accustomed to classify city churches as metropolitan, neighborhood, mission, and "fly-by-night." By metropolitan church we have meant a parish with a large membership scattered throughout the city, an imposing edifice near the downtown business district or some

[12] H. Paul Douglass and E. de S. Brunner, *The Protestant Church as a Social Institution*, Chap. 6, 1935; Lowry Nelson, *Rural Sociology.* p. 359, 1948.
[13] Kolb and Brunner, *op. cit.,* p. 524.

subcenter, a widely known clergyman, and departmentalized activities. By neighborhood church we mean a smaller group of members, most of them living within a radius of 1 mile in a residential district, a less pretentious building, usually a less famous minister, and fewer subsidiary organizations and activities. The mission is commonly a branch or outpost of some larger and more opulent church or of a whole denomination, located in an area of deterioration or among newcomers to the city; its membership is small and usually localized; and its financial support comes from outside the parish. Finally, there is a type of church for which we have no satisfactory name. It is often called a mission, whether attached to any recognized denomination or not. The Negroes call it a "store front," because it often occupies an otherwise unused store building. It may be connected with some minor sect or it may be an independent venture. It usually does not remain long at one address; indeed its whole span of life may be short. The minister or leader commonly depends on some other occupation for his means of existence, since contributions are small and irregular. The clientele is made up largely of unskilled wage earners, many of them recently from rural America.

Douglass has developed a much more satisfactory basis of classification,[14] which is based, however, on the study of Protestant churches only. It is concerned with the number and character of subsidiary organizations and activities. First he classified churches according to the number of activities he found actually carried on: smallest (1–4), small (5–8), medium (9–12), large (13–16), and largest (17–20). Then he considered the character of the activities. From his study of 1,044 Protestant city churches he discovered the relative frequency of 33 different organizations and activities. Four of them—preaching and Sunday school, ladies' aid or guild, women's missionary society, and young people's society—were found in nearly all the churches, 81 to 100 per cent. Two more—chorus choir and general social events—appeared in 61 to 80 per cent of the churches studied. Three more—men's organization, Boy Scouts, and mission study classes—were present in 41 to 60 per cent of the churches. Then there were eight activities found in only 21 to 40 per cent; five in 11 to 20 per cent; and eleven in 1 to 10 per cent of the churches studied. Churches having only those activities and organizations found in 61 to 100 per cent, *i.e.*, quite general and conventional features, were classed as having the narrowest range of activities. Those having features present in 41 to 60 per cent were considered narrow; those with features present in 21 to 40 per cent were called medium; those with features present in 11 to 20 per cent were rated broad; and

[14] H. Paul Douglass, *One Thousand City Churches*, 1926. Data used by permission of Harper & Brothers.

those with features so rare as to be found in only 1 to 10 per cent of all churches were considered broadest. Figure 26 is the chart Douglass devised for combining the two aspects of number and range of activities. The cross classification yielded 17 subvarieties of city churches, each of which was given a symbol consisting of a letter and a Roman numeral.

	Scale of Range of Activities: Per Cent Frequency				
	61–100 % Narrowest	41–60 % Narrow	21–40 % Medium	11–20 % Broad	1–10 % Broadest
1–4 Smallest	A I	A II	A III	A IV	A V
5–8 Small		B I	B II	B III	B IV
9–12 Medium			C I	C II	C III
13–16 Large			D I	D II	D III
17–20 Largest				E I	E II

Scale of Number of Activities

Fɪɢ. 26. Chart for classification of churches. (*H. Paul Douglass, One Thousand City Churches*, 1926. *By permission of Harper & Brothers, publishers.*)

The 1,044 churches under study were then assigned to the appropriate categories, whereupon it appeared that the mode, or most frequent subtype, was B-II, *i.e.*, churches with a small number and a medium range of activities. With this as a point of departure, he undertook to group the 17 subtypes into five major varieties. He added to the modal subtype the churches having the same number but a somewhat broader range of activities (B-III) and those with medium range but a somewhat larger number of activities (C-I). The combined modal type (type one) included one-third of all the churches studied and was regarded as the core, or center, about which other city churches varied. A review of the individual churches assigned to this major category showed that they really had many features in common and were different in important respects from the other subtypes. Their median membership was about 400, median age of the church about forty years, median length of time

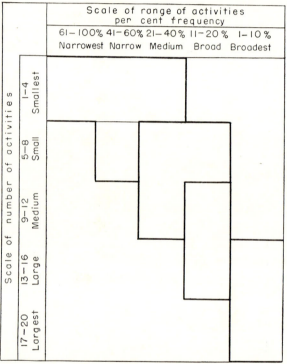

Fig. 27. Four major types of churches, combining Douglass's original categories.

in their present location twenty-five years; less than half of them had more than one paid religious worker. Most of their pastors (83.5 per cent) had full college and seminary preparation; two-thirds had been with the particular church less than five years, but nearly three-fourths had over ten years' experience; over half received salaries between $1,000 and $3,000 in 1922. Current expenses averaged about $10,000 per year (median between $6,000 and $7,000); median value of church plant was $39,000. The median Sunday school had about 300 pupils, whose average attendance was about 180; nearly half of them were between six and fourteen years of age. More than half of the churches of this type had at least three-fourths of their members living within 1 mile. For reasons elsewhere presented, Douglass designated this modal type of city church as "moderately developed and slightly adapted to urban environment."

Moving in the direction of a smaller number and a narrower range of activities, Douglass selected A-II as the center of a second type and added to it A-I, A-III, and B-I. Their combined total was nearly one-fourth of all the churches studied. In comparison with the first type, this one is properly characterized as relatively undeveloped and unadapted, for these churches had less extensive and less diversified programs. These churches were definitely smaller than those of type one, averaging about 300 members each. Two-fifths were less than twenty-five years old and nearly two-thirds had been less than twenty-five years in their present location. More than four-fifths had only a single religious worker, namely, the pastor. The ministers of these churches had the poorest education, the shortest experience, and the briefest tenure of any group of city clergy-men. There were more old men among them, and their salaries were low, 70 per cent receiving $2,000 or less. The general budget of these churches averaged about $3,000, and the median value of their church property was $20,000, or about half that of churches of type one. The Sunday school enrollment averaged about 220, which bears a relatively high ratio to the church membership. In fact, many of these churches had recently developed out of Sunday schools. Only half of them ap-peared to be well located with reference to the people they were under-taking to serve, and almost none were found in high-grade neighborhoods. Compared with type one, the parishes were less compact, only one-third having three-fourths of the members within one mile. However, they were not widely scattered, for two-thirds of the churches had at least half of their members within 1 mile.

Turning to the other side of the mode, Douglass sought to identify a type of church with a larger number and a broader range of activities. The statistical category C-II met these requirements and was also second to the most numerous subtype. To this he would naturally have added C-III and D-II, but an individual study of the small number of churches in the former subgroup showed them to be very unlike those of C-II in spite of their statistical nearness. However, C-II and D-II were found to be fairly homogeneous; hence they were combined as type three, designated as more developed and internally adapted. Their programs were so rounded as to provide in a special way for every age and sex group and cater to a wide range of human interests. Nearly three-fourths of these churches had over 500 members. More than half of them were over fifty years old; one-seventh were over a century old. They had moved more frequently than churches of any other type. Three-fourths had more than one paid religious worker; half of them had more than two. The clergy were highly educated men in the prime of life who tended to stay longer in the same parish than did those of other types. Their median salary was about $4,000, one-tenth receiving more than $7,000. The median budget was not far from $15,000, but the per capita cost was not much above the average for all city churches studied. Median value of church property was $120,000. The median Sunday school enrollment was about 400, attendance 250; it differed from the first two types in having a strong adolescent and adult participation. Because so many of these churches were located near the central business district, they tended to have scattered memberships. These "internally adapted" churches of type three constituted nearly one-fifth of all the churches studied.

The fourth major type was called "socially adapted," because of the extreme complexity of its development. It included only one-tenth of the entire group of churches, and was made up of the statistical categories D-III and E-II. Some of the distinctive elements in the programs of these churches were kindergartens and day nurseries, clinics, classes in English, civics, home economics, art, music, dramatics, vocational advice, and employment service. These churches were usually large, nearly half of them having 1,000 members or more. They were old, having a median age of fifty-five years, and only one-seventh were under twenty-five years old. While the median length of time at the present site was only thirty-six years, nearly one-third had never moved; as to location, they were more stable than the churches of any other type. The median number of paid religious workers was four. Professional equipment of the clergy often included graduate study beyond college and seminary. These churches kept more elderly men and retained them longer in a given pastorate than did other types. Salaries showed considerable variation, one-fourth being under $3,000 and one-fourth over $6,000. The median budget was over $15,000; for nearly one-third of these churches it was over $25,000. Church property was valued on the average at $240,000. The median Sunday school enrolled less than 500 and was small as compared with the church membership. However, no other type of church had so large a proportion of adolescents in its Sunday school enrollment. Half of these churches were centrally located, many of them being in the heart of the downtown section. The remainder were located in quite varied districts, ranging from high-class residential neighborhoods to slums. The membership was often quite scattered. Only type two, "unadapted," had so few compact parishes.

These four types included seven-eighths of the churches studied, leaving a scattering of variants. Subtypes A-IV and A-V represented a small number of churches with rather unusual, but not very numerous, organizations and activities. On the other hand, those of D-I had a large number of activities that were fairly conventional; that is, some of these churches varied in the direction of novelty, others in the direction of conservatism.

To make sure that important features of Douglass's classification are not lost amid the details, let us recapitulate. *Type one:* At the center he found a "core" of churches moderately developed as to size, finances, plant, number and range of activities. Their parishes were fairly compact. Their leadership was in the hands of men well trained, moderately experienced, and fairly stable. *Type two:* In the upper left-hand corner of the chart he located churches smaller, poorer (as to finance), and with fewer and more conventional activities. Their clergy had the least education, shortest experience, and briefest tenure of all the groups studied. *Type three:* To the right and below the modal type was identified a class of churches that were larger, older, better financed, with a greater number and broader range of activities. Their membership was usually scattered. Their clergy were highly educated men in the prime of life who stayed longer than those in other types of churches. *Type four:* In the lower right-hand corner was established another class of churches—largest, oldest, best financed, with the greatest number and broadest range of activities. They were located in varied districts, but half of them were downtown churches. Their membership was often quite scattered. They had several paid religious workers besides the pastors, who were the best educated, most experienced, and stayed longest of all the clergy. *Type five:* Finally there was a fringe of widely variant churches representing no particular group of characteristics.

By comparing these city churches with those of the village and open country and by studying the history of the city churches Douglass reached the conclusion that "the city church is an evolved rural church."[15] In terms of the chart, churches belonging in the upper left-hand corner, type two, were most like country churches and unadapted to city life. They were newer and had had less time to develop a program suited to the urban community. Those of the central class, type one, were less like rural churches, more developed, and somewhat adapted to city life. Types three and four were much further removed from the rural churches in age and in character; their organization was more complex and their accommodation to city life much more adequate. In still other ways city churches are evolved rural churches. Some of them have continued since the city was a village, and have never outgrown their rural traditions and practices. Others developed in villages that were later annexed to the city. Still others have been established in the city for the benefit of recent arrivals from the country. Finally, some "reflect the transplanted rural ideals of their denominations."

[15] *Ibid.*, p. 83.

It should be repeated that this study is important both for the facts it reveals and for the methods employed. It is unfortunate that we do not have equally objective studies of Catholic and Jewish churches. These latter groups would doubtless display both similarities and differences. In the case of the Catholic churches, distribution and development probably differ greatly from the Protestant churches, because the former are under a centralized authority which carefully plans locations and interrelations.

THE ECOLOGY OF PROTESTANT CHURCHES

The foregoing analysis of types of city churches has indicated that they are related to their environmental setting and that different kinds of churches may be found in different parts of the city. Another study made by the Institute of Social and Religious Research attempted to discover more precisely what relations may exist between church growth or decline and socioeconomic factors in the vicinity.[16] Sanderson studied nearly 2,000 Protestant churches in selected sectors of 6 representative large cities. In each district he assembled data of eight sorts. First he asked whether in the decade under consideration there was growth or loss of general population. It was assumed that areas of declining population would be unfavorable for the development of any institution like the church. Second, since he was concerned with Protestant churches, he asked whether there was an increase or decrease of elements likely to affiliate with a Protestant church. Obviously, if Catholics or Jews dominated a district or were increasing in numbers, it would not be a favorable location for a Protestant church. The third question pertained to changes in the characteristic economic status. We assume that these were measured by rentals paid, assessed valuation of homes, occupations, automobiles, etc. The fourth issue had to do with desirability of residence, single dwellings being rated highest and converted tenements lowest, strictly residential areas being rated higher than those partially occupied by business and industry. Fifth was a question of mobility versus stability, measured by the number of rooming houses, changes in telephones and utility meters, movers' records, school transfers, and the like. The remaining questions had to do with dependency (persons on relief), juvenile delinquency (juvenile court cases), and health (infant mortality). In all these it was expected, subject to check, that districts of declining economic status, desirability of housing, or stability, and of increasing dependency, delinquency, and mortality would be unfavorable for the development of Protestant churches.

[16] Ross W. Sanderson, *The Strategy of City Church Planning*, 1932. Data used by permission of Harper & Brothers.

Next, each city or sector of a city being studied was divided into districts which corresponded to census tracts or groups of adjacent tracts. Each district was ranked on each of the eight points. The ranks were added and the sum was divided by eight, thus giving a combined rank indicating the direction of social change, or rather the relative nature of social change, during one decade, 1917–1919 to 1927–1929. Districts were then grouped in quartiles: the best fourth, the better-than-average, the below-average, and the worst. It should be noted that this scheme, based on change, does not indicate the status of a district at any particular time. Thus a district that might be considered good may show little development or even deterioration during a decade; while a poor district may show considerable improvement and still remain on a low level.

So much for the social setting of the churches. Next the churches themselves were studied as to increase or decrease in membership, Sunday school enrollment, and total expenditure. The differences between the figures of the earlier and the later date were stated as percentages of the earlier figures. On the basis of these percentages each church was ranked on each point, after which the churches were grouped into quintiles (fifths), instead of quartiles, and lettered from A (highest fifth) to E (lowest fifth). It was then possible to determine the proportion of churches of each class in each type of district. This was done separately with reference to membership, Sunday school, and expenditures, and with reference to all three combined. The results are shown in Tables 68 to 70.

Table 68. Percentage of Churches in Each Type of Territory Ranking
A, B, C, D, E

Type of territory	A	B	C	D	E	Total
Best...................	41.0	23.0	16.4	10.4	9.2	100.0
Above average...........	25.0	23.0	20.7	18.3	13.0	100.0
Below average...........	14.0	18.6	21.4	22.0	24.0	100.0
Worst.................	10.0	14.0	19.6	24.0	32.4	100.0

SOURCE: Ross W. Sanderson, *The Strategy of City Church Planning*, p. 88, 1932. By permission of Harper & Brothers.

More recent studies in Cincinnati and St. Louis lend support to Sanderson's findings.[17] Research of this sort emphasizes the fact that

[17] H. Paul Douglass, *The Greater Cincinnati Church Study*, pp. 52–61, mimeographed, 1947; Kenneth G. Hornbuckle, *A Study of Congregational Churches in St. Louis and St. Louis County*, unpublished master's thesis, Washington University, 1943; Marcus Lang, *The Relationship of Church Progress in Missouri Synod Lutheran Churches of the St. Louis Metropolitan District to the Status of the Communities in Which They Are Located*, unpublished master's thesis, Washington University, 1946.

Table 69. Percentage of A, B, C, D, E Rankings in Each Type of Territory

Type of territory	A	B	C	D	E
Better:					
Best......................	36.1	21.9	15.2	9.9	8.4
Above average.............	32.7	32.2	28.6	25.9	17.7
Poorer:					
Below average.............	19.3	28.1	31.7	33.7	34.7
Worst.....................	11.9	17.8	24.5	30.5	39.2
Total...................	100.0	100.0	100.0	100.0	100.0

SOURCE: Ross W. Sanderson, *The Strategy of City Church Planning*, p. 91, 1932. By permission of Harper & Brothers.

Table 70. Most Frequent Rankings on Each of Three Indices of
Church Progress
(All sixteen sectors)

Type of territory	Church membership	Sunday school enrollment	Total expenditures
Best.....................	A	A	A
Above average............	A	AB	ABCD
Below average............	BCDE	DE	E
Worst...................	E	E	E

SOURCE: Ross W. Sanderson, *The Strategy of City Church Planning*, p. 98, 1932. By permission of Harper & Brothers. Where more than one letter occurs, the rankings indicated are of almost equal frequency.

churches, like other social institutions, do not exist in a vacuum but are involved in larger social situations. They vary with the whole social complex of the area in which they are located. This, of course, is exactly what could have been anticipated from the findings presented in Part 3 of this book. Moreover, the practical significance of such research should not be ignored. When a church is declining, its members moving to other parts of the city, its area being invaded by new population elements or by business, the question of what to do is very pressing. Generally speaking there are five alternatives: (1) An effort may be made to adapt the program to the changing characteristics of the district. (2) A new location may be sought which will be more convenient to the membership. (3) The congregation may disband and sell the property. (4) What often happens is that a few of the faithful hold on, vaguely hoping that something may enable them to preserve the organization. (5) Under favorable circumstances of finances and leadership, a metropolitan church may develop. Problems of this sort are frequently faced by Protestant churches and Jewish synagogues; so far less frequently by Catholic parishes.[18]

[18] Samuel C. Kincheloe, "The Behavior Sequence of a Dying Church," *Jour. Rel. Educ.*, 24 (1929), 329–345.

STRATIFICATION AND URBAN RELIGION

As we saw in Chap. 15, there is no clearly defined national pattern of social classes, but in every community there appears to be at least an informal rating of groups and categories of people. Even though we think of this in terms of a continuum rather than a set of sharply separated classes, the fact remains that differences in group prestige are real. Its relation to religious affiliation is displayed by the results of four polls taken by the American Institute of Public Opinion in 1945–1946. Table 71 shows that each of the religious bodies reported reaches across

Table 71. Class Composition of Religious Bodies, 1945–1946

Body	Per cent distribution		
	Upper class	Middle class	Lower class
Entire sample............	13	31	56
Catholic................	9	25	66
Jewish..................	22	32	46
Methodist...............	13	35	52
Baptist.................	8	24	68
Presbyterian............	22	40	38
Lutheran..	11	36	53
Episcopalian............	24	34	42
Congregational..........	24	43	33

Source: Liston Pope, "Religion and the Class Structure," *Annals Amer. Acad. Pol. Soc. Sci.*, 256 (1948), 82. By permission of the American Academy of Political and Social Science.

class lines, but that Congregational and Episcopal Churches have relatively large followings in the upper class; Baptist, Methodist, and Catholic in the lower class. Jewish congregations are more evenly distributed among the three classes. Studies already referred to show that certain sects, notably the Pentecostal and Holiness groups, draw their members almost entirely from the lower end of the prestige and status continuum. Another study shows the adherents of Christian Science to be middle- and upper-class people.[19]

Because income, occupation, education, and politics are believed to bear a positive relation to stratification in the social-psychological sense, we cite some data bearing on these traits as further indication of how stratification and religious affiliation are mutually involved. Four surveys made in 1939 to 1940 showed Catholics to be relatively more numerous on low-income levels and Protestants on high-income levels.[20] However,

[19] Joseph K. Johnson, *A Case Study of a Religion as a Form of Adjustment Behavior*, unpublished doctoral dissertation, Washington University, 1937.

[20] Hadley Cantril, "Educational and Economic Composition of Religious Groups," *Amer. Jour. Sociol.*, 48 (1943), 574–579.

both major groups were represented on all levels. Unfortunately these surveys tell us nothing about separate Protestant denominations or about Jews. As to occupation, the 1945–1946 polls showed business and professional folk relatively most numerous among the Jews, followed closely by Congregationalists, Episcopalians, and Presbyterians. Urban manual workers were relatively most numerous among Catholics, followed closely by Baptists, and at some distance by Lutherans and Methodists. As to education, the same polls showed college graduates to be relatively most numerous among Episcopalians, Presbyterians, and Congregationalists, in the order named. Persons who failed to' complete high school were relatively most numerous among Baptists, Catholics, and Lutherans, in the order named. These results correspond to those of the 1939–1940 surveys. Finally, the 1945–1946 polls inquired into the political preferences of members of religious bodies. The highest proportions of tho'se voting for Dewey in 1944 were Congregational, Presbyterian, and Episcopalian, in the order named. The highest proportions voting for Roosevelt were Jewish, Catholic, and Baptist, in the order named. Methodists were almost equally divided between the two' candidates. Thus economic, educational, and political data confirm the impression that members of different religious bodies are distributed quite differently along the social-status continuum. However, it should not be forgotten that members of most of the larger religious bodies are scattered from high to low levels, and that people o'f each social class are divided among numerous faiths.

RELATIONS BETWEEN RELIGIOUS GROUPS

Since there are so many different religious groups in every city of the United States and since these groups differ not only in creed and organization, but also in national origins, status, economic, and educational levels and political affiliation, it is not surprising that misunderstanding, suspicion, and conflict are common. Perhaps we should be surprised that there is as much tolerance, respect, and cooperation as we have actually found.

During and after World War II, the Knights of Columbus in a large city published a series of paid advertisements attacking Protestants and referring to religious tolerance as a "sign of mental confusion and personal cowardice." The Protestants responded with a mass meeting at which a Methodist bishop condemned the Catholic Church for its undemocratic structure, rigid dogmas, and political ambitions. The two groups clashed in many cities over birth control, sex education, divorce, gambling, prohibition, child labor, tax support of parochial schools, or at least provision of free textbooks, health service, school lunches, free transportation, and the like. The attempts of various religious groups to control the public schools, to censor library books, and to "get their share" from the community fund add fuel to the flames. Sometimes local struggles are bound up with international affairs. In a certain city the Knights of Columbus published a half-page advertisement headed "Shall We Help the Communists to Crucify Christian Spain?" To this the Metropolitan Church Federation (Protestant) replied with a similar advertisement headed "Shall We Help the Fascists Crucify Democracy in Spain?"

Between Jews and Christians there is prejudice which affects employment, admission to private schools and clubs, hotels, and swimming pools. But there is usually not the open religious controversy frequently displayed by Protestants versus Catholics. Among the various Protestant denominations there is some rivalry to dominate given districts, to demonstrate social usefulness through orphanages and hospitals. Occasionally there are flare-ups of "fundamentalists" against "modernists," but these divide denominations as well as pit the members of one church against those of another. On the whole, Protestant groups are tolerant of each other and engage in some real cooperation, as we shall see in Chap. 23.

In the hope of promoting mutual acceptance and collaboration in civic affairs the National Conference of Christians and Jews arranges meetings, issues publicity, holds seminars and workshops, with what results no one really knows. In community chests and councils of social agencies, members of the various groups get to know each other and sometimes work together to their mutual advantage. But even here there is a great deal of "pulling and hauling." Anyone who overlooks or minimizes religious rivalry and intolerance in cities of the United States is being unrealistic and is ignoring a potent factor in the problems of "moral integration" (consensus plus effective social organization) which we shall discuss in Chap. 23.

WHAT RELIGION MEANS TO CITY DWELLERS

The foregoing discussion suggests that organized religion does not have the same significance for all city dwellers. To members of minority ethnic groups, the church probably provides some compensation for inferior social status in the urban society as a whole. It undoubtedly strengthens group solidarity and gives some sense of security. Native white members of millennial sects probably find similar values in their churches. "Sanctification" and "life beyond the grave" compensate more or less for poverty and lack of recognition in an industrial city. However, it may be that the trade-union will prove to be a sturdy competitor of the church in this respect.

To people near the upper end of the status continuum, especially if they have wealth, sermons like Russell Conwell's "Acres of Diamonds" probably feed a sense of self-satisfaction, justify *laissez faire*, and identify wealth with righteousness. To belong to the "right" congregation is one more mark of social distinction.

Middle-class families, especially those "on their way up," find in church status, sociability, and support for their moral code. Some of them are aroused by the "social gospel" to a sense of civic obligation.

Undoubtedly many persons on all levels find in organized religion a source of comfort, courage, and guidance for daily living. But interestingly both Thorndike and Angell found the mere fact of church membership unrelated to goodness of life or moral integration of a city.[21] In other words, such matters as good government, public health, education, prevention of delinquency, control of poverty, and other practical issues of city life seem to be unaffected by the number of church members. Perhaps this finding is related to the observation of the Lynds after their second study of Middletown: "To such controversial issues . . . the churches of Middletown present the negative face of the community, or are silent, or talk such generalities that their position is equivocal."[22] Perhaps it is related to what Cuber calls "marginal participation" in religious activities.[23] In a study of Protestant churches in one metropolitan area, he found that less than 40 per cent of the members attended 20 or more times a year. He found from 18 to 37 per cent of the attendants were not members. Both members and nonmembers were inclined to ask for religious ceremonies at weddings and funerals. We do not know of corresponding studies of Catholic parishes and Jewish congregations, but Sperry cites an unofficial pamphlet which claims 2,450,000 "constituents" of synagogues and temples, leaving presumably 2,500,000 Jews unaffiliated.[24] We have no idea how accurate any of these estimates may be, but it is evident that there are vast numbers of city people who give very little time and attention to the churches. Perhaps if the religious bodies devoted less time to institutional rivalry and doctrinal disputes and more to human relations and social problems, they might play a greater role in the life of our cities.

[21] See Chap. 23.
[22] Robert S. Lynd and Helen M. Lynd, *Middletown in Transition*, p. 312, 1937. By permission of Harcourt, Brace and Company, Inc.
[23] Logan Wilson and William L. Kolb, *Sociological Analysis*, pp. 674–677, 1949. A summary of Cuber's study.
[24] Willard L. Sperry, *Religion in America*, p. 109, 1946.

SELECTED READINGS

ABRAMS, RAY H. (Editor): "Organized Religion in the United States," *Annals Amer. Acad. Pol. Soc. Sci.*, 256 (1948). A valuable symposium dealing with the Roman Catholic Church, Protestant denominations, various sects, and the relation of organized religion to other social institutions.

BERNARD, JESSIE: *American Community Behavior*, The Dryden Press, 1949. Chapters 18 and 19 deal with conflicts among Protestants, between Protestants and Catholics, among Catholics, between Christians and Jews.

DOUGLASS, H. PAUL: *One Thousand City Churches*, Harper & Brothers, 1926. Presents an objective method of classifying Protestant city churches. With slight adaptations should be usable for Catholic and Jewish. A study made under the auspices of the Institute of Social and Religious Research.

SANDERSON, ROSS W.: *The Strategy of City Church Planning*, Harper & Brothers, 1932. A study made under the auspices of the Institute of Social and Religious Research, dealing with the relation between church growth or decline and changes in socioeconomic features of the immediate vicinity.

SPERRY, WILLARD L.: *Religion in America*, The Macmillan Company, 1946. An excellent historical and descriptive account of religious denominations in the United States.

WILSON, LOGAN, and WILLIAM L. KOLB: *Sociological Analysis*, Harcourt, Brace and Company, Inc., 1949. Chapter 19, "Religious Organization," contains excerpts from the works of Becker, Pope, and Cuber referred to in the foregoing pages.

Yearbook of American Churches.

National Catholic Almanac.

American Jewish Year Book.

These three are useful for general reference.

CHAPTER 19. *Sharing in Government*

Everyone over the age of twenty-one—that is, everyone who is not an unnaturalized alien, an institutionalized mental defective, or a convicted felon—is presumably a citizen, in other words, a participant in government. However, it is well known that such participation is very uneven. Thus in 1944 in St. Louis, the percentage of adults who registered to vote ranged from 42 to 71 in various wards, and the percentage of registered voters who went to the polls in 1945 ranged from 20 to 46.[1] In addition it is sometimes found that ballots actually cast are not counted or are offset by those of "ghost" voters. When it comes to state and national issues, city dwellers are often underrepresented because of the unequal populations of legislative and congressional districts. Thus in 1948, in Missouri, metropolitan counties had in the lower house of the legislature 2 representatives for every 100,000 inhabitants, while 76 rural counties had from 7 to 12 per 100,000.[2] Evidence of this sort would be easy to multiply.

The problem of citizen participation is further complicated by the large number of governmental units in a given metropolitan area. As a result, a man may reside in one municipality, work in another, shop in a third; he may have interests in two or three different counties and in perhaps half a dozen special districts. He must pay taxes wherever he owns property, but he can vote only in the political unit where he resides. Table 72 shows how many separate governmental units there were in five metropolitan districts about 1950. This situation represents one of the most striking cultural lags in contemporary America. When the country was being settled, the area now occupied by any great city may have included many separate villages and incorporated towns and several counties. But as the central city expanded, it spread across town-

---

[1] Edward B. Olds and David W. Salmon, *St. Louis Voting Behavior*, Sec. C, 1948.
[2] Henry S. Caulfield, "Minority Rule in Missouri," *St. Louis Post-Dispatch*, Aug. 13, 1948.

Table 72. Organized Governmental Units in Metropolitan Districts

	Total	Counties	Town-ships	Munici-palities	School districts	Special districts
Chicago....................	821	5	42	115	593	66
Detroit....................	458	3	27	45	380	3
Los Angeles...............	353	3	..	56	254	40
New York–Northeastern New Jersey...................	1,039	14	78	286	520	141
St. Louis..................	539	5	18	70*	425	21

SOURCE: Adapted from *Municipal Year Book*, pp. 21–22, 1950. By permission of the International City Managers' Association.
* It is evident that this count is incomplete, for in 1951 there were 93 incorporated cities, towns, and villages in St. Louis County alone.

ship, municipal, county, and sometimes state lines. Some of these smaller units were annexed, but others remained politically independent, even though they were economically and socially one with the rest of the metropolitan area. When new needs arose, cutting across political boundaries, new governmental agencies of a special sort were created—drainage districts, park districts, port authorities, and the like. The result is a very complicated and not very efficient administrative structure.

Before considering the efforts that have been made to overcome the culture lag in metropolitan government, we shall present brief accounts of the scope of city government, important steps in its development, and some current problems other than the one just outlined, which is the object of our chief concern in this chapter.

THE SCOPE OF MUNICIPAL GOVERNMENT IN THE UNITED STATES[3]

City government has become not only an instrument of social control but also a form of big business. In 1900 our cities of over 30,000 population spent $500 million; in 1915 they spent $1 billion; in 1930, a depression year, they spent $3½ billion; in 1948 they spent $4 billion. These figures include costs of operation and maintenance, outlays for permanent improvements, and interest on debts. Considering the continued growth of cities in recent years and the lowered value of the dollar, it is evident that the increase in cost of municipal government has been remarkably small. In fact, on the basis of stable dollars per capita, it appears to have actually declined. Nevertheless it is still big business.

A second measure of the expensiveness of city government is found in

[3] Fifteenth Census, *Financial Statistics of Cities; Encyclopaedia of the Social Sciences*, Vol. 11, pp. 98–104; *Recent Social Trends*, Vol. 2, pp. 1307–1315; *Statistical Abstract of the United States*, 1949; *Municipal Year Book*, 1951.

the volume of debts. In 1903 the per capita net debt for all cities over 30,000 was about $45; in 1931 it had risen to $160. In 1934 in cities over 100,000 it was $170; in 1949 it had dropped to $155. We are not presenting these data for the purpose of adding to the worry about taxpayers' burdens, but simply to have the facts in hand. Presently we shall see that expanding functions, as well as bureaucratic waste, are responsible for these large expenditures and debts.

Another measure of the extent to which municipal government has become a great business enterprise is the number of employees. Omitting teachers and others in the school systems, 746 cities in 1935 had 445,000 full-time employees. This means that 94 out of every 10,000 city dwellers were on municipal payrolls. In 1949 all cities in the United States had together over 1 million employees, which is 128 per 10,000. Thus it appears that the numbers of municipal employees have been increasing both absolutely and relatively. In New York City they grew from 30,000 (88 per 10,000) in 1900, to 86,000 (124 per 10,000) in 1930, and to 116,000 (148 per 10,000) in 1949. This may be due in part to politicians' success in getting their supporters on the public payroll, but it represents even more the expansion of services to the inhabitants of our cities.

The functions performed by city governments may be grouped into 10 or 12 categories. Table 73 presents a common classification and the

Table 73. Per Cent Distribution of Municipal Expenditures, 397 Cities, United States, 1950

Function	Per Cent
Operation...	68.8
Safety—police, fire, etc...	16.6
Schools and libraries..	15.3
Sanitation, health, and hospitals.............................	12.2
Public welfare..	8.4
General control..	5.5
Highways and streets...	5.1
Recreation..	3.2
Other..	2.5
Capital outlay—buildings, etc.......................................	15.0
Debt retirement...	6.1
Other...	10.1
Total...	100.0

SOURCE: Adapted from *Municipal Year Book*, p. 202, 1951. By permission of the International City Managers' Association.

percentage of municipal expenditures allotted to each in 1950. The many services included under these heads have made their appearance gradually over a long period of time. This development can be well illustrated by the case of Detroit.[4] In 1830, when Detroit was a town of

[4] Lent D. Upson, *The Growth of a City Government*, Detroit Bureau of Governmental Research, 1931.

2,000 inhabitants, its government was carrying on 23 distinct activities. These included legislation, assessment and collection of revenue, enforcement of ordinances, maintenance and operation of public buildings, and fire prevention. By 1870, a population of 80,000 was served through 59 governmental activities. Some of the new functions provided for the construction of sidewalks and street pavements, sewage disposal, water supply, street lighting, elementary and high schools, a general library, an organized police patrol, and fire fighting. In 1900, the population was 285,000 and municipal activities numbered 132. Some of the additions were parks, art exhibits, evening classes, food and milk inspection, a general hospital, a system of quarantine, poor relief, garbage collection, and band concerts. By 1930, the population had increased to 1,575,000 and the activities to 306. A few of the twentieth-century developments were playgrounds, community centers, clinics, public health nurses, a probation system, women police, an employment bureau, water filtration, mosquito control, bus transportation, an airport, a lodginghouse, and zoning. These and many other municipal services represent an enormous expansion of governmental functions, not only in Detroit, but in all American cities.

Because the data in Table 73 do not include utilities, municipally owned or operated, or both owned and operated, we add Table 74. Some frightened souls would doubtless regard this as proof positive that socialism is rapidly overtaking us. For us, it is simply one more bit of evidence that we have put our cities in business on a very large scale.

Table 74. Utilities Owned or Operated by Cities over 5,000, United States, 1950

Utility	Cities reporting	
	Number	Per cent
Cities reporting...............................	2,253	100.0
Water supply and/or distribution................	1,702	75.5
Sewage treatment plant.........................	1,129	50.1
Airport..	502	22.3
Electric generation and/or distribution............	493	21.9
Incinerator....................................	411	18.2
Auditorium....................................	384	17.0
Gas manufacture and/or distribution.............	102	4.8
Port facilities.................................	31	3.6
Street railway or bus...........................	46	2.1
Slaughterhouse................................	30	1.3
Cities having none of the above..................	237	10.5
Cities not reporting............................	65	

SOURCE: *Municipal Year Book*, p. 46, 1951. By permission of the International City Managers' Association.

THE DEVELOPMENT OF MUNICIPAL GOVERNMENT

In the preceding section we pointed out that the functions now performed by municipal government in the United States have accumulated over a considerable period of time. In this section we shall show that the very nature of municipal government has undergone change. The earliest cities, those of Egypt and Mesopotamia, were not municipalities in our sense of the word. They were urban centers ruled by kings and emperors either directly or through personal representatives. Self-government was almost wholly absent. The Greek city-states were autonomous, but they combined—from our standpoint— national with municipal functions. But under the Roman law provincial cities came to be treated as corporations with certain privileges and obligations. No doubt a major purpose behind their creation was to fix the responsibility of their inhabitants to the central government. At all events, these municipia were authorized by the state to regulate their own affairs within specified limits. They were "legal persons," who could acquire and dispose of property, administer their own business, and be held responsible for meeting their obligations. This was a new idea; it became the legal basis of municipal government in the Western world.

In the late Empire, municipalities were reduced to little more than administrative districts governed by imperial officials appointed from Rome. With the collapse of Roman power in the fifth century, municipal government declined still further. As we noted in Chap. 4 the few towns that remained were neither units of a central power nor self-governing; they were often little more than the headquarters of some feudal lord, lay or ecclesiastical. However, with the revival of commerce came a struggle for local autonomy, which had varying degrees of success but made considerable headway in northern Italy, along the coasts of the Baltic and North Seas, in France, and in England. Charters were won by force from feudal nobles, purchased from kings, or otherwise acquired. In England most of them were obtained from the king by free grant or purchase. Under these charters the cities were permitted to collect their own taxes and spend their revenues, though they were required to make periodical payments in money or services. There was great lack of uniformity, but all possessed some legislative power, limited in the main to "the preservation of their ancient customs," the maintenance of their commercial privileges, and the administration of their property. It is also important to remember that the governing bodies in these English boroughs were "small, inefficient, self-continuing and self-serving bodies."[5] The Municipal Corporations Act of 1835 and that of 1882 under-

[5] *Encyclopaedia of the Social Sciences,* Vol. 11, p. 88. By permission of The Macmillan Company.

took to establish uniformity in charters and responsible local governments based on popular suffrage.

The English colonists in America of course brought their old customs and institutions with them. So in New England and New York, town governments were set up under charters granted by the royal governors. These towns were at once subordinate agencies of the colonial administration and relatively independent local units. After the Revolution the state legislatures took over the granting of charters, which came to display not only a wide variety but considerable arbitrariness as well. In the southern and middle colonies there were already established counties and townships, subordinate agents of the state. The creation of municipalities brought no little confusion. As a result of the chaos, many states sought by constitutional amendments and general statutes to make municipal charters uniform and somewhat in harmony with laws regulating coexisting local units, *i.e.*, counties, townships, etc. These efforts seem to have been partly successful, but through the device of classifying cities, legislatures were still able to regulate the affairs of individual cities rather arbitrarily.

As a reaction to the interference of rural-minded legislatures in the details of city government, a home rule movement developed. In 1875 the Missouri constitution provided that the voters of a city might elect freeholders to draft their own charter. When such a charter was ratified by popular vote, it became the controlling instrument of government in all matters of strictly local concern, provided, of course, it was consistent with the constitution and general laws of the state. Fifteen other states adopted similar provisions, but the issue remained far from solution. It is not easy to determine what matters are strictly local in significance. New inventions and new organizations, especially in the field of business, necessitate new regulations. It is natural that there should be some competition between state and municipality for exercise of the new powers.

During the nineteenth century most American cities developed rather complicated schemes of government, which were small-scale imitations of the federal system. The voters elected a mayor, a bicameral council, and various other officials. Committees of the council had charge of the administration of various departments. Later special boards, either elected or appointed by the mayor, undertook the management of public works, schools, police, parks, and the like. Inefficiency and waste were notorious. City officials were elected on the basis of their place in state and national party organizations. Franchises were practically given away. Debts mounted. Intermittently there were reform movements to "throw the rascals out." Usually they failed to win an election. If the "good government" party did elect its candidates, they were hampered by the systems of checks and balances, they sometimes proved inexperienced, good citizens often failed to stand by them—and at the next election the gang came back into power. It appeared that there was need of something more fundamental than putting good men into office.

There was more talk of home rule, of separating local elections from state politics, of simplifying city government, and of introducing business methods. But it was a catastrophe that furnished the occasion for initiating a new type of municipal government. In 1900 the city of Galveston was partially destroyed by a hurricane. In the confusion that followed, the old type of administration proved utterly incompetent to meet the urgent needs of the people. So a new form, called the commission plan, was invented. A commission of five men, elected at large, was given all executive and legislative powers. It had authority to adopt ordinances, levy taxes, vote appropriations, and make all appointments. Each individual commissioner took charge of a division, or of a group of related divisions, of the municipal activites. The idea spread rapidly, and by 1914 several hundred cities had adopted the scheme. Then the movement slowed down, and one after another cities gave up the commission form of government. It had concentrated responsibility, introduced business methods, and drawn able and honest men into public office. But it lacked administrative unity. A commission of five was too small as a legislative body and too large as an executive authority. Dissensions often arose among the members and the city's business was delayed.

Still another type of municipal government—the city manager, or council-manager, plan—made its appearance in Staunton, Va., in 1908, in Dayton, Ohio, in 1914, and during the next twenty years in 435 other cities, large and small. Under this scheme, an elected council chooses a single administrative officer, called the city manager, presumably without reference to political affiliation or local residence. He in turn appoints department heads and, sometimes with a civil service commission, subordinate employees. He plans and directs the operations of the city government, supervises the personnel, prepares the budget, and recommends policies and programs to the council, which also enacts ordinances, makes appropriations, chooses and discharges the manager. The mayor is the presiding officer of the council, the ceremonial head of the city, and sometimes political leader. Managers are more and more being trained specifically for this position; they often go from small to large cities. Thus they are becoming a group of professional city administrators. However, this form of government has not solved all problems. Much depends on the competence of the individual manager and on the alertness of the citizenry. Cincinnati, with an organized body of citizens determined to maintain good government and with an exceptionally able manager, has a noteworthy record. Kansas City, in the grip of a notorious political machine, has given a much poorer account of itself under the council-manager form of government.

The present state of affairs in the forms of municipal government is indicated in Table 75. The fact that over half of the cities reporting

Table 75. Forms of Government in Cities over 5,000 Population, United States, 1950

Population group	Total number of cities	Mayor-council		Commission		Council-manager	
		Number	Per cent	Number	Per cent	Number	Per cent
Over 500,000........	17	15	88.2	1	5.9	1	5.9
250,000–500,000......	21	7	33.3	7	33.3	7	33.3
100,000–250,000......	67	29	43.3	17	25.4	21	31.3
50,000–100,000.......	125	47	37.6	30	24.0	48	38.4
25,000–50,000........	243	112	46.1	57	21.0	80	32.9
10,000–25,000........	754	401	53.2	125	16.6	228	30.2
5,000–10,000.........	1,091	778	71.3	105	9.6	208	19.1
All cities over 5,000...	2,318	1,389	59.9	336	14.5	593	25.6

SOURCE: Adapted from *Municipal Year Book*, p. 39, 1951. By permission of the International City Managers' Association.

clung to the old forms suggests ignorance, indifference, or lack of constitutional means for adapting municipal government to present-day conditions. However, there is no city in which there have not been many changes in both structure and function. In some cases these changes have been quite profound. Already new developments are taking place in metropolitan areas, but of these we shall have more to say a little later.

It may be assumed that the modifications in city government which we have just reviewed did not arise out of vague desires to perfect a reasonably effective mechanism. On the contrary, it is obvious that some innovations, perhaps most, were deliberate efforts to solve urgent problems.

One of the perennial problems of city government is its expensiveness. Citizens demand more and more services from their municipality, but at the same time they complain about high taxes. In part because of this unwillingness to pay for desired improvements and additions, cities have accumulated a very great bonded indebtedness. In many metropolitan areas, the fiscal problems are complicated by several factors discussed earlier in this and other chapters. First of all, the multiplicity of governmental units requires a heavy overhead. Not without great administrative cost does Greater Chicago, for example, maintain over 100 separate municipalities, 600 independent school districts, and 100 other units of local government. Moreover, the fact that many middle-

and upper-class residential districts are outside the central city, while most of the slums are inside, puts an excessive burden on taxpayers of the central city.

A second problem involves the issue of state control versus home rule. As we have seen, most city charters have been granted by legislatures, first individually and then by classes of cities. Now there is increasing home rule in that locally elected boards of freeholders draw up charters which are approved by popular vote within the municipality. However, there is still some direct state control. In some states, notably Massachusetts and Missouri, metropolitan police commissions are appointed by the governor. Legislative districts are so arranged as frequently to discriminate against large cities.[6] Candidates for municipal office often run on party tickets which confuse local issues with those of state and nation. Running through all this is a rural-urban antagonism which makes it difficult to secure rational consideration of the problem.

Another difficulty lies in the complexity of local government. We have noted the growing number and variety of activities. In most cities there are many separately elected officials whose relative independence makes unified administration almost impossible. Even the commission form of government has not brought about complete integration. Often the voter is called upon to choose from dozens or even hundreds of candidates on a long ballot. He cannot possibly know much about them, and after they are elected he has difficulty in fixing responsibility upon them. As a result, he often despairs of making democratic processes effective, develops a low regard for officeholders generally, or becomes quite indifferent. Frequently his apathy is so great that he does not even go to the polls. In the 1934 elections in 760 cities only 42 per cent of the population over twenty-one years of age exercised the privilege of voting.[7] Another aspect of the same situation is the difficulty of finding competent persons to run for municipal office. Even if such a candidate appears, it is hard to arouse the "good" citizens to support him; and if he is elected, it is hard amid the complexities of municipal government and the opposition of groups with vested interests for him to give the city an effective administration. Behind the apathetic and fatalistic attitudes so often displayed toward urban politics and government, we seem to see these factors: physical mobility and heterogeneity of urban populations, our preoccupation with money-making and the absorption of "our best talents" by commerce and industry, scorn for urban politics as a career, and in general, failure to develop substitutes for the primary group controls which seem to have been relatively effective in folk and rural societies. Some reformers have urged a return to the simple ways of our

---

[6] *Recent Social Trends*, Vol. 2, p. 1493.
[7] *Municipal Year Book*, p. 169, 1936.

forefathers. We are most dubious about the possibility of such a revival and about the effectiveness of primary controls in situations dominated by secondary relationships.

To be sure, political machines may operate on a primary group basis, at least for those on the inside. Moreover, they are known to make primary group appeals for gratitude and loyalty to those whom they have favored. It is also true that some real neighborhoods continue to function as primary groups, even in the heart of a great city. But all this does little or nothing to unite the urban population as a whole for effective action toward any objective—defense against bombing, slum clearance, smoke control, expediting traffic, or any other. Somehow city dwellers must learn to operate on a basis that Tönnies would call *gesellschaftlich*, if they are to control and direct their common affairs, instead of letting them drift or be taken over by bosses and machines.

Limitations of time and space forbid our discussion of the many interesting devices employed by political machines in the exercising of their power. We must, however, guard against the notions that political corruption is peculiar to our cities, that it is altogether different from what happens in business, and that it has recently appeared on the scene. Lincoln Steffens found that the graft and incompetence he uncovered thirty-five years ago had been long in existence. He arrived at the conclusion that the morals of politicians are not worse than those of businessmen, and he might have added that municipal government in great cities was perhaps no worse than county government in rural areas. As a matter of fact, it is impossible, even now, to say definitely that the practices of city officials and employees are more to be condemned than those of many people of the business world, that municipal government is less effective and less honest than that of our rural sections

METROPOLITAN GOVERNMENT

Earlier in this chapter we indicated that one of the greatest problems in the field of city government involves the coexistence and overlapping of many different units of government in every metropolitan area. We showed that this confusing and expensive structure is related to the expansion of great cities, their economic and social absorption of suburbs and satellites, and the creation of special authorities to meet new needs. We might also have mentioned the vested interests of officeholders, the inertia of voters, and the struggles of property owners to secure or preserve advantageous tax rates. In some suburbs there is great wealth coupled with small expenditures for government; there taxes are low. In others, poverty coexists with many needs calling for public action; there taxes are high. In the central city are found both wealth and poverty; usually taxes are high. Because local government is supported primarily through the general property tax and because needs and ability to pay are very unevenly distributed over a metropolitan area, there is an acute problem of public finance. This seems clearly to call for some measure of unification.

There are many other matters which apparently can be dealt with only through some kind of centralization. There are the planning of major thoroughfares, the creation of building zones, the provision of drainage, and the control of smoke, to mention only a few items involved in metropolitan planning. The provision of such necessities as water, sewage disposal, gas, electricity, and telephone has to be made on an inclusive basis rather than in terms of separate governmental areas. Perhaps the whole thing can be more easily visualized in terms of police and fire protection, public health services, and other provisions for the public safety. Obviously, lawbreakers can operate more easily when their enemies, the police, are divided and restricted to various limited territories. As to fire protection, the story is told of a house on the line between two urban municipalities which burned to the ground while the two fire departments argued whose responsibility it was. Finally, communicable diseases can scarcely be expected to respect political boundaries. Their control must be in the hands of officials who are free to operate over an entire metropolitan area. These are only some of the more prominent issues involved in the evident need for some sort of coordination or unification.

Several methods have been devised for attacking these problems and developing a measure of metropolitan government. One of the most widely used is annexation. From time to time our cities have taken in large parts of the surrounding territories, but most annexations are of very small districts. A second, but less generally used, plan is that of city-county separation. Obviously the separation of a city from the county which might include it simplifies matters, although it does not bring about unification. It ordinarily involves the consolidation of municipal and county functions within the city limits, and the restriction of county government to what is left of the former county. This device was first employed in Baltimore in 1851. It has also been used in San Francisco, St. Louis, and Denver. Unification of city and county governments involves making the boundaries of the municipality and the county coterminous and combining the governments of the two. This was first accomplished in Philadelphia in 1854 and subsequently in New Orleans and Brooklyn. In a few instances, notably in New York City and Boston, some of the functions of city and county have been combined without a complete merger of legal or territorial identities. When city and county remain separate, some advantages have been gained through the expansion of county government to meet some of the metropolitan needs. Thus under a home rule charter Los Angeles County since 1930 has developed many of the features of a municipal government and has been enabled to serve its inhabitants to much greater advantage than it could under the usual form of county government. It assesses and collects taxes for the city of Los Angeles as well as the county, carries on regional planning, attends to sanitation, flood control, fire and police protection, health services, poor relief, street improvements, and maintains a county library and art institute. However, the relation between the county and city governments still presents some problems. The two have not been thoroughly coordinated or integrated. Similar expansions of county government have developed in Cook County (Chicago), Wayne County (Detroit), Cuyahoga County (Cleveland), and Multnomah County (Portland).

Some metropolitan problems have been attacked through intermunicipal agreements. Thus the Brooklyn Bridge was a joint undertaking between the then separate municipalities of New York and Brooklyn. The cities of Newark, Elizabeth, and the Oranges developed a joint sewer system. Detroit and Highland Park jointly established bus routes. However, the instances of such joint undertakings are few, perhaps because municipalities do not have sufficient faith in each other. Another type of intermunicipal arrangement is that in which one city furnishes services to its neighbors. Thus Baltimore, Detroit, Denver, and Seattle furnish water to neighboring municipalities. St. Louis provides high school education for Negroes from suburban communities. The efforts of a city to control its water and milk supply may incidentally prove useful to other municipalities in the same metropolitan area.

Several times we have mentioned special districts set up for the performance of particular functions, which overlap several or many governmental units in a metropolitan area. Sometimes these districts are created by the state governments and function as its divisions. Sometimes they are agents of the municipalities and thus represent a limited degree of federation. Sometimes they are quite distinct local governments operating independently of others in the area. A few are bistate in character. As long ago as 1850, there were 10 special authorities in the Philadelphia district. In Greater New York the first one was created in 1857. From then on they have become increasingly numerous in many of our metropolitan centers. Their functions include the provision of a water supply, sewage disposal, local transportation, bridges, tunnels, parks, seaports, and health services. Perhaps these special districts represent about as near an approach to metropolitan government as we have in the United States, but there have been proposals looking toward much more completely federated government. Boston in 1896, Oakland in 1922, Pittsburgh in 1928, and Cleveland in 1929 were some of the battlegrounds on which this issue has been fought. The schemes have varied, but all had in mind a far-reaching measure of unification. Some of them propose making the county a central government for the metropolitan area. Some would preserve the existing municipality divisions much as they are, while others would abolish them in favor of new and larger subdivisions. In some plans the central metropolitan government is to be one of specific delegated powers, leaving all other powers to the separate localities. In other plans, the exact reverse of this is proposed. We are in no position to pass on the relative merits of these but have no hesitation in insisting upon the importance of a coordinated and a unified system of government for every metropolitan district.

HOW CITY DWELLERS VOTE

In an earlier section of this chapter we referred to a study of voting behavior in St. Louis.[8] We noted that in one year the percentage of adults who registered ranged from 42 to 71 in the city's 28 wards; for the city as a whole it was 59. This means that approximately two-fifths of the citizens did not even bother to register. Table 76 shows the proportions

Table 76. Per Cent of Registered Voters Who Cast Ballots in Specified Elections in St. Louis

Election	Percentage who voted in		
	Whole city	Individual wards	
		Minimum	Maximum
Presidential, 1944...............	83.8	70.1	87.6
Mayoralty, 1945................	42.7	34.4	54.5
Constitution, 1945..............	33.1	19.3	45.9
Library tax, 1946...............	51.9	23.5	64.3
Antidiscrimination, 1946.........	22.4	16.7	27.9
Rent control, 1948..............	38.6	31.8	48.6
Slum clearance, 1948............	74.0	50.0	83.3

SOURCE: Adapted from Edward B. Olds and David W. Salmon, *St. Louis Voting Behavior Study*, Sec. C, 1948. By permission of the authors.

of registered voters who went to the polls. As a matter of fact, in one city-wide election only 13 per cent of the potential voters cast ballots, and in the Sixteenth Ward only 9 per cent voted.[9]

On closer examination it was found that "the non-voting and non-

[8] Olds and Salmon, *op. cit.*
[9] Since St. Louis has very few nonnaturalized aliens, we have computed these percentages on the assumption that all persons over twenty-one are eligible to vote. In any case the margin of error is small.

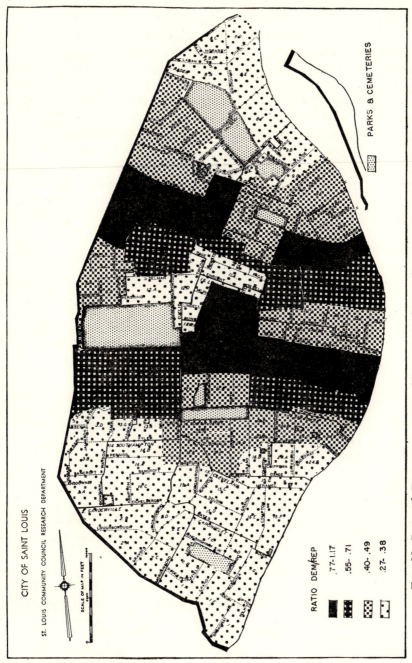

Fig. 28. Ratio of Democratic to Republican votes, by wards, mayoralty election, St. Louis, 1945.

registering population tends to come from the lower income strata, from areas which contain old apartment and rooming houses with low rents, and from districts in which racial minorities are segregated."[10] In the precincts so characterized, citizens who did vote gave most support to the Democratic party and to an antiracial discrimination charter amendment; they gave least support to the new state constitution and to a slum clearance bond issue.[11] Given precincts tended to remain consistently Republican or Democratic in nine candidate races. Figure 28 indicates the general distribution of voting areas. If compared with maps presented in earlier chapters, relationships between voting behavior and other socioeconomic factors will become apparent.

A similar study in Seattle[12] yielded results very much like those obtained in St. Louis. There was the same consistency in voting Republican or Democratic, the same type of division on other issues, the same general relationship to various socioeconomic factors. Precincts which regularly voted Republican opposed a state income tax and favored strike control, a referendum to limit the tax levy on real and personal property, and an initiative measure regarded as favorable to the public utilities. The precincts which regularly went Democratic favored old-age pensions and the income tax; they opposed strike control and limitation of the property tax levy. As in St. Louis, the Democratic districts were marked by low rentals, low percentage of homeownership, and low percentage of native-born of native parentage.

SUMMARY

We have traced in rough outline the rise of municipal government in response to the increasing number of specialized problems in urban centers. The people of cities wanted to manage some of their own affairs, and central governments often found it convenient to deal with cities as corporations. On the other hand, some state and national governments have been loath to give up direct control of municipal affairs. In America this tendency has been accentuated by rural-urban antagonisms and by party politics. On the whole, the trend has been in the direction of home rule.

The management of cities has become a matter of big business requiring more and more business methods of the best type. Yet most municipalities in the United States cling to outworn forms of government, quite unsuited to the performance of many functions for large popu-

[10] Olds and Salmon, *op. cit.*, p. A-4.

[11] The explanation for this apparent anomaly is that Negroes, who occupied most of the area which it was proposed to clear, had no assurance that the new housing would be available to them; hence they voted against the issue.

[12] Calvin F. Schmid, *Social Trends in Seattle*, pp. 257ff., 1944.

lations. Municipal government has become very complex and expensive. With voters indifferent and spoilsmen alert, political machines have often dominated our cities. Efforts to promote the short ballot, proportional representation, nonpartisan elections, the council-manager form of government, civil service, and the like have made headway in many places but have been unsuccessful in others.

A major problem in political structure is how to coordinate or unify the agencies and activities of the many governmental units in some of our metropolitan areas. Annexation, consolidation, special districts, federation —all have advantages and disadvantages. Resistance comes from politicians who fear loss of patronage, suburbanites who fear rising taxes, and all who hesitate to risk change.

SELECTED READINGS

ENCYCLOPAEDIA OF THE SOCIAL SCIENCES: See articles on municipal government, municipal corporation, municipal finance, home rule, civil service, political machines, political corruption, city manager, county-city consolidation.

GOSNELL, H. F.: *Machine Politics: Chicago Model,* University of Chicago Press, 1937. One of several concrete studies which form the basis for generalizations in this field.

LEPAWSKY, ALBERT, *et al.: Urban Government,* Vol. 1 of the Supplementary Report of the Urbanism Committee to the National Resources Committee, 1940. See especially Part 1, "Development of Urban Government," and Part 2, "Federal Relations to Urban Governments."

MCKEAN, D. D., *Party and Pressure Politics,* Houghton Mifflin Company, 1949. Deals with party structure and behavior, registrations and elections, pressure groups from business, labor, religion, race, and nationality.

MERRIAM, CHARLES E., *et al.: The Government of the Metropolitan Region of Chicago,* University of Chicago Press, 1933. Displays the chaotic condition of local government in one great metropolitan area.

STEFFENS, LINCOLN: The Autobiography of Lincoln Steffens, Harcourt, Brace and Company, Inc., 1931. Reveals the inside story of American city politics in the late nineteenth and early twentieth centuries.

STUDENSKI, P.: *Government of Metropolitan Areas in the United States,* National Municipal League, 1930. Presents the case for integration of governmental machinery in metropolitan areas and attempts that have been made in that direction.

CHAPTER 20. *Getting Help in Time of Trouble*

Trouble comes to people in every sort of community and in every walk of life, but there are differences in kinds of trouble, in attendant circumstances, and in ways of meeting it. Sickness, accident, death, poverty, marital discord, juvenile delinquency seem to occur everywhere, but there are variations in the way they strike and in people's reactions. The congestion, heterogeneity, anonymity, and mobility which characterize the social life of the city make it hard for old-fashioned neighborliness and mutual aid to function. Residents of large cities more often than those in small communities work for wages, live in rented quarters, travel some distance between home and work, and depend on formal organizations for many purposes.

In colonial days families and individuals in need of food, shelter, nursing, guidance, or other goods or services received them most often from kinsmen or neighbors. But even in those days there were persons without friends or relatives nearby, whose misfortune the town or church was called upon to relieve. Orphaned and illegitimate children, forsaken old folks, blind, deaf, crippled, insane, and feeble-minded persons were occasionally provided for by local government or, less often, by a religious order. But by and large the numbers not cared for by kinsmen were small, the costs were not great, and attention to them was an incidental responsibility of men busy with other affairs.[1] Specialization and professionalization were to come much later, and primarily in cities.

As towns developed into cities, spontaneous neighboring and mutual aid declined, relatively if not absolutely. There were too many people; they were too diverse in language and custom; they lived physically near

[1] Those interested in studying American social work in its preurban stage will find a number of monographs at their disposal, *e.g.*, Robert W. Kelso, *The History of Public Poor Relief in Massachusetts, 1620–1920,* 1922; Roy M. Brown, *Public Poor Relief in North Carolina,* 1928; Isabel C. Bruce and Edith Eickhoff, *The Michigan Poor Law,* 1936. They will also find valuable data in a collection of documents by Sophonisba P. Breckinridge, *Public Welfare Administration in the United States: Select Documents,* 1927.

but socially distant; they moved about too much. Primary social relations gave way to secondary. Hence when a person lost his job, fell ill, had an accident, or suffered other misfortune, he was likely to be stranded in the midst of strangers. Even if not socially isolated, he was often among friends who were little better off than himself and unable to render much assistance. At the other end of the economic ladder were nice ladies with leisure and gentlemen with money. They were shocked by mass poverty and unassimilated foreigners and were intrigued by the idea of doing something about it. What that something should be was not always clear. Certainly there was little notion of social and economic reorganization. But with a mixture of sympathy, fear, and self-importance the middle and upper classes undertook many sorts of philanthropic ventures.

Thus as cities grew, there appeared increasing numbers of organizations designed to meet a great variety of human needs. Some provided food and shelter for the homeless; some gathered in street waifs; some taught English to foreigners, thrift to the impoverished, and religious doctrines to the wayward. Most of these agencies were established in slum districts near the centers of large cities. They were sponsored mainly by middle- and upper-class folk who lived in outlying residential sections. As the numbers of these organizations grew, problems of coordination appeared. Also, with mounting costs of charity and never-ending lines of applicants, interest turned somewhat toward the prevention of poverty, disease, and crime. In the twentieth century the movement took a definite professional turn. Gradually the activities we call social work were diffused into small towns and rural districts. Even yet professional work is predominantly urban both in character and in distribution.

One of the most intimate glimpses we have of the troubles encountered by people of modest or small means and of the ways in which they meet them is that presented by Koos.[2] In the early 1940's he made an unusually intensive study of 62 families in one New York City block selected as representative of the Kips Bay–Yorkville Health District. For two years he was practically "one of them." The difficulties faced by these families included those experiences mentioned at the beginning of this chapter, but there was something more than being sick, losing a loved one, being "fired," and the like. One man put it this way: "A jamb is something you aren't used to handling, and there don't seem to be any rules for doing anything about it."[3] In other words, the troubles of these humble New Yorkers involved a disturbance of the normal pattern of life, a sharpened sense of insecurity, worry, and an effort to find a way out of the new and troublesome situation. Two-thirds of the families not only encountered trouble, as defined, during Koos's two years among them, but were suffer-

[2] Earl L. Koos, *Families in Trouble*, 1946.
[3] *Ibid.*, p. 9. By permission of Columbia University Press.

ing from troubles experienced earlier. Of the other one-third all but five were in trouble either during or before the period of study.

Where did these families turn for help? Especially, what use did they make of formal health and welfare agencies? Koos found that 57 families used some health agency other than the visiting nurse associations; 19 were helped by the Department of Public Welfare (relief); only 5 were clients of a family service society. It appeared that most of the families used these formal agencies only in case of extreme need. In some instances no help seemed to be available from a social work organization. In still other instances help was both available and known to the family, but rejected because of the stigma attached to charity or resentment against what was regarded as "snooping" by social workers. In the families which received no "institutional" aid, there were 52 troubles muddled through without any outside help. In 57 cases the families obtained advice, consolation, or material help as indicated in Table 77. These 109 troubles were experienced by 46 families who on these occasions had no assistance from social work or public health agencies. However, an even larger number of families did turn to professional social workers, visiting nurses, and physicians.

SOME TYPES OF SOCIAL WORK

Earlier in this chapter we mentioned some kinds of social service which are available to people in trouble and we reported their emergence in relation to the growth of cities. In the pages to follow we shall describe a few varieties of social work a bit more fully and shall tell more about their development in response to certain characteristics of urban life.

Table 77. Sources of Help and Times Consulted in 57 Emergencies

Source of Help	Times Consulted
Relatives................	36
Druggist...............	31
Bartender.............	29
Priest or minister........	16
Labor leader...........	6
Political leader.........	4
Policeman.............	2
Total................	124

SOURCE: Adapted from Earl L. Koos, *Families in Trouble*, p. 86, 1946. By permission of Columbia University Press.

RELIEF AND FAMILY SERVICE

It would be interesting, if space permitted, to review the entire history of relief and family service to see what relation, if any, they have borne to the growth of cities. But that would be far beyond the scope of this work. We shall be content with reminding the reader that Christian charity may be said to have begun with the appointment of deacons in the Jerusalem church to care for widows and orphans in that large bilingual group. Jewish charity has a genuine rural background, but its organization took definite shape in the ghettos of medieval cities. Public relief began in the cities of northwestern Europe, becoming rather general in the fifteenth and sixteenth centuries. The idea of governmental responsibility for the needy was brought over from England by the colonists from that country, and poor laws were in operation long before the American Revolution. But life was hard in the colonies; there was no margin to warrant the toleration of loafers or any number of dependents of any sort. Hence both the laws and their administration were intended to discourage possible applicants for relief.

So long as the United States was predominantly a rural, agricultural nation the chief support of needy children, the aged, and other unfortunates appears to have come from relatives and neighbors. It was only the exceptional cases that became public burdens. But as cities grew, spontaneous neighborliness and mutual aid became less and less adequate. The mobility and anonymity of city life meant that masses of people did not know one another or sympathize with one another's need. Moreover, there were increasingly crowded together in slum areas great numbers of folk who had not the means to assist even when they knew and cared. Hence there developed formal machinery to make some provision for the most needy. In part this took the form of ecclesiastical charities, especially those of the Roman Catholic Church. Then after the War between the States and with the rise of the middle class, it very often took the form of private, nonsectarian philanthropy. A host of petty, ill-managed organizations arose, whose functions appear to have been to occupy the leisure time of well-to-do folk and to save their souls even more than to feed, clothe, nurse, or discipline the lower classes.

Even before the War between the States, there appeared a few larger organizations called Provident Association or Association for Improving the Condition of the Poor. These societies depended on volunteer visitors but insisted on investigation; they urged temperance and thrift; they sought the cooperation of other charitable organizations. But their success was limited. They neither rescued their clients from poverty nor won the affiliation of their fellow philanthropists. When the depression of 1873 came on, private charity was described as having "sunk into the sea of common almsgiving"; it was "profuse and chaotic, while still behind the demands made upon it, and was dispersed in tantalizing doles miserably inadequate for effectual succor where the need was genuine, and dealt out broadcast among the clamorous and impudent."[4]

[4] *Nat. Conf. Char. & Cor.*, p. 53, 1893.

It was during the depression of 1873 that the charity organization movement was brought over from London, where it had arisen in response to a similar situation. By 1880 there were 14 societies of this type. Their basic policies were (1) "mediating" between the client and possible sources of relief rather than giving directly, (2) abolition of public outdoor (home) relief on the ground of its hopeless immersion in partisan politics, (3) coordination of the work of other agencies, (4) central registration of persons helped, (5) friendly visiting among the poor, (6) district conferences to serve "as a popular school for teaching charity," (7) "provident schemes," (8) the repression of street begging, (9) housing reform. Later came intercity cooperation and a transportation agreement to eliminate "passing the buck." All this represented a rather ambitious program, although there were some who charged that it failed to get at the root of poverty. But it may be that the most important contribution of the charity organization movement was its development of a philosophy and a set of skills that have come to be called social casework. Gradually a professional literature came into being; formal training courses were established; and in 1904 the first professional school of social work was launched in New York.

Since the turn of the century, the charity organization movement in American cities has become a family welfare movement. In this transition, material relief has paradoxically become both less and more important. What we mean is this: Instead of concentrating on the physical needs of families in distress, agencies in this field have concerned themselves with the family as a social group, its unity and adaptability. They have used relief as a "tool in treatment," more or less incidental and subsidiary to other services, especially counseling. They have given particular attention to relations between husband and wife, parents and children, to family pride, loyalty, and "we-feeling" as against individualization, tension, and open conflict. On the other hand, during this same period these agencies have given up the policy of merely mediating and have given increasing amounts of direct relief. This trend was marked throughout the twenties and reached its climax in the early years of the depression. Originally an affair of private charity, the family welfare movement has come to include public departments that have adopted the principles under discussion and have employed a professionally trained personnel. The notion that public relief must be abolished has given way to cooperation between public and private agencies in the field. It is generally agreed that large-scale relief must be the responsibility of some governmental unit or units; it is less generally accepted that personal service of the sort called casework should accompany much relief; but it is not at all clear just what functions belong distinctively to private family welfare societies. Those variously urged include: supplementation of the relief and service of public agencies, development of new services and methods, public education.

Two episodes of the last half century involve rapid and extensive diffusion of family welfare work into rural areas. The first took place during World War I, when the American Red Cross organized chapters in many small towns and rural counties to aid in family adjustments necessitated by the sudden removal of many men to the army and navy. The sheer number of persons to be aided made it unlikely that spontaneous neighborliness and mutual aid among relatives would suffice. Also, there were technical matters requiring attention: soldiers' allotments, war risk insurance, and compensation. Many experienced social workers were drafted from the cities to organize and conduct the new home service. The second episode occurred in 1933, when the Federal Emergency Relief Administration required the states, as a condition of participation in Federal funds, to create suitable organizational machinery where such did not exist and to employ reasonably competent personnel. Again city-trained social workers invaded rural districts, and again some rural folk were given at least short courses in family casework. The result is that through the influence of the Federal Social Security system and state departments of public welfare there are now many professional social workers in rural counties.

CHILD WELFARE WORK

It is difficult to measure the urbanization of child welfare work because many agencies, public and private, serve both urban and rural areas. Thus in colonial days, before the rise of cities, orphans, illegitimates, and troublesome children were sometimes apprenticed or indentured by the local officials. About the middle of the nineteenth century, Massachusetts developed a state-wide system of boarding out needy children in foster homes. Several states authorized the establishment of county homes for dependent children, and half a dozen states set up state public schools, as centers for distributing such children in foster homes. Nevertheless, it is correct to say that a large part of the child welfare movement has been urban.

The earliest orphanages were established in seaboard cities under religious or municipal auspices. The number of such institutions has grown to an estimated 1,400, and most of them are located in or near large cities. However, we have no data as to the number of young charges drawn from urban and from rural areas.

Child placing received a great stimulus from the New York Children's

Aid Society, which was established in 1853 to save the "young outcasts" from the "great lower class." The founder announced "emigration to be the best remedy for juvenile pauperism," and hoped to drain the city of these "vagrant children," placing them in "respectable country homes." After reaching the children through lodginghouses and Sunday schools, he gathered together a carload lot and transported them to a small town in Michigan, where they were placed in farm and village homes recommended by clergymen and justices of the peace. Over a forty-year period more than 90,000 New York City children were scattered from Manitoba to Florida, and from New Jersey to California. From this wholesale shipment of boys and girls in the mid-nineteenth century to modern casework with needy children is a long road. But there has developed, first and chiefly in large cities, a program which includes careful inquiry into the physical health, intelligence, emotions, family ties, and other "resources and liabilities" of each child for whom care is asked. It involves similarly thorough study of each foster home that is discovered or offered. Great care is taken in the effort to fit home and child to each other. After placement, there is continuing supervision and guidance. For some children board is paid; others are given free homes; a minority are adopted; and a small number work for their keep. Obviously the limited diagnostic facilities and the great distances make it hard to adapt such a program to the country, yet the diffusion is taking place through state-wide children's home societies and children's bureaus of the state government.

Protective work with and for children began under private auspices and developed first in large cities. In the nineteenth century there were humane societies and societies for the prevention of cruelty to children. Later came juvenile protective associations and other organizations to make investigations, issue publicity, and bring pressure to bear on legislative bodies and administrative officials. Since 1910 and especially since 1930, both investigations and direct service to neglected children have been largely shifted from private to public auspices. Protective work for children is now carried on largely through juvenile courts and departments of public welfare (child welfare services).

Another type of public child welfare work began with mothers' pensions which first developed in Kansas City and Chicago in 1911. These spread rapidly over the country and have now been absorbed into the "aid to dependent children" which is part of the social security system. Finally, mention may be made of work carried on under boards of education, particularly the work of attendance officers and visiting teachers. The former are to all intents and purposes police officers, while the latter are social caseworkers. However, in some large school systems the functions of attendance departments have been extended to include many problems of pupil-teacher-parent relationships.

OTHER VARIETIES OF SOCIAL WORK

The types of social work discussed so far are by no means the only ones that deserve consideration, but limitations of space forbid more than passing mention of others. One of the important varieties of social case-work that arose in large cities is medical social work, which is essentially the study of the social and economic situation of patients in hospitals and clinics and the carrying through of programs intended to help patients to recover and retain their health. It is based on recognition of the fact that financial conditions, home responsibilities, working conditions, personal attitudes, religious beliefs, and many other social factors contribute both to health and to disease. Hence, starting in Boston and spreading throughout the nation, this has become one of the major varieties of American social casework.

Beginning with World War I and accelerated during World War II, psychiatric social work has become increasingly important in cities of the United States and in hospitals under the Veterans' Administration. This specialty began as social service to patients in institutions for the mentally sick and the mentally defective. Presently it became apparent that the point of view, the insights, and the skills of psychiatric social work might profitably be applied to problems of family disorganization, delinquency, educational and vocational maladjustment.

Another type of social agency to which people in trouble sometimes turn for help is the social settlement. This, like the charity organization society, supposedly originated in London in the latter part of the nineteenth century. It may be said to have arisen in part out of the—to an Englishman—amazing discovery that in the metropolis there were great populations devoid of any "gentlemen" to assume leadership and responsibilty in civic affairs. It was preceded by city missions and by a few ventures on the part of Christian Socialists, but the settlement was an adventure of university men who wanted to make a contribution in service rather than in cash and in a secular rather than a religious fashion. A number of them settled in a slum area, seeking to participate as fully as possible in the lives of its inhabitants, promoting and conducting classes, recreational activities, semiformal investigations, and participating sometimes in politics.

About 1890 the idea was transplanted to the United States, whose cities had not only slums but great immigrant populations whose lack of assimilation distressed many civic leaders. The early American settlements were established in New York, Chicago, Boston, and Philadelphia. As in England, they represented to a large degree the interest of college and university folk in the working classes of large cities. They were a true form of "bourgeois benevolence." Young college graduates of some means settled in slum districts and established centers of educational, recreational, and civic activities. They sought to make these settlements not merely "service stations" but also points for the development of contacts between social classes. It was hoped that a better understanding might be promoted and that each class might learn from the other. That is to say, there is a note of democracy in the settlement despite a seemingly contradictory note of condescension and uplift.

The social settlements were among the first, if not the first, agencies to develop the sort of thing that has come to be known as social group work. They concerned themselves not merely with teaching English to foreigners and home economics to young girls, not merely with supervising playgrounds for small children and dramatics for adults, but with the promotion of organized group activities as such. In other words, they wanted to give to their clientele experience in organized group life whereby they might learn to play their parts, "to lead and follow, to meet and handle propaganda, to integrate conflicting loyalties, to cooperate at certain points and to exert group pressure at others."[5] Social group work has been gradually developing a body of technical knowledge and skills for bringing people together into groups, utilizing or promoting common interests, discovering and training leaders, guiding the conduct of meetings, and dealing with other aspects of human relations in small groups. It is not primarily concerned with people in trouble, but group work is sometimes used as a means of social therapy.

URBAN CONCENTRATION OF SOCIAL WORK

From a historical review of social work it is evident that this kind of professional service originated in cities and has had its most marked development in cities. Various series of data support the generalization that the numbers of social workers and of social agencies vary with the size of population aggregate. Table 78 is based on a study of over 3,800 localities ranging in population from 2,000 to over 1 million.

From the 1951 *Directory of Member Agencies* of the Family Service Association of America we have determined that agencies of this type are found in less than 1 per cent of cities under 25,000; in one-sixth or cities between 25,000 and 50,000; in two-fifths of cities between 50,000 and 100,000; in four-fifths of cities between 100,000 and 250,000; and in all but two cities over 250,000. It should be noted that membership in the Family Service Association of America represents not only participation in the field of activity, but also the maintenance of professional standards. From the 1950 *Directory of Community Chests and Councils of Social*

---

[5] Grace L. Coyle, "Group Work and Social Change," *National Conference of Social Work*, p. 395, 1935.

Table 78. Percentages of Communities of Different Size Groups Possessing Different Social Welfare Facilities

	2,000–2,500	2,500–5,000	5,000–10,000	10,000–25,000	25,000–50,000	50,000–100,000	100,000–250,000	250,000–500,000	500,000–1,000,000	1,000,000 and over
At least one social worker.......	2	3	17	19	49	79	96	96	100	100
Day nursery..................	1	1	4	11	32	63	88	96	100	100
Home for dependent children....	4	7	15	29	61	79	89	92	100	100
Home for the aged.............	3	4	10	18	47	62	82	96	100	100
Juvenile court.................	14	17	30	45	74	84	95	88	100	100
Psychiatric clinic...............	1	3	7	16	27	48	63	83	100	100
Legal aid bureau...............	0	0	0	0	1	10	41	83	100	100
Community chest..............	0	1	4	15	51	65	84	92	100	100

SOURCE: Adapted from Fenton Keyes, *The Correlation of Social Phenomena with Community Size*, unpublished doctoral dissertation, Yale University, p. 99, 1942. By permission of the author and Yale University.

Agencies we find that these coordinating bodies are still overwhelmingly metropolitan, although in recent years many have been established in small cities. In 1950 there were community chests in one-ninth of places under 5,000; in one-sixth of places between 5,000 and 10,000; in nearly one-half of places between 10,000 and 25,000; in over nine-tenths of places between 25,000 and 50,000; and in nearly every city over that size. In 1950 New York was the only city of more than a million inhabitants which had no community chest; it did, however, have a council of social agencies (Welfare Council of New York City). Table 78 shows clearly the distribution of social workers in relation to size of community, as computed by Keyes in 1942. The sample statistics concerning the labor force compiled by the Bureau of the Census in 1943 provide added evidence. From these data it appears that 72 per cent of those who listed their usual occupation as social and welfare worker were urban, and 83 per cent of those employed in March, 1940, as social and welfare workers were urban.[6] We ourselves checked the membership directory of the American Association of Social Workers for 1936 and found over two-thirds of all professional social workers at that time listed as residents of cities of 100,000 or over. Thus the evidence is decisive as to the urban concentration of social work.

MEDICAL CARE IN CITIES

Like the history of social work, the history of medical care is associated with the development of cities. The physicians of antiquity

[6] Bureau of the Census, *The Labor Force, Usual Occupation, Sample Statistics*, 1943; *The Labor Force, Occupational Characteristics, Sample Statistics*, 1943.

and of medieval Europe were city men. The medieval hospital, though very unlike the modern institution of the same name, was nearly always located in a town or city. So today in the United States we find medical facilities and services more common and more adequately developed in cities than in the country.

Table 79. Relative Distribution of Physicians, General Hospital Beds, and Population, by Rural-Urban Type of Counties, 1942

Type of county	Per cent of population	Per cent of physicians	Per cent of hospital beds
All counties..............................	100.0	100.0	100.0
Metropolitan counties.....................	53.3	67.9	70.6
Bordering metropolitan counties...........	16.0	11.9	10.7
Not bordering metropolitan counties with largest urban place:			
10,000 or more........................	9.5	8.1	9.9
5,000–10,000.........................	6.7	4.4	
2,500–5,000..........................	6.3	3.7	8.8
Under 2,500..........................	8.2	4.0	

SOURCE: Adapted from F. D. Mott and M. I. Roemer, *Rural Health and Medical Care*, pp. 152, 218, 1948. By permission of McGraw-Hill Book Company, Inc.

Table 80. Percentages of Communities of Different Size Groups Possessing Different Medical Facilities

Size of community	Hospital	Tuberculosis sanitarium	Public health nurse
2,000–2,500.................	23	1	18
2,500–5,000.................	37	2	35
5,000–10,000...............	61	3	59
10,000–25,000..............	74	6	81
25,000–50,000..............	86	19	87
50,000–100,000.............	94	29	97
100,000–250,000............	100	55	100
250,000–500,000............	100	63	100
500,000–1,000,000...........	100	38	100
1,000,000 and over..........	100	100	100

SOURCE: Adapted from Fenton Keyes, *The Correlation of Social Phenomena with Community Size*, unpublished doctoral dissertation, Yale University, p. 99, 1942. By permission of the author and Yale University.

Tables 79 and 80 represent two ways of measuring the concentration of certain medical facilities in metropolitan centers. Table 81 is a different approach to the same issue. It shows not only that the numbers of physicians are relatively greater in urban states than in rural states, but that this condition has continued over a quarter of a century. As a matter of fact, we have data, compiled in somewhat different form, which indicate that this urban concentration has been going on for half a century and that it is becoming steadily greater.[7] Table 82 shows the same general disparity between the ratios of dentists and of hospital beds to total population in urban and in rural states at two different dates. Table 83 makes it plain that urban states are more adequately supplied with trained nurses and drugstores than are rural states. In varying forms,

Table 81. Number of Physicians per 100,000 Population in Selected Urban and Rural States, 1927, 1938, and 1949

	Per cent urban, 1940	Ratio of physicians to population		
		1927	1938	1949
Seven Most Urban States in 1940				
District of Columbia..............	100.0	342	336	293
Rhode Island.....................	91.6	111	135	135
Massachusetts....................	89.4	147	173	185
New York........................	82.8	163	190	210
New Jersey......................	81.6	100	133	133
Illinois..........................	73.6	149	152	152
California.......................	71.0	200	169	158
Seven Least Urban States in 1940				
West Virginia....................	28.1	103	100	90
North Carolina...................	27.3	80	77	86
South Dakota....................	24.6	87	82	76
South Carolina...................	24.5	71	74	75
Arkansas........................	22.2	109	96	85
North Dakota....................	20.6	78	79	79
Mississippi......................	19.8	94	70	69
United States....................	56.5	126	131	135

SOURCE: 1927 data from R. I. Lee and L. W. Jones, *The Fundamentals of Good Medical Care*, p. 116, 1933. 1938 and 1949 data from American Medical Association, Bureau of Medical Economic Research, Bulletin 78, p. 7, 1950. By permission of the University of Chicago Press and the American Medical Association.

the evidence is available to show that as we go from open country to metropolis there is both absolute and relative increase in physicians' and dentists' services and in hospital care.[8]

These data naturally raise the question of whether city people are more frequently and more seriously ill than country people. If so, they evidently need the extra medical care that is at hand. Unfortunately the facts are elusive; diagnostic facilities are less adequate in rural than in

[7] R. G. Leland, *Distribution of Physicians in the United States*, pp. 48, 51, 1936.
[8] F. D. Mott and M. I. Roemer, *Rural Health and Medical Care*, pp. 282, 286, 297, 1948; I. S. Falk, M. C. Klem, and N. Sinai, *The Incidence of Illness*, pp. 92, 100, 279, 1933.

Table 82. Number of Dentists per 100,000 Population, Number of General Hospital Beds per 1,000 Population in Selected Urban and Rural States, 1927–1930 and 1940–1942

	Per cent urban, 1940	Ratio of dentists to population		Ratio of general hospital beds to population	
		1927–1930	1940	1927–1930	1942
Seven Most Urban States in 1940					
District of Columbia..........	100.0	98	70	10.3	6.4
Rhode Island.................	91.6	55	49	4.5	4.0
Massachusetts................	89.4	80	64	4.9	5.5
New York....................	82.8	63	72	4.1	4.9
New Jersey..................	81.6		62	3.3	3.9
Illinois.....................	73.6	75	71	3.9	3.8
California...................	71.0	103	74	4.7	4.5
Seven Least Urban States in 1940					
West Virginia................	28.1	40	30	2.5	2.9
North Carolina..............	27.3	29	21	1.7	2.4
South Dakota................	24.6	49	44	3.0	3.5
South Carolina..............	24.5	24	18	1.5	2.0
Arkansas....................	22.2	23	18	1.8	1.7
North Dakota................	20.6	46	39	2.9	3.9
Mississippi..................	19.8	19	18	1.4	1.6
United States...............	56.5	56	50	3.3	3.5

SOURCE: 1927–1930 data from R. I. Lee and L. W. Jones, *The Fundamentals of Good Medical Care*, p. 116, 1933; 1940–1942 data from F. D. Mott and M. I. Roemer, *Rural Health and Medical Care*, pp. 188–189, 226–227, 1948. By permission of the University of Chicago Press and McGraw-Hill Book Company, Inc.

Table 83. Number of Persons per Trained Nurse and per Drugstore in States Grouped by Percentage of Population Urban, 1940

Per cent urban (state populations)	Number of persons per trained nurse	Number of persons per drugstore
Over 70...............	306	2,089
61–70.................	452	2,247
51–60.................	492	2,062
41–50.................	597	2,049
31–40.................	771	2,650
30 and under...........	958	3,308
United States..........	454	2,273

SOURCE : Adapted from F. D. Mott and M. I. Roemer, *Rural Health and Medical Care*, pp. 193, 258, 1948. By permission of McGraw-Hill Book Company, Inc.

urban areas, and what different people say about their aches and pains is hardly to be accepted as reliable evidence. This much we do know: urban death rates are higher than rural, although individual cities have very low mortality, and since 1900 the urban death rates have declined much more than the rural death rates.[9] With reference to particular diseases the death rates vary as follows:

Table 84. Relative Differences in Urban and Rural Death Rates

Disease	Higher death rate	
	In cities	In rural areas
Heart diseases...................	x	
Tuberculosis....................	x	
Syphilis.......................	x	
Cancer........................	x	
Diabetes......................	x	
Pneumonia....................	..	x
Influenza......................	..	x
Diarrhea and enteritis..........	..	x
Typhoid.......................	..	x
Malaria.......................	..	x
Diphtheria....................	..	x

Speaking generally, this means that the degenerative diseases are more frequently recognized as causes of death in cities than in rural districts; while most communicable diseases, especially those of childhood, are more frequently found in rural districts.[10]

To sum up the whole matter, cities frequently confront people with situations in which they are unable to meet their troubles by themselves or with the aid of friends and relatives. In rural districts this happens less often and less dramatically. It is in cities that the need of specialized, professional services has been most recognized. Cities also have been able to provide more adequate finances and education for professional services. It is for these reasons that there has been a concentration of social work and medical care in urban centers. However, while social work programs and facilities have been recently diffused steadily into rural areas, medical facilities and personnel have been concentrated more and more in large cities. While it is true that country people can go to cities for some of their medical care and even for some kinds of social service, the present distribution of personnel and agencies obviously does not correspond to the distribution of need. It rather suggests the stronger drawing power of cities in terms of prestige, income, and facilities with which to work.

[9] Mott and Roemer, *op. cit.*, p. 54.
[10] *Ibid.*, Chap. 4.

SELECTED READINGS

BRUNO, FRANK J.: *Trends in Social Work as Reflected in the Proceedings of the National Conference of Social Work, 1874–1946.* Columbia University Press, 1948. The proceedings themselves are issued annually and contain very useful articles.

FINK, ARTHUR E.: *The Field of Social Work,* Henry Holt and Company, Inc., 1942 and 1949. A description of social work as a whole and of its specialized fields, their philosophy and processes illustrated by case summaries.

HOLLIS, ERNEST V., and ALICE L. TAYLOR: *Social Work Education in the United States,* Columbia University Press, 1951. Chapter 2 describes the status and scope of social work with some data as to rural-urban differences.

KOOS, EARL L.: *Families in Trouble,* Columbia University Press, 1946. The report of an intensive study of urban families, their troubles, and where they turned for help.

MOTT, FREDERICK D., and MILTON I. ROEMER: *Rural Health and Medical Care,* McGraw-Hill Book Company, Inc., 1948. Contains many tables and charts comparing rural and urban health and services.

STROUP, HERBERT H.: *Social Work,* American Book Company, 1948. Description and history of American social work, its structure and procedures in a dozen specialized fields.

Social Work Year Book, 1951, American Association of Social Workers. See classified list of topical articles. Issued in alternate years.

PART 5

Social Change and the City

CHAPTER 21

Changes in American Life Associated with Urbanism

In the preceding parts of this book we have undertaken to answer such questions as these: When, where, and under what circumstances have cities developed? What is their spatial pattern? To what extent and in what ways are the activities of city people localized? How does social life vary as one proceeds along the rural-urban continuum? In Part 5 our concern is with the city and social change. What general changes in the life of a people accompany the development of urbanism? Are there characteristic series of changes in cities themselves? Can these be predicted or controlled?

First of all, let us remind ourselves that urbanism did not begin in the United States. Cities of the Near East and of Europe preceded and set patterns of life that have had their impact on us. This means that urbanism is older than Americanism. Nevertheless, cities are relatively new in human experience. Five thousand years ago there were practically none. Today there are thousands, including 40 of over a million inhabitants each. Second, the development of cities is bound up with general cultural development. We saw in Chap. 4 how the earliest cities of which we have any knowledge appeared in river valleys of the Near East. They followed or accompanied the cultivation of grains, domestication of animals, drainage and irrigation, stable residence, fortifications, trade and government over expanding areas. During classical antiquity, tribal villages grew into city-states with elaborate systems of government, religion, and trade. New methods of warfare and transportation helped Rome to become a city of perhaps a million people, ruling a vast empire. Then the *Völkerwanderung* brought hordes of Barbarians who knew not city life; Rome fell to perhaps 20,000; and Europe became a multitude of petty feudal units. With the Crusades came a renewal of commerce; old towns were revived and new ones sprang up. In these towns and cities appeared gilds, universities, and new outlooks on life.

But the development of urbanism on a large scale came with and after the Industrial Revolution, which involved new means of transportation and communication, improved agriculture, new kinds of building, a re-alignment of social classes, a philosophy of *laissez faire*, and the spread of nationalism.

In the changes to which we have just referred we note that the development of cities has followed and depended on other phases of social life. We also observe that cities have been centers of cultural innovations which are diffused to the hinterland. In many ways large cities dominate their regions. This we have found in the city-states of classical antiquity, in the imperial capitals of modern times, and in metropolitan regions of the United States.

In the foregoing chapters we have found indications that cities in the United States have passed through similar sequences of change. These are not duplicated in detail in other countries, but further study may reveal some features that are generic to the life cycle of cities everywhere. Here it is our purpose to review the scattered evidence with the hope of finding a more adequate answer to the question: Is there a typical sequence of events in the life history of North American cities? Do the same sorts of things happen in approximately the same order? Are there stages which might be identified as youth, maturity, and perhaps decline? We shall deal with this problem in terms of history—physical growth, relations to the surrounding area and to other cities, economic base, and social institutions or established ways of carrying on major activities —and the Index of Urbanism and its correlates.

THE PHYSICAL GROWTH OF CITIES

From the data set forth in Chaps. 4 to 7 it seems clear that our present great cities typically started as relatively self-sufficient villages, developed into towns which were small trading centers, then became genuine cities serving larger areas and involved in commercial relations with other cities, and finally expanded into metropolitan structures.

As to rates of growth, cities show great diversity. Thus St. Louis developed slowly for seventy-five years; it grew rapidly from 1840 to 1870, after which it settled down to a moderate rate of expansion. Detroit's development was fairly slow and steady until the automobile era began, about 1910, after which it grew at a rapid rate until the depression of 1929. Chicago started later than St. Louis and Detroit but since its first few years has maintained a rapid growth. Philadelphia's population has increased steadily at a moderate rate except during the 1850's, when it quadrupled, and during the 1930's, when it suffered a small loss. Seattle was an unimportant town until 1880; then it had thirty years of very rapid development, from 3,500 to 237,000; since 1910 it has grown steadily but moderately. Until 1930 no United States city of 100,000 showed an intercensal decline. But the 1930 census showed that 4 large cities had lost population, 1940 showed 28, and 1950 showed 9. It is understood, of course, that these were incorporated municipalities; in most cases the metropolitan areas of which they were parts actually grew. As a matter of fact, the 1930 census was the first to show a loss of population in a metropolitan district. In the 1920's three metropolitan districts lost population, in the 1930's nine, and the 1940's three.

As to sources of population, our earliest cities—Boston, New York, Philadelphia, Baltimore—were established by newcomers from Europe. They grew by attracting to themselves descendants of Europeans who had settled first in rural America. From the War between the States to World War I the urban increase was chiefly due to European immigration. Since then the most noticeable additions have been of rural Americans, especially Negroes. Southern cities have received fewer immigrants from abroad than have those of the North, and more migrants from rural areas, both white and Negro. Western cities have just begun to acquire large Negro populations. Some cities, *e.g.*, Boston, New York, Chicago, and San Francisco, have depended longer and to a greater extent on immigration from abroad than have others, *e.g.*, Baltimore, Detroit, St. Louis, and Los Angeles. Los Angeles has attracted chiefly native whites; St. Louis, Detroit, and Baltimore have drawn Americans of both major races.

As a city grows, there are characteristic internal movements. Starting as a small, compact unit, it spreads out in several directions, occupying more and more territory. In time it approaches and surrounds outlying towns, which are gradually absorbed into the metropolis. As business and industry invade residential districts, old families move farther from the center. But factories and stores usually do not occupy the entire area evacuated by old residents. Single dwellings become converted tenements and house newcomers to the city. The centrifugal flight continues until the inner city begins to lose population. Then realtors, downtown merchants, and tax collectors manifest alarm. New housing programs have been undertaken with a view to rehabilitating the districts which have become blighted and drawing population back toward the heart of the city. These characteristic internal movements have been more fully described in Chaps. 7, 9, 11, and 12.

THE EXTERNAL RELATIONS OF CITIES

As we pointed out in earlier chapters, no city can live unto itself. Also, urbanism as a characteristic way of life depends upon the existence of many cities among which there are various relations. Hence the dominant mode of transportation must be considered in its bearing on the life cycle of our cities. From the beginning of our history as a nation until the War between the States, the principal mode of transportation was by water. Our earliest cities were along the Atlantic seaboard; later cities grew up on the Great Lakes and along the Ohio and Mississippi Rivers. In view of this fact, cities not only appeared where there were good harbors or suitable river landings; they were in the nature of water-bound settlements, *i.e.*, business houses had to be near the water front. Trade was carried on for the most part with other places which could be reached by water. Trade consisted largely in the handling of goods which would not be damaged by slow transit.

About 1850 railroads began to be an important means of transportation. After the War between the States, they spread over the country very rapidly. Railroads not only stimulated the growth of existing towns like Rochester and Chicago but brought new towns and cities into existence, *e.g.*, Indianapolis, Wichita, and Oklahoma City. The railroads brought about a redistribution of business activities in individual cities. Terminals, warehouses, and factories no longer had to cluster about the water front; they could be located on any piece of ground conveniently reached by rail. The railroads also promoted suburban development and hastened the absorption of outlying communities by the growing city.

Since 1900, cities have been particularly affected by the enormous increase in the number of automobiles. These have still further stimulated suburban development and have caused it to take place in sections not easily reached by rail. The automobile has also created new traffic problems. It has facilitated outdoor recreation, particularly week-end trips into the country. The truck and bus have further consolidated business relations between great cities and outlying towns.

Finally we have the airplane, whose influence on cities we are only beginning to understand. It enables people to get back and forth very quickly from one city to another, thus enchancing intercity movement in contrast with other kinds of mobility.

In keeping with the varied means of transportation, there have been characteristic changes in the hinterland, or sphere of influence, belonging to each city. In most cases this was initially small, although there have been some exceptions, as in the cases of San Francisco and St. Louis. As transportation facilities developed, the trade area expanded until it overlapped that of some other city. Later, with the rise of additional urban centers and with changes in major lines of transportation, these trade areas, or spheres of influence, contracted, until they now seem to be approaching stabilization. The momentum of great cities is such that the smaller places in the same region have long since ceased to be rivals of the metropolis. Instead, they take their place in a constellation centering about the great city. To a certain extent, even metropolitan centers are ceasing to be rivals. Each has its own hinterland; each has certain major products which it distributes to other cities for redistribution to their respective hinterlands. Hence the businessmen in each place tend to look somewhat tolerantly upon those of other centers. In other words, after expansion and contraction, after several changes in transportation facilities, and after the opening of natural resources, cities seem to be settling down temporarily to fairly well-defined relations to each other and to their own hinterlands.

THE ECONOMIC BASES OF CITIES

Another important aspect of the life cycle of a city is its changing economic base. However, the diversity here is so great that we find it very difficult to identify a characteristic sequence of events to which any large number of cities seem to conform. The few points which stand out are these. Initially the community is approximately a self-sufficient unit. There are local trade, handicraft, and agriculture. Then there develop gradually manufacturing on a larger scale and trade with a larger area. Sometimes wholesaling appears first and sometimes manufacturing. Also, the manufacturing may be confined to a single industry or it may be diversified. As cities grow large, they develop increasingly as financial and managerial headquarters for the major enterprises of their regions. Finally, a few great cities, such as New York, have moved into positions of national and international dominance.

In detail, the economic base may change as one after another new natural resources are discovered and developed. Thus Duluth has depended in succession on furs, lumber, iron, and wheat. Seattle started with lumber, later added fishing and mining, and subsequently became an important financial and administrative center. Los Angeles was initially a sleepy agricultural town. Then it became a booming tourist center. Presently oil, later the movies and aircraft made their important contributions to its economic life. On the whole it appears that the economic life of our cities is becoming more and more diversified, so that in each metropolitan district there are manufacturing, wholesale and retail trade, banking, and in fact almost all the major types of business activity. Along with internal diversity has come intercity resemblance; so that every city presents, within limits, a miniature of American life.

SOCIAL INSTITUTIONS OF CITIES

Turning to what are sometimes called the social institutions, we find characteristic changes in the family, in recreation, in education, in religion, in social work, and in government.

The Family. Many of our cities were settled primarily by single men; others were settled at the very beginning by family groups. Such families as existed were commonly patriarchal in form. However, with the coming of people of various cultural backgrounds, the city came to display numerous forms, until today there is not only the patriarchal family of the older immigrant from abroad and rural America, but the so-called emancipated family with working wife and few children, the equalitarian family on somewhat higher economic level with few children and with the wife engaged in social activities outside the home, and the mother-dominated family from which the husband and father is absent most of the time in the conduct of his business or profession.

In general, the changes that have taken place in American families, especially in cities, involve an increase in the number of married women working outside their homes, a decrease in the number of relatives, lodgers, and servants, a declining birth rate, the diffusion of knowledge of contraception, an increase in divorce,[1] and increased living in multiple dwellings. It is impossible to arrange these various changes in any particular order, but taken together they seem to represent a general direction of change in American city families. It is a change involving fewer functions, fewer members, more scattered activities, narrower quarters, and more democratic control. These changes have been already discussed in Chap. 16.

Recreation. It is somewhat easier to identify a generalized sequence of events in the development of recreation in cities of the United States. In an early day, this was chiefly informal in character. There were dances, picnics, card parties, church socials, weddings, and funerals. During the nineteenth century, there developed numerous recreational agencies on a commercial basis. These included the theater, public dance hall, skating rink, bowling alley, billiard parlor, and saloon. Perhaps to these should be added places with varied activities centering, however, about gambling and prostitution. Many of these commercial recreational institutions were condemned by substantial citizens; in fact, the condemnation sometimes extended not only to the saloon and the brothel but also to the theater and well-conducted dance halls, billiard parlors, etc. In the last quarter of the nineteenth century there arose a number of semiphilanthropic recreational agencies which were in part attempts to offset the commercial agencies and in part efforts to provide recreation for people who previously had none. Among these semiphilanthropic agencies were the YMCA and YMHA, social settlements, institutional churches, and such organizations as Boy Scouts and Campfire Girls. Finally, and almost entirely since the beginning of the twentieth century, there have developed

---

[1] At all periods for which we have data, the urban divorce rate has exceeded the rural, and with the exception of a very few years the increase has been unbroken.

public, tax-supported, recreational facilities. These include parks, playgrounds, gymnasiums, bathing beaches, summer camps, and supervised sports of many kinds.

Education. In early colonial days education was largely informal, supplemented by some tutoring. But in New England there were early established public elementary schools. In the middle colonies there were parochial schools and in the South some private schools charging tuition. Later came public high schools and private academies, carrying education to what is now called the secondary level. Some of these academies developed into privately endowed colleges and universities. The next important development was that of vocational education, first in the trades and later in business. This came about under both private and public auspices. Still later came junior colleges and municipal universities, carrying public education to a higher level than any reached heretofore except in the state universities and teachers' colleges. Finally, there has been a significant development of adult education under both public and private auspices. Thus we find both public and private schools from colonial times until now, but there has been a steady increase in the relative importance of tax-supported education. Also, there has been a steady increase in the length of school terms, in the number of years attended, and in the variety of schools available.

Religion. In colonial times it was common for a town to have only one type of church, although some places in the middle colonies early had several. As time passed and the population became more heterogeneous, there was an increasing diversity of sects until, as we showed in Chap. 18, the typical North American city now contains a great variety of religious groups. These have become somewhat stratified, depending in part on the date of arrival and in part on the economic status of the communicants. Nevertheless, despite diversity and stratification, there has arisen, among Protestant churches at least, a fairly strong federation movement as a result of which more tolerance obtains and cooperation of several sorts is carried on. Finally, there is some indication that the churches may be suffering a decline in prestige in our cities. The evidence of this last is circumstantial, hence subject to dispute.

Social Work. In the early years of our history on the frontier, and even now in small communities, it has been customary for people who experience misfortune to be helped informally by their friends and neighbors. But as the numbers of strangers and detached persons increased, neighborliness and mutual aid were supplemented by minimum public assistance, limited to residents, as under the English Poor Law. With the growth of cities came an increasing number of ecclesiastical and then private nonsectarian charities accompanied by systematic efforts to abolish public assistance. In the twentieth century came consolidation and coordination of private agencies with a tremendous expansion of public welfare systems, social insurance, and the development of social work as a profession. Stated in other terms, the sequence has been roughly this: mutual aid, private charity, public assistance, social insurance. These changes have been national rather than urban, but initiative and leadership have come from the cities; diffusion from urban centers has been promoted especially by the Red Cross during the 1920's and by the Federal Security Agency in the next two decades.

Government. When Europeans settled on our shores, they established colonies, some of which later became states. In New England they early developed town (really township) government with direct citizen participation. In the South they created magisterial districts and counties. As the West was gradually occupied, territories, counties, and school districts took form. In general, towns came later and municipal government was something of an afterthought. As towns grew into cities, they were often misfits in the general structure of government.

With the growth of small cities into large cities and metropolitan centers, population spilled over into unincorporated areas and surrounded incorporated towns. By the opening of the twentieth century, some of our metropolitan areas had become a confused tangle of overlapping and conflicting authorities. There have been some attempts at integration, but so far they have had very limited success.

Along with other changes there has been a steady increase in the number and variety of functions performed by municipal government. Personnel has expanded and costs have multiplied. However, since 1940 per capita costs have actually declined, and city government fades almost into insignificance alongside of the Federal colossus.

INDEX OF URBANISM AND ITS CORRELATES

In Chaps. 14 to 20 we have shown the relation between various statistical series and the Index of Urbanism. These data display the relationships between the Index and such items as multiple dwellings, employment of women, schooling completed, and medical facilities, but they pertain to 100 different areas at only a single date. However, after viewing them in relation to other evidence we have assembled, we believe that they represent the kinds of changes that may be expected as any single area becomes more urban.

LIFE CYCLE OR MATURATION?

From the evidence which we have just summarized, it is apparent that in some respects cities of the United States have passed through similar stages in about the same order, but that in other respects there is considerable variation. However, it is not at all certain—in fact, it is rather unlikely—that cities of the future will repeat the sequences of events we have identified. The airplane, the atomic bomb, the radio, national advertising, and factors which have not yet appeared make it difficult to predict how our cities will develop in the future.

Perhaps the most important and most valid generalization we can make in the face of our somewhat confusing data is that cities are losing those characteristics associated with pioneering and rapid growth. Urban populations are still highly mobile, as we noted in Chap. 13. There has been a relative decline in rural-urban migration, but people are moving about within the same city and are moving from city to city. Whenever there is a slowing down of the rate of growth, cities may be able to provide more adequately for the populations they have instead of struggling to build more schools, more churches, more stores, more transportation facilities, etc.[2] Then they can concentrate on securing better schools and better facilities of every kind. It may not be amiss to call this a form of maturity. We may be justified in saying that our cities are getting over their youthful period of growth and boom and settling down to a more quiet and stable development.

McKenzie has made much of the point that our cities are becoming increasingly alike.[3] While his data cover a shorter period of time than we would like, they cannot be ignored. First of all, there is increasing occupational uniformity. Less and less frequently are the workers of a given city concentrated in one type of employment. More and more they are distributed among various kinds of gainful work. Moreover, the populations in the major occupational groups are more and more alike from city to city. Next McKenzie notes increasing industrial diversification. In this as in the preceding item his data are convincing as far as they go, and they accord with common observation, but the analysis should cover more cities and a longer period of time. Another mark of what McKenzie calls maturation is the wider distribution of large banks and of bank deposits. Still another is the standardization of merchandise through the development of chain stores and national advertising. Finally he displays a decline in the differences between regions—it is unfortunate that this is not between cities—in newspaper circulation, post-office receipts, motor-vehicle registration, telephones, health services, church membership and expenditures, and listings in *Who's Who*. We ourselves made similar computations pertaining to education but were not able to identify any well-defined trend. However, despite incompleteness of the evidence available, it is our impression that

---

[2] One should not forget that some cities are still growing rapidly and that our urban population as a whole is still increasing.

[3] R. D. McKenzie, *The Metropolitan Community,* Chap. 9, 1933.

cities of the United States are becoming more alike and that the period of most rapid growth is probably over. But this does not mean the end of dramatic changes. The threat of atomic bombs and other demands of national defense may bring about decentralization of a sort never seen before. Moreover, the use of electric power, new and more rapid means of transportation, plus gradual acceptance of the necessity for both national and local planning, may greatly facilitate the development of more medium-sized cities scattered more widely over the country.[4]

SOCIAL PROBLEMS IN CITIES

In the course of the other changes which we have noted, there appear from time to time situations which arouse and disturb the citizenry, or some segments of it, and which often involve serious controversy. For example, the people of nearly all our cities have experienced shortage of housing, dilapidation, and high rents. Few if any cities have not been troubled about their traffic, crowded streets, inadequate bus and streetcar service, lack of parking space, and high costs of transportation. City slums have for years received the attention of journalists, muckrakers, reformers, administrators, and many others besides the people who have to live in them. Periodically crime waves are featured in the metropolitan dailies and, at all times, there is no lack of juvenile and adult delinquents. Intergroup conflict has plagued every city in the land. Perhaps its most dramatic forms are the strike and race riot, but there are many other manifestations of prejudice and hostility between economic, ethnic, and religious groups. Then there are problems pertaining to public services and their financing—police and fire protection, public schools, sanitation, parks, playgrounds, public assistance, etc.—which were particularly urgent during the depression of the 1930's but which have not ceased to worry city dwellers.

There are other problems which concern the people of our great cities but which call for action on a regional or national scale. These include matters of railroad rates, development of new transportation routes like the proposed St. Lawrence seaway, economic planning and control having to do with prices, wages, and credit, location of industries involved in national defense, military and naval installations, flood control, and regional organization like that of the Tennessee Valley Authority.

[4] To check this notion of what might happen against what has happened, we have calculated the relative distribution of the United States population in incorporated places of varying sizes in 1890, 1930, 1940, and 1950. The ratio of 1930 to 1890 percentages was lowest in places of 2,500 to 5,000 and greatest in places of 500,000 to 1,000,000. The ratio increased steadily from one category to another until the class over 1 million was reached. The minima and maxima were in the same class intervals for 1940/1890 and 1950/1890 ratios, but the ratios for other categories did not display a steady progression.

In the following chapter we shall be concerned with these questions: Are our cities changing only in response to blind, impersonal forces or is their development being directed? Do the people of the United States have any clear notions about what they want their cities to be like? If so, have they any effective means of achieving their goals?

SELECTED READINGS

CHURCHILL, HENRY S.: *The City Is the People*, Reynal & Hitchcock, Inc., 1945. A well-illustrated little book on development and problems of cities in the United States.

FARIS, ROBERT E. L.: *Social Disorganization*, The Ronald Press Company, 1948. The major hypothesis of this book is that the basic cause of social disorganization is the transition from folk society to urban, industrial society.

MUMFORD, LEWIS: *City Development: Studies in Disintegration and Renewal*, Harcourt, Brace and Company, Inc., 1945. A collection of critical essays with a challenging point of view but a minimum of evidence.

SCHLESINGER, ARTHUR M.: *The Rise of the City*, The Macmillan Company, 1933. Depicts the lure of North American cities in the nineteenth century and cultural changes that accompanied their growth.

Our Cities, Their Role in the National Economy, Report of the Urbanism Committee to the National Resources Committee, 1937. A graphic and verbal presentation of cultural changes in the United States from 1790 to 1930 with special reference to the growth of cities.

Recent Social Trends in the United States, Report of the President's Research Committee on Social Trends, McGraw-Hill Book Company, Inc., 1933. An analysis of cultural changes from 1900 to 1930, including urbanism and related factors.

CHAPTER 22. *Can Urban Change Be Directed?*

IS THERE CONSENSUS ABOUT OBJECTIVES?

Throughout this book we have noted many characteristics of cities which are inacceptable (displeasing, annoying, or obnoxious) to many people. Can anything be done about them? The answer is "yes," for some persons and some groups are getting at least some of the things they want. Well-to-do families establish exclusive residential districts in which they enjoy the amenities of life without intrusion of the *hoi polloi*. Middle-class families form neighborhood improvement associations through which they protect their districts against the invasion of taverns, mortuaries, and people of other races and religions. Political machines capture and retain power in the interest of men who want jobs, contracts, and protection against police or gangsters. Social work agencies, churches, and police departments carry on programs for the reduction of juvenile delinquency. Wage earners form trade-unions which often obtain increased pay, decreased hours, and modified conditions of work. Negroes organize to fight or plead for fair employment practices, civil liberties, or the abolition of Jim Crow. In other words, many separate groups in our cities seem to know what they want and have ways of getting at least part of what they want. This much is clear.

But what some groups want may be opposed by others. If they do not actively fight, they may consider each other's goals undesirable and offer passive resistance. In still other cases they may simply be indifferent. Obviously there is far from being complete agreement on values in any city. Even without unanimity on all points, may there not be some measure of consensus? Are there not some goals on which a strong majority agrees? Objectives which most people deem desirable, important, and worth serious effort to attain? This is a difficult question, yet some answer must be found. For if there is no consensus as to ends, there can hardly be a general program of social control.

One reason why it is hard to identify values is that often they are

350

implicit rather than explicit. We must infer them from what people do and say in everyday life, as well as from their formal declarations in creeds, constitutions, and resolutions. Another difficulty inheres in the fact that verbalized codes and accepted behavior do not always correspond. Witness "even-handed justice" versus "fixing" tickets for traffic violations, "sanctity of the family" versus prostitution, integrity in public office versus "honest graft," prohibition of gambling versus "bingo" games at church socials and slot machines in veterans' clubs, ethical concepts of truth versus much advertising and salesmanship.

Without pursuing further the general issue of values and their consistency, let us consider a few items on which there is likely to be considerable agreement among city dwellers in the United States.

1. People value health and expect their city to do something about it through sewage disposal, garbage collection, inspection of markets and dairies, quarantine, emergency medical care, and free medical service to people of very low incomes. To be sure, there are cultists who dissent, and there is disagreement about organization and procedure, but there is a fairly wide area of consensus manifested by the support of public health departments and semipublic health agencies, by report and comment in the press, and by casual conversation.

2. There is majority support for formal education, specifically through the public schools. At the same time there is diversity in that adherents of some churches prefer parochial schools and there is conflict over racial segregation. Also there are arguments about "frills," un-American textbooks, "atheistic" teachers, high school fraternities, and football. But by and large the people of our cities accept and support public education.

3. There is considerable evidence of agreement that the American standard of living includes many creature comforts such as housing with private bath, central heating, electricity, and gas.[1] The responsibility of a city with reference to these comforts and conveniences is suggested by building codes and housing ordinances, slum clearance, and public housing projects. But the persistence of blighted areas and the pressures of real estate boards indicate that the citizens are by no means in agreement as to how much the city "owes" its residents.

4. It seems to be accepted that man does not live by bread alone. Both in municipal and in family budgets some provision is made for recreation. Almost every city now provides playgrounds, parks, and supervised sports. Not a few have zoological gardens, municipal theaters, field houses, and summer camps.

[1] Actually, the 1950 census shows that 63.5 per cent of all dwelling units had exclusive bathtub or shower, private toilet, and hot running water. The percentage with central heating, electricity, and gas had not been reported as this book went to press. However, the standard of housing considered "properly and truly American" includes all these items.

5. Both our literature and common behavior indicate that every normal adult is expected to "pay his (or her) own way," either by work outside the home or by keeping house. By the same token, it is assumed that he will have a chance to earn a living. Unfortunately the facts do not always support this assumption, since members of minority groups often labor under a handicap, and in times of depression masses of people are without ordinary means of subsistence. Cities as such assume little responsibility in the areas of fair employment practices, unemployment compensation, and relief generally. Moreover, there are lively debates about the desirability of such measures.

6. Less tangible than any of the preceding items, development of character is stressed in our literature and particularly by our religious institutions. Officially at least, we want our citizens to tell the truth (except perhaps in advertising), not to take other people's property (unless it belongs to government or a corporation), to be considerate and respectful to other persons (of one's own race, class, and religion), and in general to abide by the laws and regulations intended to maintain order (unless they interfere with one's own convenience or business). In other words, almost everybody believes in character building as a general proposition but has a lot of exceptions or "patterned evasions," as they are sometimes called. Moreover, outside of law enforcement, wholesome recreation, and formal education, it is not clear what people expect their city to do about character.

STUDIES OF OBJECTIVES, CONSENSUS, AND IMPLEMENTATION

Some years ago, E. L. Thorndike made a study of about 300 cities in the United States, rating them according to a G Score of "general goodness of life for good people." The components of this score or index were items of health, education, recreation, "creature comforts," and some miscellaneous social and economic conditions. After elaborate computations, using data of varying relevance and reliability, he came to the conclusion that

if perfect measures of every fact about these cities and their inhabitants were available, the differences among the 295 cities in the goodness of life for good people would be attributable—about 60 per cent to differences in the mental and moral qualities of the populations, about 25 per cent to differences in their incomes.[2]

This is a curiously individualistic interpretation. It seems to imply acceptance of the nineteenth-century notion that if every individual is doing what he can for himself, the body politic will thrive. In contrast

[2] E. L. Thorndike, *Your City*, p. 117, 1939. By permission of Harcourt, Brace and Company, Inc.

with Thorndike's study we have one by Angell, who concerned himself with the residents of a city as at least potentially members of a social group. He focused his attention on "moral integration," which he defined in terms of "a set of common ends and values toward which all are oriented and in terms of which the life of the group is organized."[3]

Angell devised an index of moral integration which comprised two major components. The first he called a "welfare effort index," in which he utilized (1) per capita local expenditure for health and welfare services adjusted for level of living and (2) the percentage of all expenditures for such services which were derived from local sources: taxes, contributions, and endowments. This welfare effort index was presumed to be a measure of the "intentional moral integration," or perhaps the determination of the local population as a whole to achieve declared objectives. The second component was a crime index, or the number of certain offenses reported to the FBI per 100,000 of the local population. This was considered a negative index of the "habitual moral integration" of a city, that is, an indicator of the relative extent to which people do or do not behave in accord with norms set forth in the law. Finally, the crime scores were reversed and combined with the welfare effort scores.

To determine the validity of the index of moral integration, Angell compared the integration ratings of selected cities with their support of schools, recreation, libraries and museums, sanitation, health, and public safety; their birth rates, size of family, home ownership; all of which varied directly with the index of moral integration. He found a negative correlation between the index and homicides, suicides, illegitimate births, deaths from syphilis and gonorrhea. He found sufficient consistency in the relationship of his index of moral integration to all these items to give him confidence that his scores really indicate relative degrees of consensus about values and effectiveness in attaining them. Whether we fully accept the components of his index or not, we must admit that most of his items are relevant and that so far no one has offered a better device for quantitative treatment of this important but elusive phase of social life.

Angell did not stop with the devising of his index and its application to 43 large cities. He sought next to find what factors were associated with high and low scores. The two which stood out as most significant were mobility and heterogeneity.[4] (Coefficient of correlation between

---

[3] Robert C. Angell, *The Moral Integration of American Cities*, p. 2, 1951. This is Part 2 of No. 1 of Vol. 57 of the *American Journal of Sociology*. By permission of the University of Chicago Press.

[4] Mobility and heterogeneity were found to vary independently of each other (coefficient of correlation, $-.06$), and jointly to account for 63 per cent of the variation in integration between cities (multiple coefficient of correlation, $.79$). Angell, *op. cit.*, p. 18.

moral integration and mobility was —.49, and with heterogeneity was —.59.) Other factors were correlated with the integration index—rate of growth (—.43); employment of married women (—.54); variation or spread of rentals (—.65)—but when combined with mobility and heterogeneity, the multiple correlations showed little or no change. In other words, no combination of three factors accounted for significantly more of the variation in moral integration than did the first two, mobility and heterogeneity. Factors which showed no significant relation to the integration index were size (but note that all 43 cities were over 100,000), per capita retail sales (as a measure of level of living), church membership, percentage of all gainfully employed persons who were clerical and skilled manual workers (as indication of the size of a middle class mediating between the extremes). The percentage of small businessmen among all proprietors and managers (low when there are large corporations with absentee ownership) surprisingly showed a negative correlation with the integration index.

Not content with these gross statistics, Angell finally proceeded to a careful study of four cities selected thus:

City	Actual integration score	Relation of actual score to score predicted on basis of mobility and heterogeneity
A	High	Higher
B	High	Lower
C	Low	Higher
D	Low	Lower

He and his assistants interviewed a cross section of the population in each city plus leaders nominated by heads of the school system, principal newspaper, principal radio station, police department, labor-union council, principal private social work organization, public welfare agency, federation of religious organizations, community businessmen's organization, and council of women's clubs. From this more intensive study, Angell concluded that *leadership* is a very important element in the moral integration of a city, that is, in development of consensus as to values and effective efforts toward their realization. According to his findings an optimal leadership group would be:

1. Composed of well-educated persons;
2. Composed of those whose original involvement in community affairs sprang from their own interest, the involvement of their friends, or the nature of their profession;
3. Widely representative of the socioeconomic groups within the city;
4. Made up in somewhat equal proportions of those who were born in the

city, those who were born elsewhere but have lived in the community a long time, and those who have lived in the community a decade or so;

5. Composed of those who have had enough contacts with other segments of the population to enable them to understand their points of view (social realism);

6. Marked by congeniality but not "cliquishness";

7. Composed of those who realize the importance of effort and informal organization in overcoming public apathy toward community problems.[5]

This inquiry finally included popular estimates and leaders' estimates of the contribution of various agencies to "good for the city as a whole." We have so many doubts about the adequacy of this part of the study that we shall not describe the methods or the findings except to cite the conclusion that "the school and the church can probably exercise a powerful influence in the direction of moral integration if they will but apply themselves to the task."[6]

With this background we turn now to a consideration of some of the program making, promotion, and execution which go on in our cities. These may be regarded as indicators, though, of course, not measures, of the consensus and effectiveness of urban populations.

PHYSICAL PLANNING OF CITIES

There are in the United States over 2,000 municipal planning commissions and more than 400 county planning commissions, plus a smaller number of metropolitan, state, and regional planning bodies.[7] Most of these are relatively new, have restricted budgets and authority, and hence show limited accomplishments. However, their existence and the results which they have achieved display partial agreement among city dwellers as to the necessity of joint effort to bring order out of the confusion apparent in every large city.

In previous chapters we have described blighted areas, centrifugal flight, unexpected redistribution of population upsetting the operation of schools, churches, and small business; breaking up old neighborhoods; and other changes which are unforeseen, unplanned, and threatening to the interests of many persons and groups. We have noted the intermingling of commercial and industrial properties with residences and of apartment buildings with single dwellings. Out toward the periphery we have found a veritable hodgepodge, some sections being quite undeveloped while others, farther out, are closely built up. Almost side by side we have discovered "swank" residential districts and suburban slums. In general, we have found that about twice as many lots are

[5] Angell, *op. cit.*, pp. 108–109. By permission of the University of Chicago Press.
[6] *Ibid.*, p. 114.
[7] *Social Work Year Book, 1951*, p. 237.

staked out as are occupied by residences or other buildings. For vast numbers of city dwellers, places of residence, work, shopping, and recreation are so scattered that much time has to be spent coming and going in the midst of heavy traffic. Streets are not wide enough for the number of cars, busses, and trucks; streetcars and other public transportation facilities are often crowded, slow, and infrequent, failing to serve some districts at all. Freight to and from distant places is routed through metropolitan terminals, crowding docks and railroad yards. River cities are subject to floods; all cities need storm sewers to carry off rain water. Growing cities find their sanitary sewers overloaded, drinking water inadequate, utilities unable to serve new subdivisions as fast as they are opened up. Old cities display the ugliness of dirt and dilapidation; new cities display the ugliness of jerry-building.

As a reaction to the conditions we have just enumerated and ·others which they suggest, city planning (usually restricted to physical planning) has spread throughout the United States. This has been defined as "the ordering of the physical elements of a region or a city so that each will serve most effectively in an economical, efficient, healthful, and agreeable development of the entire area."[8] City planning may be divided into four parts: (1) There is research into the situation as it exists and has developed, (2) the civic design, the drawing up of plans and specifications for the urban layout, (3) regulation by law, which involves legislation and its enforcement in order to make possible the carrying out of a plan which may be devised, (4) the influencing of public relations; seeking to induce homeowners, industrialists, and others to work together in development of a city plan; trying to persuade rather than to compel compliance with a legally adopted plan. Stated a little differently, city planning may be said to have these six aspects: engineering, architectural, landscape architectural, economic, legal, and sociological.[9]

There is one phase of planning which has been so widely adopted and is so generally known that it is frequently mistaken for city planning as a whole. This is commonly known as zoning and is the regulation of land use and buildings. It deals with such matters as types of buildings, uses to which they may be put, height, building lines, and the percentage of a lot which may be occupied. The need for zoning has been partly indicated in considering the need for city planning in general. But the factors which make city fathers most ready to adopt zoning ordinances are the unsettling of property values, the destruction of neighborhoods and

---

[8] *Social Work Year Book, 1937,* p. 416. By permission of the Russell Sage Foundation.
[9] *Ibid.,* p. 418.

communities, unsightliness due to the hodgepodge of all sorts of build-ings of irregular lines and heights. However, early zoning was very far from solving these problems, for there was rather limited information available and there was much pressure from real estate speculators and other groups. Hence there was, and is, very unsatisfactory division of land for various uses. Commonly too little has been zoned for single dwellings, too much for multiple dwellings and commercial and in-dustrial properties. Whenever a residential district has been threatened with invasion, property owners who became panic-stricken wanted the district immediately zoned for business or industry in order that they might quickly realize hoped-for gains from the sale of land. Because this has been overdone, many old residential sections are partly occupied by stores, factories, etc., instead of a few sections being completely taken over for these purposes. In addition, owners of filling stations, mortuaries, beauty parlors, and the like ask for "spot zoning" in order that they may locate in otherwise restricted residential districts. As a result of all these pressures, a zoning ordinance is hardly adopted until it begins to be amended; presently the actual land use bears little resemblance to what was intended by the planning commission.

In addition to zoning there are several other activities which may be carried on separately or as parts of a city plan. These include the laying out of new suburbs, the establishment of civic centers, the development of railway terminals and port facilities, slum clearance, park systems, air-ports, major thoroughfares, reorganization of the city into neighborhoods, etc.

Over and over again we have had occasion to emphasize the fact that a city rarely ends at its official limits. This is relevant to city planning as well as to other aspects of urbanism which we have considered. What we are interested in here is a master plan intended as a guide for the planning of separate municipalities within a metropolitan area and as a means of coordinating them so that there may be harmony, convenience, and efficiency in the whole. Metropolitan and regional planning are often confused. The latter term should be restricted to plans for the use of natural resources and the integration of rural and urban interests throughout an extended region; metropolitan planning is strictly urban in character.

The reasons for metropolitan planning should by this time be obvious to any student of the city. Not only plural government and the common problems of traffic, police, fire, drainage, sanitation, and all the rest, but the convenience of having a well-devised system of through streets, the regulation of real estate subdivisions, the distribution of trading sub-centers, all emphasize the importance of unified planning for a metropolitan area. Already the idea has spread so widely that there are something like 100 official boards and unofficial associations devoted to such metropolitan planning.

Undoubtedly the most comprehensive and best known metropolitan plan is that which bears the title of Regional Plan for New York and its Environs.[10] This venture was initiated by some private individuals and sponsored by the Russell Sage Foundation. A Regional Planning Association was set up on an unofficial basis but with the cooperation of public officials in and about metropolitan New York. The territory covered is much larger than that which the Bureau of the Census considers to be the metropolitan area New York–Northeastern New Jersey, but it is smaller than what we would ordinarily consider to be the region dependent upon and tributary to the city. Specifically, this plan has to do with an area of 5,500 square miles covering parts of 3 states, all or part of 22 counties, 400 municipalities, and a population of over 13 million people. The survey conducted by the Regional Planning Association dealt with the geography, history, and population of the area. It included an especially careful study of the economic life with particular emphasis on recent trends such as the gravitating of manufacturing to a belt about halfway between the central city and the periphery of the area. The inquiry sought answers to such questions as these: What activities can be carried on at the center? What ones must be carried on at the center? What others would be more advantageously located farther out? The study of industries and their location was, of course, directly related to population trends and to traffic problems. Hence the study of trafficways and transportation was another significant part of the survey. Still others had to do with parks, housing, government.

The plan itself was similarly comprehensive. First of all, it proposed a definite scheme of railroads, including trunk lines, outer and inner belt lines, commuters' lines, and terminals conveniently located in various sections of the metropolitan area. It provided a system of highways and byways, broad through streets, express highways, either elevated or depressed loops or belt lines, and by-passes. It proposed several major north and south routes, a few diagonals and grade separations. Closely related to the general system of highways and streets was the program for parkways and boulevards which were intended to expedite traffic and to afford pleasure. A large part of the planning had to do, of course, with land use. It proposed that certain districts should be built up while others should be open. It proposed that certain sections should be residential, others industrial, still others commercial. It was based on the

[10] The committee which fostered this plan published eight volumes based on an extensive and intensive survey, and two volumes which set forth the plan which grew out of this research. This whole is interestingly and simply summarized by R. L. Duffus, *Mastering a Metropolis*, 1930.

proposition, adequately demonstrated by the survey, that "there is ample room in our great regional apartment if we arrange the furniture sensibly."[11] The development which was indicated in the plan was for Manhattan to continue as the center of marketing, banking, finer manufacturing, and commercial recreation. Brooklyn, Queens, the Bronx, and Staten Island were to expand as centers of industry and residence. Heavy industry was to move gradually into New Jersey, where ocean and railroad terminals could be provided, where relatively inexpensive land was available. Residential sections were to be settled conveniently near, but unspoiled by, industries. For many of these projects, especially on the New Jersey side of the Hudson River, extensive reclamation projects were shown to be necessary. All through the area, parks, parkways, golf courses, and other open spaces were to be carefully distributed. Land for these purposes was to be purchased in advance of close settlement whenever possible, in order to make sure of providing the needed open spaces and to avoid excessive cost. Other parts of the plan had to do with the development and protection of neighborhoods, civic centers, airports, and, in fact, nearly every aspect of the physical city.

The devising and carrying out of a complete city plan, desired and supported by the people as a whole, is something for the future. But it should not be supposed that city planning is altogether new. There are indications of it in the ancient world, in Babylon, Ninevah, some of the Greek cities, and Roman provincial towns. In the Middle Ages there was not much city planning, although it appears that some towns were established by various rulers as fortresses. In the seventeenth and eighteenth centuries there were some cases that merit attention, notably those of Paris, Edinburgh, Berlin, and St. Petersburg. In North America some colonial towns were systematically laid out. In 1811 a street plan on the gridiron pattern was prepared for New York. In 1791 Pierre L'Enfant was invited to draw up a comprehensive plan for Washington, D.C. He took full advantage of his remarkable opportunity to lay out a new city unhampered by long-existent conditions and interests. His plan was marked by spaciousness, by the settings and approaches to buildings, and by their reciprocal relation. He used a rectangular scheme, on which he superimposed diagonal streets adjusted to the topography. At important intersections he provided large circles and squares. Later there were established building lines and regulations of material and height. According to Adams, "the plan remains as the one monumental example of comprehensive planning in the United States."[12] A few other cities were planned during the nineteenth century, some wealthy suburbs were skillfully designed, and some industrial suburbs were rather carefully

[11] *Ibid.*, p. 186.
[12] Thomas Adams, *Outline of Town and City Planning*, p. 127, 1935.

planned. But the chief development of city planning in this country has come in the twentieth century.

The hopes of city planners have been great; the general body of citizens has given rather lukewarm support. In actual practice very serious limitations have been encountered. First of all, there are few chances to plan new cities from the start. For the most part we are restricted to the expensive task of remodeling existing cities. To be sure, there are bound to be some rebuilding and some expansion, both of which afford opportunities for taking advantage of a definite plan. But because much of the land is already occupied and because there are many vested interests, city planning in practice involves a multitude of compromises. There are other difficulties. Sometimes those who deal in real estate wish to have a plan which will aid them in their business but not do much else. Sometimes ambitious public officials promote the development of expensive ornamental features when there are many more urgent needs at hand. Because of the plurality of governmental units which we described in Chap. 19, there is usually no single authority with power to make and enforce plans for an entire metropolitan district. Finally, it is hard for people to visualize a master plan. They can conceive and understand the limited program of a drainage system, or a civic center, or a railroad terminal, but they find it difficult to think in terms of a comprehensive program. Hence our conclusion with reference to the physical planning of cities is that consensus is only moderately developed; most people seem to be ambivalent in their feelings and limited in their understanding. Under these conditions it is no wonder that city planners find themselves frustrated, and planning commissions are given small budgets and restricted powers. As a result, the physical layout of our cities does not really suit anybody.

SELECTED READINGS

ANGELL, ROBERT C.: *The Moral Integration of American Cities,* Supplement to the *American Journal of Sociology,* July, 1951. An attempt to define, measure, and account for agreement on urban values and organization for their attainment.

CHURCHILL, HENRY S.: *The City Is the People,* Reynal & Hitchcock, Inc., 1945. A simple statement of the need for city planning, efforts made, difficulties encountered, and prospects.

DUFFUS, R. L.: *Mastering a Metropolis,* Harper & Brothers, 1930. A readable summary of the voluminous survey and plan for New York and its environs.

GALLION, ARTHUR B.: *The Urban Pattern, City Planning and Design,* D. Van Nostrand Company, Inc., 1950. History and principles of city planning with many concrete examples and illustrations.

HILLMAN, ARTHUR: *Community Organization and Planning,* The Macmillan Company, 1950. See especially Chap. 4, "The Scope of City Planning," Chap. 5, "The Role of the Expert and the Citizen in City Planning," and Chap. 6, "Community Life in Planned Communities and Housing Projects."

THORNDIKE, EDWARD L.: *Your City,* Harcourt, Brace and Company, Inc., 1939. An attempt to measure "the goodness of life" in cities and factors responsible for the degree to which it is realized.

CHAPTER 23. *Social Planning of Cities*

Although in the preceding chapter we concentrated our attention on planning the physical structure of cities, we were drawn inevitably into a consideration of many less tangible aspects of urban life—earning a living, making a home, finding recreation, carrying on religious activities, etc. From the standpoint of social structure the physical layout of a city has been shown to have a close relation to stratification, localization, mobility, organization and disorganization of neighborhoods and families, conflict and accommodation among ethnic and religious groups.

Now it happens that most of the urban planning recognized as such has dealt primarily with physical aspects of single municipalities. But there has been a great deal of unlabeled planning in the realms of business, government, social work, education, and religion. Chambers of commerce, bureaus of municipal research, councils of social agencies, boards of education, and church federations have been studying the city from the standpoints of their particular interests, have been outlining programs for the fulfillment of their purposes, and have been trying to "sell" their ideas to the public. Only to a very limited extent have these several groups worked together. Still less have they united people in various parts of a metropolitan area in comprehensive planning.

ECONOMIC PLANNING

We have seen that physical planning necessarily involves one phase of economic planning, namely, the location of various types of business and industry. The allocation of certain districts to heavy industry, others to light manufacturing and wholesaling, others to retail establishments, and still others to terminal facilities is well under way. But many errors have been committed, especially in the form of assigning to commerce and industry more space than they are able to use. Much zoning has been based—not altogether unwisely—on present land uses and those anticipated on the basis of recent trends. But careful study, such as accompanied the making of a plan for New York and its environs, shows that business and industry are not always successful in finding the most

362

appropriate sites. Separate efforts, even joint guesses, often lead business-men astray or leave them helpless in the face of forces beyond their individual control. The problem is very complicated, for the location of industrial and commercial establishments involves relations to other businesses, dwellings and transportation for employees, transportation of raw materials and finished products, accessibility to customers, and the possibility that they may be nuisances to the occupants of adjacent land.

In the United States economic planning for cities has not gone far beyond the attempt to direct the spatial distribution of economic activities over a metropolitan area. However, this does not mean that there has been no attention to the integration of supply services and the disposal of waste, the provision of public utilities, the adaptation of urban com-merce and industry to the region's needs, or the utilization of natural resources in the hinterland. What we mean is that there has been little evidence that these matters were viewed as integral parts of metropolitan planning.

Many cities have, through one agency or another, given attention to marketing facilities, both wholesale and retail. But this has been largely from the standpoint of promoting the sales of individual firms or groups of firms, rather than from the standpoint of consumer needs and a balanced economic life for the city and its region. In some instances municipalities have established public markets, but these are rarely distributed throughout the city; their location is determined with reference to their own success as business ventures rather than with reference to supplementing or supplanting existing stores. Zoning, which might be expected to control the distribution of marketing activities, has followed rather than guided the development of retail outlets along string streets and in subcenters.

In contrast to markets, the disposal of waste has come to be planned for an entire municipality, though not for a whole metropolitan area. Garbage, ashes, and trash are collected by municipal departments or by contractors who assume responsibility for the municipality. Sewage dis-posal is commonly a municipal function, not a metropolitan one.

The diversification of industry, which was discussed in Chap. 14, has been urged by businessmen's organizations and by newspapers, but it seems to be developing more spontaneously than under direction. The bringing in of a new industry is often heralded not as an instance of diversification but as an increase in the number of customers of merchants and realtors, clients of professional men, members of churches, etc.

Likewise the adaptation of city and region goes forward more or less haphazardly. Individuals and corporations, of course, consider how they may secure raw materials cheaply and how they may sell finished products to advantage in their trade area. But there has been little joint effort to develop in an urban center industries that could make maximum use of regional resources—human and natural—and could offer maximum service to the region's population.

Such economic planning as we find has often been the work of chambers of commerce, although they are not, strictly speaking, planning bodies. Perhaps one reason why they have not devoted more attention to comprehensive planning is that their general pattern of activity was set long ago in an era of commercial and industrial expansion on a thoroughly competitive basis. The New York Chamber was founded in 1768. Before the War between the States, there were 30 such bodies. However, their greatest development numerically has come in more recent years, reaching by 1950 a total of about 2,250.

Chambers of commerce are essentially businessmen's organizations, to which are sometimes attached professional men, public officials, and even farmers. They are private organizations, built up by membership campaigns, supported by dues, and usually managed by paid secretaries. In general they perform two kinds of function: (1) technical and administrative services for their members and (2) representation of business interests before governmental bodies. In the first group are included efforts to secure better transportation, provision of labor supply, advertising local products, attracting tourists and conventions, arranging sales days, etc. In the second group are included issuing publicity about pending legislation, calling on public officials, holding hearings, and otherwise seeking to exert pressure on government in the interest of merchants and manufacturers of the city or region.

Sometimes chamber of commerce members mistakenly imagine that they represent the entire populace. Frequently they undertake to act in the name of a whole community, metropolitan area, or region. They initiate or support civic programs which they regard as beneficial to everybody. Thus they get behind movements to reorganize municipal government, to construct express highways, to provide parking space, to develop parks, to increase the water supply, to get "chiselers" off relief, to balance the municipal budget. But it is reasonable to suppose that such efforts are exerted primarily for the benefit of business—not in conscious opposition to the welfare of labor, agriculture, or consumers— but with the somewhat dubious assumption that what is good for business is good for everybody. Further support for this statement may be drawn from the facts that chambers of commerce commonly oppose municipal ownership of gas, electricity, street railway, and other public utilities; that they often seek to maintain or to establish the "open shop," or the so-called "American plan"; that they discourage consumers' cooperation. Sometimes they are identified with campaigns against liberals and radicals. Thus it seems clear that chambers of commerce, though perfectly legitimate organizations of businessmen, have not functioned to any great extent as general economic planning bodies, nor have the plans they project always been integrated into a more comprehensive program of social planning.

Perhaps it is inevitable that, in a culture whose economic complex rests on the principles of private ownership and "free" competition, economic planning should be undeveloped. As a matter of fact, it is popular in some circles to declare oneself opposed to all planning. Yet it would appear more realistic to state the issue in terms of what kind of planning, by whom, and for what ends. For it is evident that corporations, trade associations, chambers of commerce, labor unions, farmers' organizations, and governmental agencies are now engaged in planning, but not jointly. The question that interests us is this: Can we achieve a measure of agreement on goals and on methods of economic planning for whole cities, regions, and the nation?

REPLANNING CITY GOVERNMENT

In Chap. 19 we pointed out the grounds for replanning the governmental structure of metropolitan areas. We showed that political units have been brought into being one at a time, often with overlapping and even conflicting jurisdictions. This happened in part because previously separate communities were growing together, in part because citizens distrusted established authorities, in part because local bureaucracies were loath to relinquish their prerogatives. We described in that chapter the partial development of metropolitan government and the struggles that are still going on.

Within individual municipalities, and sometimes extending throughout a state or the nation, there are voters' leagues, taxpayers' associations, bureaus of governmental research, and all sorts of good government movements. These are usually concerned with particular issues, such as civil service, the council-manager form of government, a balanced budget, or simply the ejection of a powerful machine. Occasionally such a group may study the whole political structure of a metropolitan area and outline a plan for its reorganization. Most frequently, its attention is confined to details and to segments of the metropolitan area. Such replanning of government as occurs is almost inevitably bound up with city planning in the physical sense. It also overlaps the planning of recreation, education, public health, social work, neighborhoods, and communities.

One aspect of government in urban areas concerning which there has been much discussion and little action is the tax structure. The general property tax, special assessments, license fees, and fines do not constitute a satisfactory basis for the support of local government under urban conditions. They are particularly inadequate, confusing, and irritating when, as in Boston, Chicago, and St. Louis, there are numerous independent bodies with power to assess and levy taxes on the same body of citizens.

A minority of citizens believe that an integrated metropolitan government would bring economy, efficiency, and other results difficult or impossible of attainment under the present scheme of plural government. But most people are bound by tradition, and those with vested interests are always ready to defend the *status quo*. Hence efforts to promote metropolitan government have been partial and halting. As we reported in Chap. 19, these programs have taken the forms of annexation, city-county consolidation, expansion of county functions, intermunicipal agreements and joint undertakings, special districts and authorities having to do with water, sewage, transportation, and health services. Such limited programs of coordination and unification have been put into effect in various places. No comprehensive plan has been adopted anywhere in the United States, although inclusive schemes of government have been seriously considered in Oakland, Pittsburgh, and Cleveland.

EDUCATIONAL PLANNING

The story of city planning for education is simply told. With the development of public school systems having governing boards and superintendents, there came partial integration of urban education. But city boards of education have little or no authority over private schools. Usually they enforce the attendance laws, sometimes they provide school health service. But compulsory aspects of the curriculum are usually set forth by state rather than by municipal authorities. There is little or no central planning that covers parochial, commercial, progressive, and workers' education. Furthermore, there are in every metropolitan area several, or many, independent school districts. Both within and without municipalities are found separate boards of education with separate taxing and spending powers, separate administrative officers, and separate programs of work. There is some informal consultation but little comprehensive planning.

RELIGIOUS PLANNING

In the field of urban religion there have been some definite efforts to bring about joint planning but, as in the realms of business, government, and education, they have been partial and not especially successful. It has been well said that "the American city is a veritable jungle of religious organizations."[1] In every urban center of 100,000 or over may be found from 20 to 50 denominations. Representing each denomination or sect there are varying numbers of local churches, sometimes care-

[1] H. Paul Douglass, *Protestant Cooperation in American Cities*, p. 14, 1930.

fully located and jointly controlled but often established and conducted with little reference to other churches even of their own faith. In general, the Catholic parishes are located in accordance with a diocesan plan, while the Protestant and Jewish congregations, like Topsy, "just growed." To be sure, there are some intra- and interdenominational affiliations which promote and facilitate joint action. Among them are ministerial alliances, Sunday school associations, women's missionary unions, men's brotherhoods, and leagues of young people. But these are not planning bodies.

Now, in so far as churches agree on moral codes and general theological beliefs they might be expected to work together. As a matter of fact, it appears that their division, mutual indifference, and occasional conflict interfere with the achievement of the common aims implied in their doctrines and creeds. Institutional glory, denominational self-satisfaction, and sectarian hostility, in various forms and degrees, separate religionists and seem to limit the results of their efforts. The outsider finds it difficult to reconcile the professions of brotherhood and righteousness with the aloofness and petty squabbles which so often appear on the ecclesiastical scene.

To achieve some measure of coordination there have grown up, especially in large centers, city or metropolitan church federations, numbering by 1950 about 150. But they are limited both in membership and in activity. In the first place they are restricted to Protestant churches; no Catholic or Jewish groups have joined them. Sometimes their membership is even more narrowly confined to "evangelical" churches. These include only those that believe in the Trinity and hold to the importance of a special emotional experience called conversion; they exclude Unitarians, Lutherans, and Christian Scientists. In addition, Negro churches are sometimes left out, as are non-English-speaking congregations. Often we note the absence of "fundamentalist" groups, small churches, and suburban parishes. The lines are not consistent; in recent years they have been broadened; but universally church federations omit many religious groups.

The functions of church federations are of two general kinds. The first covers joint efforts in evangelism (*e.g.*, revival meetings), religious education (*e.g.*, daily vacation Bible schools), social service (*e.g.*, girls' protective leagues), and moral reforms (*e.g.*, prohibition). The second is called comity and is really an attempt to engage in social planning as it pertains to religion.[2] Sometimes comity is involved in new situations, as when several denominations unite directly or through a federation to make a religious survey of a newly developed suburban district. Or they may consult together with reference to the organization of new congregations, the selection of church sites, the establishment of

[2] H. Paul Douglass, *Church Comity*, 1929.

missions or Sunday schools. Sometimes comity has to do with existing churches when there are problems of relocation, mergers, splits, transfers of a congregation from one denomination to another, and federation. It may be concerned with new policies, such as the undertaking or abandoning of work for foreign language groups. All these provide opportunities for joint planning of religious activities and facilities.

The federation movement may be said to have started with the Evangelical Alliance just after the War between the States. In the eighties and nineties, it was promoted through the establishment of ministerial alliances. In 1900 the National Federation of Churches was founded; in 1908 it became the Federal Council of Churches, and in 1950 it was reorganized as the National Council of the Churches of Christ in the United States of America. This body has promoted the formation of local federations, many of which were started during and immediately after World War I.

The Roman Catholic Church, being established on a hierarchical basis, with highly centralized control, does plan the location of parishes carefully, though it does not display such unified action in the founding and conduct of its charities. The Jewish congregations exercise a large degree of local autonomy. Protestants, Catholics, and Jews have in no city combined to make comprehensive plans for religious work. The National Conference of Christians and Jews, with local offices in several cities, is dedicated to the promotion of good will among religious and other groups, but it could hardly be called a joint planning body, especially since many religionists are skeptical of its methods if not its goals. Perhaps there is something about formal religion which makes cooperation among denominations inherently difficult. In general, each group believes that it has "the true doctrine," "the right way of salvation." Assuming that, the others must be wrong, hence too close association might endanger "the true faith" and its hold on the communicants. Moreover, it may well be that intragroup strength depends on a certain measure of intergroup hostility. At all events, consensus in regard to religion seems not to have developed beyond that in respect to economics.

SOCIAL WORK PLANNING

Possibly the most comprehensive planning of social institutions in cities that we have had so far is that pertaining to social work. To be sure, the structure of social work, like that of business, government, education, and religion, has grown up without coordinated planning; but recently there have been attempts to view the field as a whole and to plan for its orderly development. Councils of social agencies, under various names, have attempted since 1909 to cover social casework, group work, institutions in the narrow, popular sense, and a multitude of miscellaneous activities. The casework with which they are concerned includes relief giving, family counseling, child guidance and protection, vocational advice and placement, probation and parole, medical and psychiatric social work. The group work includes the promotion and guidance of clubs, classes, and less formal groups of young and old, supervision of recreational activities, leadership and administration of social centers. The institutions include homes for children, old people, delinquents, mental defectives, and physically handicapped persons. In addition, councils of social agencies have engaged in research, propaganda, lobbying, and in general the promotion of legislative changes, administrative efficiency, and moral reforms. Sometimes these are merely a lot of separate interests that happen to converge in one office. Sometimes their interrelations are studied and comprehensive programs are developed. Occasionally a large-scale survey is conducted to view the metropolitan situation as a whole and plan social work accordingly.

Sometimes the planning of social work is undertaken by a community fund, either in cooperation with a council or in lieu of one. Since community funds do not include public welfare services and frequently omit some private agencies (*e.g.*, Red Cross, Tuberculosis Society, YMCA, Boy Scouts), their planning and coordinating activities can hardly be community-wide. Councils organized separately from community funds are usually more inclusive and may be expected to win wider acceptance. They too have their limitations. They are associations or organizations established to carry on social work. They usually accept the existing situation and seek to promote teamwork, raise standards, and increase public interest. But out of the coordinating function has grown some social planning, or at least the planning of social work. Nevertheless, these councils have several limitations. They commonly devote most of their attention to private agencies; they usually deal with only part of a metropolitan area; they are frequently dominated by people who are more interested in maintaining the *status quo* than in planning social reorganization.

Unfortunately many people have used the words "social planning" and "community organization" as synonyms of social work planning. Now the last would be a significant part of comprehensive social planning and would overlap the promotion of local communities, but it is after all somewhat specialized. The whole matter would be clarified by more careful use of terms.

NEIGHBORHOOD PLANNING

Social workers have sometimes engaged in what might be called neighborhood planning. Thus the social settlements in blighted areas are often intended to be the headquarters of neighborhoods actual or potential. It is generally assumed that the people living near a settlement house either do or should constitute a neighborhood. Sometimes this appears to be a fairly accurate characterization, but often the nigh-dwellers are a heterogeneous and mobile lot, who have little to do with one another. Under such circumstances the settlement becomes a social service station rather than the center of local group life. The social workers make efforts to promote mutual acquaintance and respect among various ethnic groups, to bring united pressure to bear on public officials, and to develop urban nigh-dwellers into neighbors. Their labors are not wholly in vain, but they cannot point to large accomplishments in the realm of neighborhood organization.

In Chap. 11 we described the work of the Urban League which has to do with organizing residents of blocks and small districts as "neighbors." We noted that the principal projects of these organized groups have had to do with the appearance of houses, yards, and streets, the promotion of health programs, adult education, and various kinds of propaganda. The degree of their success is difficult to determine. But it is probably correct to say that neighborhood planning has been subordinate to other objectives.

More genuine neighborhood planning has preceded and accompanied the establishment of private streets and places, like those described in Chap. 11. Here there has often been careful design of the physical layout, selection of residents, organization of a property owners' association. Often the aims of securing a congenial group of families, of protecting property values, of escaping from traffic, and of living in a stable, attractive, and accessible neighborhood are achieved. But these advantages are available chiefly to the well to do.

In the plan for New York and its environs, considerable attention was given to the development of neighborhoods.[3] The metropolitan area was not laid out in potential neighborhood and non-neighborhood districts, as was later done by Harland Bartholomew for St. Louis, but plans were drawn up for such neighborhoods as might come into being. These plans involved a physical aspect, an economic organization, and the development of social institutions. Arterial highways were to form the boundaries but never to pass through a neighborhood. Dwellings were to be reached by winding cul-de-sacs, preferably approaching from the rear. Houses were to face on open spaces occupied by grass and flowers and by playgrounds. Pedestrian and vehicular traffic would be separated in the interest of safety. Distinctly neighborhood institutions, such as elementary schools, would be centrally located. Those serving the population of a larger area, such as retail stores, would be located on the

[3] Clarence A. Perry, *et al.*, *Neighborhood and Community Planning*, 1929, Vol. 7 of the *Regional Survey of New York and Its Environs.*

through streets, preferably at or near intersections. The residents of a neighborhood were expected to join a property owners' association or neighborhood improvement association. This organization was to consider not merely economic problems, but recreational, educational, and any other problems that might affect the group as a whole. Separate plans were designed for neighborhoods in different parts of the metropolitan area: suburban, industrial, and apartment districts. These were to differ both in physical plan and in economic organization. In suburban neighborhoods homeownership by individual families was anticipated. In the others corporate ownership of multiple dwellings was to be the rule. Something of this sort seems to have become a standard part of city planning, but emphasis has been placed very heavily on the physical rather than on the social aspects. Thus one textbook on city planning says "the neighborhood unit is not some sociological phenomenon. . . . It is simply a physical environment in which . . . " and so on.[4]

In view of the evident decline of neighboring in cities and the gradual substitution of nonlocal for local groups, it may fairly be asked: Why bother about planning neighborhoods? The answer is in part that this is a means of promoting quiet, safety, health, beauty, acceptable associates, and availability without annoyance of service agencies. Neighborhood life seems to mean most to families with small children. Perhaps it is not necessary or even desirable for groups of adults and single individuals. Even for families with small children and with adequate incomes, there are problems of changing business and professional connections. If urban populations become much more mobile, neighborhoods can hardly survive. Even a well-integrated neighborhood will be threatened by the removal of families from its membership. Replacements may not prove congenial, or they may have so many interests in other parts of the city that they may never identify themselves wholly with the neighborhood. Hence we are inclined to view neighborhood planning as an attractive goal, but probably not practical for large numbers of city dwellers.

COMMUNITY PLANNING

A logical development would be the grouping of neighborhoods into communities. But as a matter of fact the planning of communities seems to be older than the effort to develop neighborhoods. All through the nineteenth century there appeared books and pamphlets urging the establishment of model communities. Fourier in 1822, Wakefield in 1849, and Howard in 1898 urged the creation of new communties on unused land. Howard's plan in particular was to establish small urban units

---

[4] Arthur B. Gallion, *The Urban Pattern, City Planning and Design*, p. 278, 1950. By permission of D. Van Nostrand Company, Inc.

which might combine the advantages of city and country life. There would be single dwellings with plenty of open spaces. Separate, but close by, would be places of employment and a shopping center. Round about would be a permanent agricultural belt. Thus the community would be to a considerable degree independent and self-sufficient. It would be sub-urban in location, thus having access to the facilities of the great city, but with much less commuting than is usually necessary for suburban dwellers.

Probably the best known example we have in the United States is Radburn, N.J., about 15 miles from the heart of New York City. This venture was promoted by a limited dividend company, the City Housing Corporation. Advantage was taken of land not previously used for urban purposes and hence available at a wholesale, "undeveloped" price. A complete town was laid out; homes were erected; some factories were attracted. Residential sections were planned essentially as neighborhoods. There is a conveniently located shopping center. At one side is an in-dustrial district. There cannot be a permanent agricultural belt, because Radburn is too near the heart of the metropolitan area; but it is hoped that there will always be parks on all sides. The inhabitants are expected to buy their homes. They do not get the property at cost, but ultimately, after the fixed dividends have been paid, they are to receive the increased value of the land. To exercise eventual control over the whole develop-ment, the Radburn Association was established. Every householder is ex-pected to be a member.

About 1935 the Resettlement Administration planned four "green-belt" towns, three of which have been built as "dormitory villages" for people who earn their livings in nearby cities. The physical development has been often described,[5] but we have no adequate account of their social organization. It was hoped that in each case the elementary school would become a community center and that the residents would become a well-knit social group. Unfortunately we have no satisfactory report on the extent to which community of life has been achieved.

It seems to be generally assumed that communities cannot be de-veloped in the heart of great cities. But in 1917 there was an interesting attempt to do this very thing. In Cincinnati the Mohawk-Brighton district was selected for the experiment known as the Social Unit.[6] Here was a population of 15,000 occupying 31 blocks. It was a rather stable lot of folks, mostly of German descent, many of them owners of small homes. The plan was presented to them; it aroused their interest; and to its development they gave much time and effort.

<hr />

[5] *Ibid.*, pp. 144–147.
[6] Courtenay Dinwiddie, *Community Responsibility: A Review of the Cincinnati Social Unit Experiment*, 1921.

The program was not one of physical construction or reconstruction. It was a genuine scheme of community organization. Its purpose was to provide a mechanism whereby the citizens could all share in devising and carrying out programs of social action. To make this possible, there was devised a system of dual representation, geographical and occupational. All the adults living in a given block were to elect a block council of seven, who were to choose their representative, to be known as the block worker, to discuss local needs and to consider proposals made by the unit executive, the occupational council, or any other individual or group. Some of the block councils seem to have met rather frequently, while others came together rarely if ever. At all events every block had a "worker," however chosen. All the block workers met as members of the citizens' council. This was really the policy-making body for the community. Since the members lived very near to their constituents and put in several hours a week seeking their opinions and guiding them to specialists whose services they might need, the citizens' council was representative in a very unusual sense.

The occupational organization was intended to include everyone whose trade or profession was conducted in whole or in part in the district, rather than the gainfully employed persons who lived in the district. They were organized first by occupations. Thus there was a physicians' council, to which dentists were later admitted, a nursing council, a social workers' council, and a teachers' council. The clergymen, businessmen, and wage earners never united, and they took rather less part in the whole venture than was hoped. Representatives of these professional and trades groups were to form the occupational council, which was to promote better understanding and cooperation. Members of the citizens' council and occupational council were to meet together as the general council to consider matters of general interest.

It happened that during the three years of the experiment, 1917 to 1920, more attention was devoted to public health than to anything else. This was stimulated by the U.S. Children's Bureau, but it was enthusiastically supported by the people of the district. Had it not been for the short life of the unit, the general preoccupation with World War I, and the opposition of politicians, doubtless other phases of the local life would have received similar consideration. At all events, the venture came to an end when the outside subsidy ceased, and nothing quite like it has been elsewhere developed.

During the years immediately following World War I there was much loose talk about community organization, but the underlying ideas were rather vague. Some people identified the term with public recreation. Others meant by it the enlisting of popular support for social work organizations. Still others had in mind church unity, consolidated schools,

Americanization, and doubtless other limited projects. All these efforts contained the germ of social planning, but none of them was sufficiently comprehensive to warrant the use of that label.

THE REVOLUTIONARY NATURE OF CITY AND REGIONAL PLANNING

If we were to have really effective physical and social planning of cities, metropolitan areas, and regions, there would have to be a thoroughgoing modification, if not abandonment, of our traditional individualism and "free" competition. To project and enforce specified land uses and institutional development would inevitably restrict the theoretic and sacred right of every citizen to do as he pleases. Consider how the regulation of subdivisions might hamper the conventional real estate business, how the control of social work might cramp the style of private agencies, how comity might interfere with the effort to lure everyone into some particular religious faith. Whether the planning were done by an ambitious dictator, a selfish oligarchy, or a democratic society, it would mean a complete abandonment of *laissez faire*. To devise and carry out comprehensive plans for urban areas would require fundamental changes in our social philosophy.

We say this not to frighten any timid soul or to excite those who are already restless, but to emphasize the vast difference between the unguided scramble amid which our cities have developed in the past, and social planning. We do not like our cities as they are. Are we ready to pay the price of making them over? Can we come to some agreement as to objectives and work together for their attainment? On the answer to these questions rests the future of urbanism in the United States.

SELECTED READINGS

DINWIDDIE, COURTENAY: *Community Responsibility: A Review of the Cincinnati Social Unit Experiment,* New York School of Social Work, 1921.

GALLION, ARTHUR B.: *The Urban Pattern, City Planning and Design,* D. Van Nostrand Company, Inc., 1950. Chapter 7 deals with garden cities, Chap. 21 with neighborhood units.

HILLMAN, ARTHUR: *Community Organization and Planning,* The Macmillan Company, 1950. Describes planning for various types of services and planning in general as a process of developing consensus and coordination.

McMILLEN, WAYNE: *Community Organization for Social Welfare,* University of Chicago Press, 1945. A detailed treatment of the planning and organization of social work.

ZORBAUGH, HARVEY W.: *Gold Coast and Slum,* University of Chicago Press, 1929. Chapter 12, "Reform, Realism and City Life," questions the possibility of integrating the social elements in an urban area.

Name Index

A

Abrams, Ray H., 304
Adams, Thomas, 359
Ames, E. S., 287
Angell, Robert C., 15, 304, 353–355n., 360
Aquinas, Thomas, 49
Atwood, R. S., 52n.
Augustus, Philip, 49

B

Barnes, Harry Elmer, 244n.
Bartholomew, Harland, 370
Beals, Ralph, 19n., 27
Beard, Charles A., 80
Becker, Howard, 244, 287, 289, 305
Beegle, J. Allan, 24, 26, 27, 243–245, 255n., 271, 286
Bernard, Jessie S., 156, 157, 305
Black, J. Bertram, 110n.
Bogue, Don J., 81, 86–91, 188, 201, 222
Braden, Charles S., 289n.
Bradshaw, Nettie P., 38
Breasted, J. H., 45n.
Breckinridge, Sophonisba P., 322n.
Breese, Gerald W., 200, 202
Brown, Roy M., 322n.
Bruce, Isabel C., 322n.
Brunner, Edmund de S., 85, 86, 91, 131, 290n., 291
Bruno, Frank J., 336
Buck, Paul H., 273n., 279n., 285
Burgess, Ernest W., 27, 44n., 52, 81n., 100, 113, 115, 134, 270

C

Caesar, Julius, 49
Cantril, Hadley, 301n.
Caplow, Theodore, 115n.
Carpenter, David B., 33n., 227n., 228
Carpenter, Niles, 43, 44, 46

Casis, Ana, 55n.
Caulfield, Henry S., 306n.
Cavan, Ruth Shonle, 267–270
Cayton, Horace R., 154, 238, 243
Centers, Richard, 260, 281, 283
Chase, Stuart, 34n.
Child, Irwin L., 153
Childe, V. Gordon, 43n., 52
Churchill, Henry S., 349, 360
Clark, Carroll D., 189
Colodesch, Max, 101n.
Conwell, Russell, 304
Cottrell, Leonard S., 270n.
Cowgill, Donald O., 101n., 110n., 150, 196
Cowgill, Mary S., 150
Coyle, Grace L., 330n.
Cuber, John F., 304, 305

D

Dahir, James, 169
Davie, Maurice R., 15, 115, 154
Davies, Vernon, 266n.
Davis, Allison, 232n.–234, 243, 266
Davis, Kingsley, 55n.
Dean, John P., 184
Dee, Wm. L. J., 177
Demangeon, A., 49n.
Deutschberger, Paul, 168, 169
Dewey, Richard, 169
Dickinson, Robert E., 91
Dinwiddie, Courtenay, 131, 372n., 374
Douglass, H. Paul, 291–295, 297, 299n., 305, 366, 367
Drake, St. Clair, 154, 238, 243
Duffus, R. L., 358n., 360
Dunham, H. Warren, 176
Durkheim, Emile, 24

E

Edward III, 51
Eels, Kenneth, 242n., 243
Eickhoff, Edith, 322n.

Subject Index